ALICE IN THE COUNTRY OF HEARTS
My Fanatic Rabbit

1

STORY BY ♥ QuinRose

ART BY ♥ Delico Psyche

SCENARIO BY ♥ Owl Shinotsuki

ALICE IN THE COUNTRY OF HEARTS

~ My Fanatic Rabbit ~

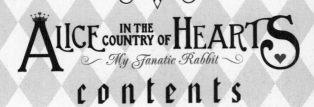

contents

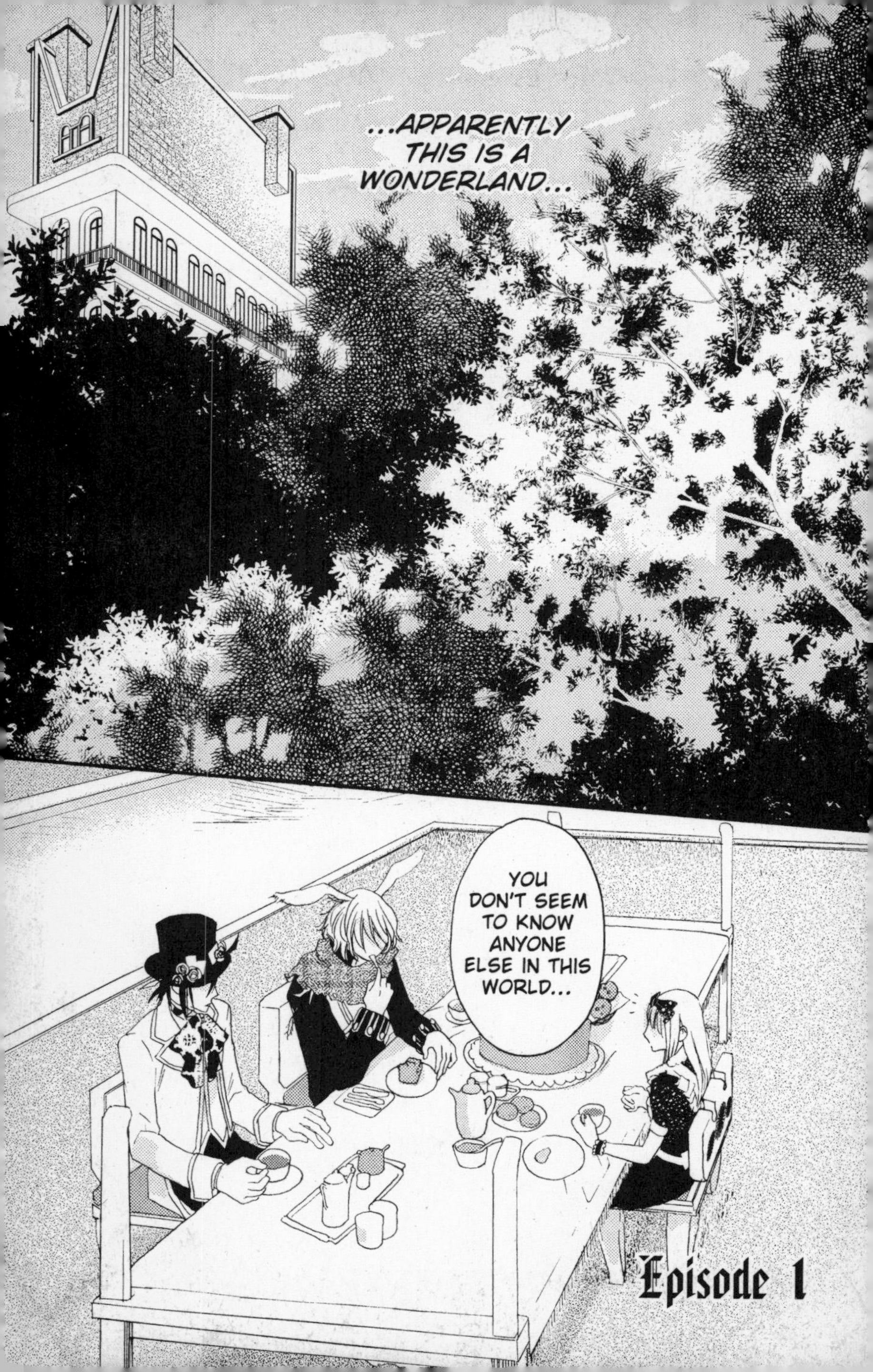
...APPARENTLY THIS IS A WONDERLAND...
YOU DON'T SEEM TO KNOW ANYONE ELSE IN THIS WORLD...
Episode 1

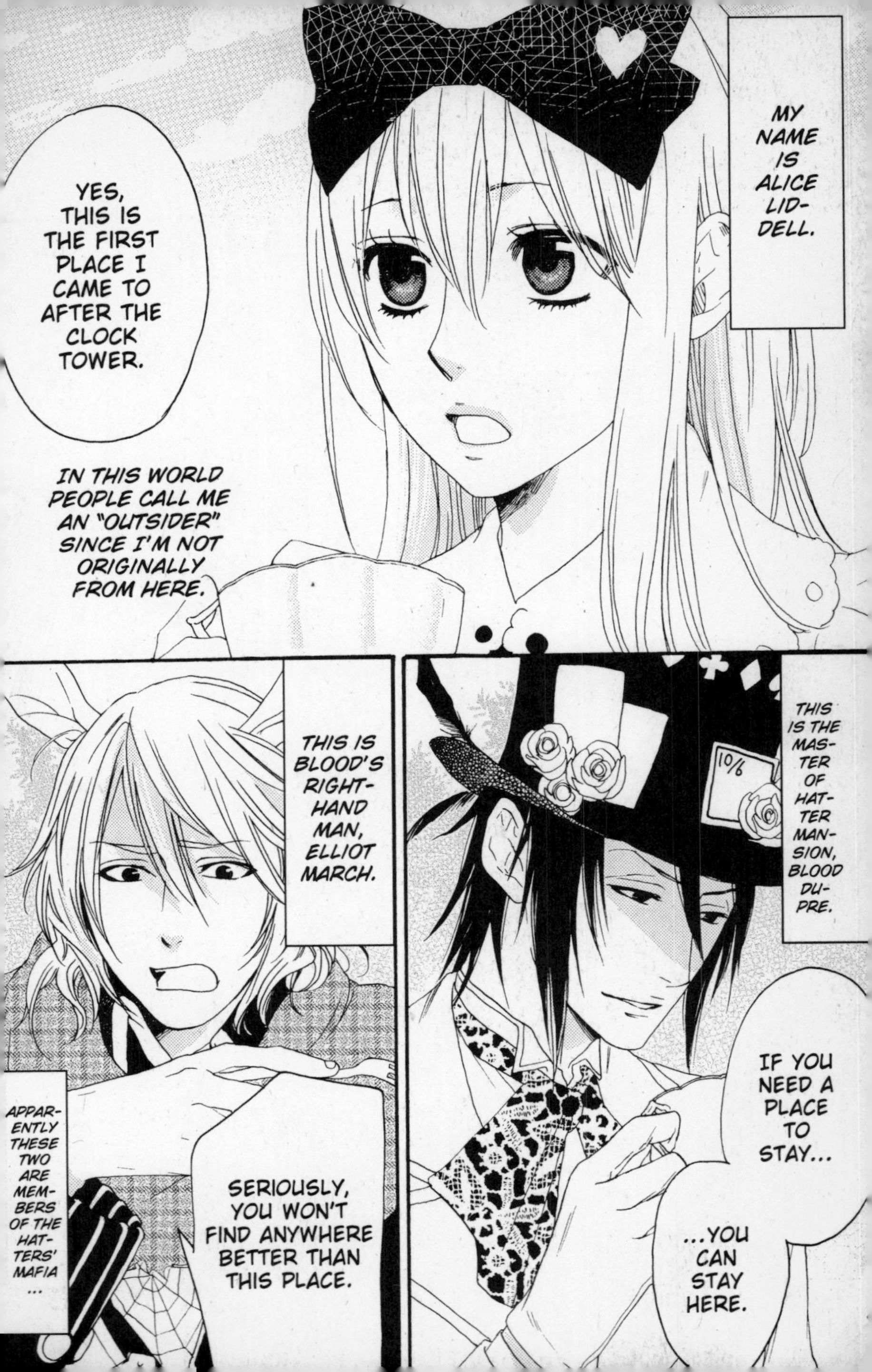
MY NAME IS ALICE LIDDELL.
YES, THIS IS THE FIRST PLACE I CAME TO AFTER THE CLOCK TOWER.
IN THIS WORLD PEOPLE CALL ME AN "OUTSIDER" SINCE I'M NOT ORIGINALLY FROM HERE.
THIS IS THE MASTER OF HATTER MANSION, BLOOD DUPRE.
IF YOU NEED A PLACE TO STAY...
...YOU CAN STAY HERE.
THIS IS BLOOD'S RIGHT-HAND MAN, ELLIOT MARCH.
SERIOUSLY, YOU WON'T FIND ANYWHERE BETTER THAN THIS PLACE.
APPARENTLY THESE TWO ARE MEMBERS OF THE HATTERS' MAFIA...

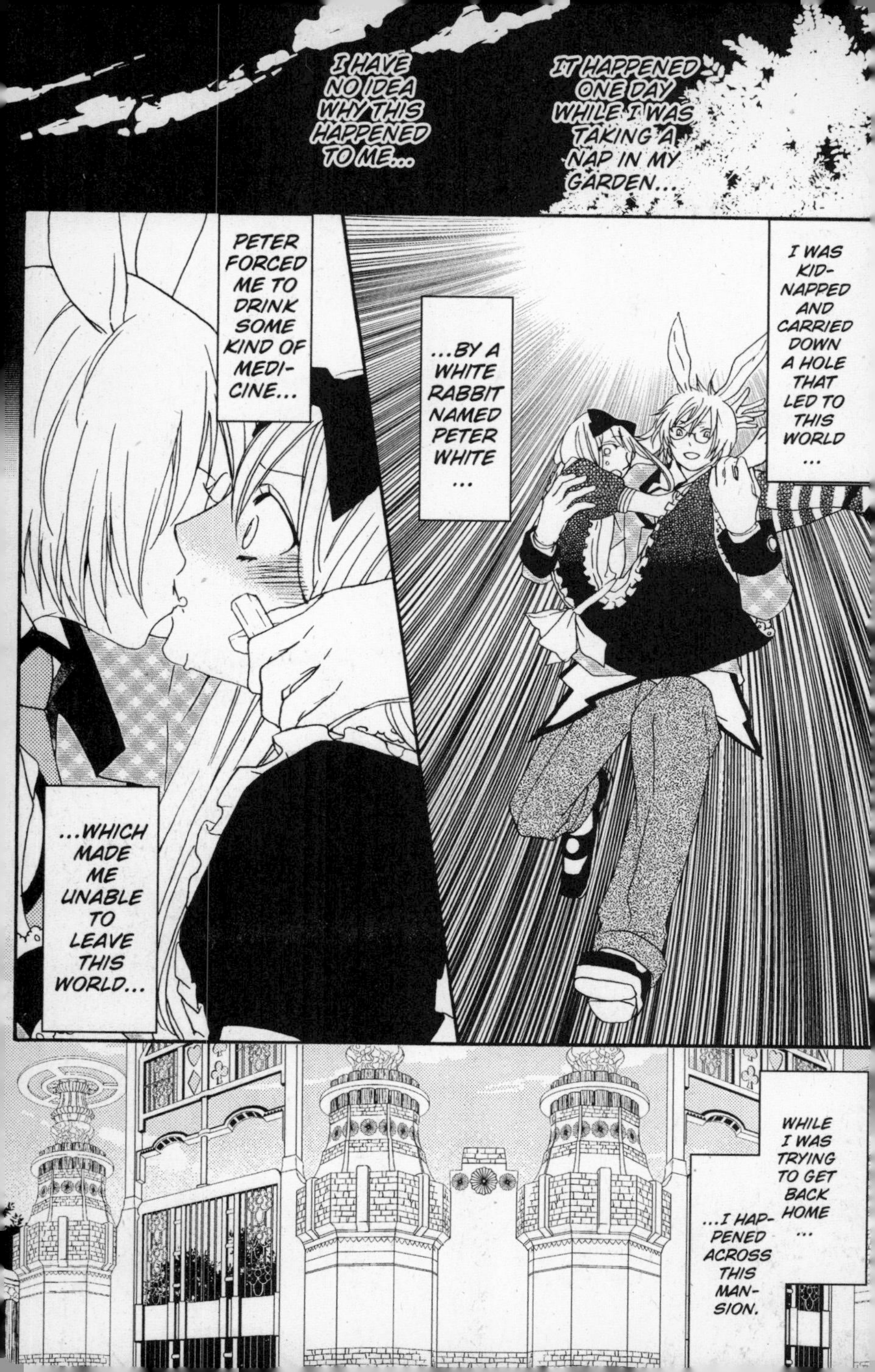
IT HAPPENED ONE DAY WHILE I WAS TAKING A NAP IN MY GARDEN...
I HAVE NO IDEA WHY THIS HAPPENED TO ME...
I WAS KID-NAPPED AND CARRIED DOWN A HOLE THAT LED TO THIS WORLD...
...BY A WHITE RABBIT NAMED PETER WHITE...
PETER FORCED ME TO DRINK SOME KIND OF MEDI-CINE...
...WHICH MADE ME UNABLE TO LEAVE THIS WORLD...
WHILE I WAS TRYING TO GET BACK HOME...
...I HAP-PENED ACROSS THIS MAN-SION.

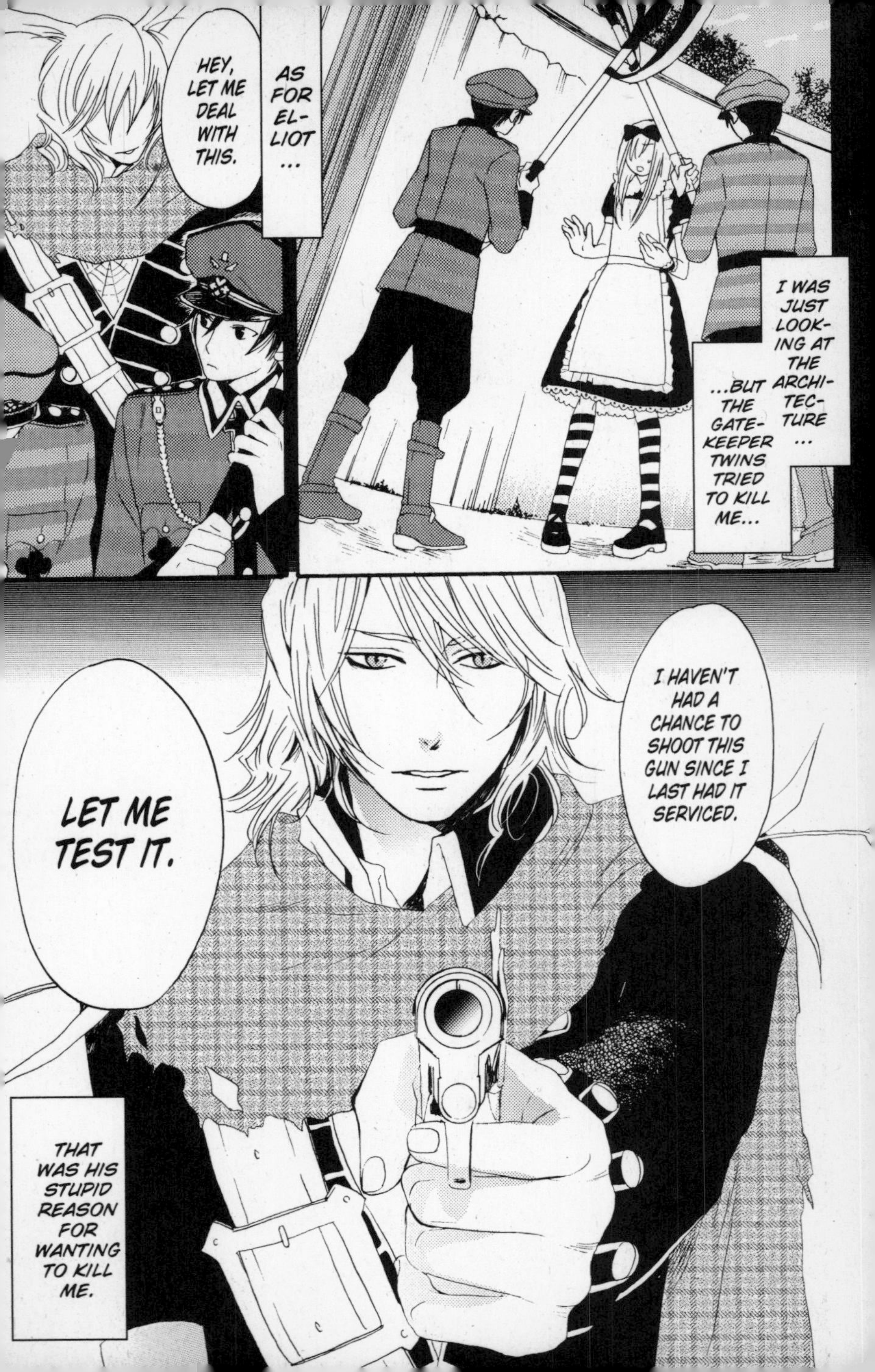
I WAS JUST LOOKING AT THE ARCHITECTURE...
...BUT THE GATEKEEPER TWINS TRIED TO KILL ME...
AS FOR ELLIOT...
HEY, LET ME DEAL WITH THIS.
I HAVEN'T HAD A CHANCE TO SHOOT THIS GUN SINCE I LAST HAD IT SERVICED.
LET ME TEST IT.
THAT WAS HIS STUPID REASON FOR WANTING TO KILL ME.

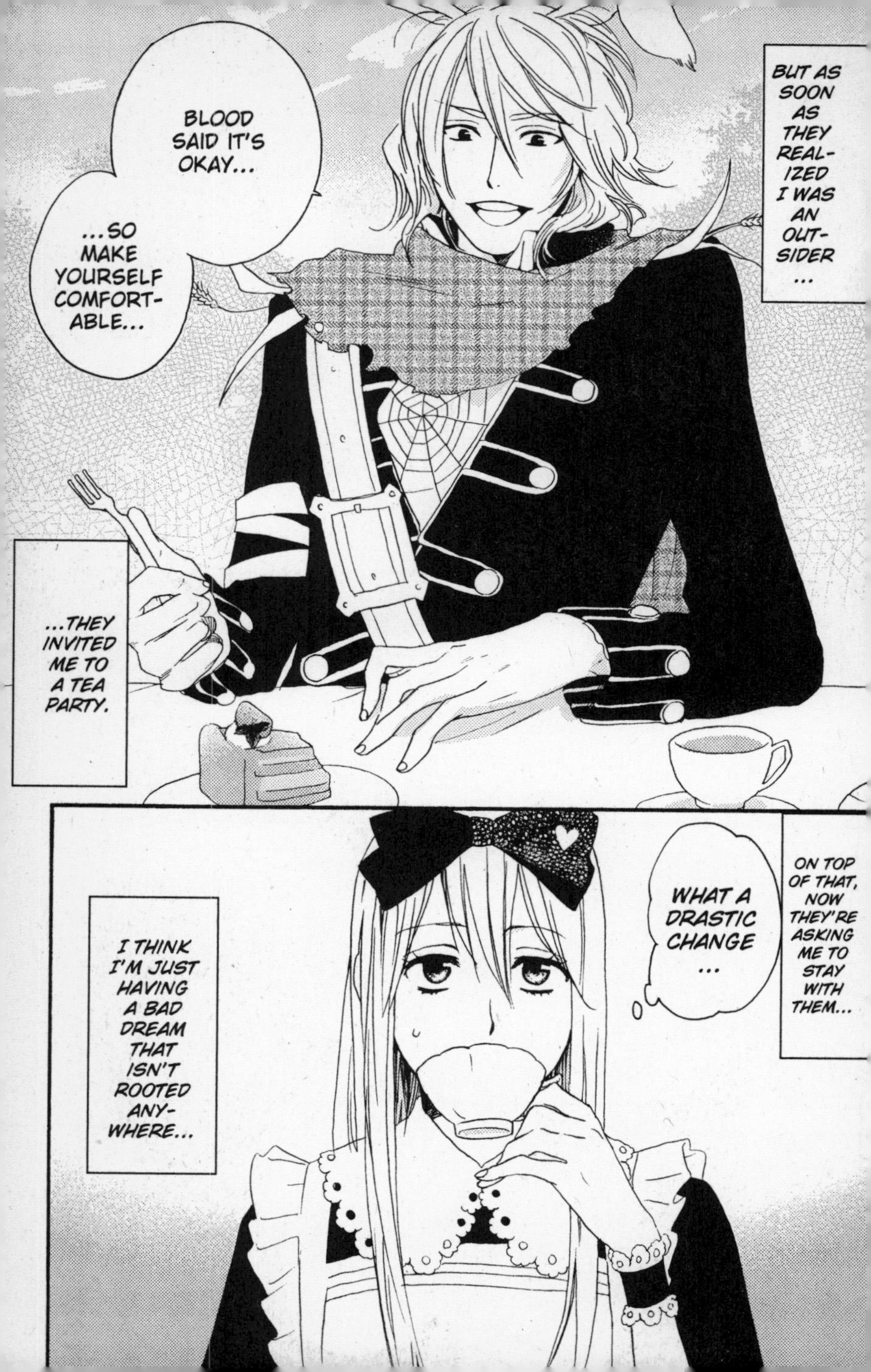
BUT AS SOON AS THEY REAL-IZED I WAS AN OUT-SIDER...
BLOOD SAID IT'S OKAY...
...SO MAKE YOURSELF COMFORT-ABLE...
...THEY INVITED ME TO A TEA PARTY.
ON TOP OF THAT, NOW THEY'RE ASKING ME TO STAY WITH THEM...
WHAT A DRASTIC CHANGE...
I THINK I'M JUST HAVING A BAD DREAM THAT ISN'T ROOTED ANY-WHERE...

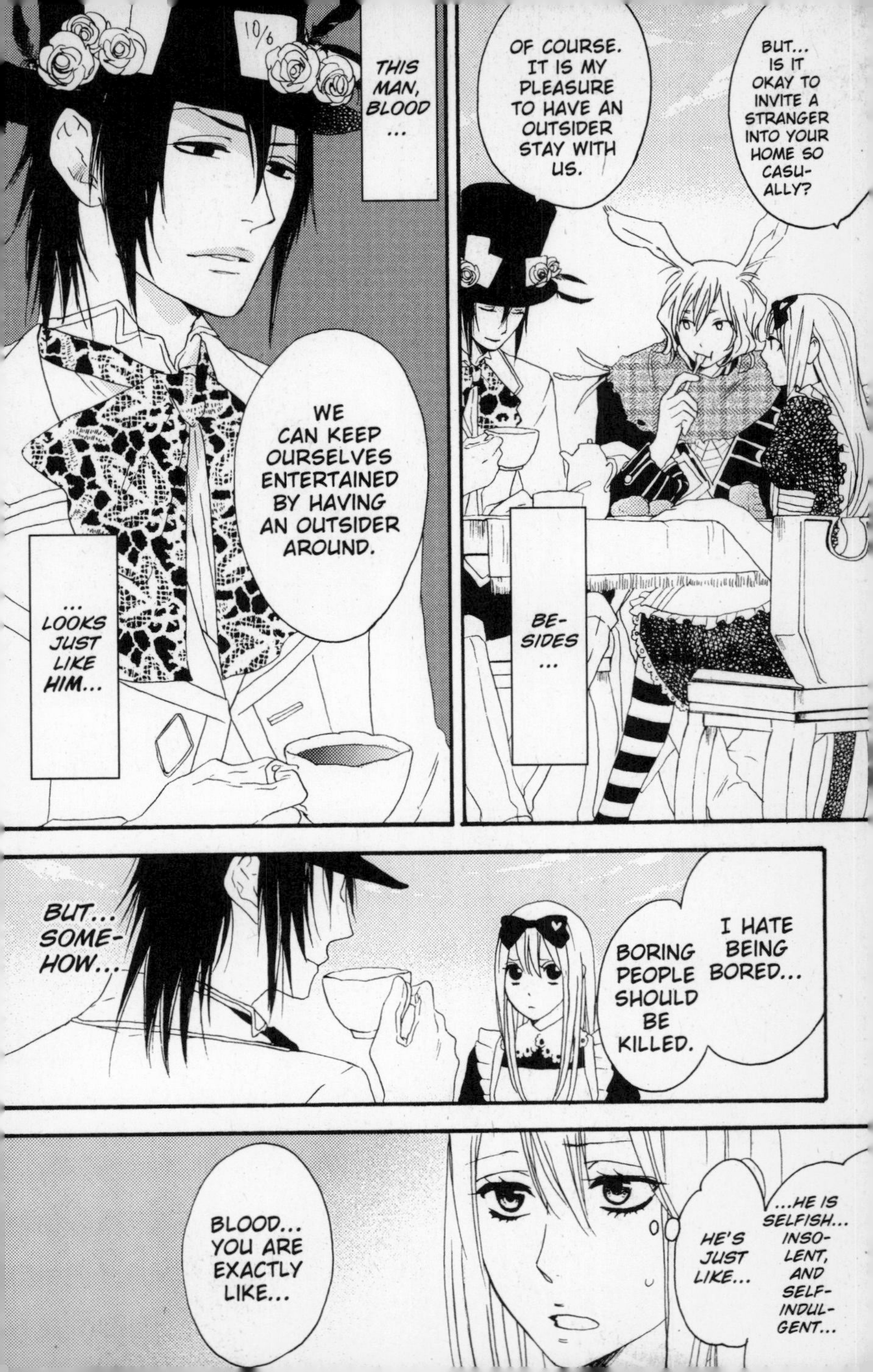
BUT... IS IT OKAY TO INVITE A STRANGER INTO YOUR HOME SO CASUALLY?
OF COURSE. IT IS MY PLEASURE TO HAVE AN OUTSIDER STAY WITH US.
BESIDES...
THIS MAN, BLOOD...
WE CAN KEEP OURSELVES ENTERTAINED BY HAVING AN OUTSIDER AROUND.
...LOOKS JUST LIKE HIM...
I HATE BEING BORED...
BORING PEOPLE SHOULD BE KILLED.
BUT... SOMEHOW...
...HE IS SELFISH... INSOLENT, AND SELF-INDULGENT...
HE'S JUST LIKE...
BLOOD... YOU ARE EXACTLY LIKE...

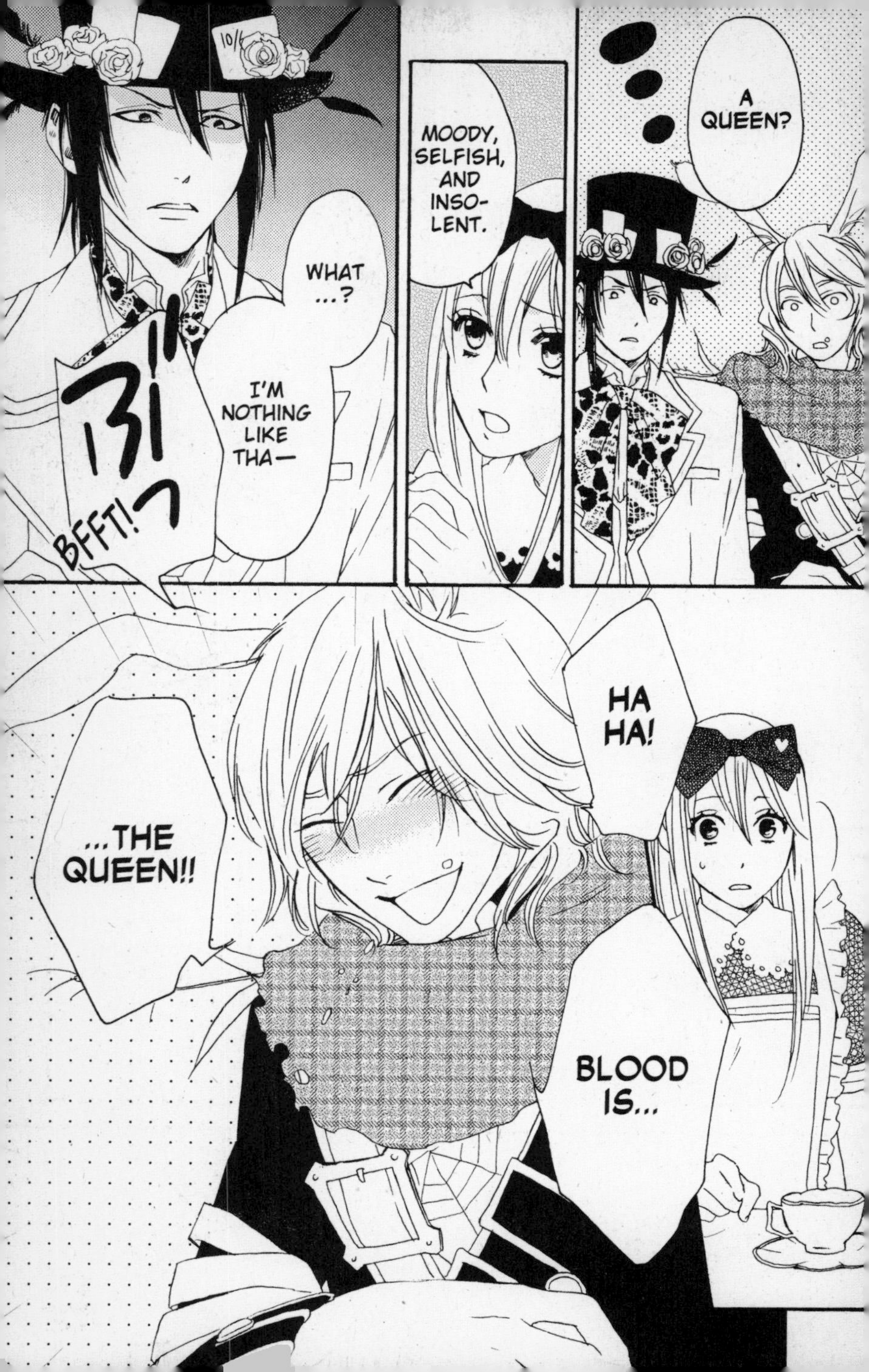
A QUEEN?
MOODY, SELFISH, AND INSO- LENT.
WHAT ...?
I'M NOTHING LIKE THA—
BFFT!
HA HA!
BLOOD IS...
...THE QUEEN!!

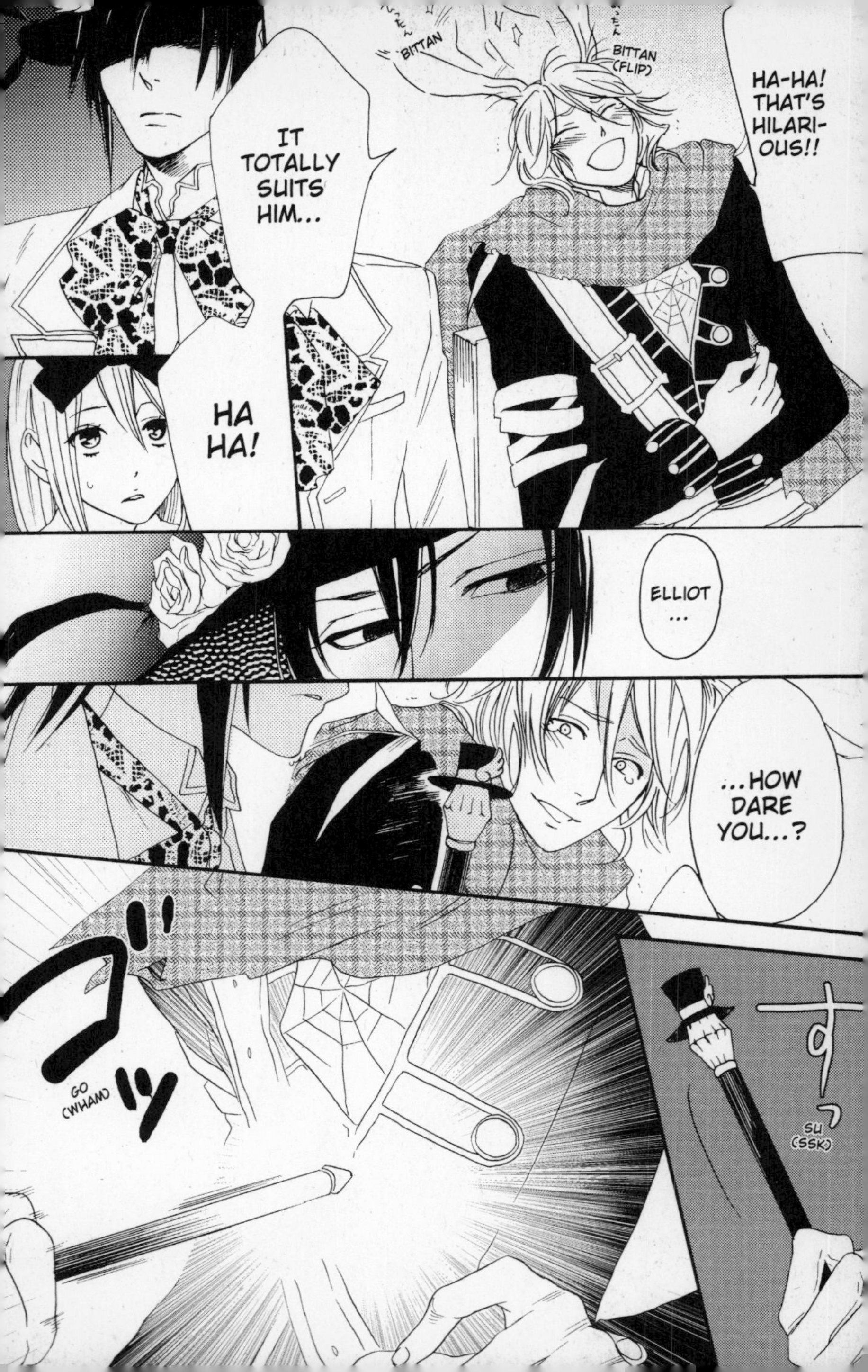
BITTAN (FLIP)
BITTAN
HA-HA! THAT'S HILARI-OUS!!
IT TOTALLY SUITS HIM...
HA HA!
ELLIOT ...
...HOW DARE YOU...?
すっ
SU (SSK)
ゴッ
GO (WHAM)

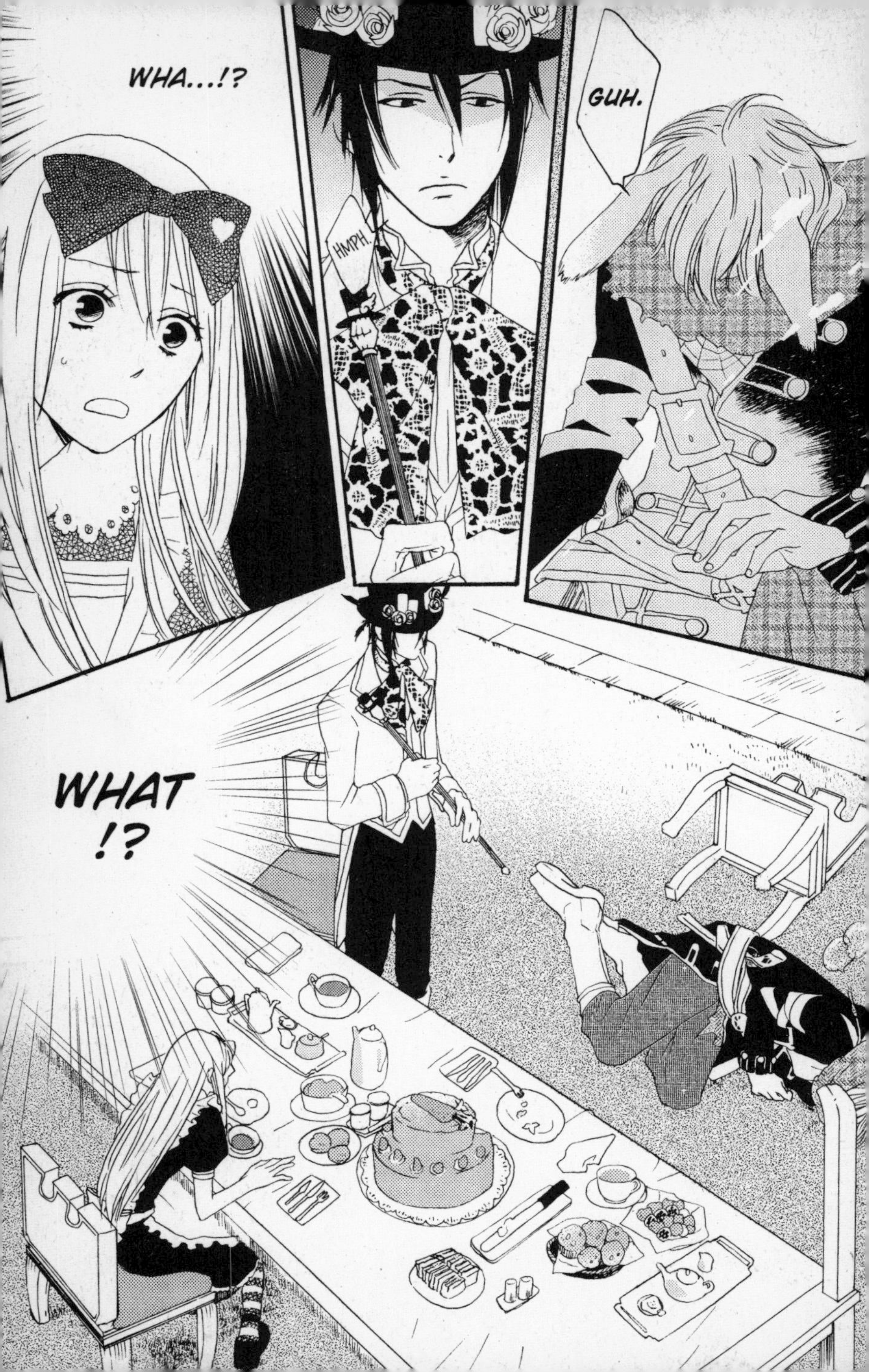
GUH.
HMPH.
WHA...!?
WHAT !?

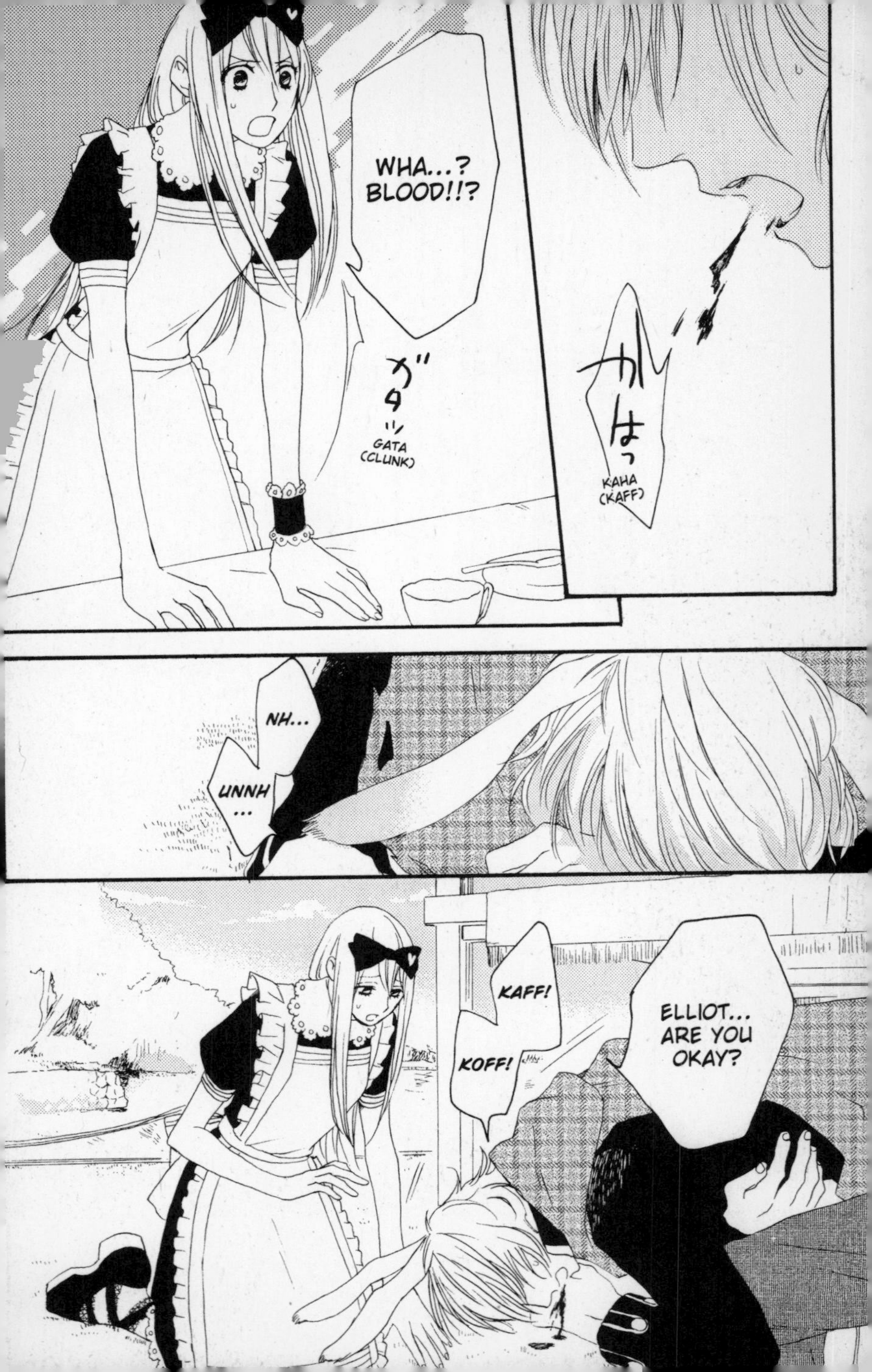
かはっ
KAHA (KAFF)
WHA...? BLOOD!!?
ガタッ
GATA (CLUNK)
NH...
UNNH ...
ELLIOT... ARE YOU OKAY?
KAFF!
KOFF!

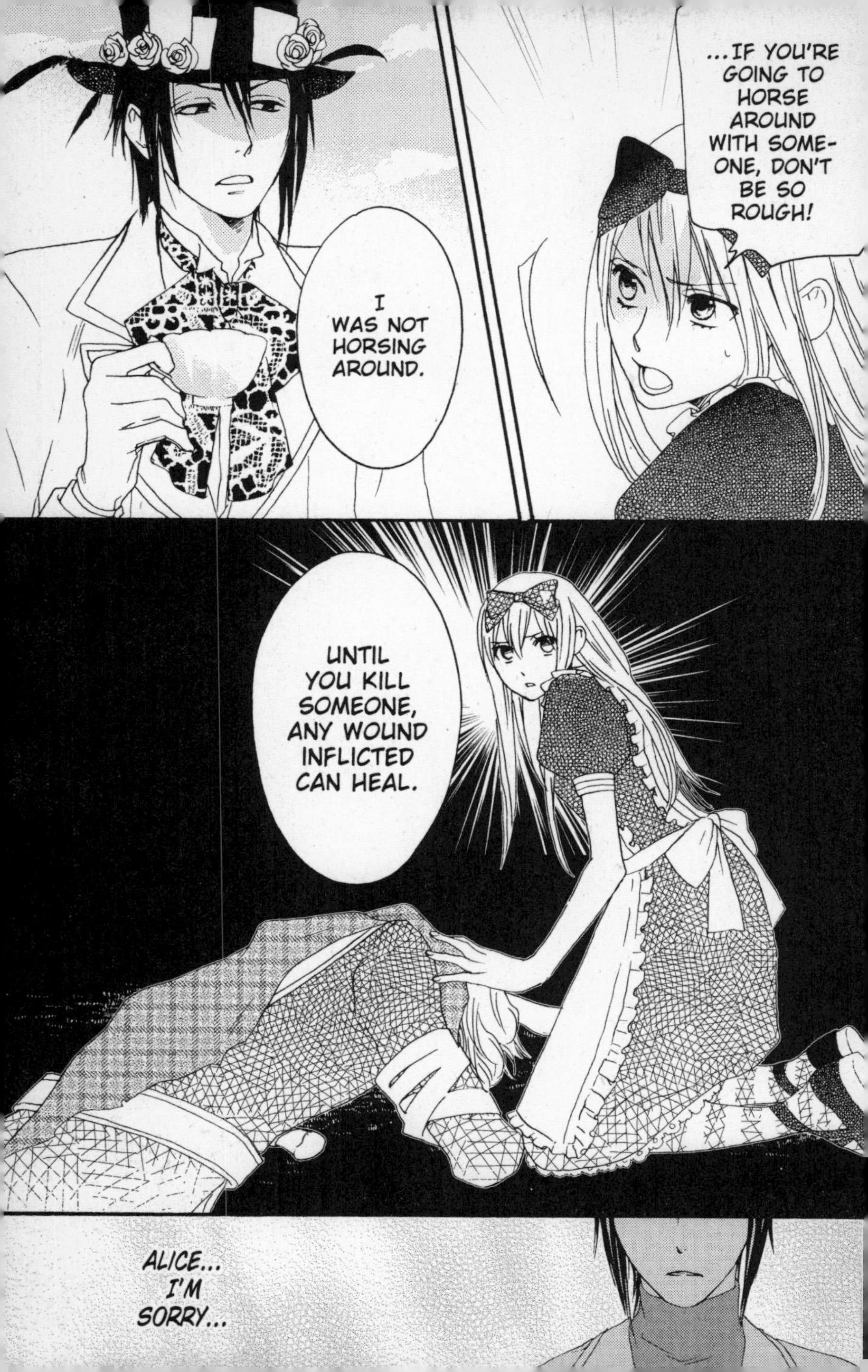
...IF YOU'RE GOING TO HORSE AROUND WITH SOME-ONE, DON'T BE SO ROUGH!
I WAS NOT HORSING AROUND.
UNTIL YOU KILL SOMEONE, ANY WOUND INFLICTED CAN HEAL.
ALICE... I'M SORRY...

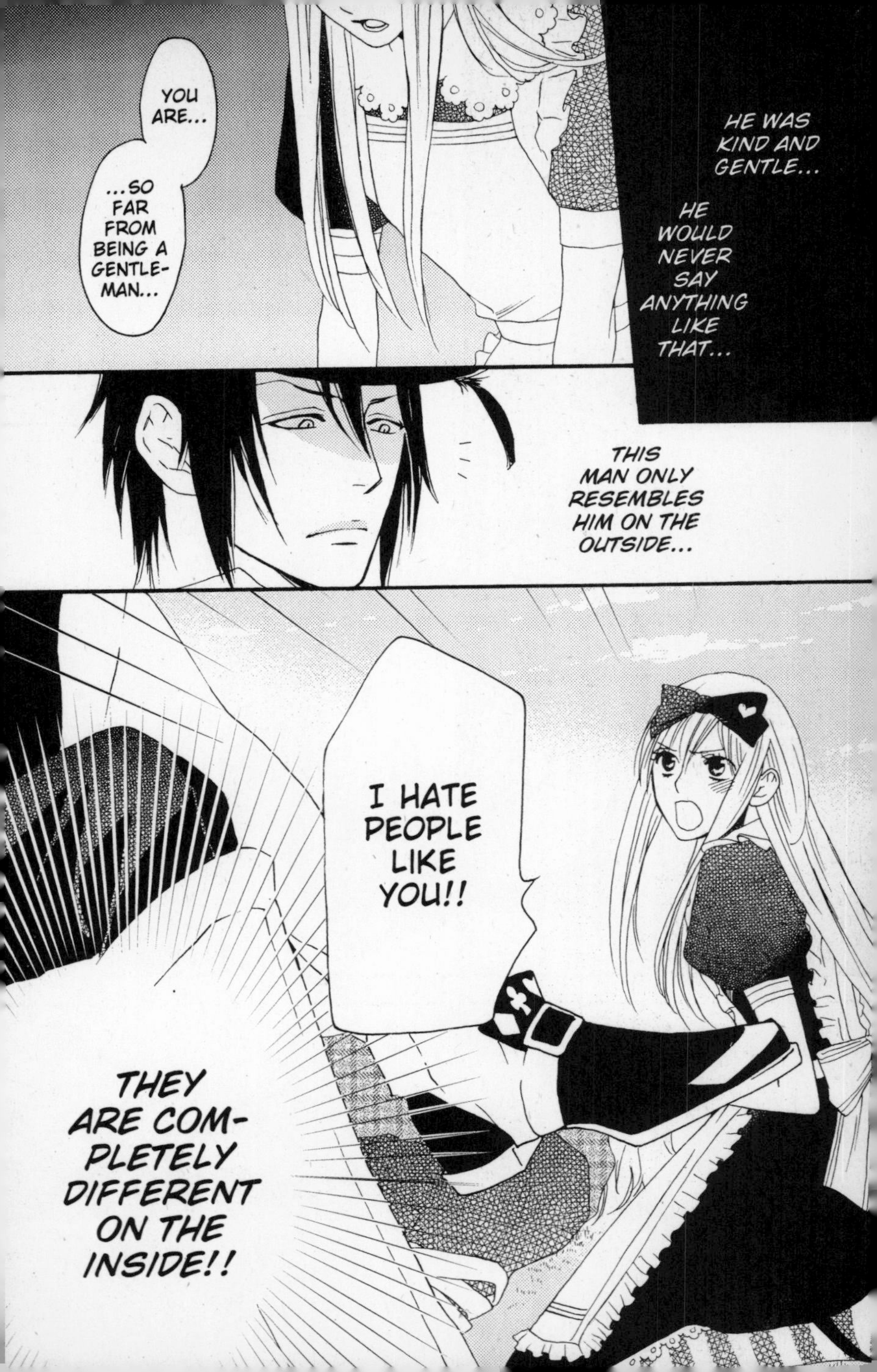
HE WAS KIND AND GENTLE...
HE WOULD NEVER SAY ANYTHING LIKE THAT...
YOU ARE...
...SO FAR FROM BEING A GENTLE-MAN...
THIS MAN ONLY RESEMBLES HIM ON THE OUTSIDE...
I HATE PEOPLE LIKE YOU!!
THEY ARE COM-PLETELY DIFFERENT ON THE INSIDE!!

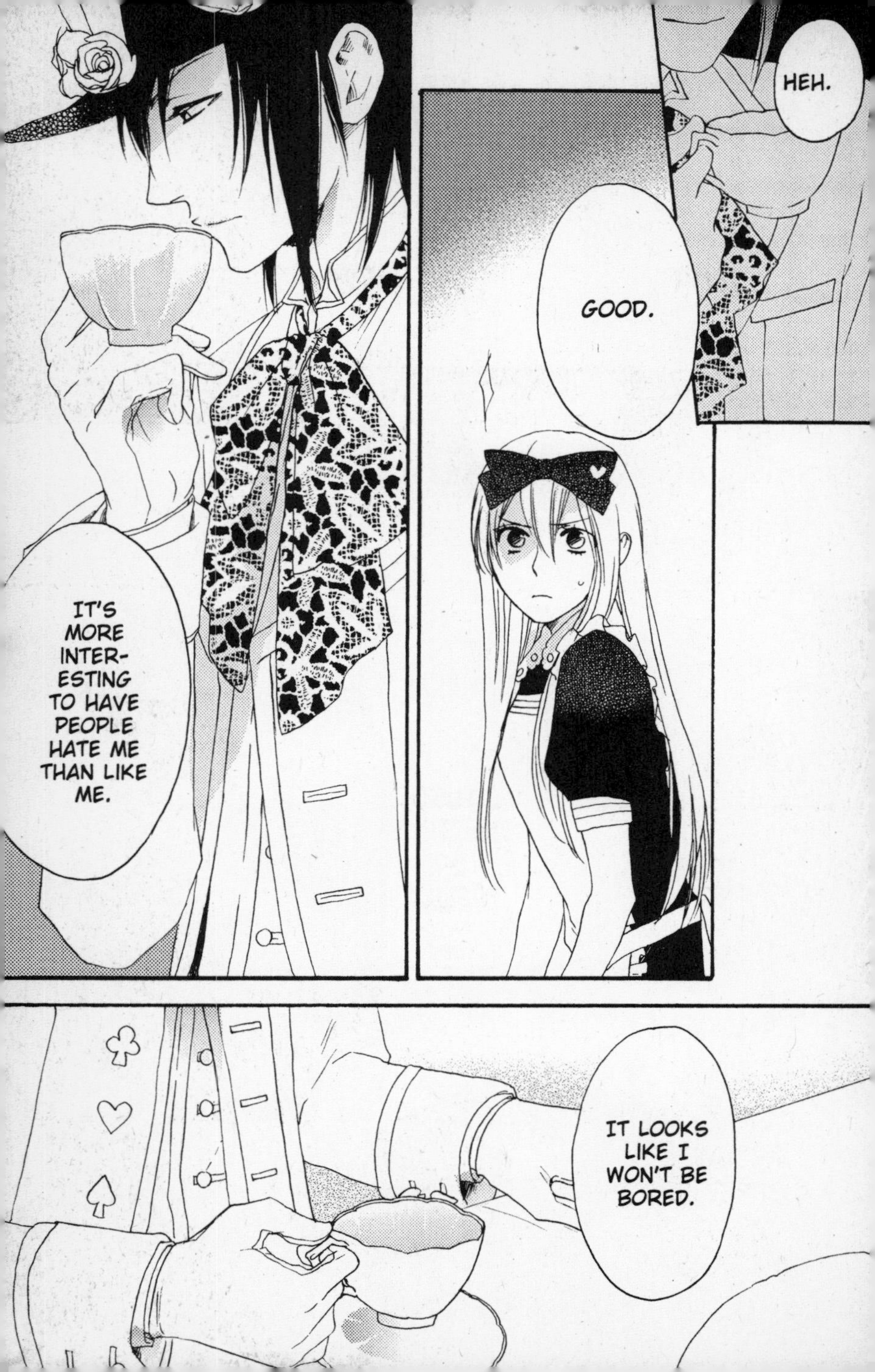
HEH.
GOOD.
IT'S MORE INTER-ESTING TO HAVE PEOPLE HATE ME THAN LIKE ME.
IT LOOKS LIKE I WON'T BE BORED.

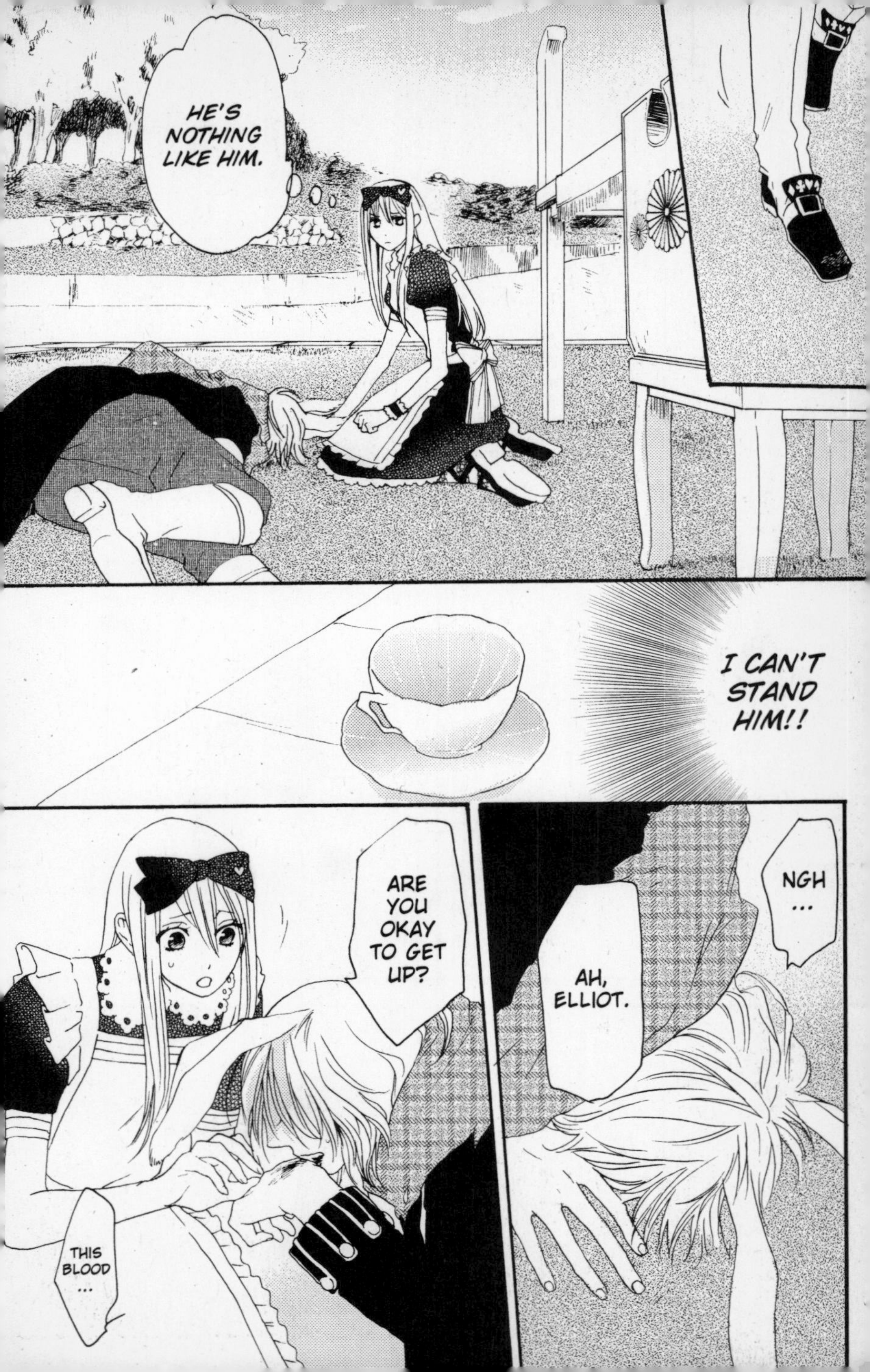
HE'S NOTHING LIKE HIM.
I CAN'T STAND HIM!!
NGH ...
AH, ELLIOT.
ARE YOU OKAY TO GET UP?
THIS BLOOD ...

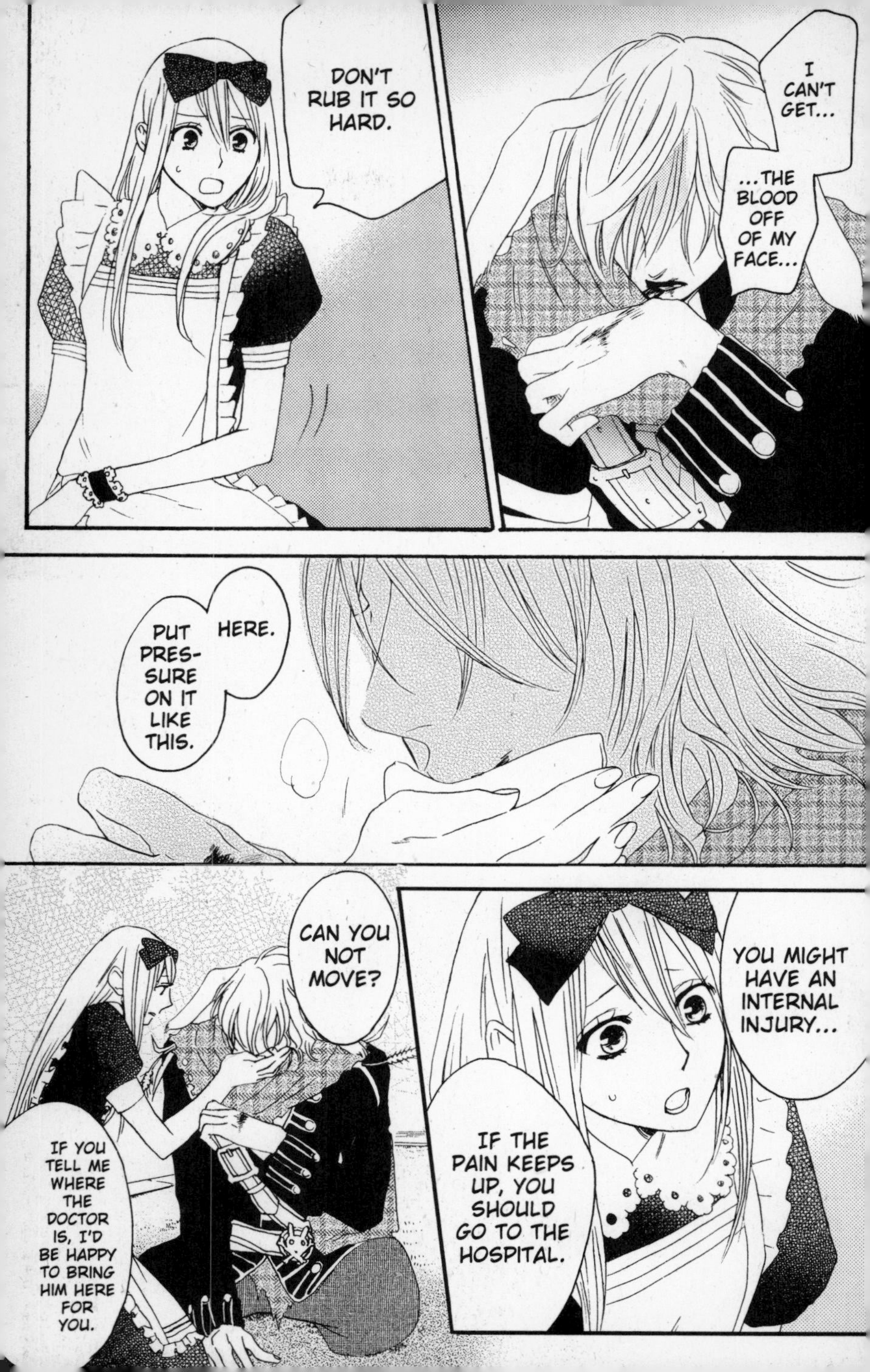
I CAN'T GET...
...THE BLOOD OFF OF MY FACE...
DON'T RUB IT SO HARD.
HERE. PUT PRES-SURE ON IT LIKE THIS.
YOU MIGHT HAVE AN INTERNAL INJURY...
IF THE PAIN KEEPS UP, YOU SHOULD GO TO THE HOSPITAL.
CAN YOU NOT MOVE?
IF YOU TELL ME WHERE THE DOCTOR IS, I'D BE HAPPY TO BRING HIM HERE FOR YOU.

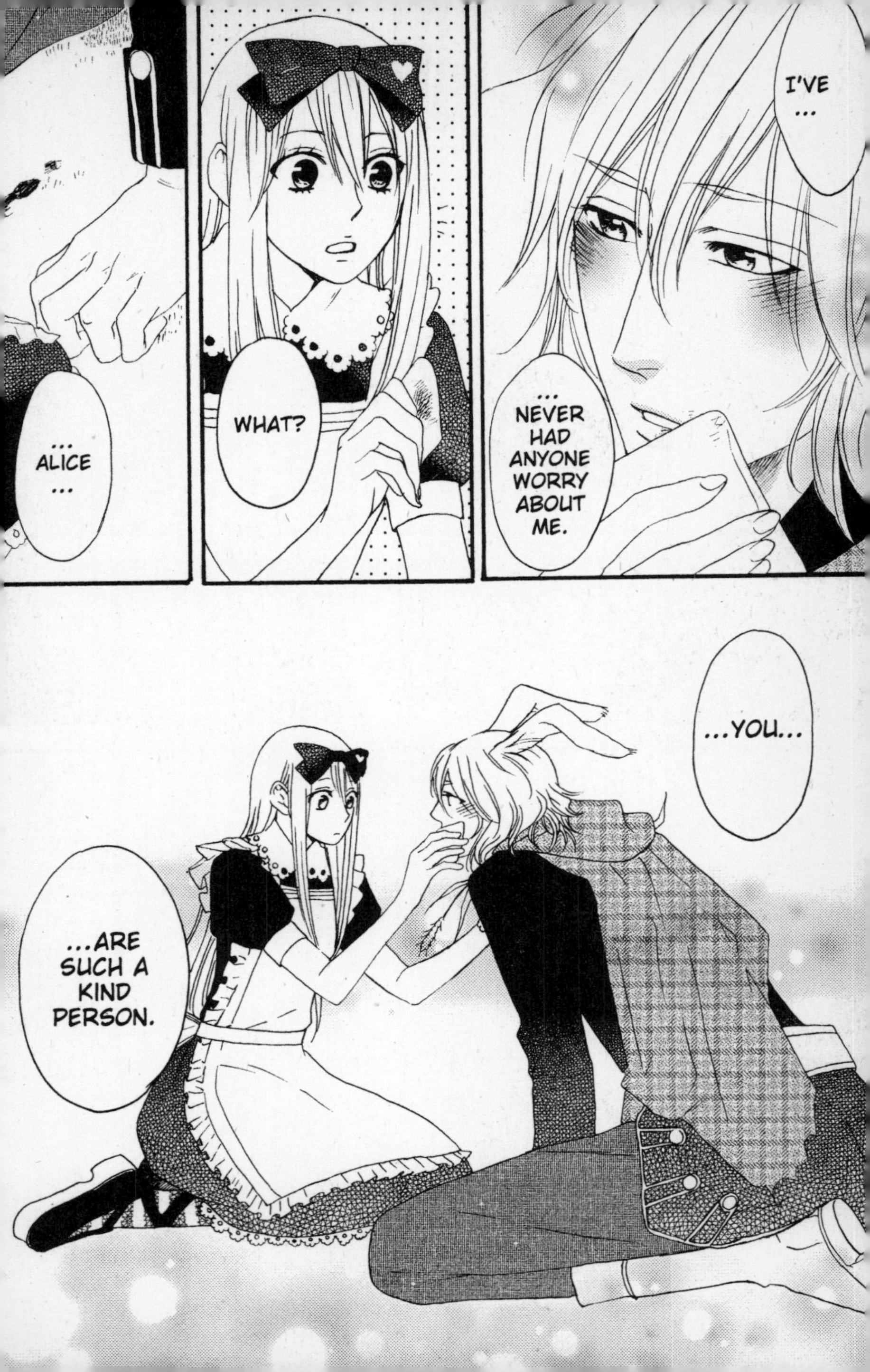
I'VE ...
... NEVER HAD ANYONE WORRY ABOUT ME.
WHAT?
... ALICE ...
...YOU...
...ARE SUCH A KIND PERSON.

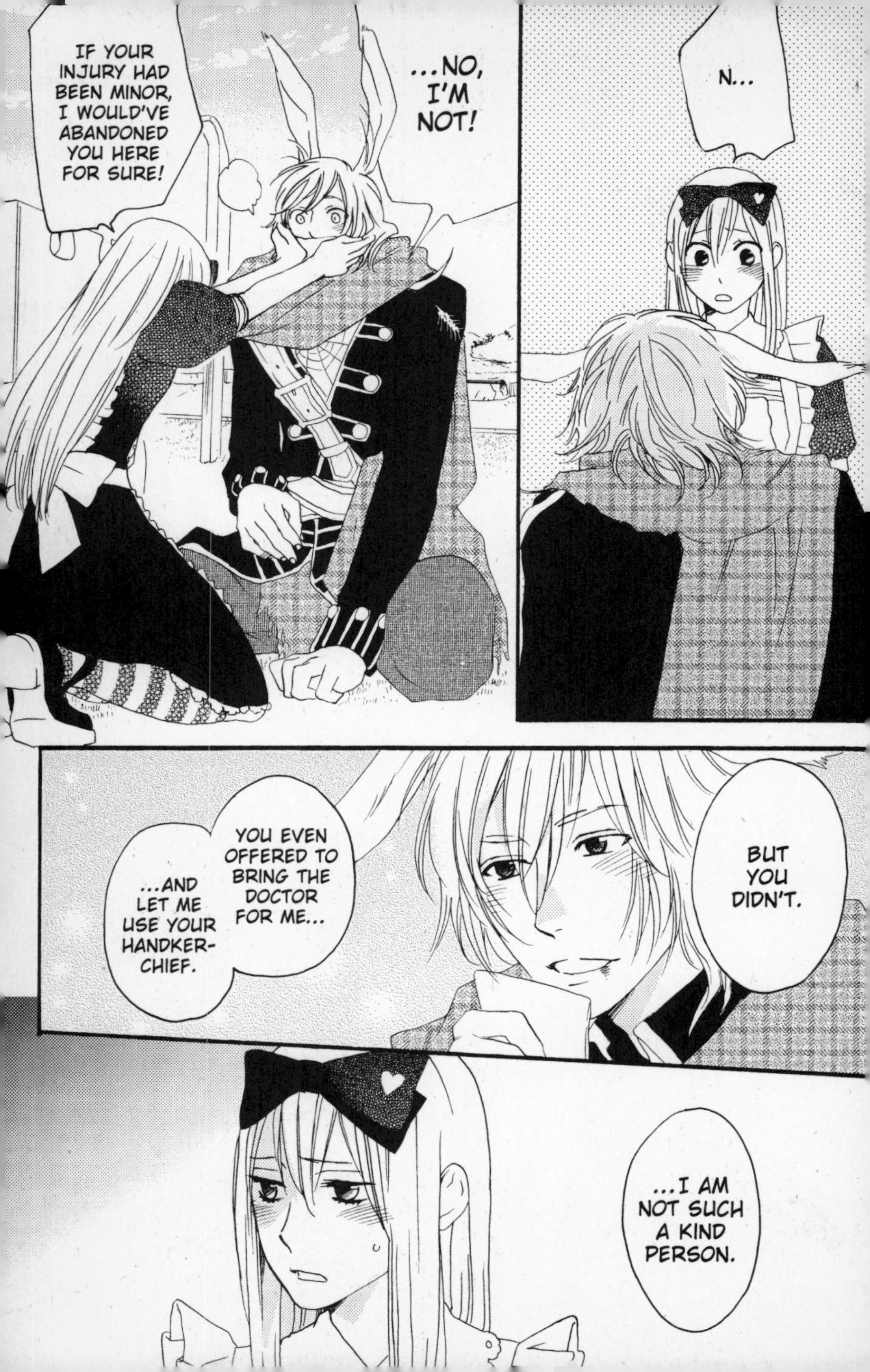
N...
...NO, I'M NOT!
IF YOUR INJURY HAD BEEN MINOR, I WOULD'VE ABANDONED YOU HERE FOR SURE!
BUT YOU DIDN'T.
YOU EVEN OFFERED TO BRING THE DOCTOR FOR ME...
...AND LET ME USE YOUR HANDKER-CHIEF.
...I AM NOT SUCH A KIND PERSON.

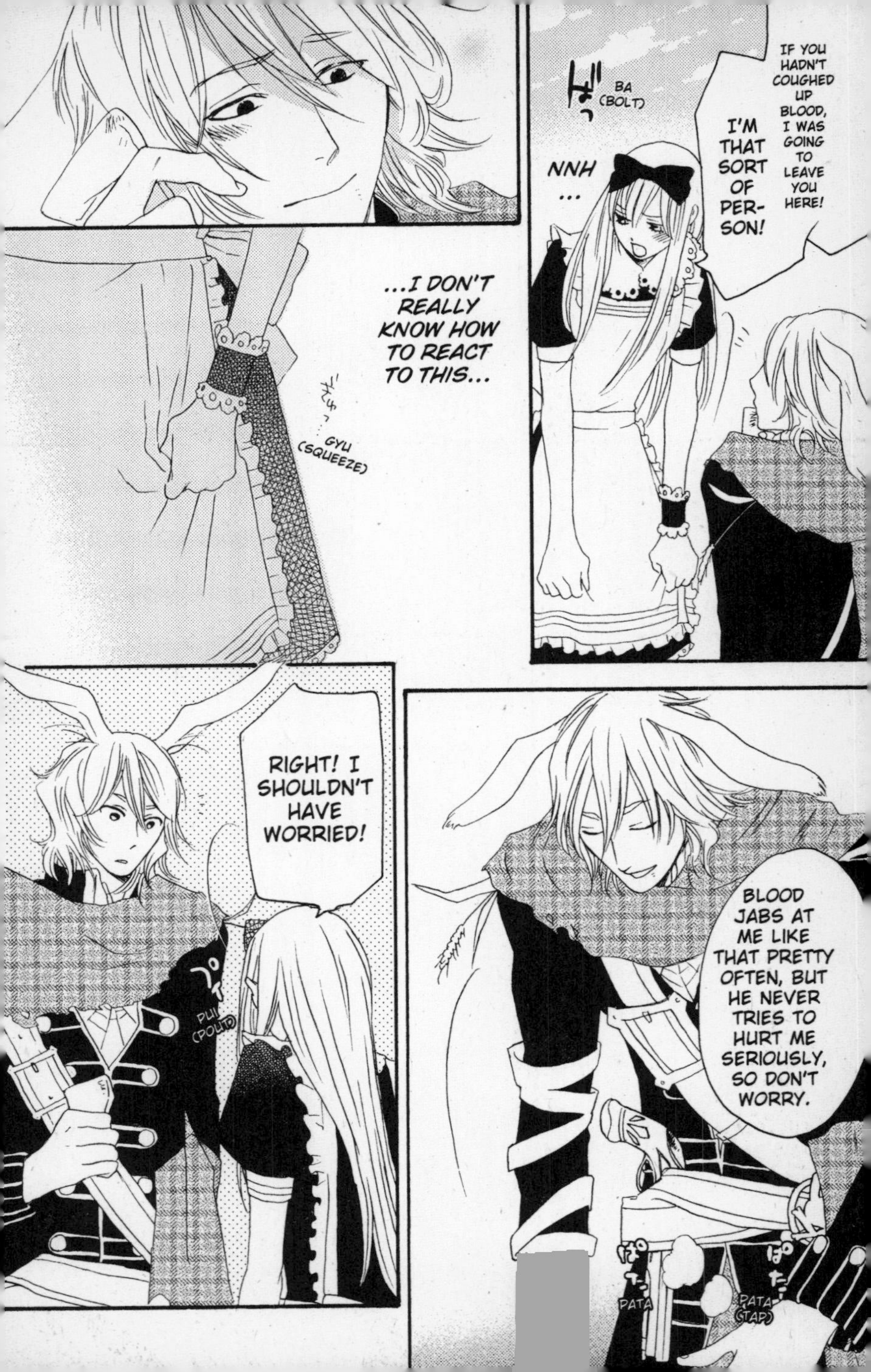
IF YOU HADN'T COUGHED UP BLOOD, I WAS GOING TO LEAVE YOU HERE!
I'M THAT SORT OF PER-SON!
BA (BOLT)
NNH ...
...I DON'T REALLY KNOW HOW TO REACT TO THIS...
GYU (SQUEEZE)
BLOOD JABS AT ME LIKE THAT PRETTY OFTEN, BUT HE NEVER TRIES TO HURT ME SERIOUSLY, SO DON'T WORRY.
PATA
PATA (TAP)
RIGHT! I SHOULDN'T HAVE WORRIED!
PUI (POUT)

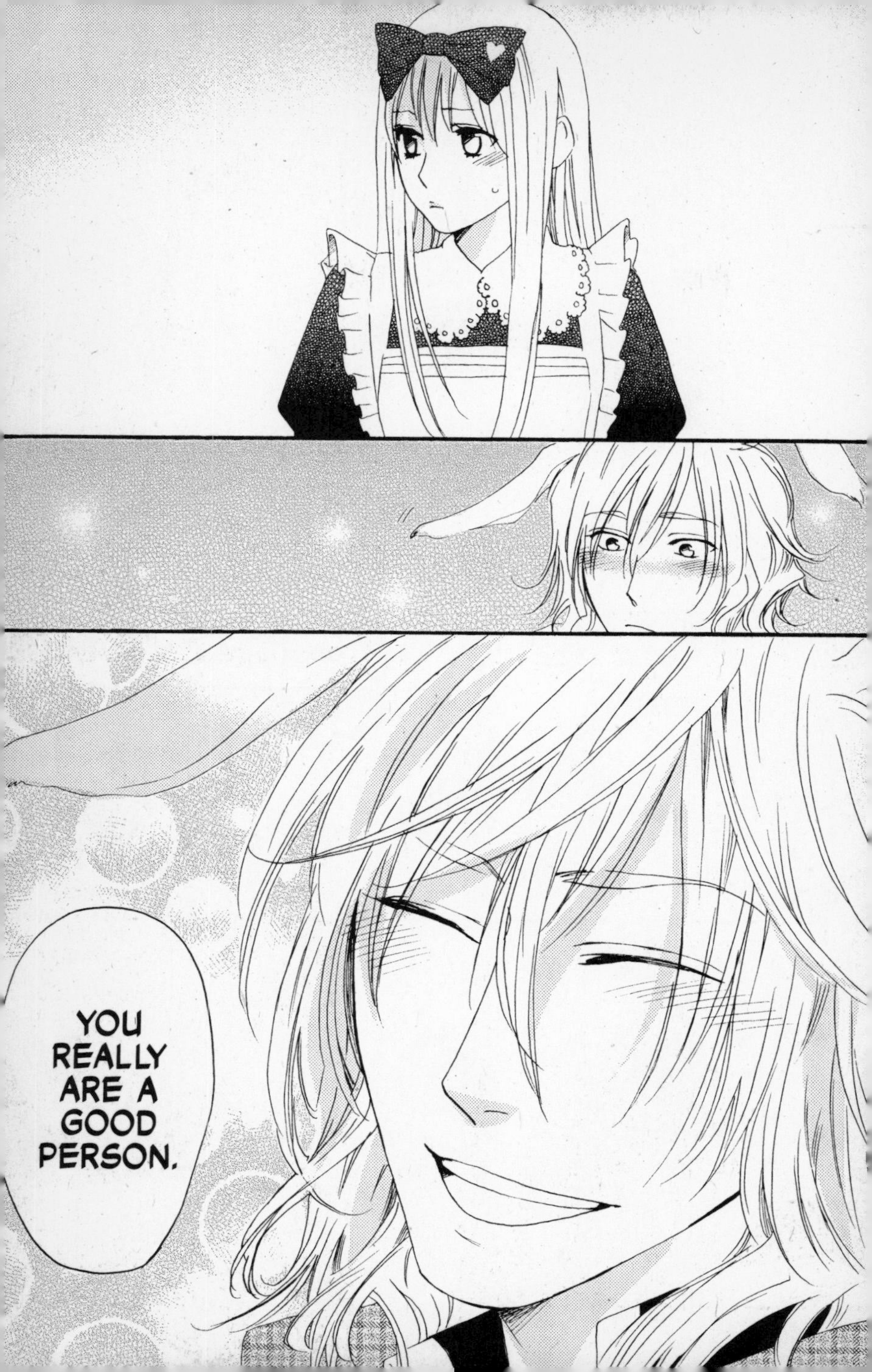
YOU REALLY ARE A GOOD PERSON.

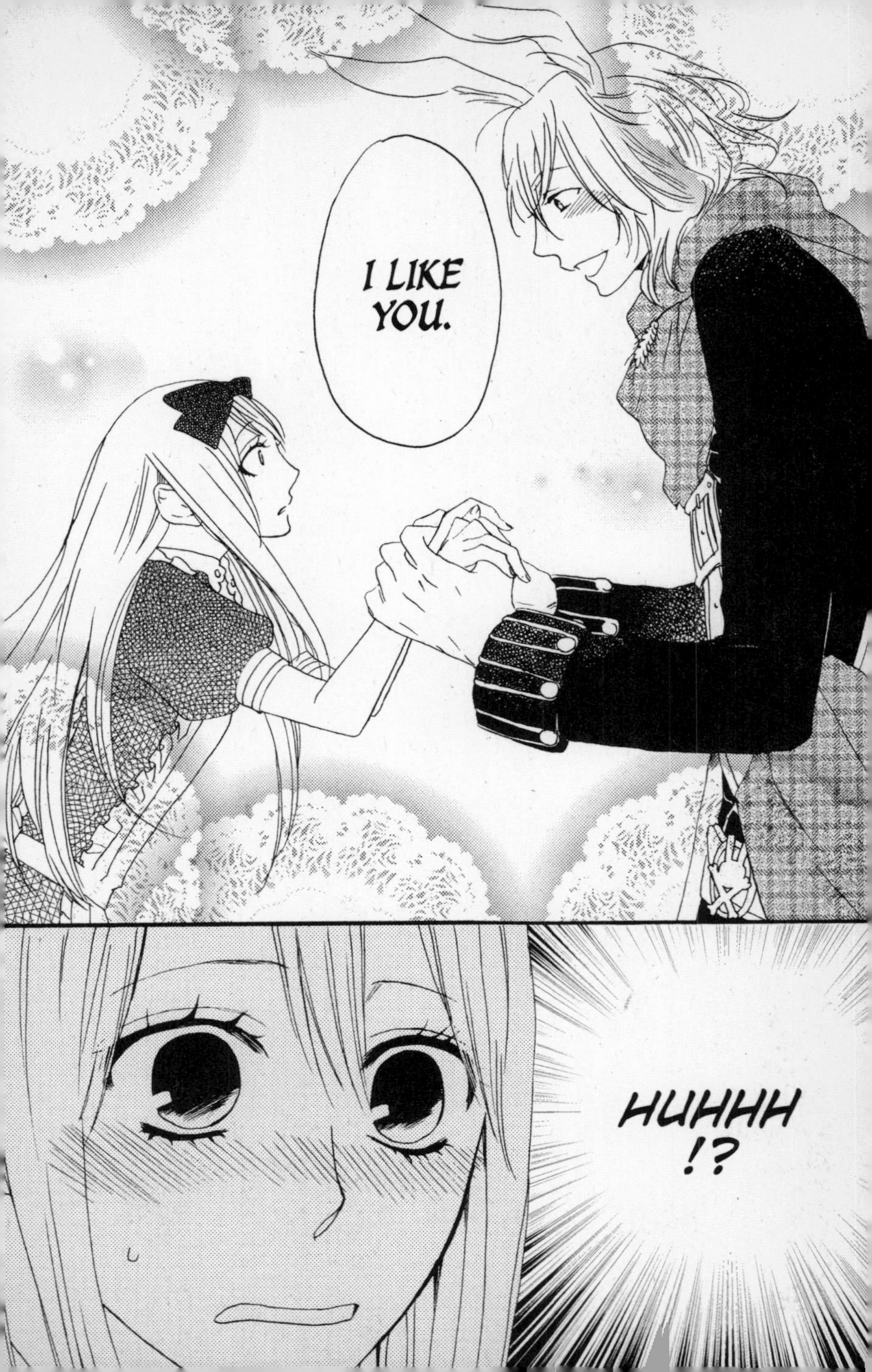
I LIKE YOU.
HUHHH !?

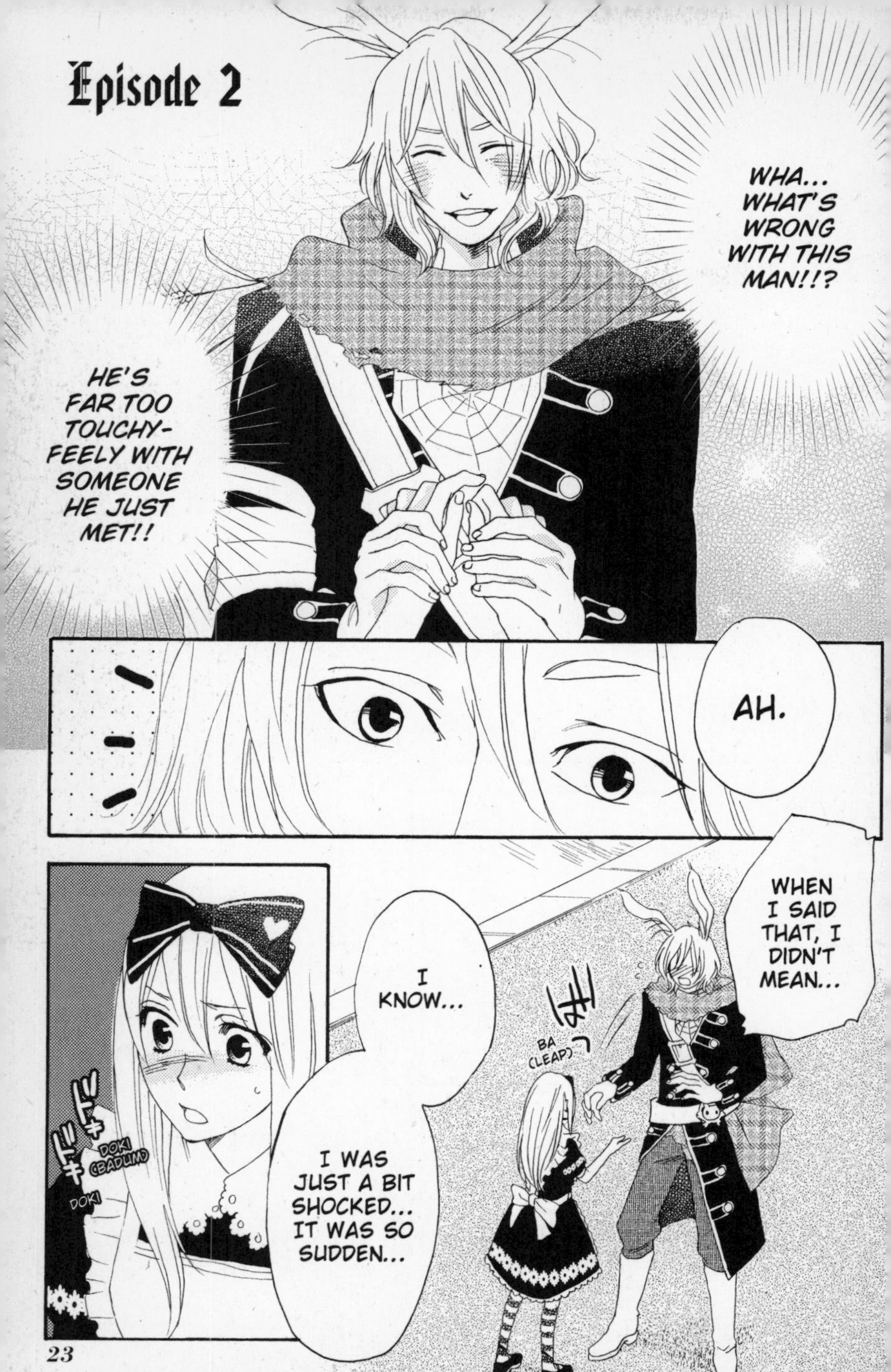
Episode 2
WHA... WHAT'S WRONG WITH THIS MAN!!?
HE'S FAR TOO TOUCHY-FEELY WITH SOMEONE HE JUST MET!!
AH.
WHEN I SAID THAT, I DIDN'T MEAN...
ばっ
BA (LEAP)
I KNOW...
I WAS JUST A BIT SHOCKED... IT WAS SO SUDDEN...
ドキ ドキ
DOKI (BADUM)
DOKI

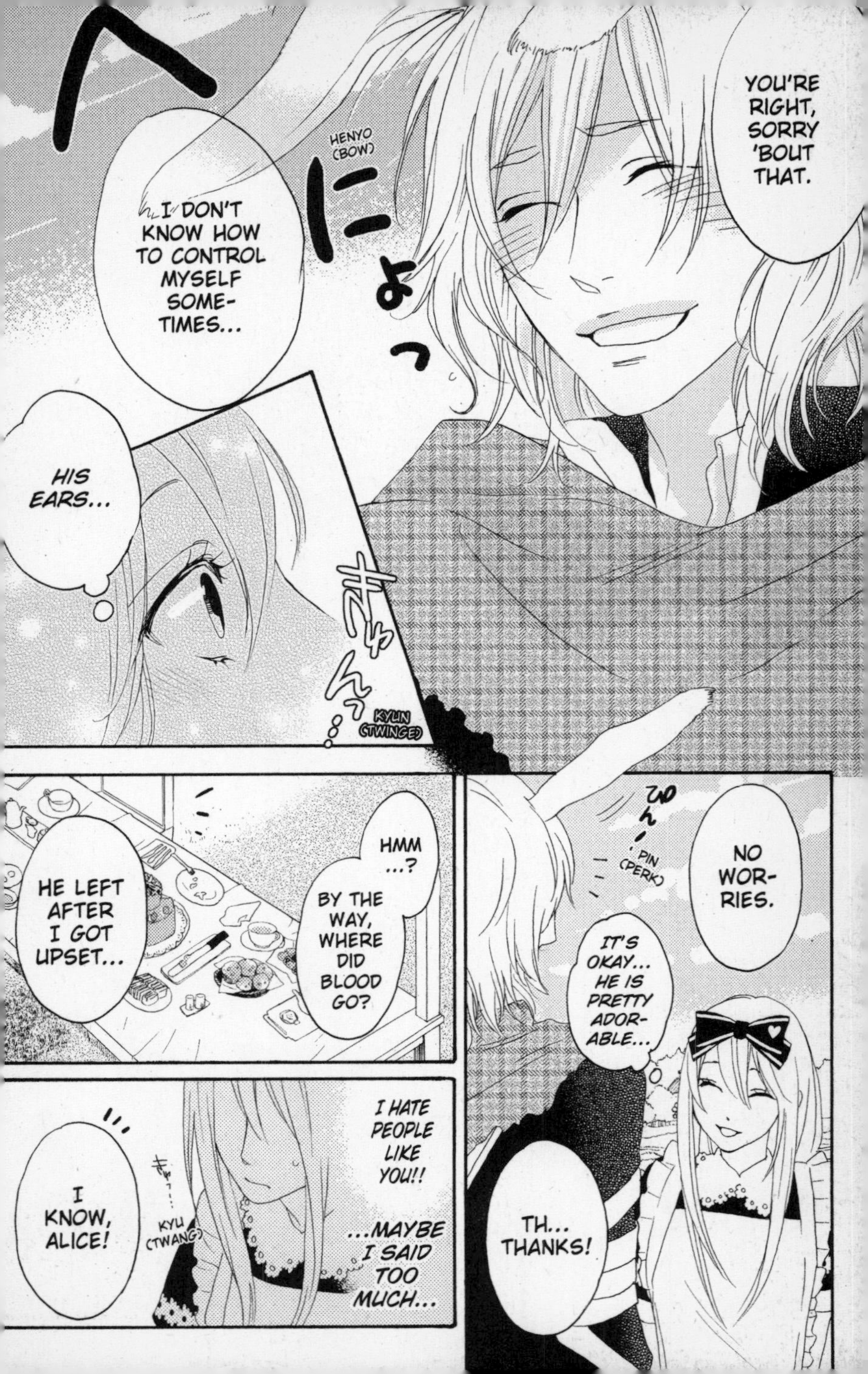
YOU'RE RIGHT, SORRY 'BOUT THAT.
HENYO (BOW)
I DON'T KNOW HOW TO CONTROL MYSELF SOME-TIMES...
HIS EARS...
KYUN (TWINGED)
PIN (PERK)
NO WOR-RIES.
IT'S OKAY... HE IS PRETTY ADOR-ABLE...
TH... THANKS!
HMM ...?
BY THE WAY, WHERE DID BLOOD GO?
HE LEFT AFTER I GOT UPSET...
I HATE PEOPLE LIKE YOU!!
...MAYBE I SAID TOO MUCH...
KYU (TWANG)
I KNOW, ALICE!

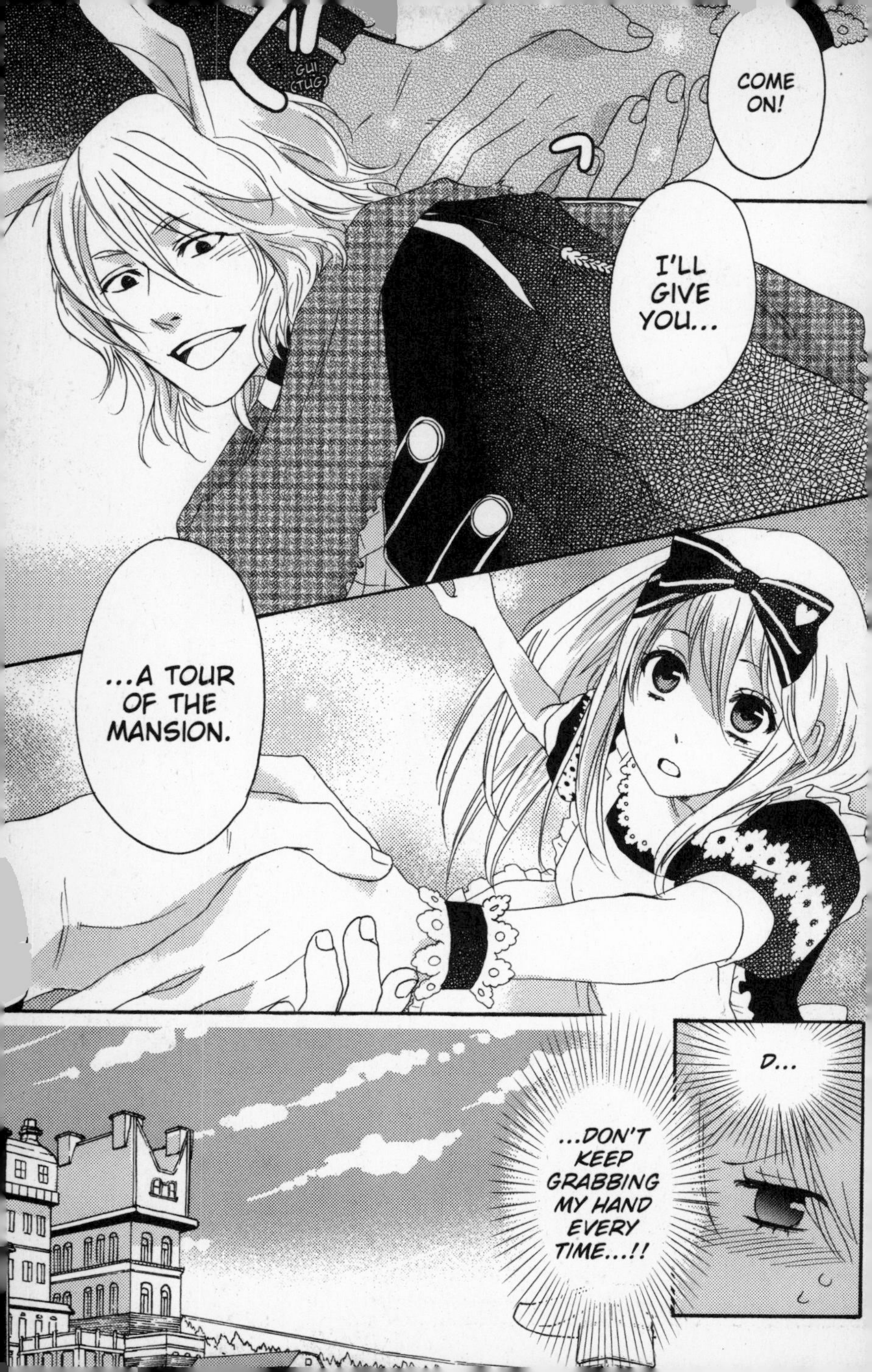
COME ON!
GUI (TUG)
I'LL GIVE YOU...
...A TOUR OF THE MANSION.
D...
...DON'T KEEP GRABBING MY HAND EVERY TIME...!!

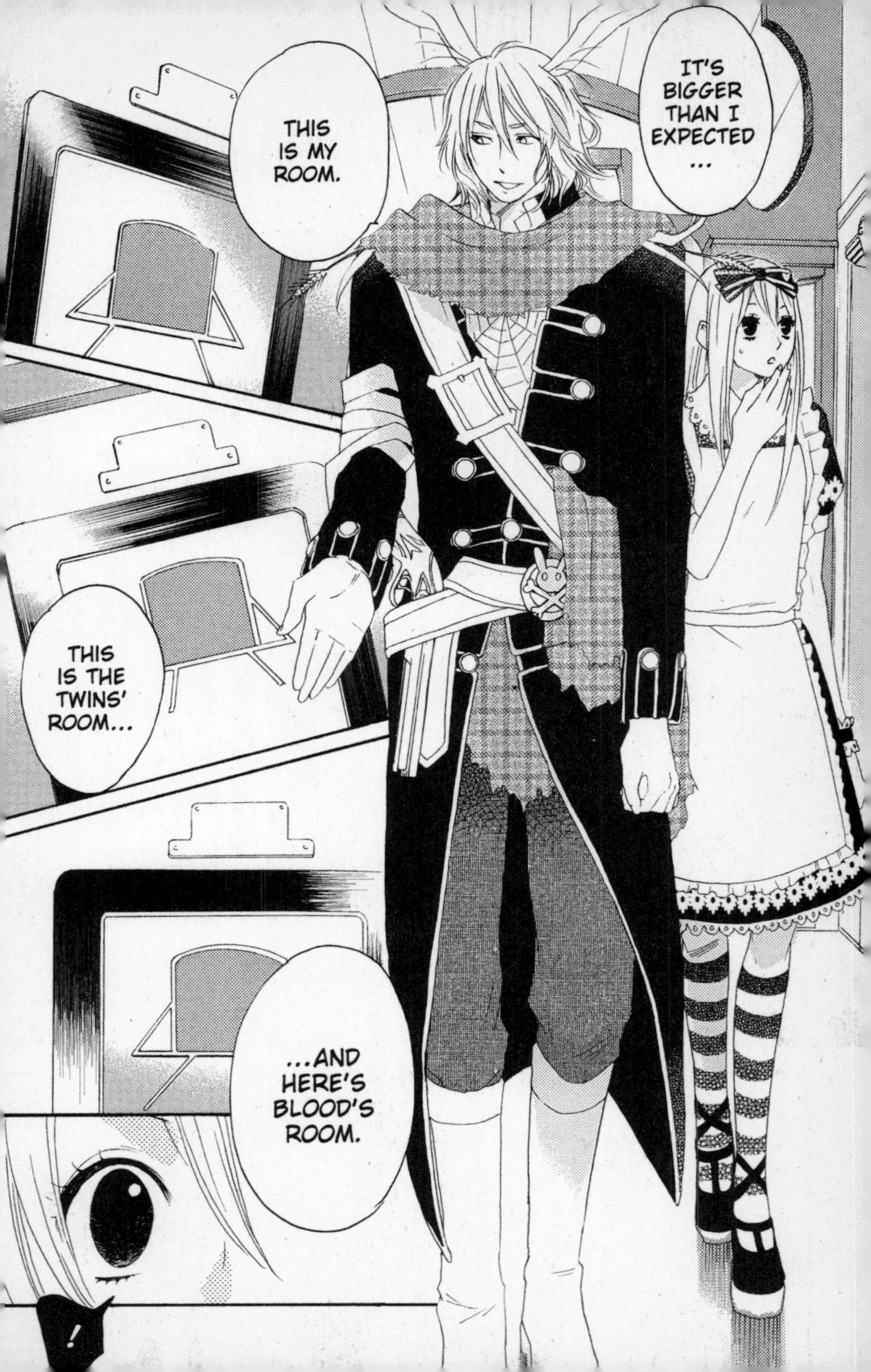
IT'S BIGGER THAN I EXPECTED ...
THIS IS MY ROOM.
THIS IS THE TWINS' ROOM...
...AND HERE'S BLOOD'S ROOM.
!

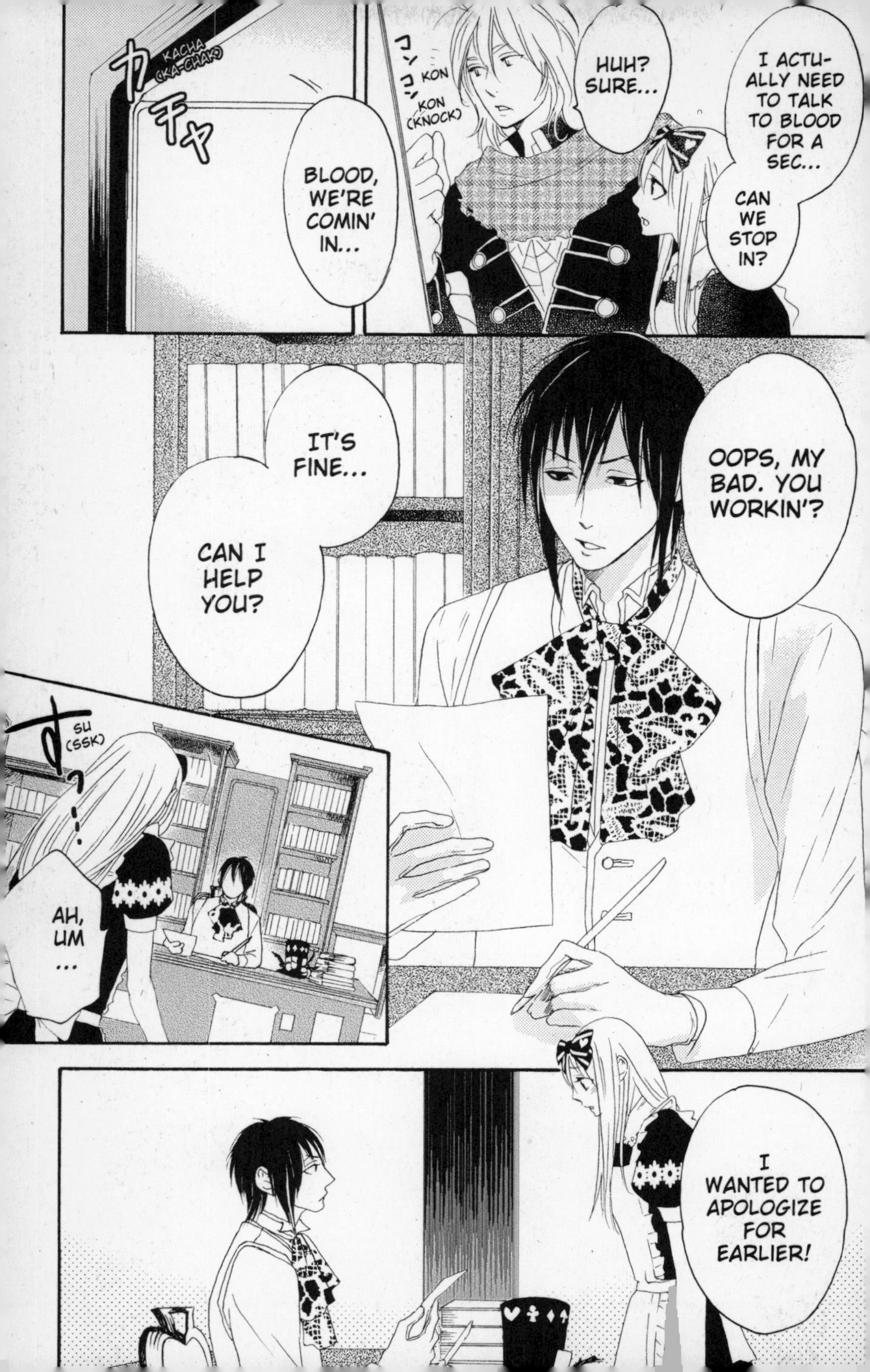
I ACTUALLY NEED TO TALK TO BLOOD FOR A SEC...
CAN WE STOP IN?
HUH? SURE...
コンコン
KON KON (KNOCK)
BLOOD, WE'RE COMIN' IN...
カチャ
KACHA (KA-CHAK)
OOPS, MY BAD. YOU WORKIN'?
IT'S FINE...
CAN I HELP YOU?
す
SU (SSK)
AH, UM...
I WANTED TO APOLOGIZE FOR EARLIER!

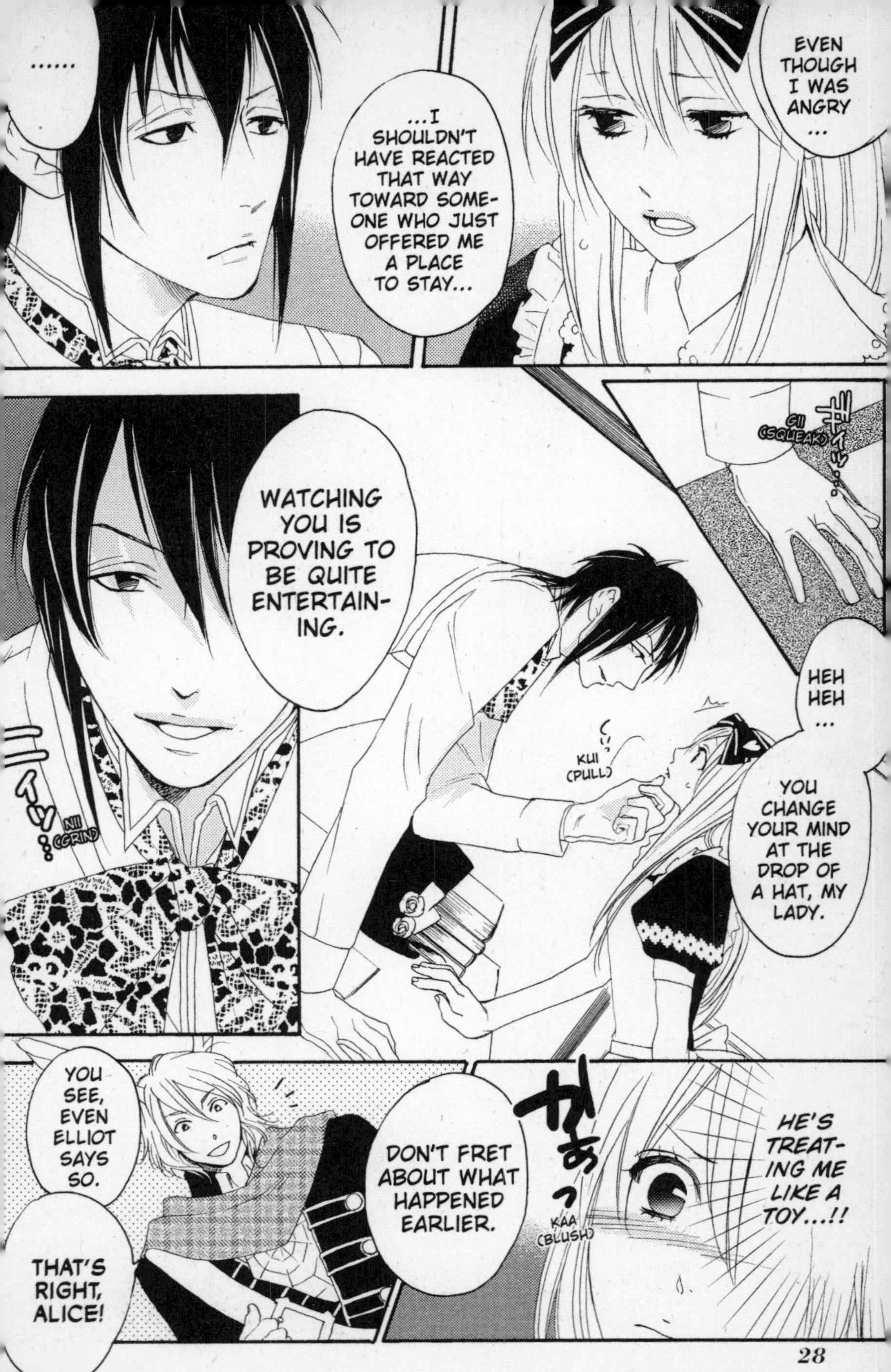
EVEN THOUGH I WAS ANGRY ...
...I SHOULDN'T HAVE REACTED THAT WAY TOWARD SOME-ONE WHO JUST OFFERED ME A PLACE TO STAY...
......
GII (SQUEAK)
HEH HEH ...
YOU CHANGE YOUR MIND AT THE DROP OF A HAT, MY LADY.
KUI (PULL)
WATCHING YOU IS PROVING TO BE QUITE ENTERTAIN-ING.
NII (GRIN)
HE'S TREAT-ING ME LIKE A TOY...!!
KAA (BLUSH)
DON'T FRET ABOUT WHAT HAPPENED EARLIER.
YOU SEE, EVEN ELLIOT SAYS SO.
THAT'S RIGHT, ALICE!

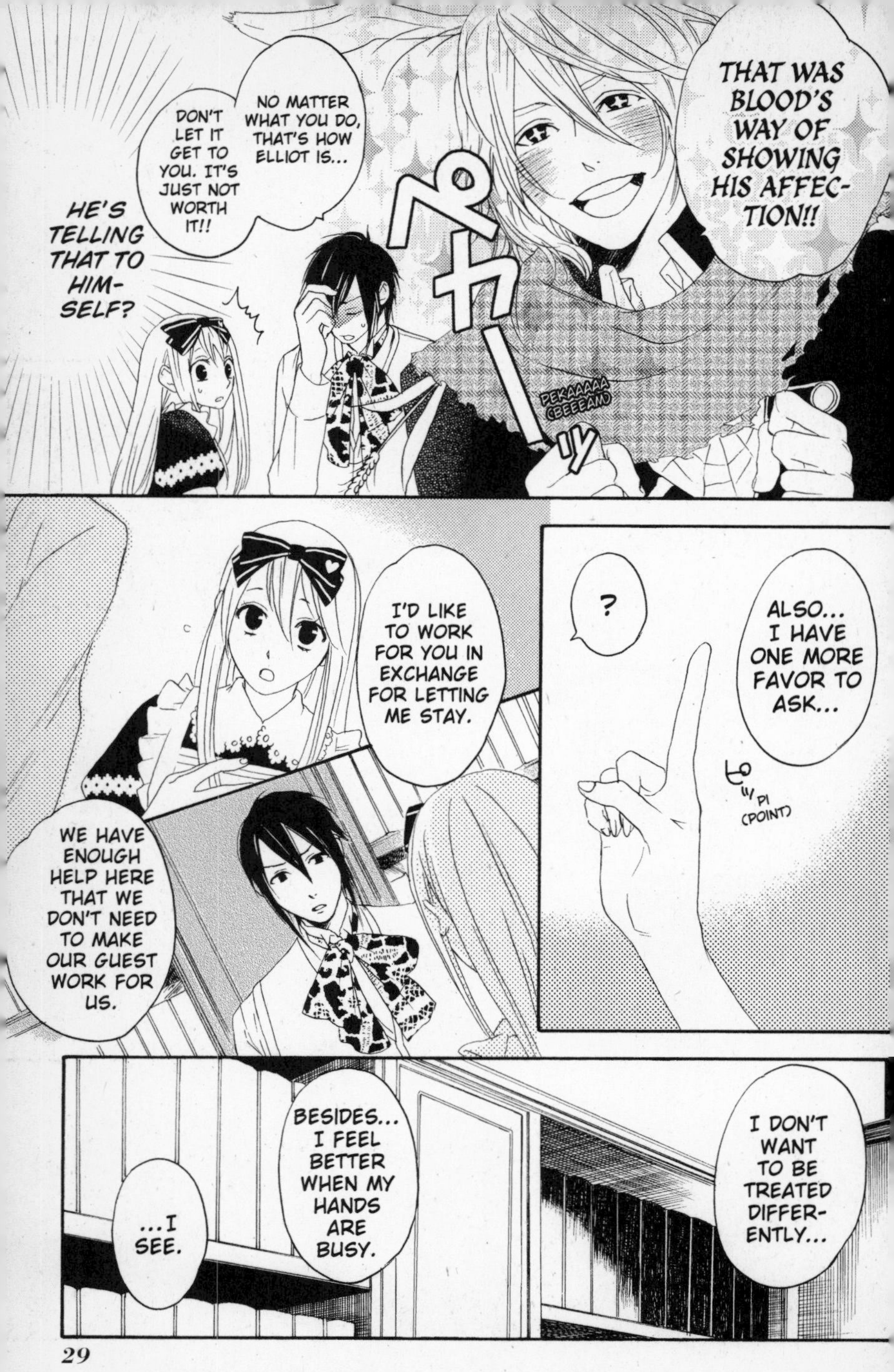
THAT WAS BLOOD'S WAY OF SHOWING HIS AFFECTION!!
ペカーッ
PEKAAAAA (BEEEAM)
NO MATTER WHAT YOU DO, THAT'S HOW ELLIOT IS...
DON'T LET IT GET TO YOU. IT'S JUST NOT WORTH IT!!
HE'S TELLING THAT TO HIMSELF?
ALSO... I HAVE ONE MORE FAVOR TO ASK...
PI (POINT)
?
I'D LIKE TO WORK FOR YOU IN EXCHANGE FOR LETTING ME STAY.
WE HAVE ENOUGH HELP HERE THAT WE DON'T NEED TO MAKE OUR GUEST WORK FOR US.
I DON'T WANT TO BE TREATED DIFFERENTLY...
BESIDES... I FEEL BETTER WHEN MY HANDS ARE BUSY.
...I SEE.

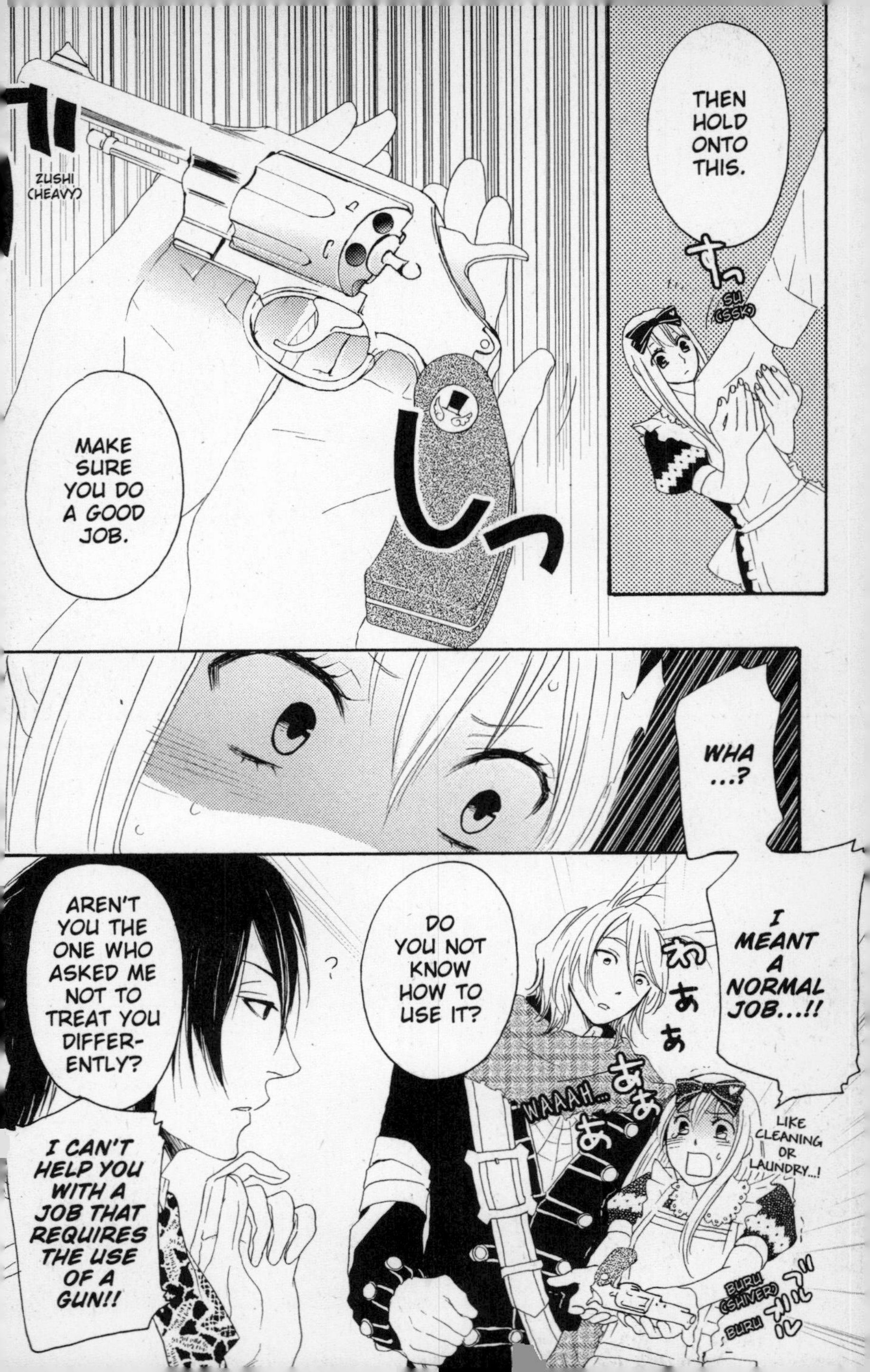
THEN HOLD ONTO THIS.
SU (SSK)
ZUSHI (HEAVY)
MAKE SURE YOU DO A GOOD JOB.
WHA ...?
I MEANT A NORMAL JOB...!!
LIKE CLEANING OR LAUNDRY...!
WAAAH...
BURU (SHIVER) BURU
DO YOU NOT KNOW HOW TO USE IT?
AREN'T YOU THE ONE WHO ASKED ME NOT TO TREAT YOU DIFFER-ENTLY?
I CAN'T HELP YOU WITH A JOB THAT REQUIRES THE USE OF A GUN!!

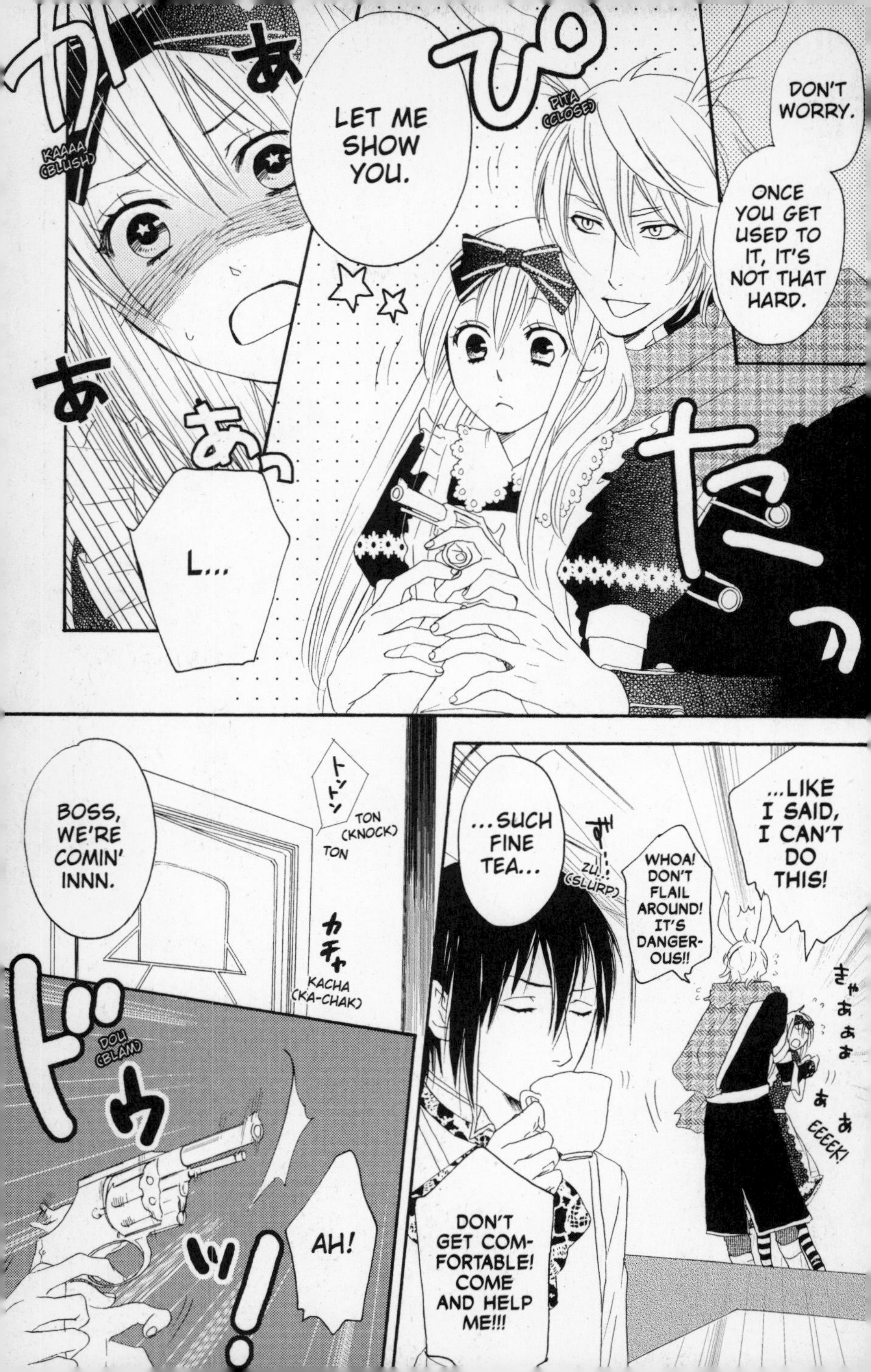
DON'T WORRY.
ONCE YOU GET USED TO IT, IT'S NOT THAT HARD.
たっ
ぴ
PITA (CLOSE)
LET ME SHOW YOU.
かーぁ
KAAAA (BLUSH)
あ あっ
L...
...LIKE I SAID, I CAN'T DO THIS!
WHOA! DON'T FLAIL AROUND! IT'S DANGER-OUS!!
きゃあぁぁ あ あ
EEEEK!
...SUCH FINE TEA...
ずー
ZU (SLURP)
DON'T GET COM-FORTABLE! COME AND HELP ME!!!
トントン
TON (KNOCK) TON
BOSS, WE'RE COMIN' INNN.
カチャ
KACHA (KA-CHAK)
ドゥッ!
DOU (BLAM)
AH!

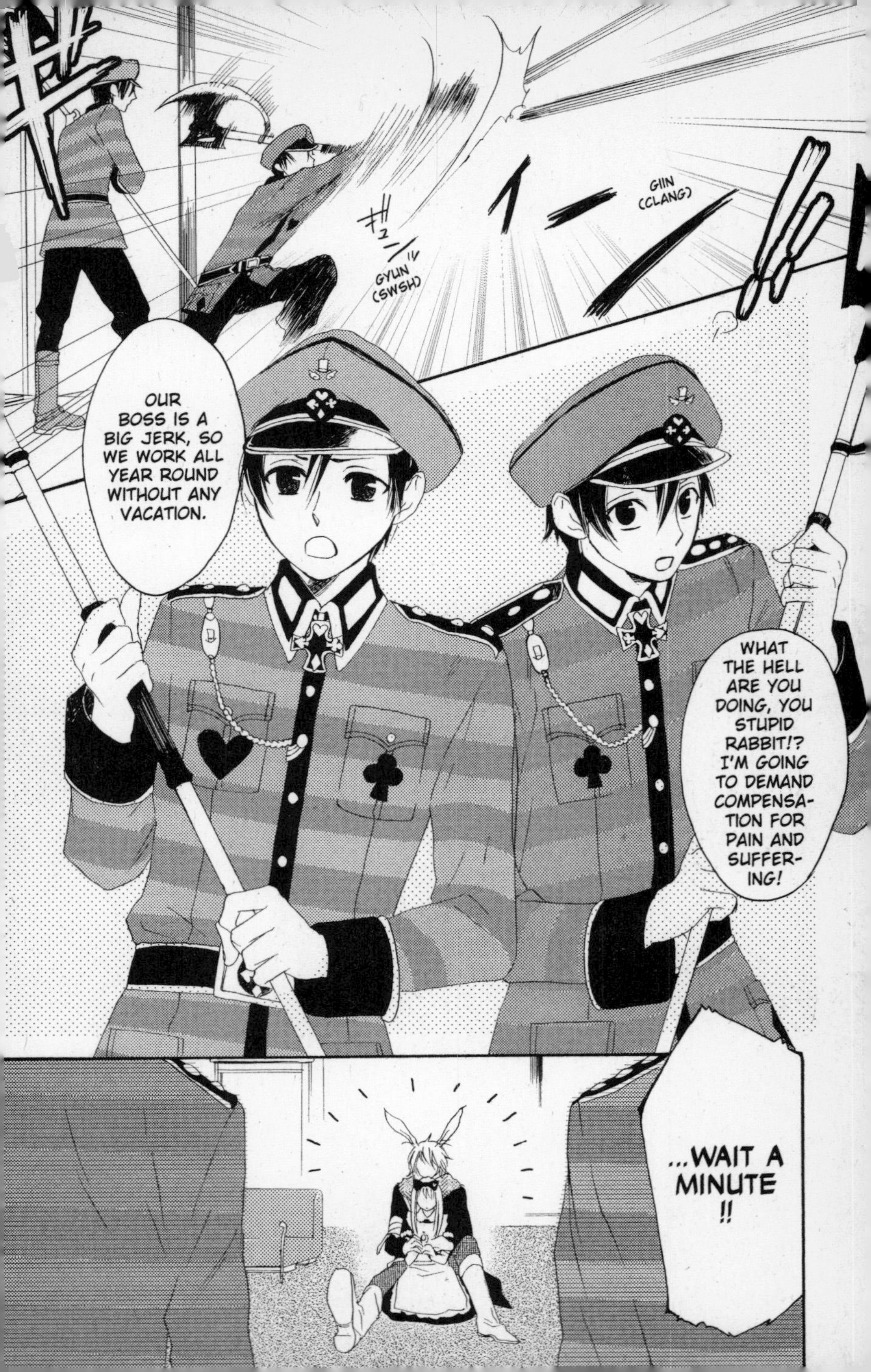
GIIN (CLANG)
GYUN (SWSH)
WHAT THE HELL ARE YOU DOING, YOU STUPID RABBIT!? I'M GOING TO DEMAND COMPENSA-TION FOR PAIN AND SUFFER-ING!
OUR BOSS IS A BIG JERK, SO WE WORK ALL YEAR ROUND WITHOUT ANY VACATION.
...WAIT A MINUTE !!

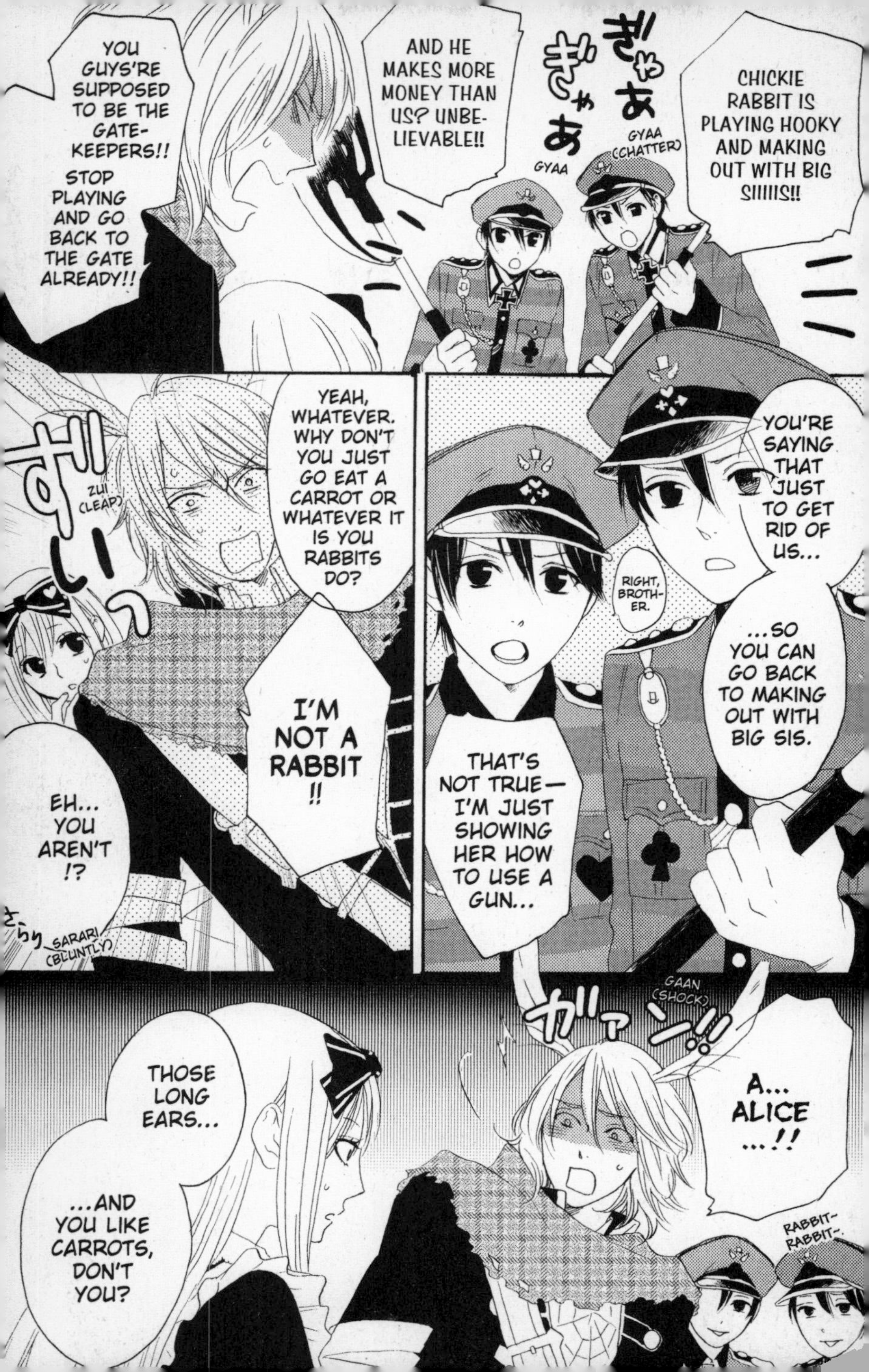
ぎゃあ ぎゃあ
GYAA (CHATTER)
GYAA
CHICKIE RABBIT IS PLAYING HOOKY AND MAKING OUT WITH BIG SIIIIIS!!
AND HE MAKES MORE MONEY THAN US? UNBE-LIEVABLE!!
YOU GUYS'RE SUPPOSED TO BE THE GATE-KEEPERS!!
STOP PLAYING AND GO BACK TO THE GATE ALREADY!!
YOU'RE SAYING THAT JUST TO GET RID OF US...
RIGHT, BROTHER.
...SO YOU CAN GO BACK TO MAKING OUT WITH BIG SIS.
THAT'S NOT TRUE— I'M JUST SHOWING HER HOW TO USE A GUN...
YEAH, WHATEVER. WHY DON'T YOU JUST GO EAT A CARROT OR WHATEVER IT IS YOU RABBITS DO?
ずいっ
ZUI (LEAP)
I'M NOT A RABBIT!!
EH... YOU AREN'T!?
さらり
SARARI (BLUNTLY)
ガァン!!
GAAN (SHOCK)
A... ALICE...!!
RABBIT-RABBIT-.
THOSE LONG EARS...
...AND YOU LIKE CARROTS, DON'T YOU?

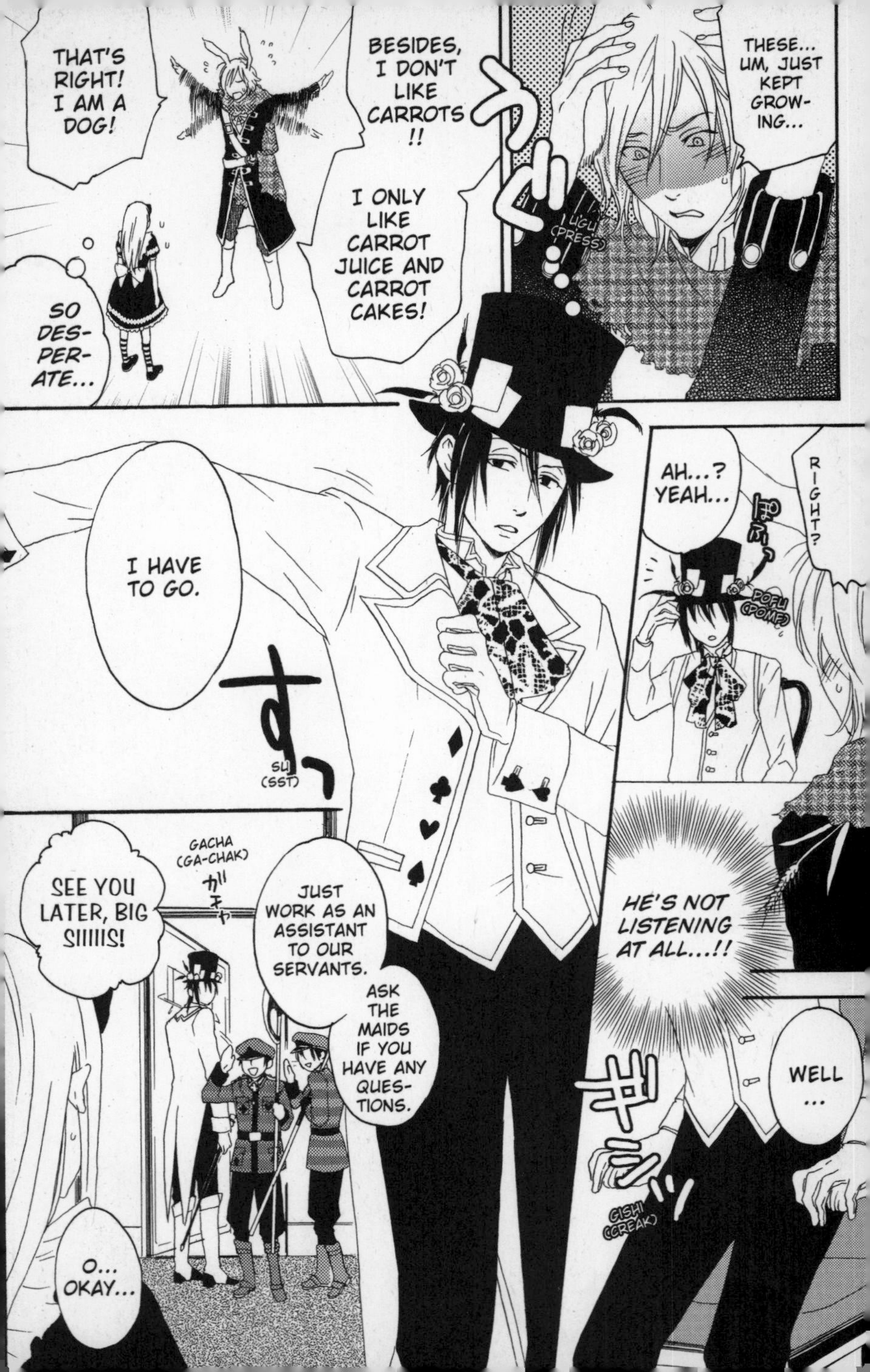
THESE... UM, JUST KEPT GROW-ING...
UGU (PRESS)
THAT'S RIGHT! I AM A DOG!
BESIDES, I DON'T LIKE CARROTS!!
I ONLY LIKE CARROT JUICE AND CARROT CAKES!
SO DES-PER-ATE...
RIGHT?
AH...? YEAH...
POFU (POMF)
HE'S NOT LISTENING AT ALL...!!
WELL...
GISHI (CREAK)
I HAVE TO GO.
SU (SST)
JUST WORK AS AN ASSISTANT TO OUR SERVANTS.
ASK THE MAIDS IF YOU HAVE ANY QUES-TIONS.
GACHA (GA-CHAK)
SEE YOU LATER, BIG SIIIIIS!
O... OKAY...

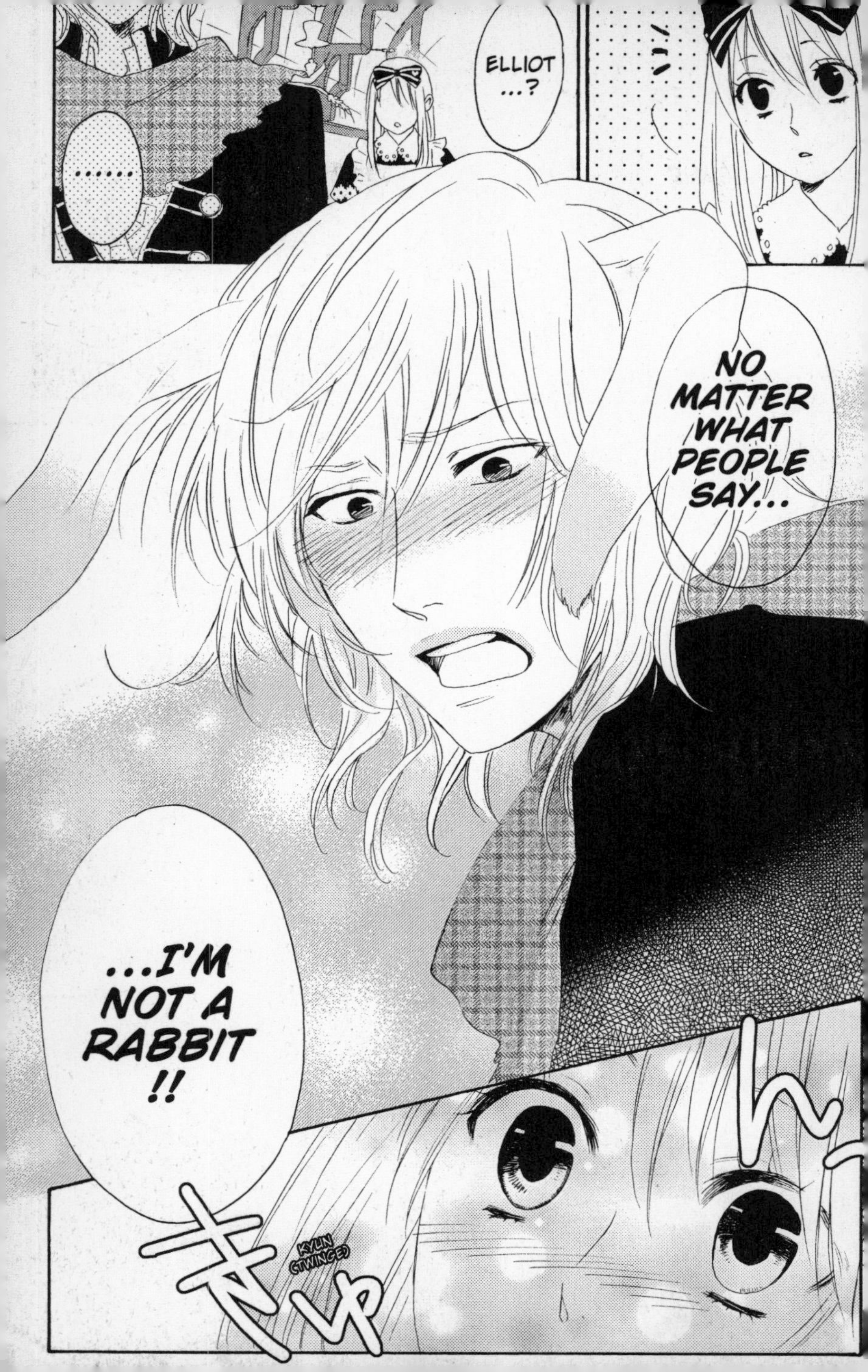
ELLIOT ...?
......
NO MATTER WHAT PEOPLE SAY...
...I'M NOT A RABBIT !!
きゅん
KYUN (TWINGE)

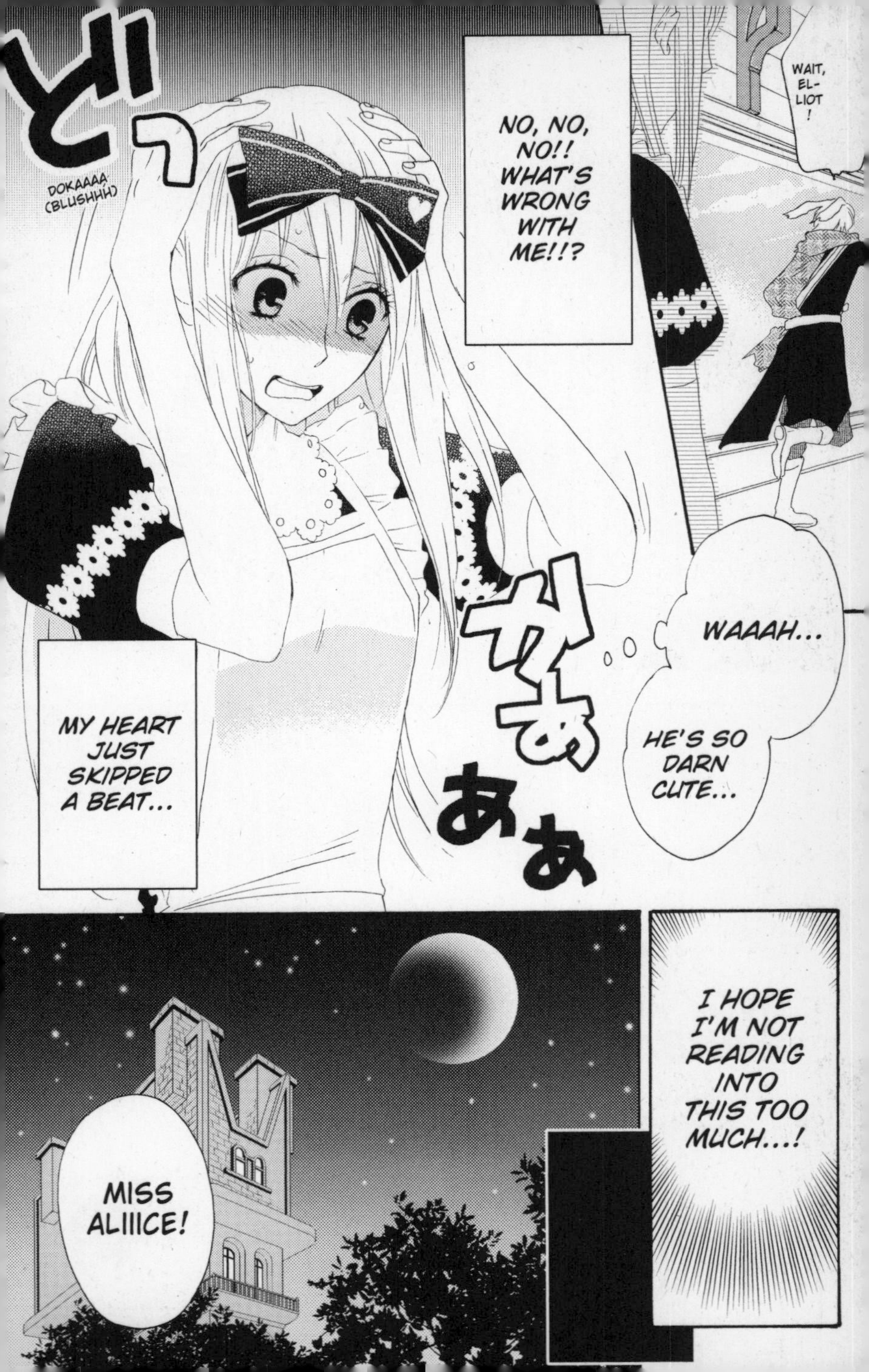
WAIT, EL-LIOT!
NO, NO, NO!! WHAT'S WRONG WITH ME!!?
どっ
DOKAAAA (BLUSHHH)
WAAAH...
HE'S SO DARN CUTE...
MY HEART JUST SKIPPED A BEAT...
I HOPE I'M NOT READING INTO THIS TOO MUCH...!
MISS ALIIICE!

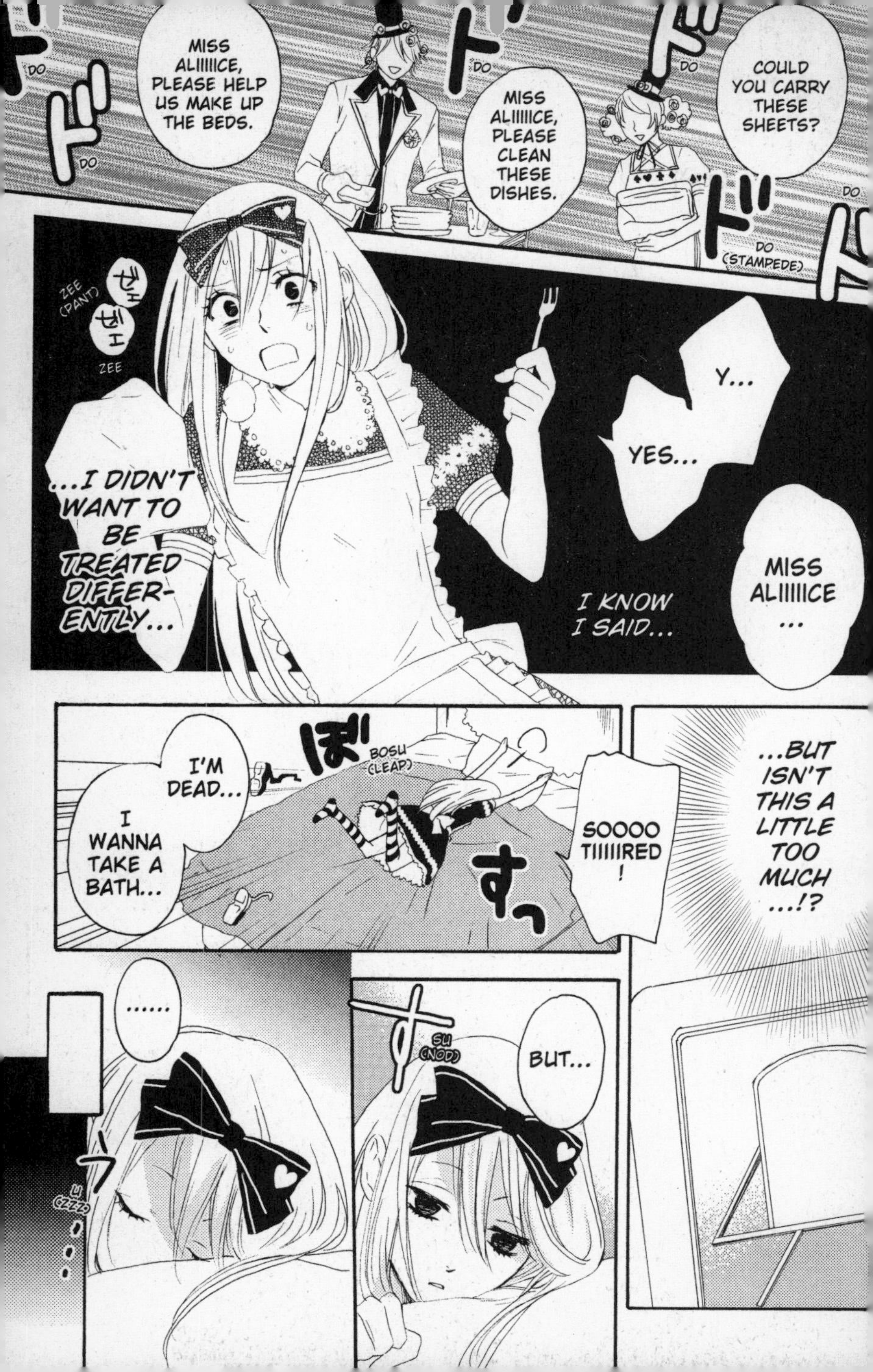
DO
COULD YOU CARRY THESE SHEETS?
DO (STAMPEDE)
DO
MISS ALIIIIICE, PLEASE CLEAN THESE DISHES.
DO
MISS ALIIIIICE, PLEASE HELP US MAKE UP THE BEDS.
DO
DO
Y...
YES...
MISS ALIIIIICE...
I KNOW I SAID...
...I DIDN'T WANT TO BE TREATED DIFFERENTLY...
ZEE (PANT)
ZEE
...BUT ISN'T THIS A LITTLE TOO MUCH...!?
SOOOO TIIIIIRED!
BOSU (LEAP)
I'M DEAD...
I WANNA TAKE A BATH...
BUT...
SU (NOD)
......
U (ZZZZ)

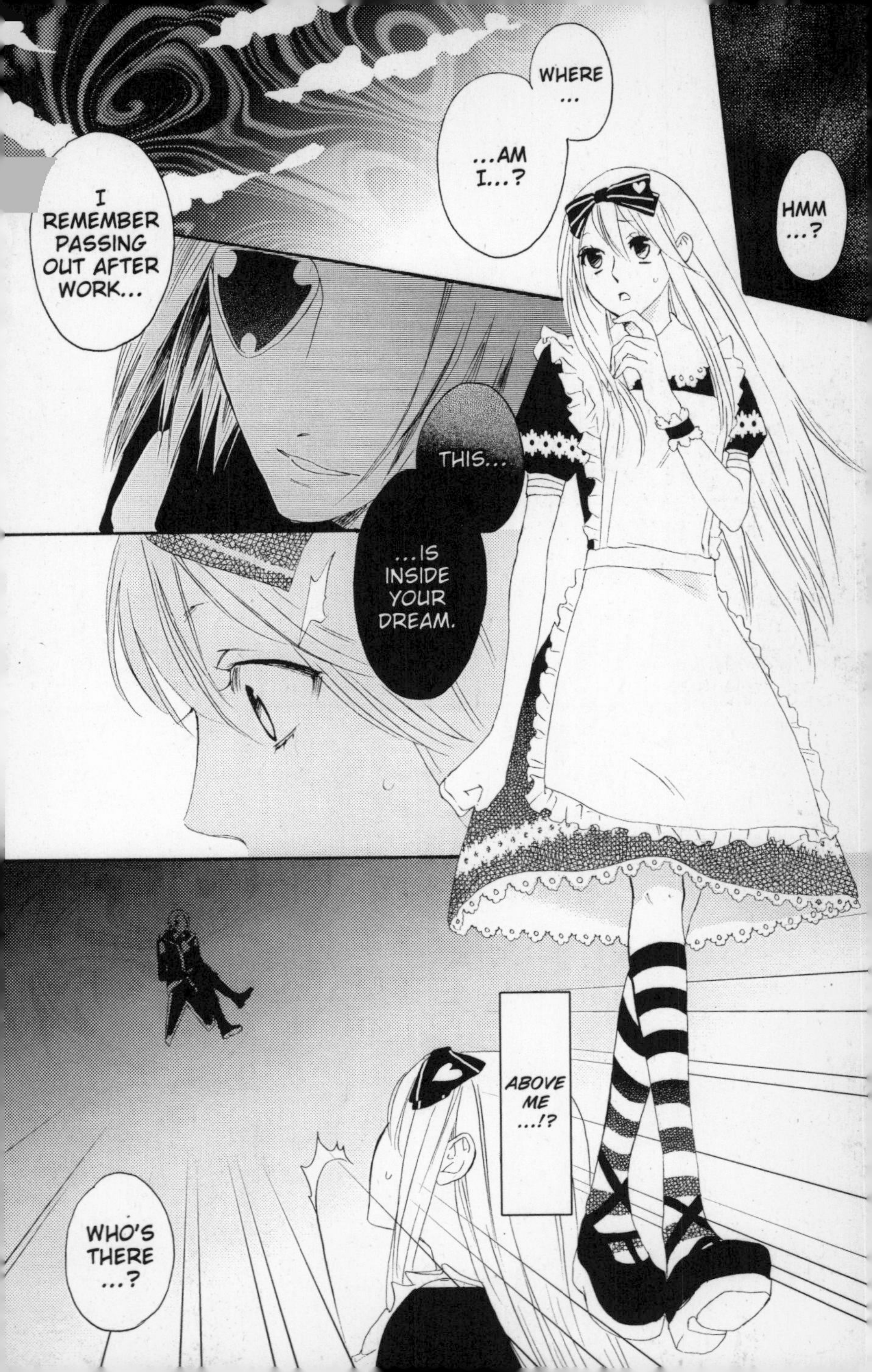
HMM ...?
WHERE ... ...AM I...?
I REMEMBER PASSING OUT AFTER WORK...
THIS...
...IS INSIDE YOUR DREAM.
ABOVE ME ...!?
WHO'S THERE ...?

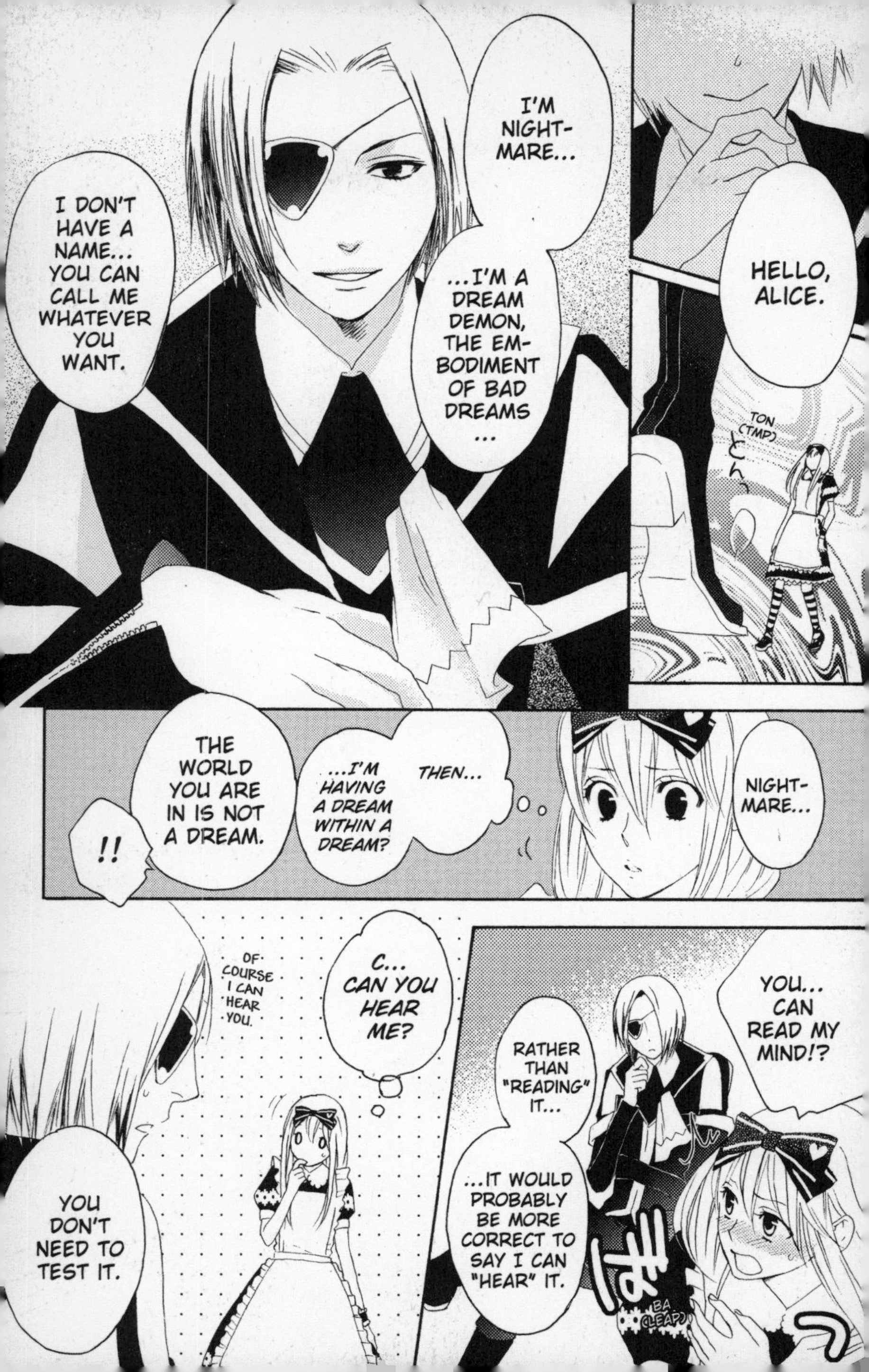
HELLO, ALICE.
TON (TMP)
I'M NIGHTMARE...
...I'M A DREAM DEMON, THE EMBODIMENT OF BAD DREAMS...
I DON'T HAVE A NAME... YOU CAN CALL ME WHATEVER YOU WANT.
NIGHTMARE...
THEN...
...I'M HAVING A DREAM WITHIN A DREAM?
THE WORLD YOU ARE IN IS NOT A DREAM.
!!
YOU... CAN READ MY MIND!?
BA (LEAP)
RATHER THAN "READING" IT...
...IT WOULD PROBABLY BE MORE CORRECT TO SAY I CAN "HEAR" IT.
C... CAN YOU HEAR ME?
OF COURSE I CAN HEAR YOU.
YOU DON'T NEED TO TEST IT.

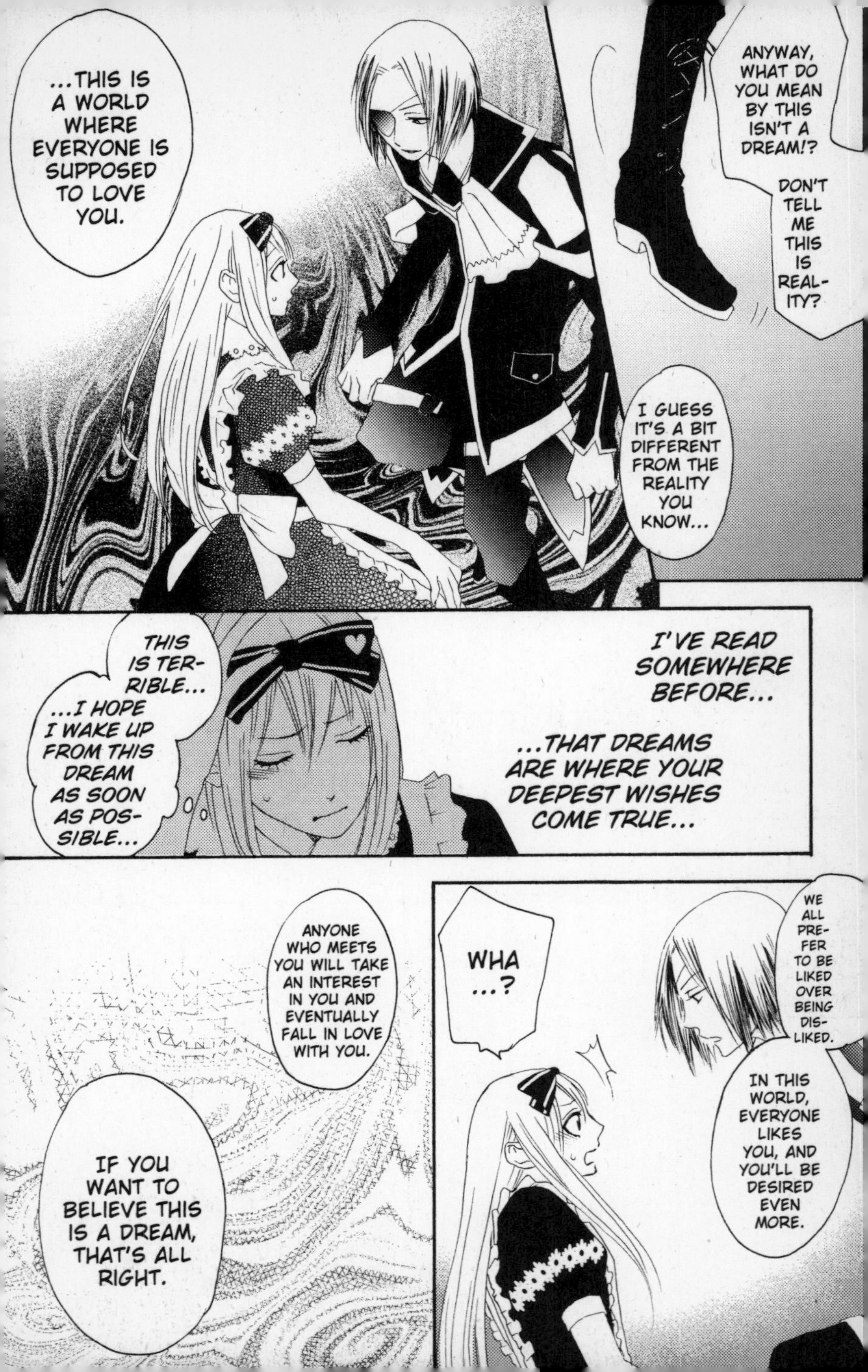
ANYWAY, WHAT DO YOU MEAN BY THIS ISN'T A DREAM!?
DON'T TELL ME THIS IS REALITY?
I GUESS IT'S A BIT DIFFERENT FROM THE REALITY YOU KNOW...
...THIS IS A WORLD WHERE EVERYONE IS SUPPOSED TO LOVE YOU.
I'VE READ SOMEWHERE BEFORE...
...THAT DREAMS ARE WHERE YOUR DEEPEST WISHES COME TRUE...
THIS IS TERRIBLE...
...I HOPE I WAKE UP FROM THIS DREAM AS SOON AS POSSIBLE...
WE ALL PREFER TO BE LIKED OVER BEING DISLIKED.
WHA ...?
IN THIS WORLD, EVERYONE LIKES YOU, AND YOU'LL BE DESIRED EVEN MORE.
ANYONE WHO MEETS YOU WILL TAKE AN INTEREST IN YOU AND EVENTUALLY FALL IN LOVE WITH YOU.
IF YOU WANT TO BELIEVE THIS IS A DREAM, THAT'S ALL RIGHT.

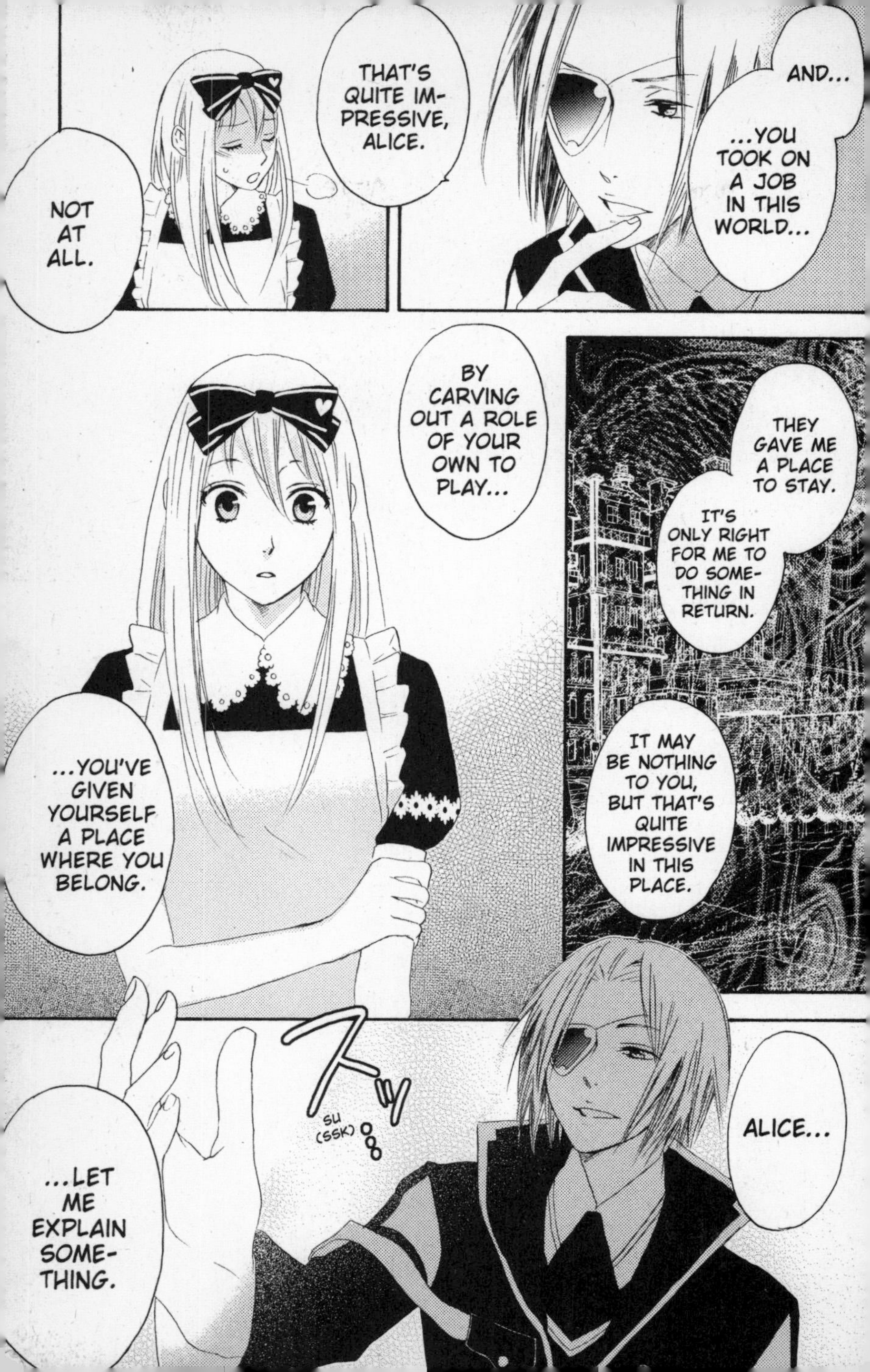
AND...
...YOU TOOK ON A JOB IN THIS WORLD...
THAT'S QUITE IM-PRESSIVE, ALICE.
NOT AT ALL.
THEY GAVE ME A PLACE TO STAY.
IT'S ONLY RIGHT FOR ME TO DO SOME-THING IN RETURN.
IT MAY BE NOTHING TO YOU, BUT THAT'S QUITE IMPRESSIVE IN THIS PLACE.
BY CARVING OUT A ROLE OF YOUR OWN TO PLAY...
...YOU'VE GIVEN YOURSELF A PLACE WHERE YOU BELONG.
ALICE...
SU (SSK)
...LET ME EXPLAIN SOME-THING.

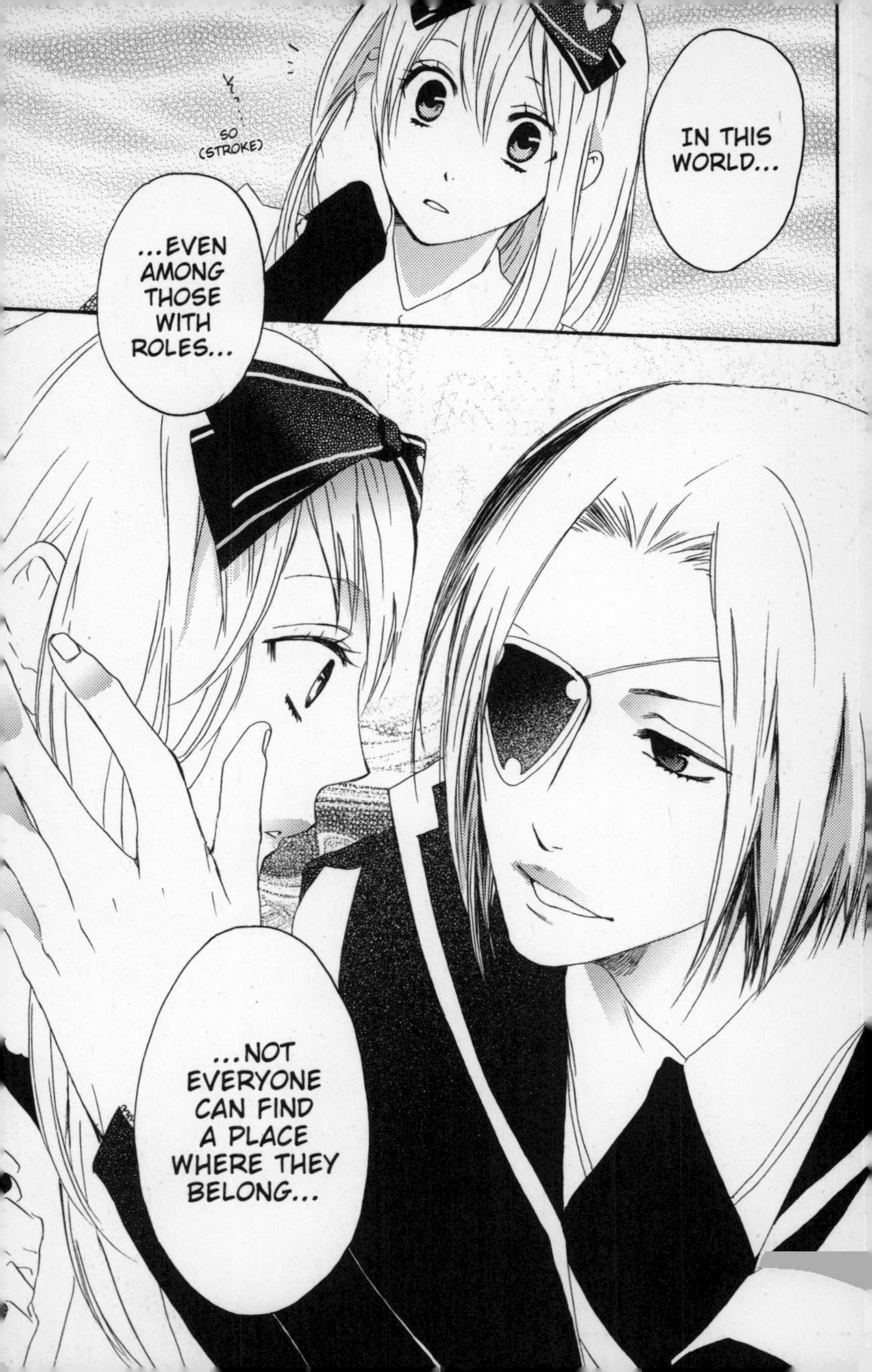
IN THIS WORLD...
SO (STROKE)
...EVEN AMONG THOSE WITH ROLES...
...NOT EVERYONE CAN FIND A PLACE WHERE THEY BELONG...

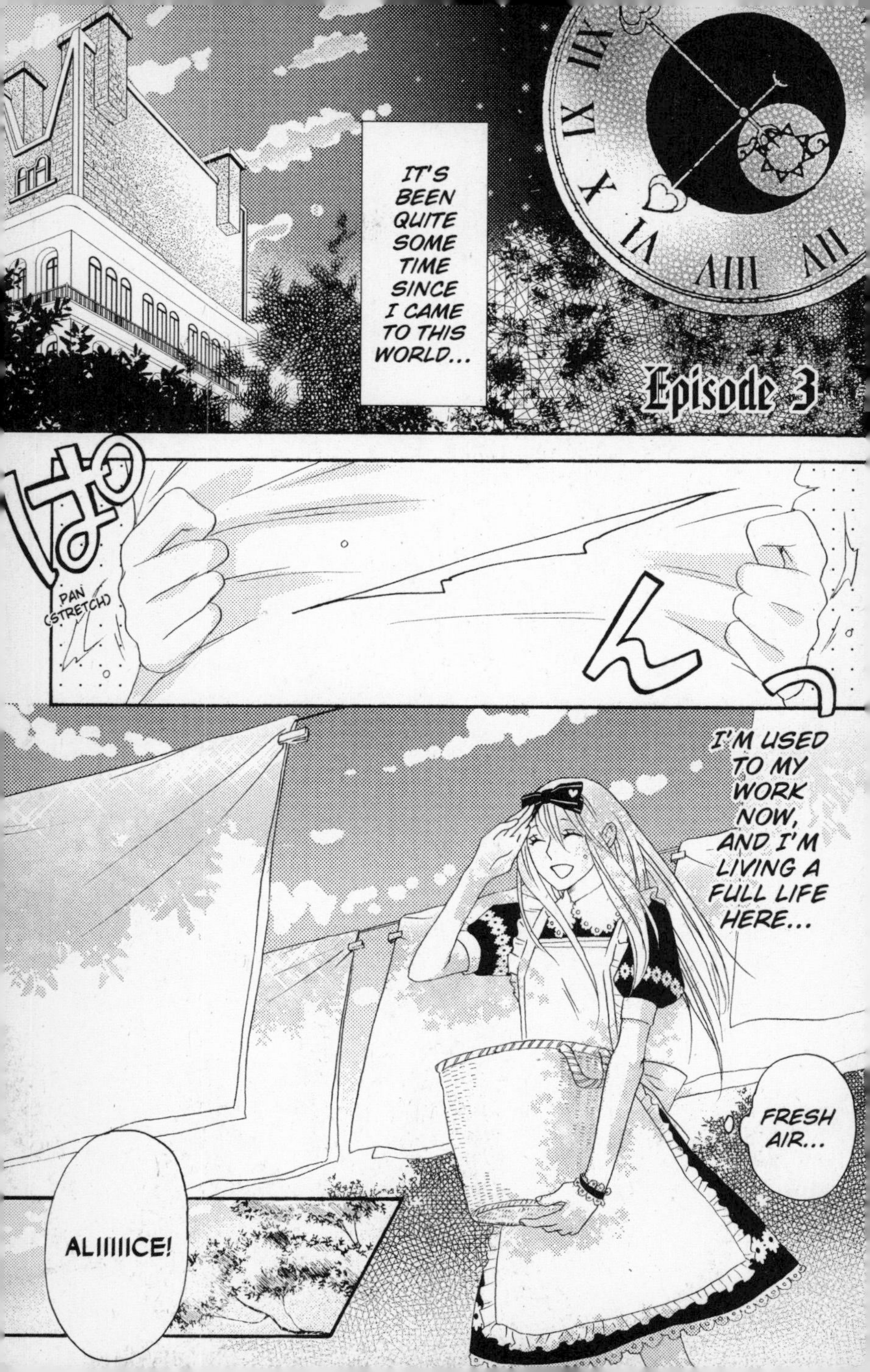

IT'S BEEN QUITE SOME TIME SINCE I CAME TO THIS WORLD...
Episode 3
んっ
ぱ
PAN (STRETCH)
I'M USED TO MY WORK NOW, AND I'M LIVING A FULL LIFE HERE...
FRESH AIR...
ALIIIIICE!

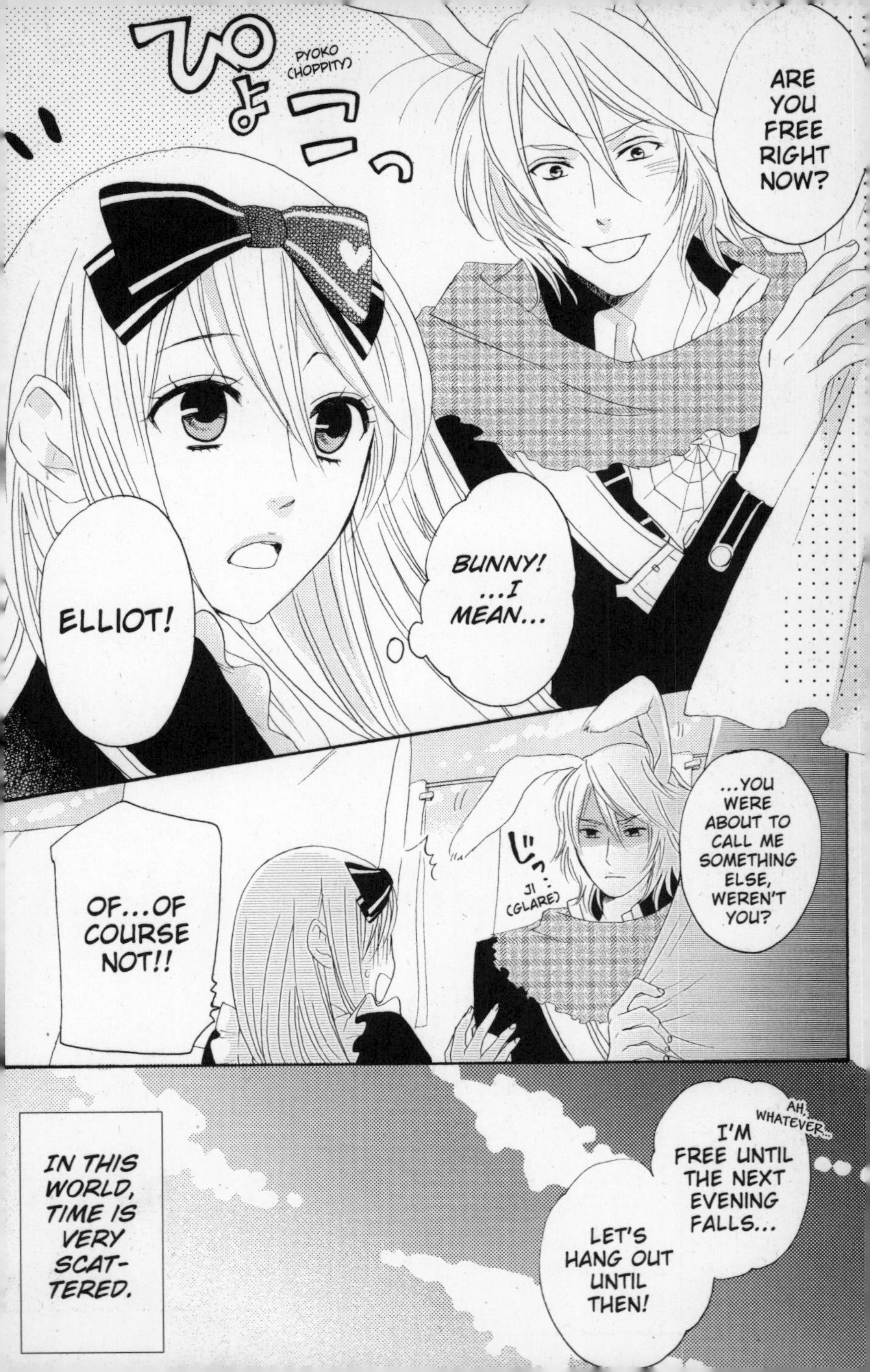
ARE YOU FREE RIGHT NOW?
ぴょこっ
PYOKO (HOPPITY)
BUNNY! ...I MEAN...
ELLIOT!
...YOU WERE ABOUT TO CALL ME SOMETHING ELSE, WEREN'T YOU?
じっ
JI (GLARE)
OF...OF COURSE NOT!!
AH, WHATEVER...
I'M FREE UNTIL THE NEXT EVENING FALLS...
LET'S HANG OUT UNTIL THEN!
IN THIS WORLD, TIME IS VERY SCAT-TERED.

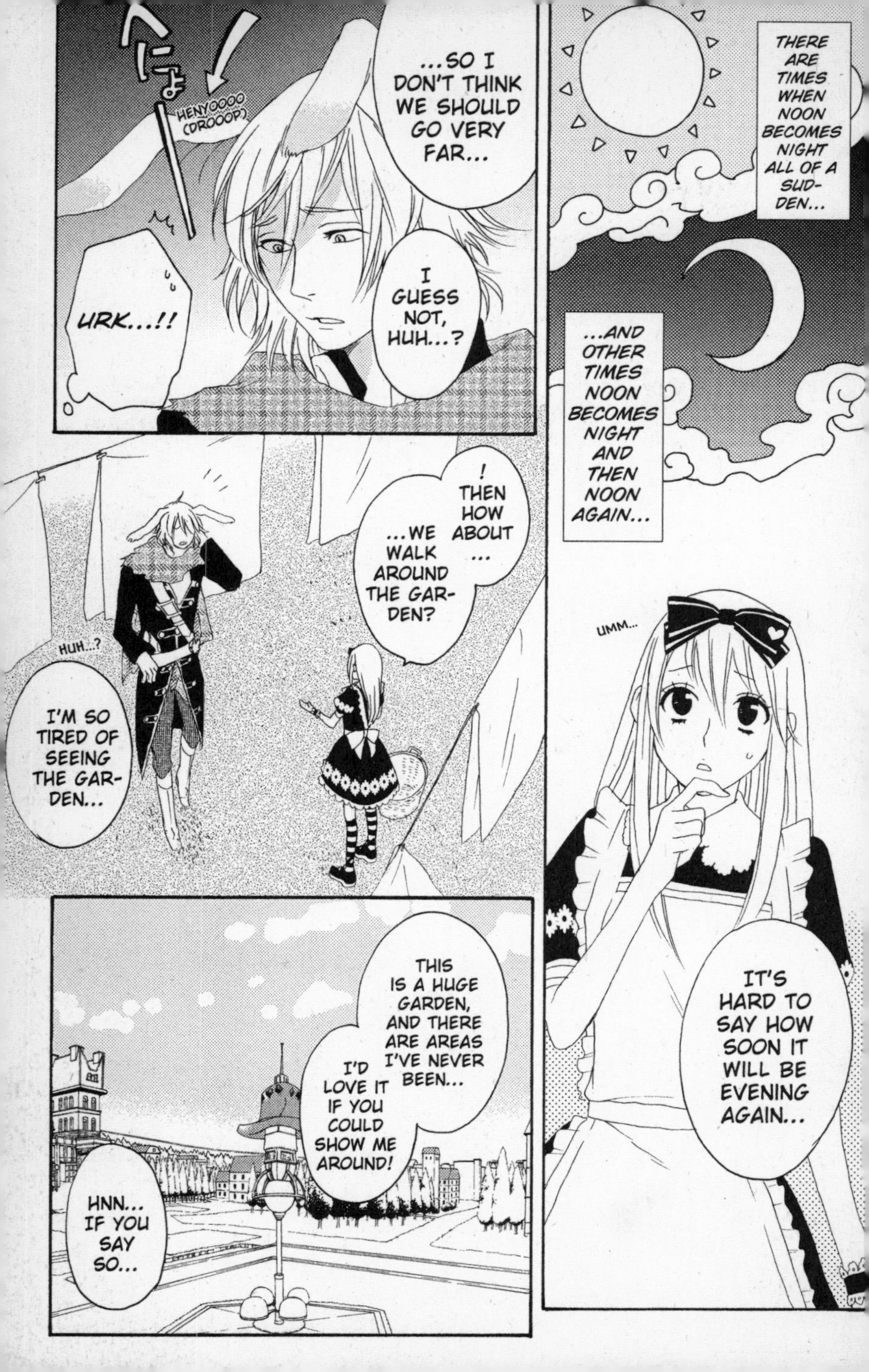
THERE ARE TIMES WHEN NOON BECOMES NIGHT ALL OF A SUD-DEN...
...AND OTHER TIMES NOON BECOMES NIGHT AND THEN NOON AGAIN...
UMM...
IT'S HARD TO SAY HOW SOON IT WILL BE EVENING AGAIN...
...SO I DON'T THINK WE SHOULD GO VERY FAR...
へにょ
HENYOOOO (DROOOP)
URK...!!
I GUESS NOT, HUH...?
! THEN HOW ABOUT...
...WE WALK AROUND THE GAR-DEN?
HUH...?
I'M SO TIRED OF SEEING THE GAR-DEN...
THIS IS A HUGE GARDEN, AND THERE ARE AREAS I'VE NEVER BEEN...
I'D LOVE IT IF YOU COULD SHOW ME AROUND!
HNN... IF YOU SAY SO...

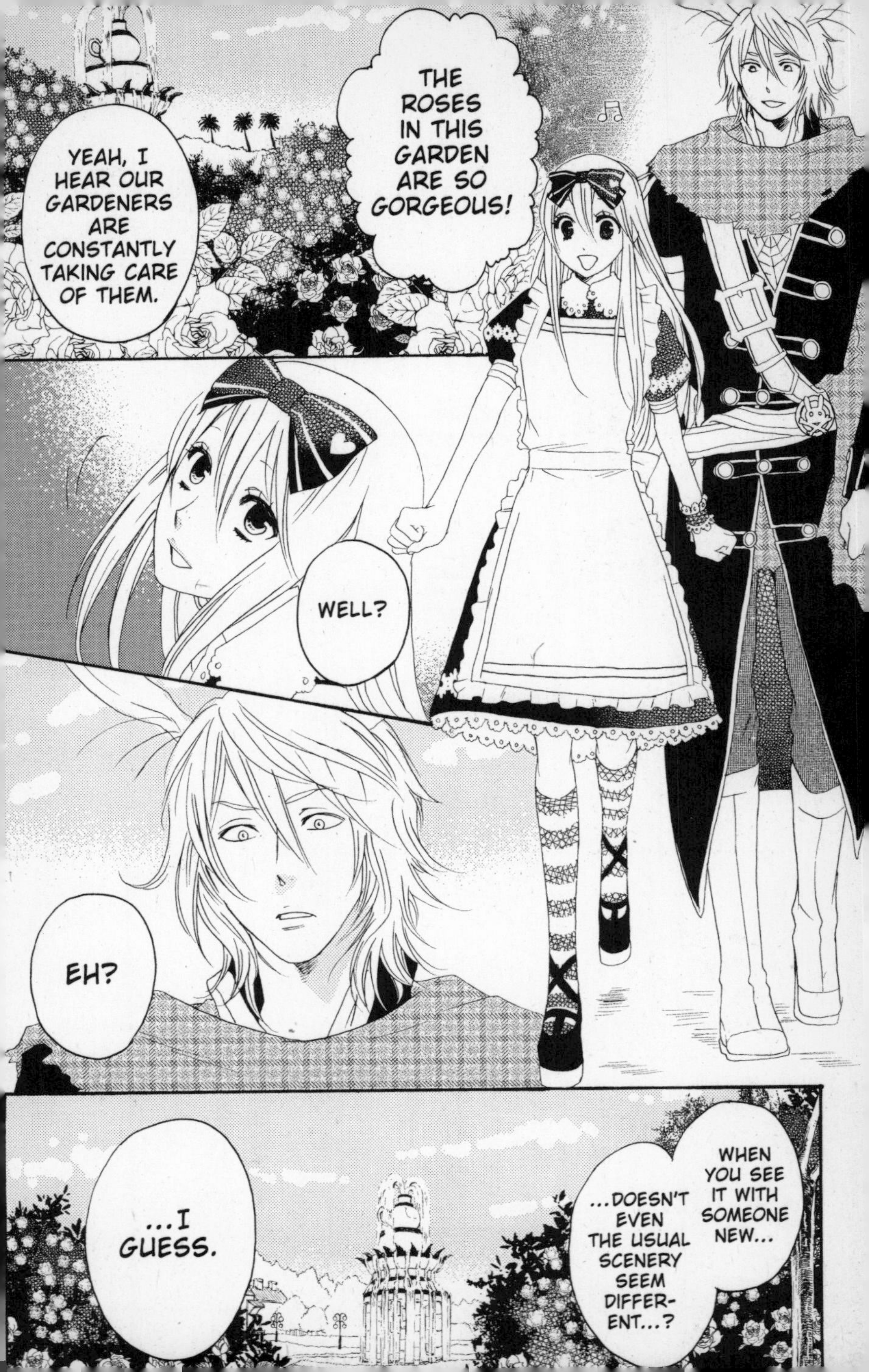
THE ROSES IN THIS GARDEN ARE SO GORGEOUS!
YEAH, I HEAR OUR GARDENERS ARE CONSTANTLY TAKING CARE OF THEM.
WELL?
EH?
WHEN YOU SEE IT WITH SOMEONE NEW...
...DOESN'T EVEN THE USUAL SCENERY SEEM DIFFER-ENT...?
...I GUESS.

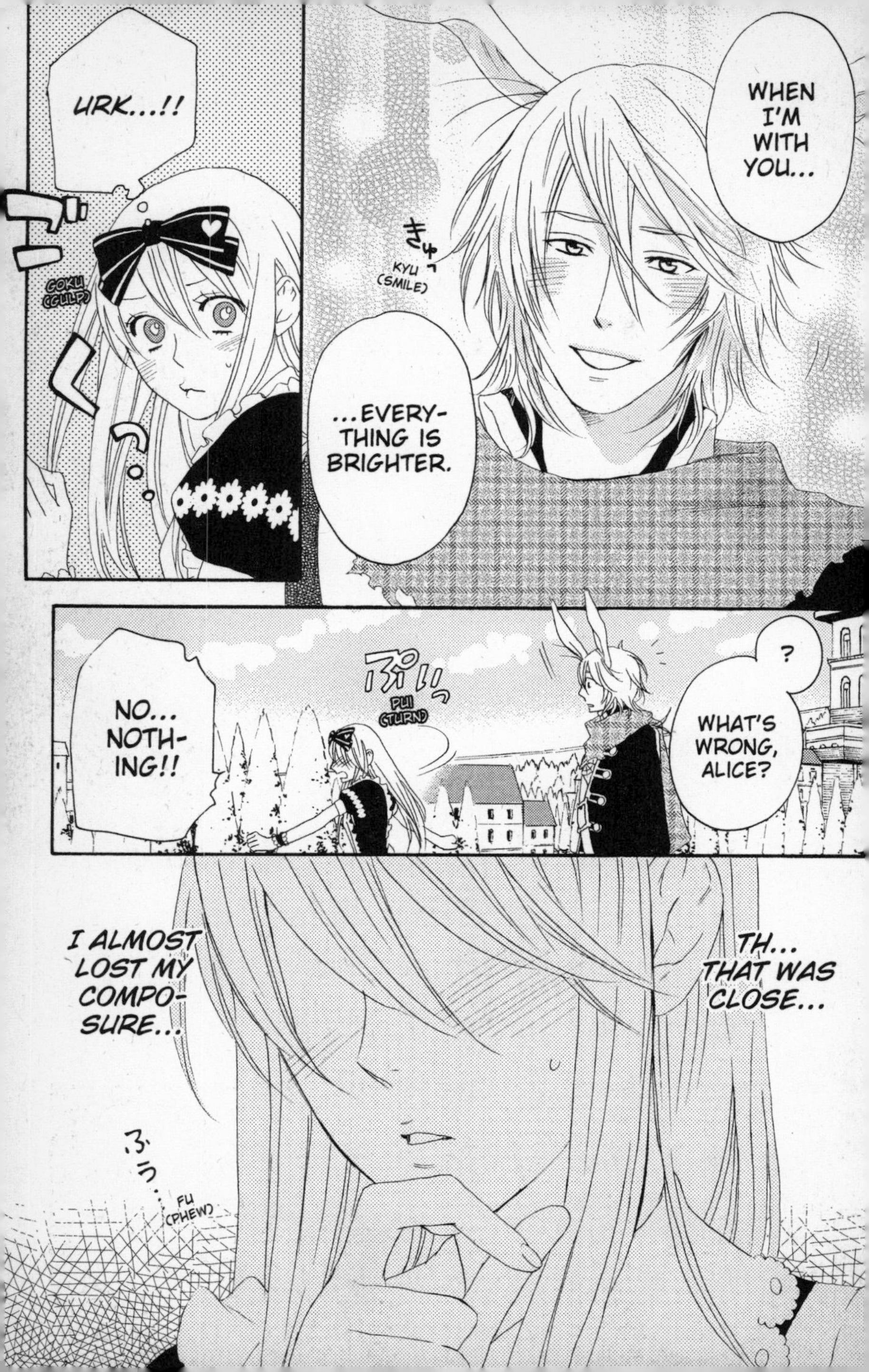
WHEN I'M WITH YOU...
きゅっ
KYU (SMILE)
...EVERY-THING IS BRIGHTER.
URK...!!
GOKU (GULP)
?
WHAT'S WRONG, ALICE?
ぷいっ
PUI (TURN)
NO... NOTH-ING!!
TH... THAT WAS CLOSE...
I ALMOST LOST MY COMPO-SURE...
FU (PHEW)

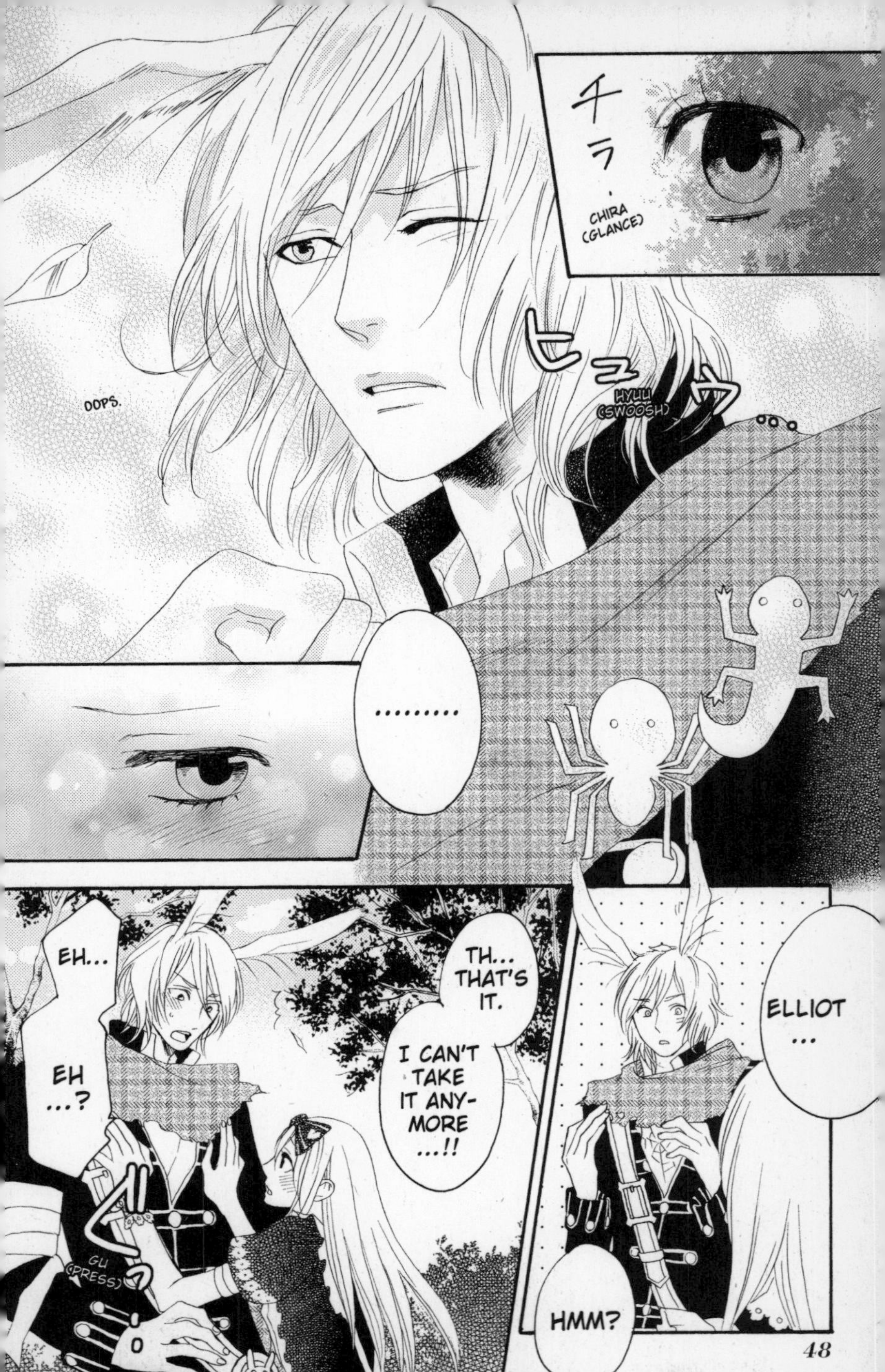
チラ・
CHIRA (GLANCE)
DOPS.
ヒュウ…
HYUU (SWOOSH)
....
ELLIOT ...
HMM?
TH... THAT'S IT.
I CAN'T TAKE IT ANYMORE ...!!
EH...
EH ...?
GU (PRESS)

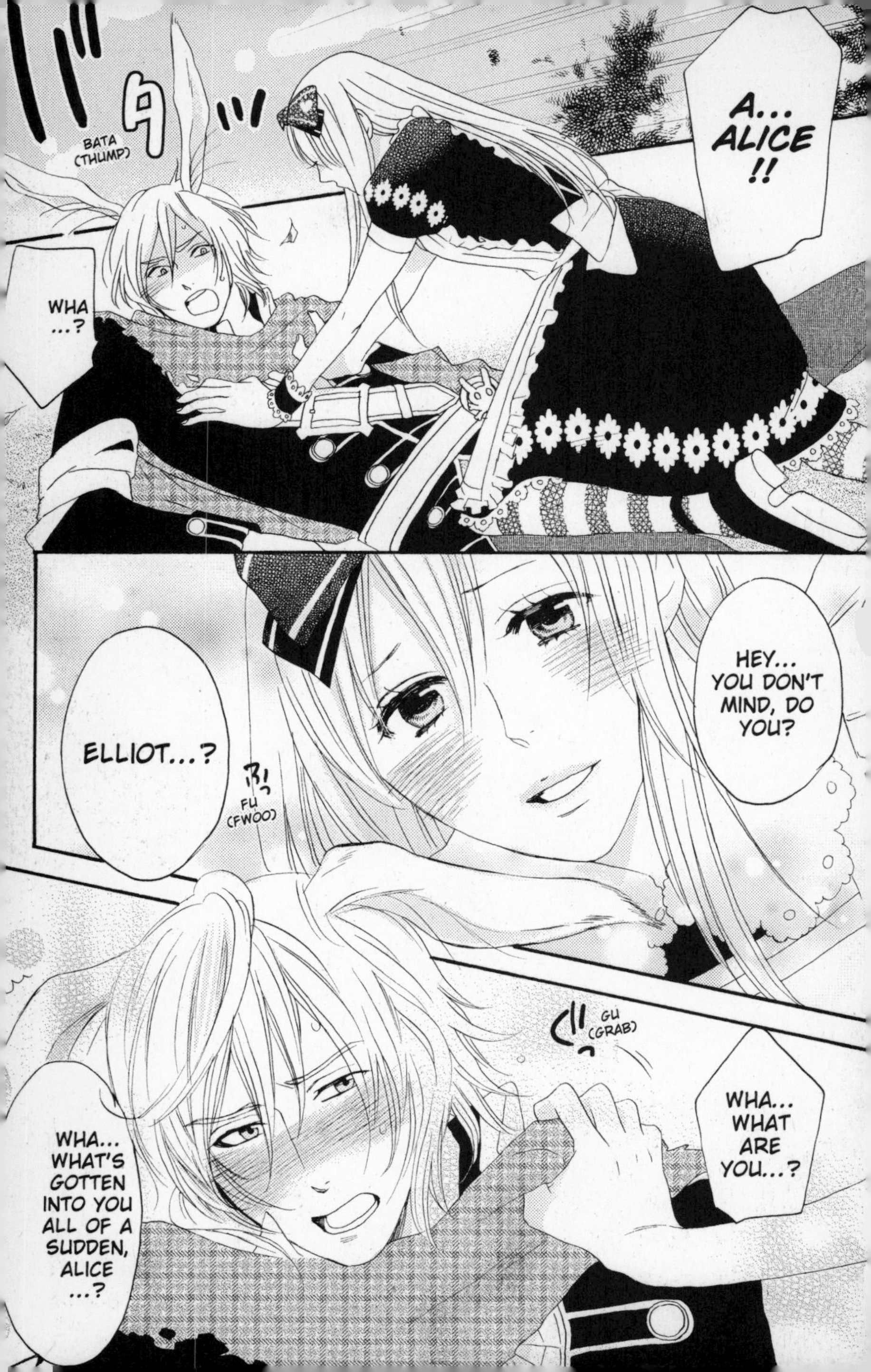
A... ALICE!!
バタッ
BATA (THUMP)
WHA...?
HEY... YOU DON'T MIND, DO YOU?
FU (FWOO)
ELLIOT...?
GU (GRAB)
WHA... WHAT ARE YOU...?
WHA... WHAT'S GOTTEN INTO YOU ALL OF A SUDDEN, ALICE...?

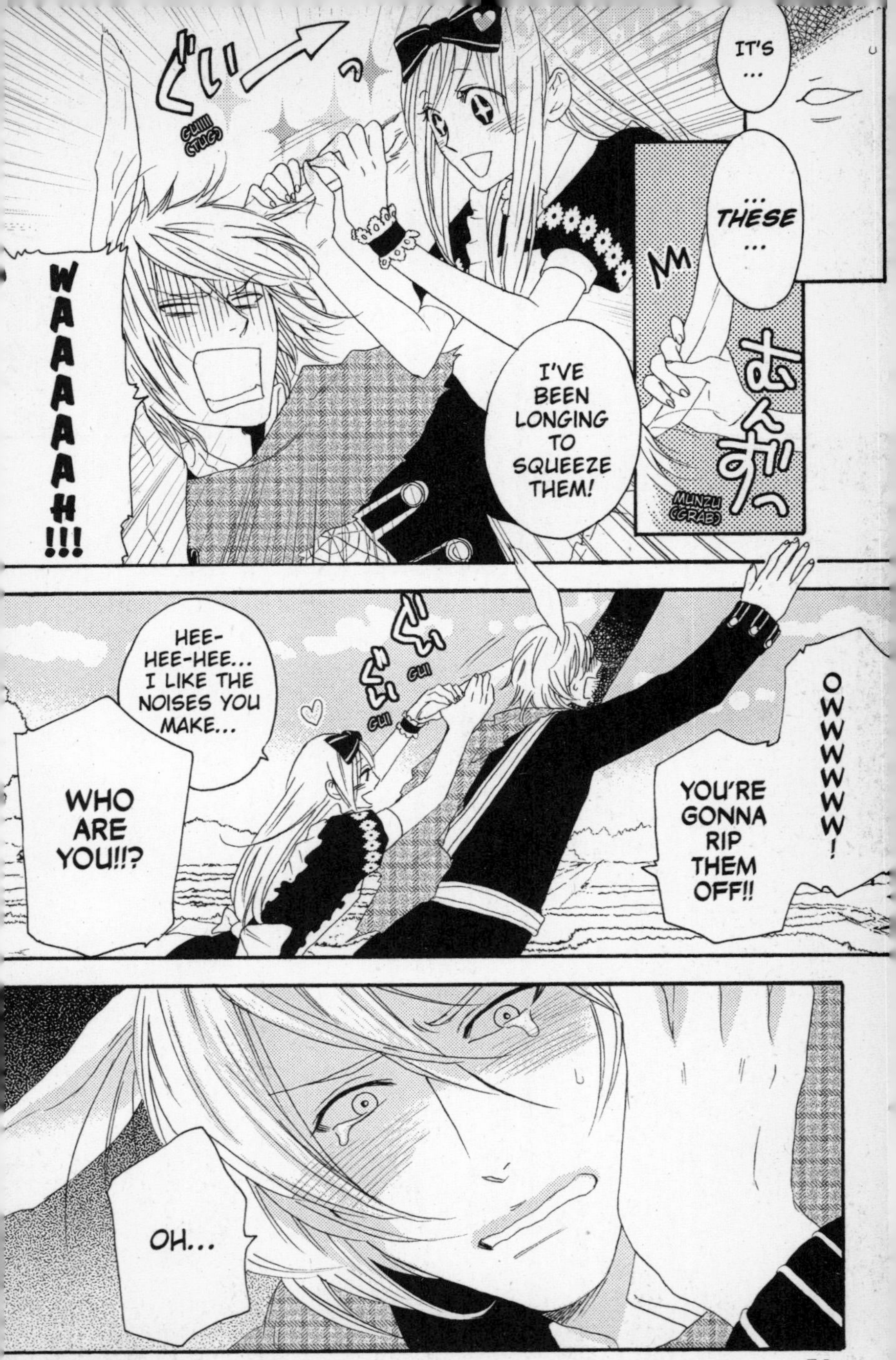
IT'S ...
... THESE ...
MUNZU (GRAB)
I'VE BEEN LONGING TO SQUEEZE THEM!
GUIIII (TUG)
WAAAAAAAH!!!
OWWWWWW!
YOU'RE GONNA RIP THEM OFF!!
GUI
GUI
HEE-HEE-HEE... I LIKE THE NOISES YOU MAKE...
WHO ARE YOU!!?
OH...

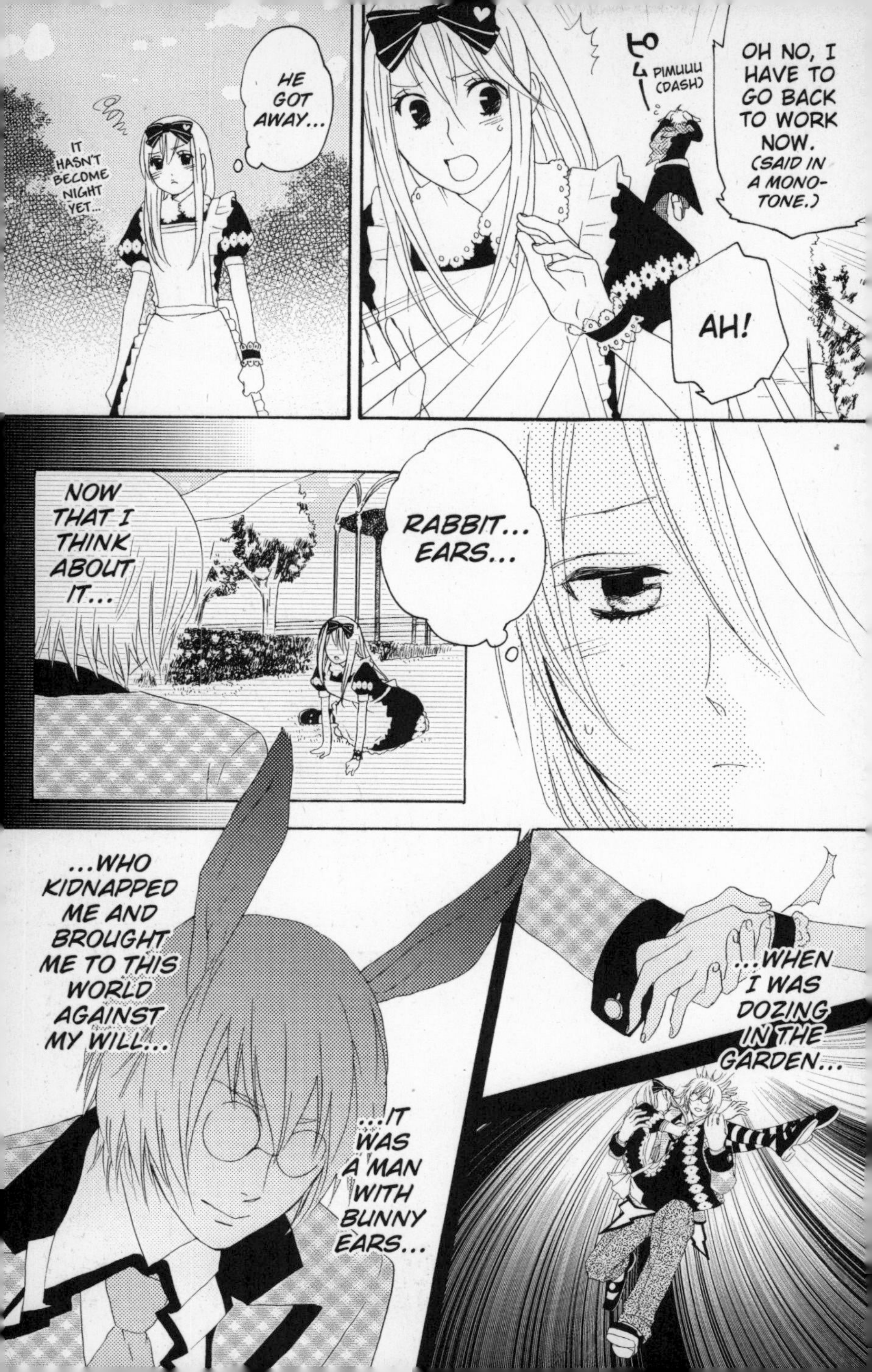
OH NO, I HAVE TO GO BACK TO WORK NOW. (SAID IN A MONOTONE.)
PIMUUU (DASH)
AH!
HE GOT AWAY...
IT HASN'T BECOME NIGHT YET...
RABBIT... EARS...
NOW THAT I THINK ABOUT IT...
...WHEN I WAS DOZING IN THE GARDEN...
...WHO KIDNAPPED ME AND BROUGHT ME TO THIS WORLD AGAINST MY WILL...
...IT WAS A MAN WITH BUNNY EARS...

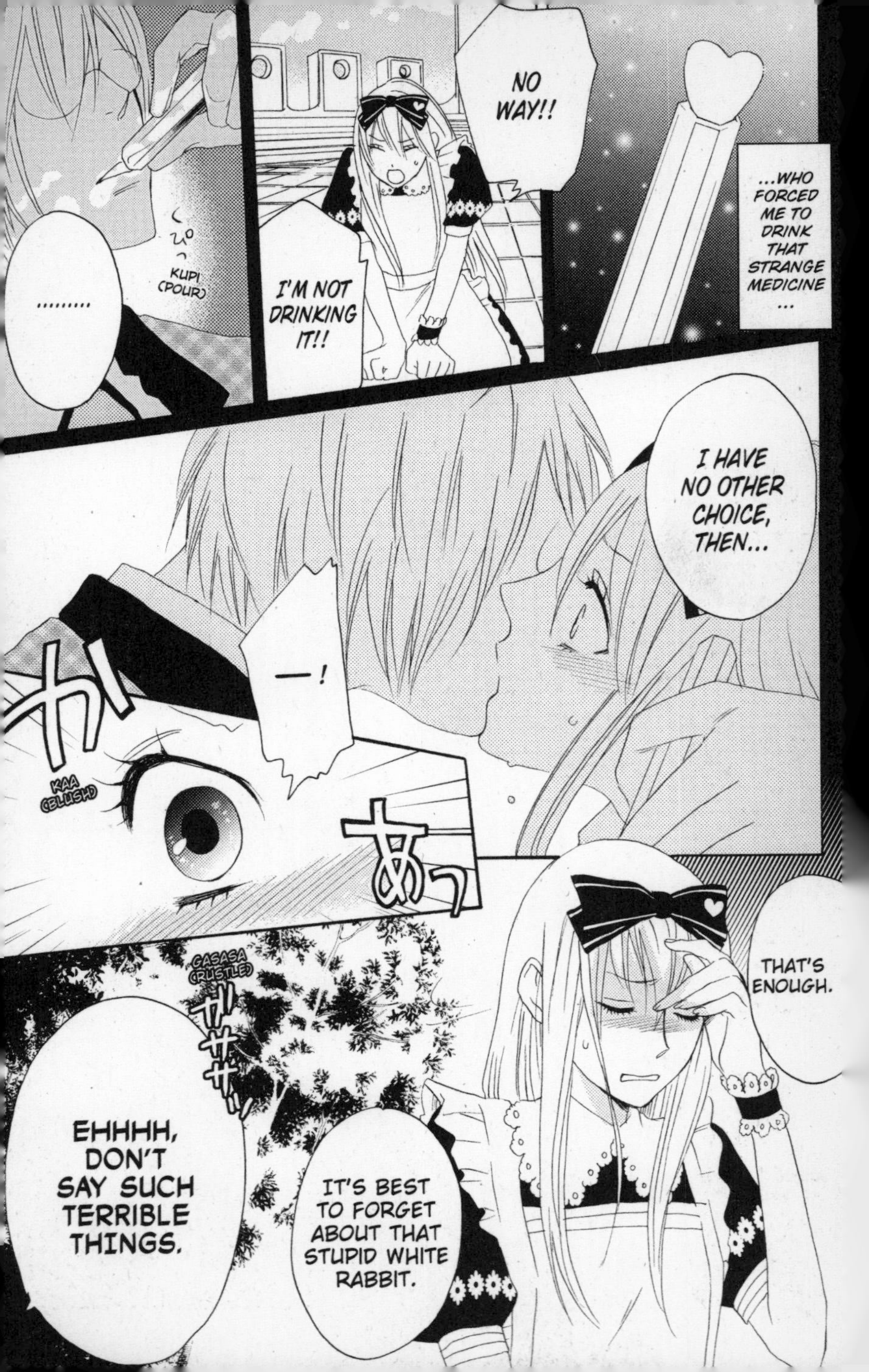
...WHO FORCED ME TO DRINK THAT STRANGE MEDICINE...
NO WAY!!
I'M NOT DRINKING IT!!
KUPI (POUR)
....
I HAVE NO OTHER CHOICE, THEN...
—!
KAA (BLUSH)
THAT'S ENOUGH.
IT'S BEST TO FORGET ABOUT THAT STUPID WHITE RABBIT.
GASASA (RUSTLED)
EHHHH, DON'T SAY SUCH TERRIBLE THINGS.

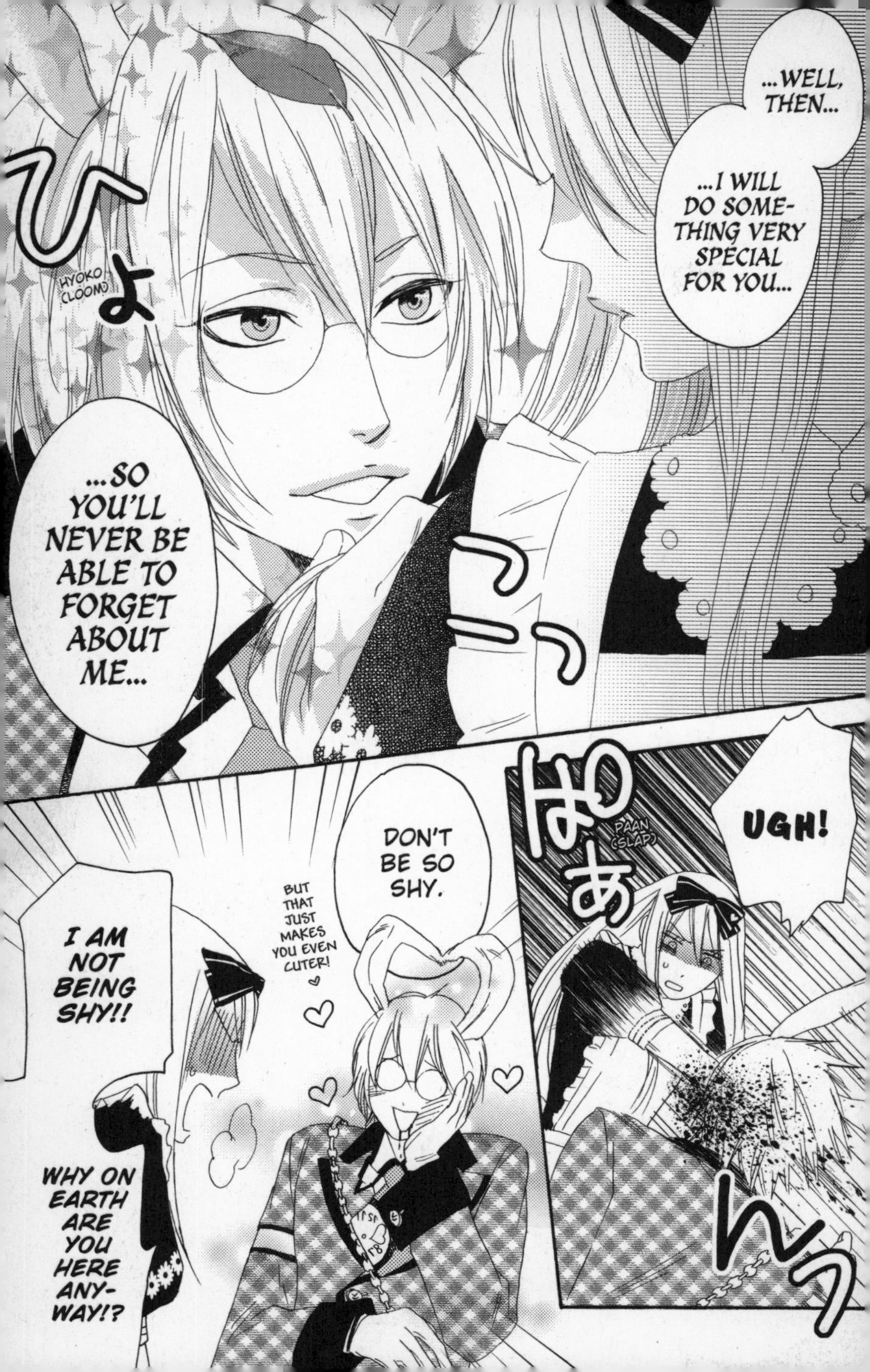
...WELL, THEN...
...I WILL DO SOME-THING VERY SPECIAL FOR YOU...
HYOKO (LOOM)
...SO YOU'LL NEVER BE ABLE TO FORGET ABOUT ME...
PAAN (SLAP)
UGH!
DON'T BE SO SHY.
BUT THAT JUST MAKES YOU EVEN CUTER!
I AM NOT BEING SHY!!
WHY ON EARTH ARE YOU HERE ANYWAY!?

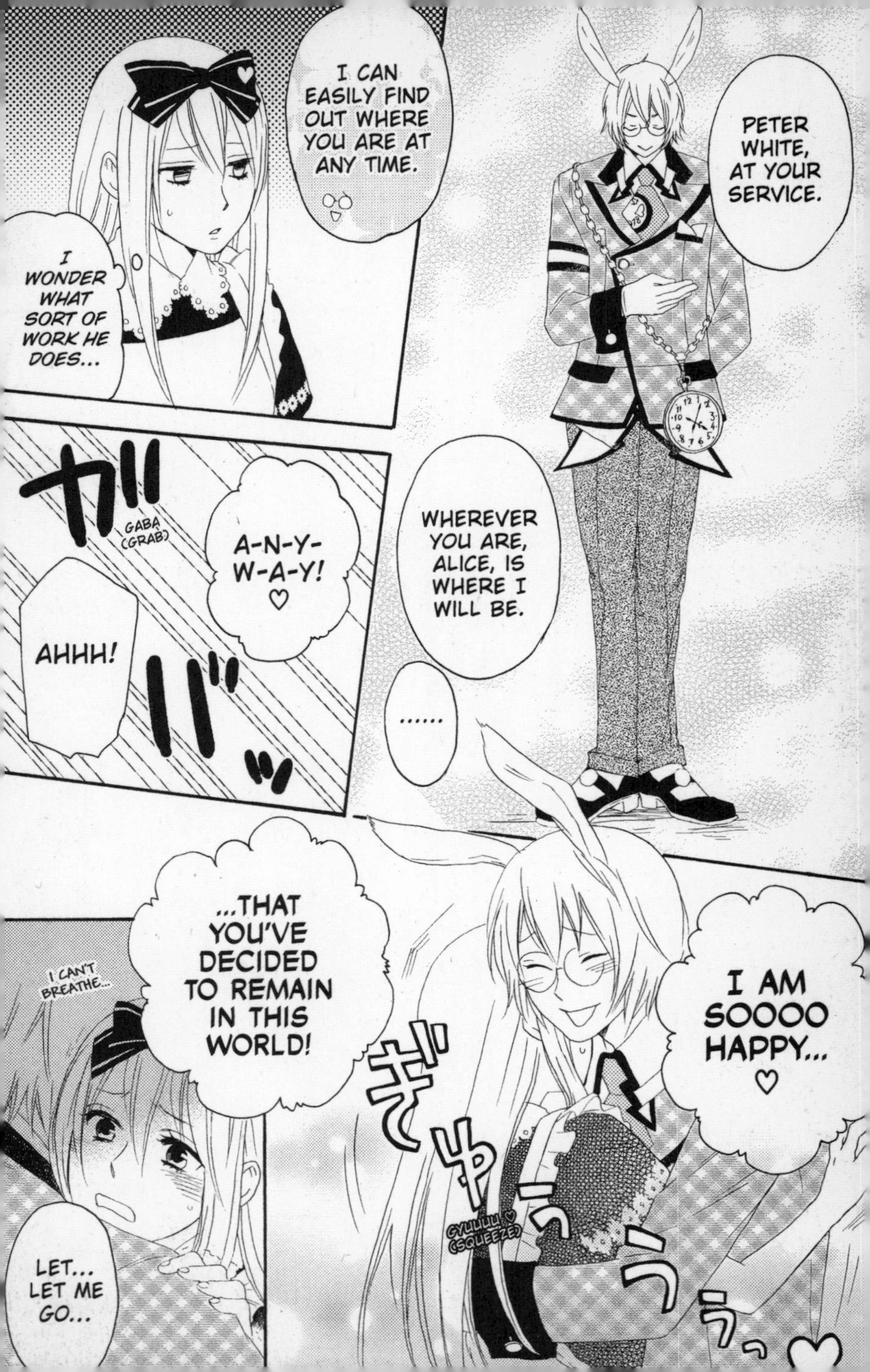
PETER WHITE, AT YOUR SERVICE.
WHEREVER YOU ARE, ALICE, IS WHERE I WILL BE.
......
I CAN EASILY FIND OUT WHERE YOU ARE AT ANY TIME.
I WONDER WHAT SORT OF WORK HE DOES...
A-N-Y-W-A-Y! ♡
ガバッ
GABA (GRAB)
AHHH!
I AM SOOOO HAPPY... ♡
...THAT YOU'VE DECIDED TO REMAIN IN THIS WORLD!
ぎゅううっ
GYULLLL ♡ (SQUEEZE)
I CAN'T BREATHE...
LET... LET ME GO...

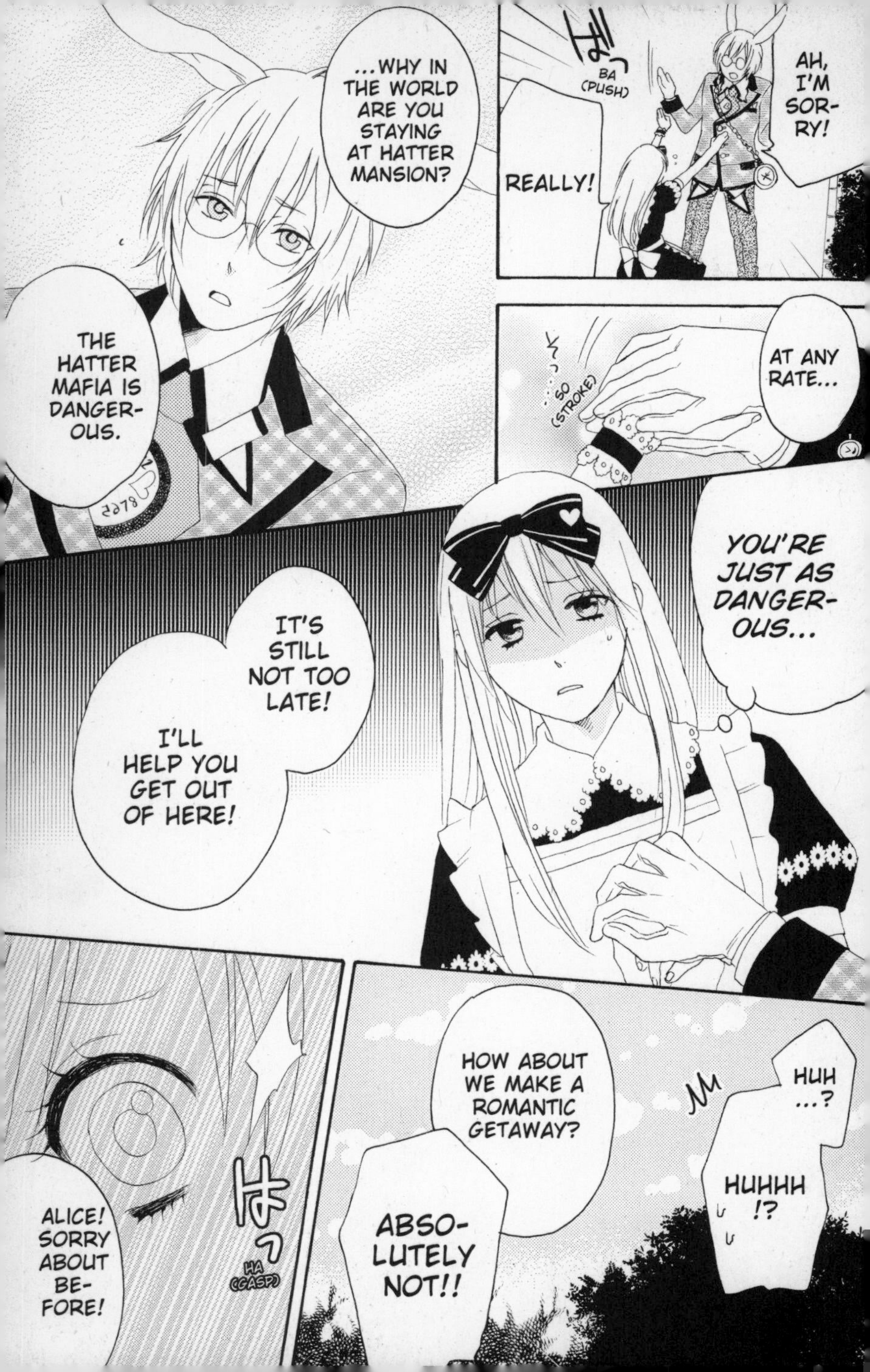
AH, I'M SORRY!
BA (PUSH)
REALLY!
AT ANY RATE...
SO (STROKE)
...WHY IN THE WORLD ARE YOU STAYING AT HATTER MANSION?
THE HATTER MAFIA IS DANGEROUS.
YOU'RE JUST AS DANGEROUS...
IT'S STILL NOT TOO LATE!
I'LL HELP YOU GET OUT OF HERE!
HUH ...?
HOW ABOUT WE MAKE A ROMANTIC GETAWAY?
HUHHH !?
ABSOLUTELY NOT!!
HA (GASP)
ALICE! SORRY ABOUT BEFORE!

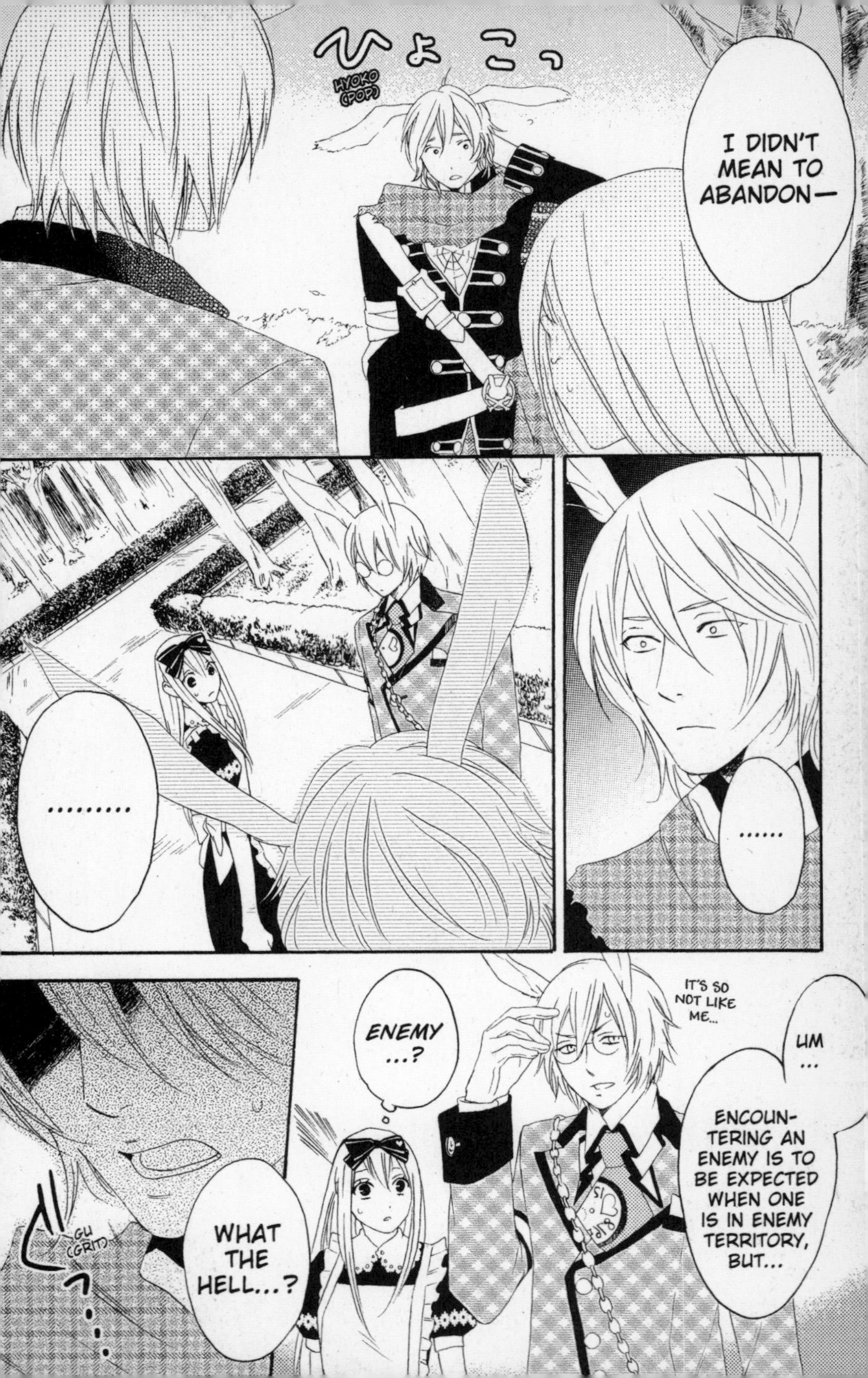
I DIDN'T MEAN TO ABANDON—
ひょこっ
HYOKO (POP)
......
....
UM ...
ENCOUN-TERING AN ENEMY IS TO BE EXPECTED WHEN ONE IS IN ENEMY TERRITORY, BUT...
IT'S SO NOT LIKE ME...
ENEMY ...?
WHAT THE HELL...?
GU (GRIT)

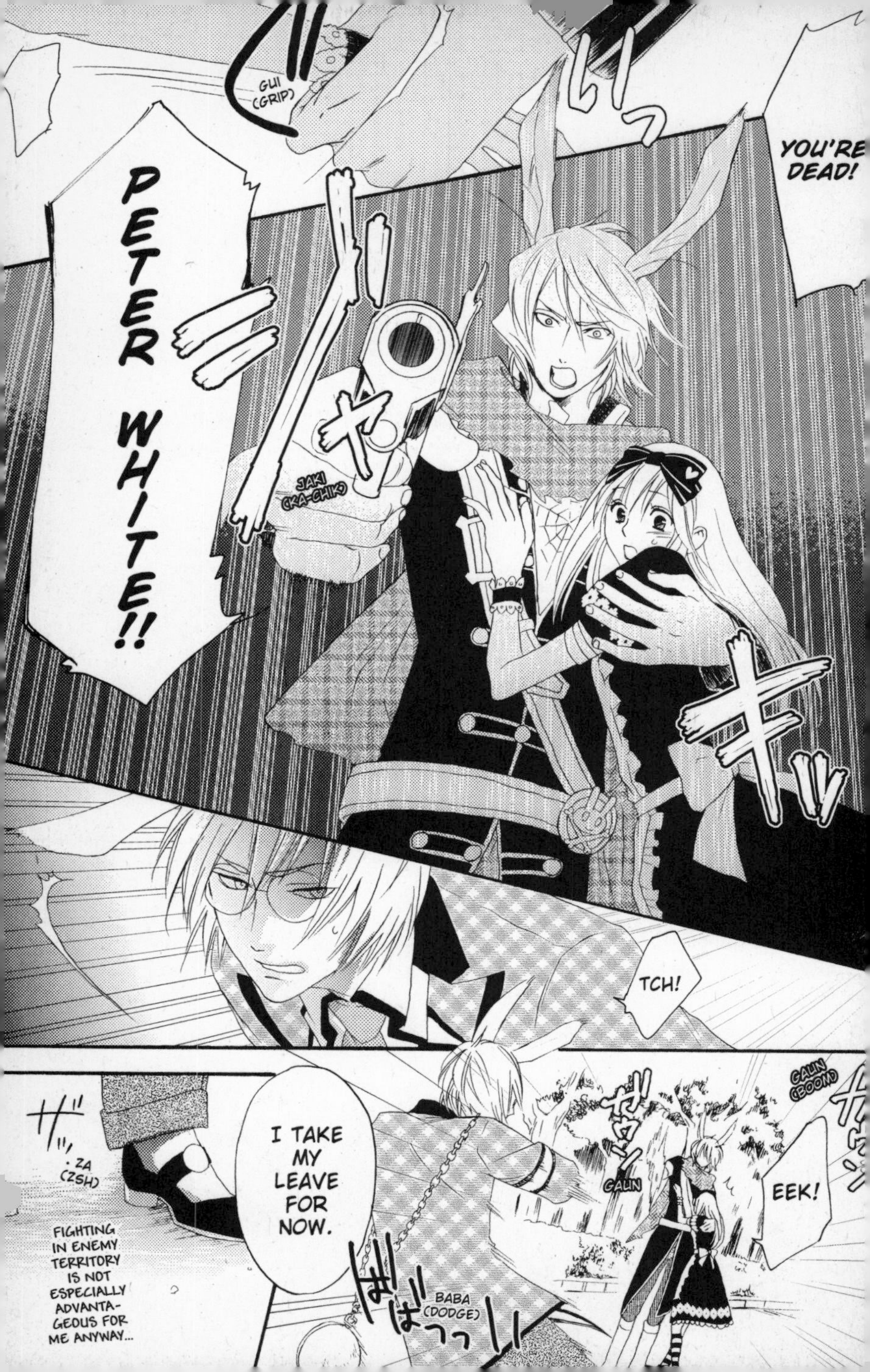
YOU'RE DEAD!
GUI (GRIP)
PETER WHITE!!
JAKI (KA-CHIK)
TCH!
GAUN (BOON)
EEK!
GAUN
I TAKE MY LEAVE FOR NOW.
BABA (DODGE)
ZA (ZSH)
FIGHTING IN ENEMY TERRITORY IS NOT ESPECIALLY ADVANTA-GEOUS FOR ME ANYWAY...

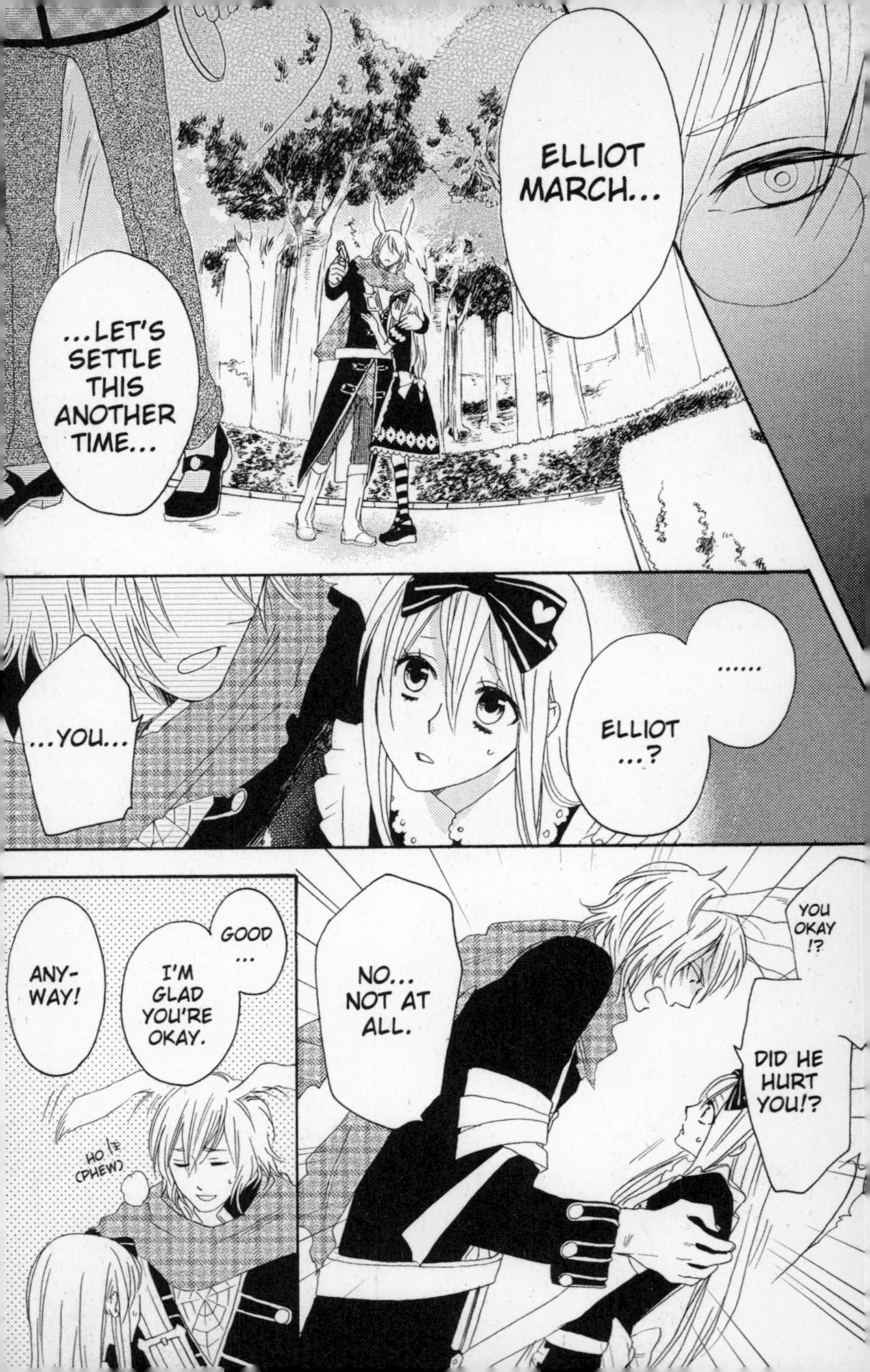
ELLIOT MARCH...
...LET'S SETTLE THIS ANOTHER TIME...
......
ELLIOT ...?
...YOU...
YOU OKAY !?
DID HE HURT YOU!?
NO... NOT AT ALL.
GOOD ...
I'M GLAD YOU'RE OKAY.
ANY-WAY!
(PHEW)

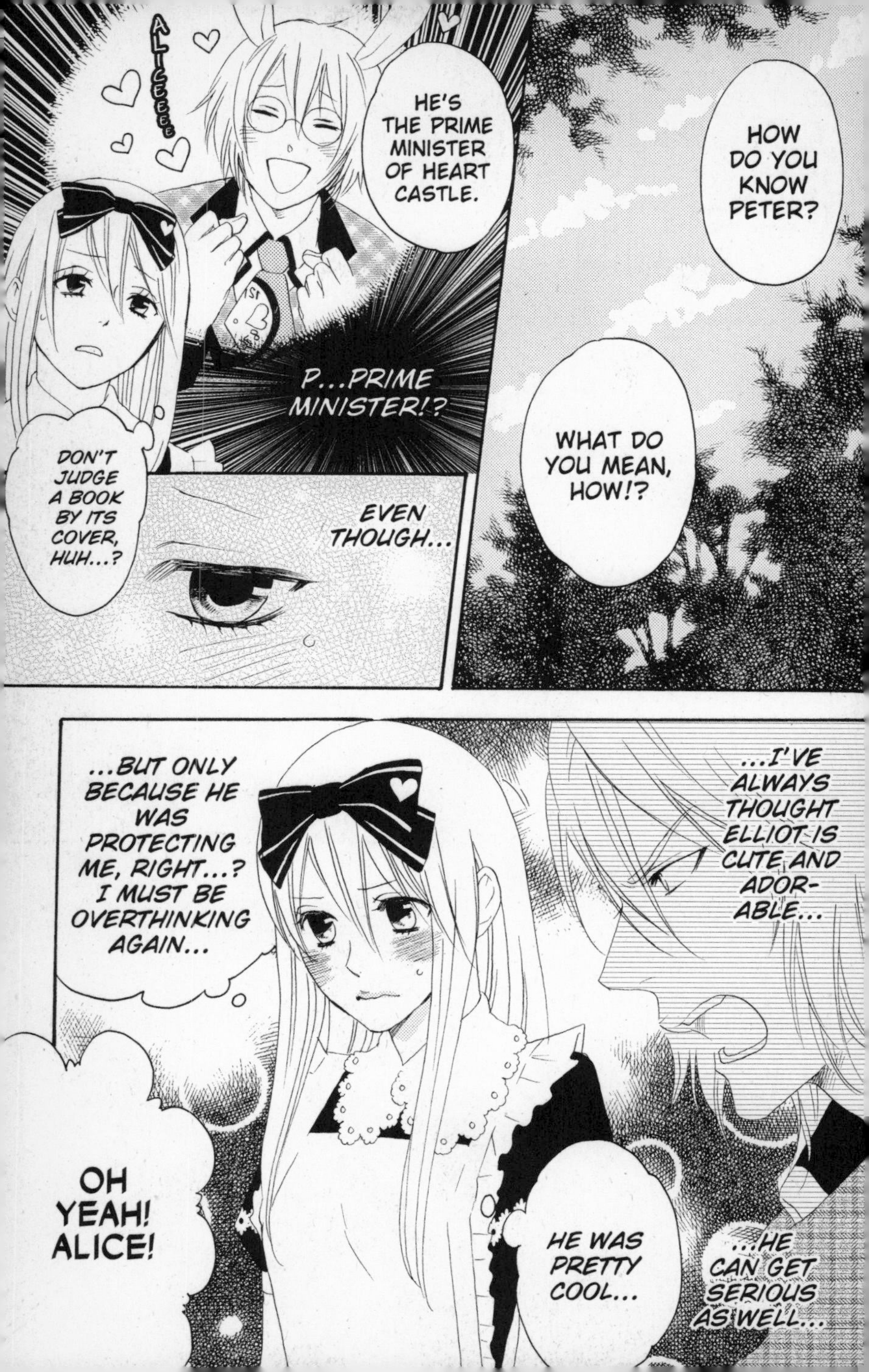
HOW DO YOU KNOW PETER?
WHAT DO YOU MEAN, HOW!?
ALICEEEE
HE'S THE PRIME MINISTER OF HEART CASTLE.
P...PRIME MINISTER!?
EVEN THOUGH...
DON'T JUDGE A BOOK BY ITS COVER, HUH...?
...I'VE ALWAYS THOUGHT ELLIOT IS CUTE AND ADORABLE...
...HE CAN GET SERIOUS AS WELL...
HE WAS PRETTY COOL...
...BUT ONLY BECAUSE HE WAS PROTECTING ME, RIGHT...? I MUST BE OVERTHINKING AGAIN...
OH YEAH! ALICE!

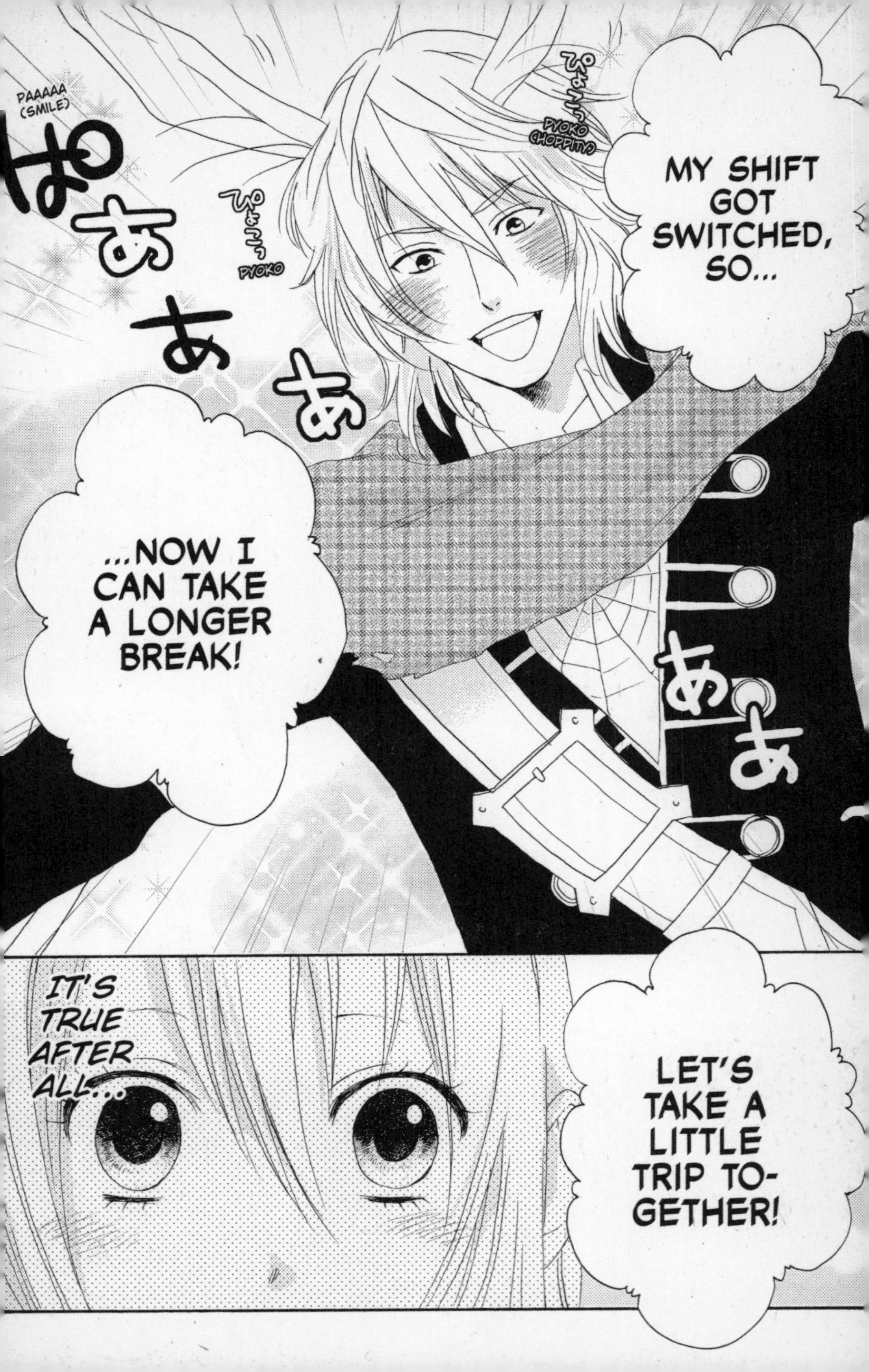
ぴょこっ
PYOKO (HOPPITY)
MY SHIFT GOT SWITCHED, SO...
ぴょこっ
PYOKO
ぱあぁぁぁぁ
PAAAAAA (SMILE)
...NOW I CAN TAKE A LONGER BREAK!
LET'S TAKE A LITTLE TRIP TO-GETHER!
IT'S TRUE AFTER ALL...

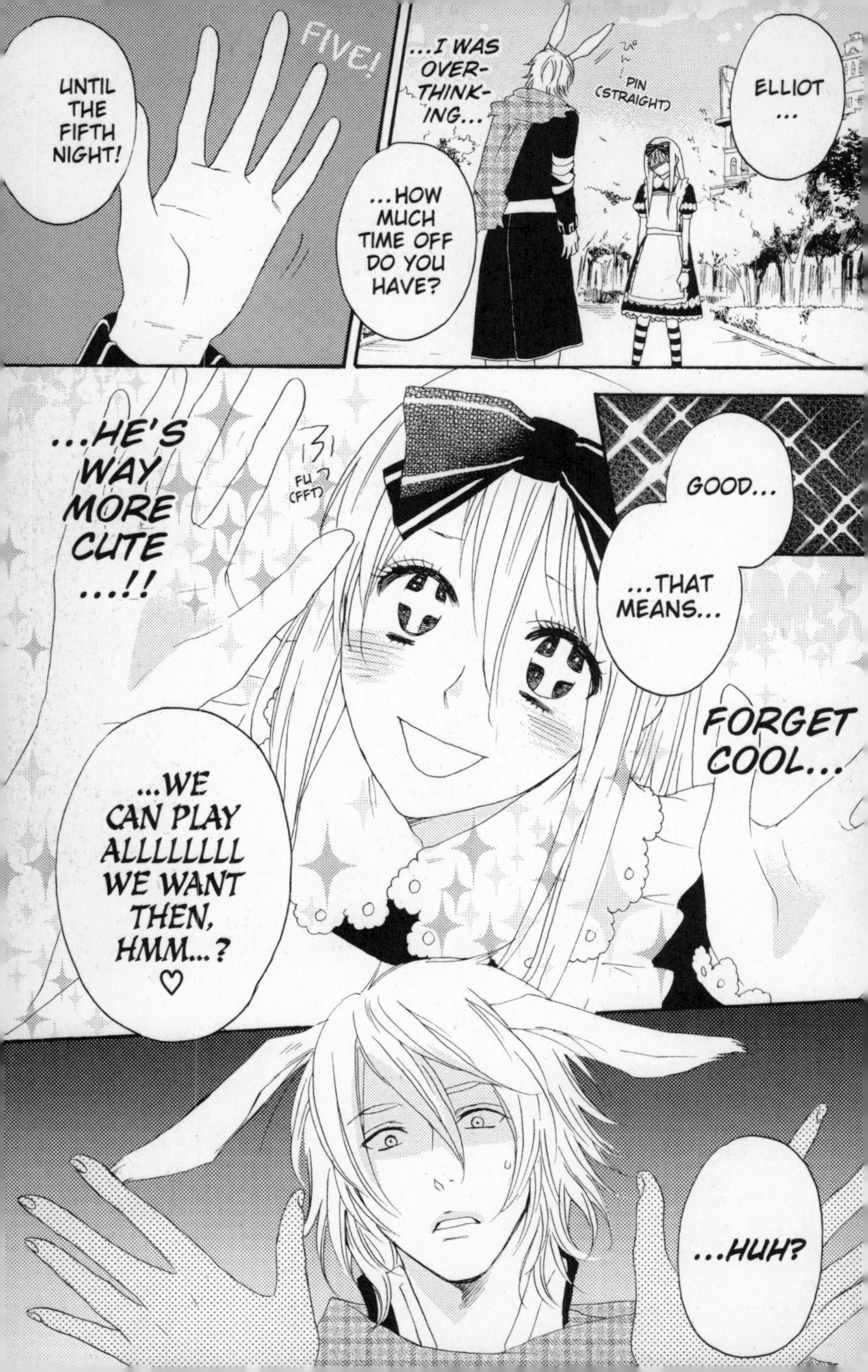
ELLIOT ...
PIN (STRAIGHT)
...I WAS OVER-THINK-ING...
...HOW MUCH TIME OFF DO YOU HAVE?
FIVE!
UNTIL THE FIFTH NIGHT!
GOOD...
...THAT MEANS...
FORGET COOL...
FU (FFT)
...HE'S WAY MORE CUTE ...!!
...WE CAN PLAY ALLLLLLLL WE WANT THEN, HMM...? ♡
...HUH?

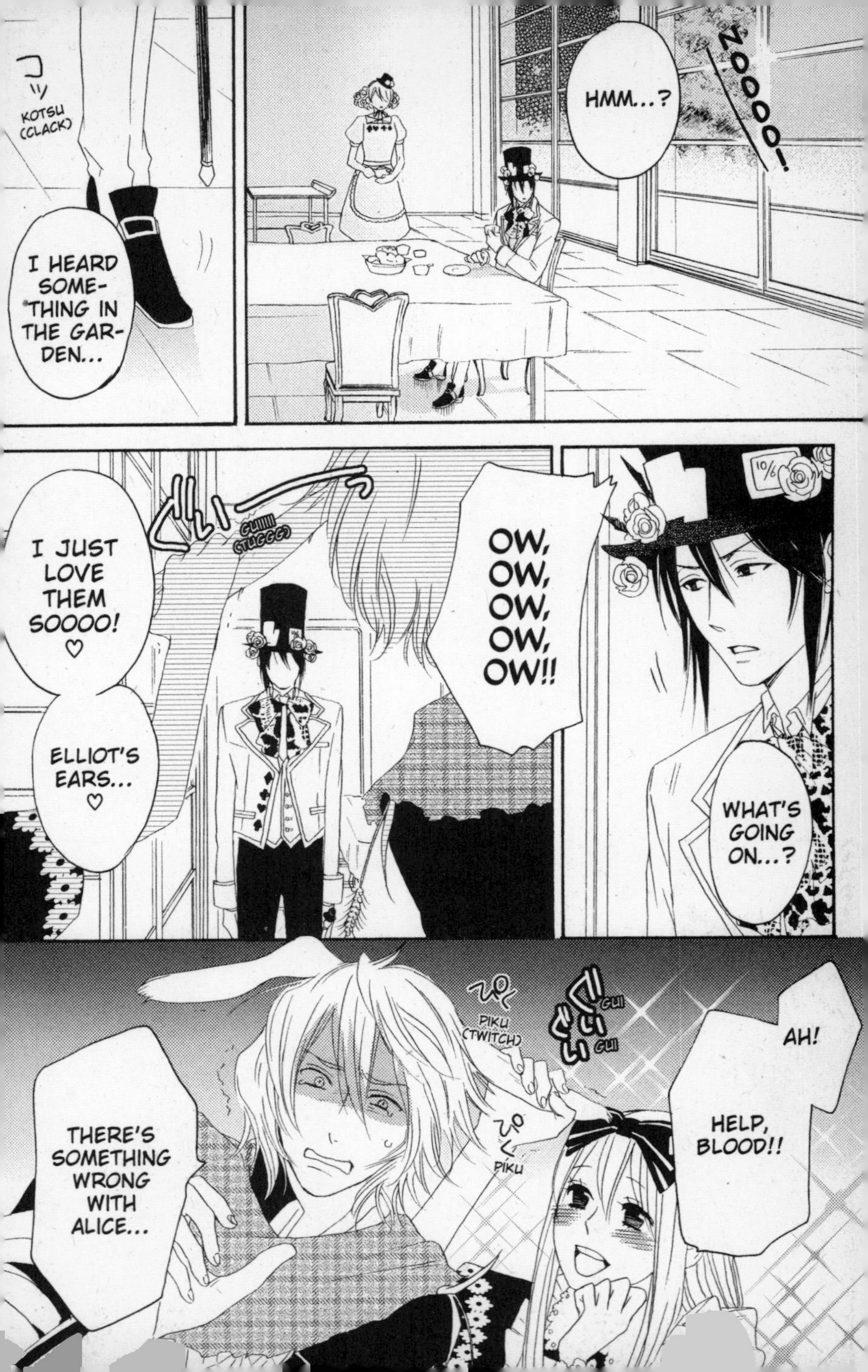

HMM...?
NOOOOO-!
コッ
KOTSU (CLACK)
I HEARD SOMETHING IN THE GARDEN...
WHAT'S GOING ON...?
OW, OW, OW, OW, OW!!
ぐいーっ
GUIIIII (TUGGG)
I JUST LOVE THEM SOOOO! ♡
ELLIOT'S EARS... ♡
AH!
HELP, BLOOD!!
ぐいぐい
GUI GUI
ぴく
PIKU (TWITCH)
ぴく
PIKU
THERE'S SOMETHING WRONG WITH ALICE...

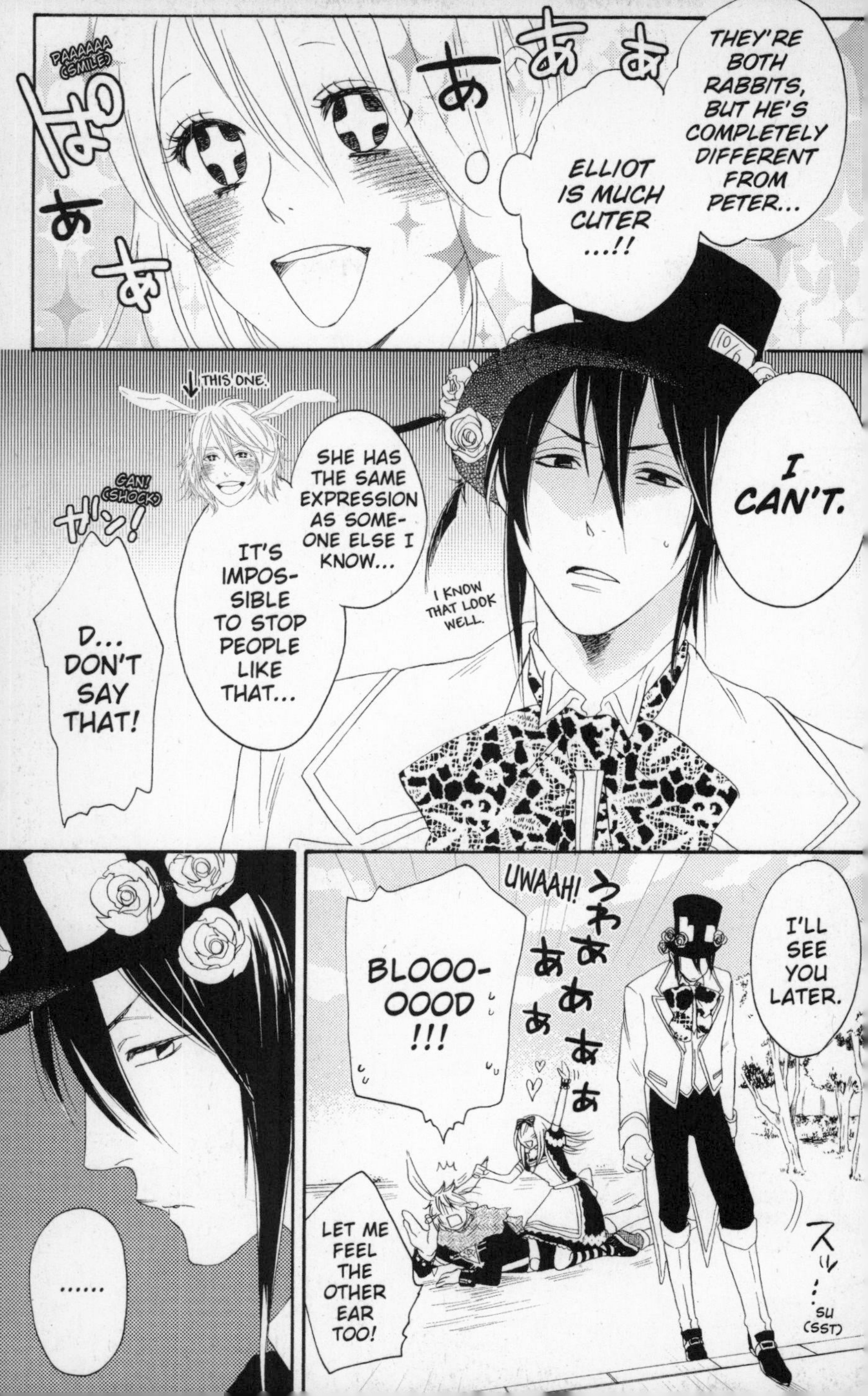
THEY'RE BOTH RABBITS, BUT HE'S COMPLETELY DIFFERENT FROM PETER...
ELLIOT IS MUCH CUTER ...!!
ぱあああああ
PAAAAAA (SMILE)
I CAN'T.
I KNOW THAT LOOK WELL.
SHE HAS THE SAME EXPRESSION AS SOME-ONE ELSE I KNOW...
IT'S IMPOS-SIBLE TO STOP PEOPLE LIKE THAT...
THIS ONE.
ガーン!
GAN! (SHOCK)
D... DON'T SAY THAT!
I'LL SEE YOU LATER.
UWAAH!
うわあああああああ
BLOOO-OOOD!!!
LET ME FEEL THE OTHER EAR TOO!
スッ…
SU (SST)
......

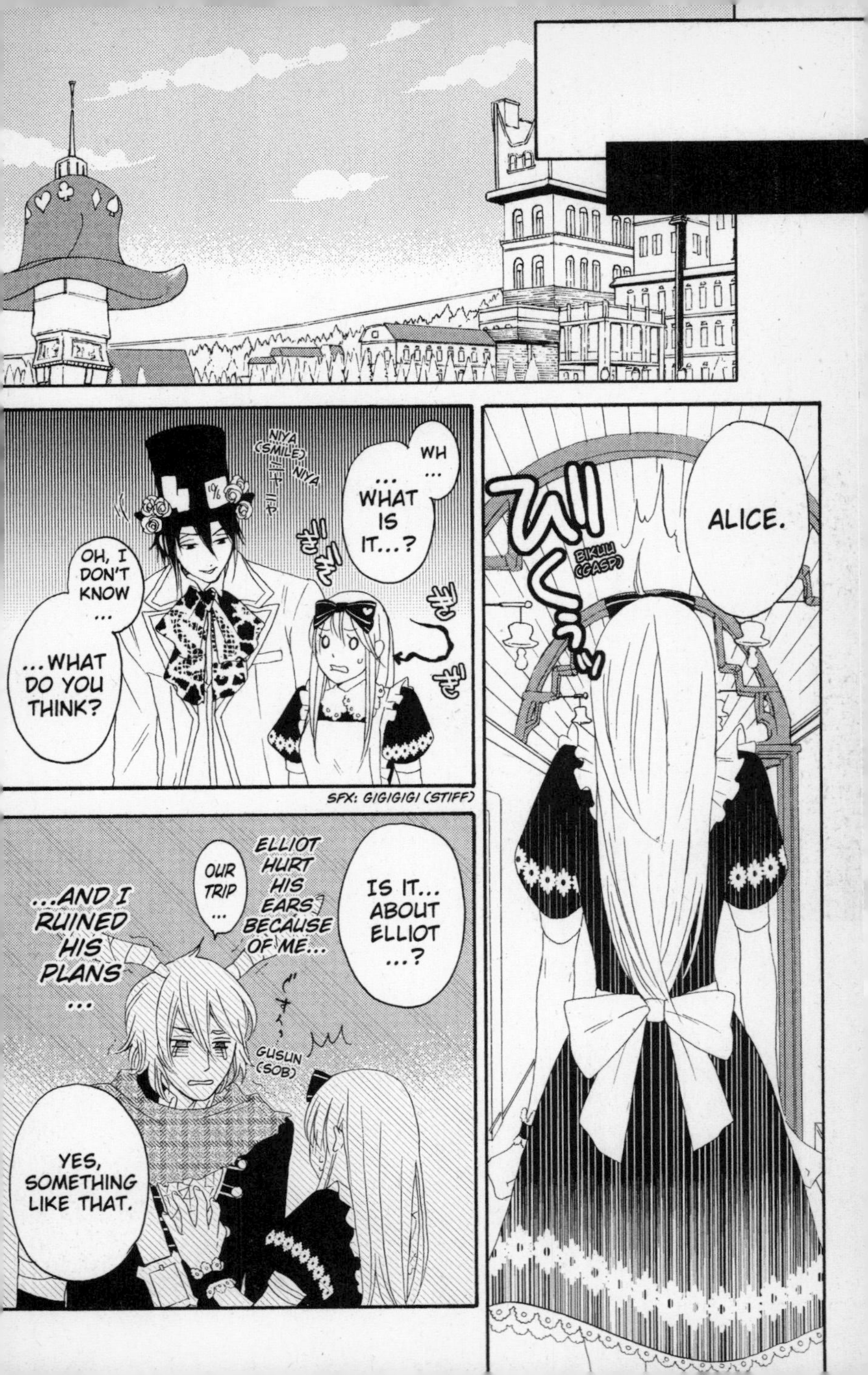
ALICE.
BIKUU (GASP)
WH ... ...WHAT IS IT...?
NIYA (SMILE) NIYA
OH, I DON'T KNOW ...
...WHAT DO YOU THINK?
SFX: GIGIGIGI (STIFF)
IS IT... ABOUT ELLIOT ...?
ELLIOT HURT HIS EARS BECAUSE OF ME...
OUR TRIP ...
...AND I RUINED HIS PLANS ...
GUSUN (SOB)
YES, SOMETHING LIKE THAT.

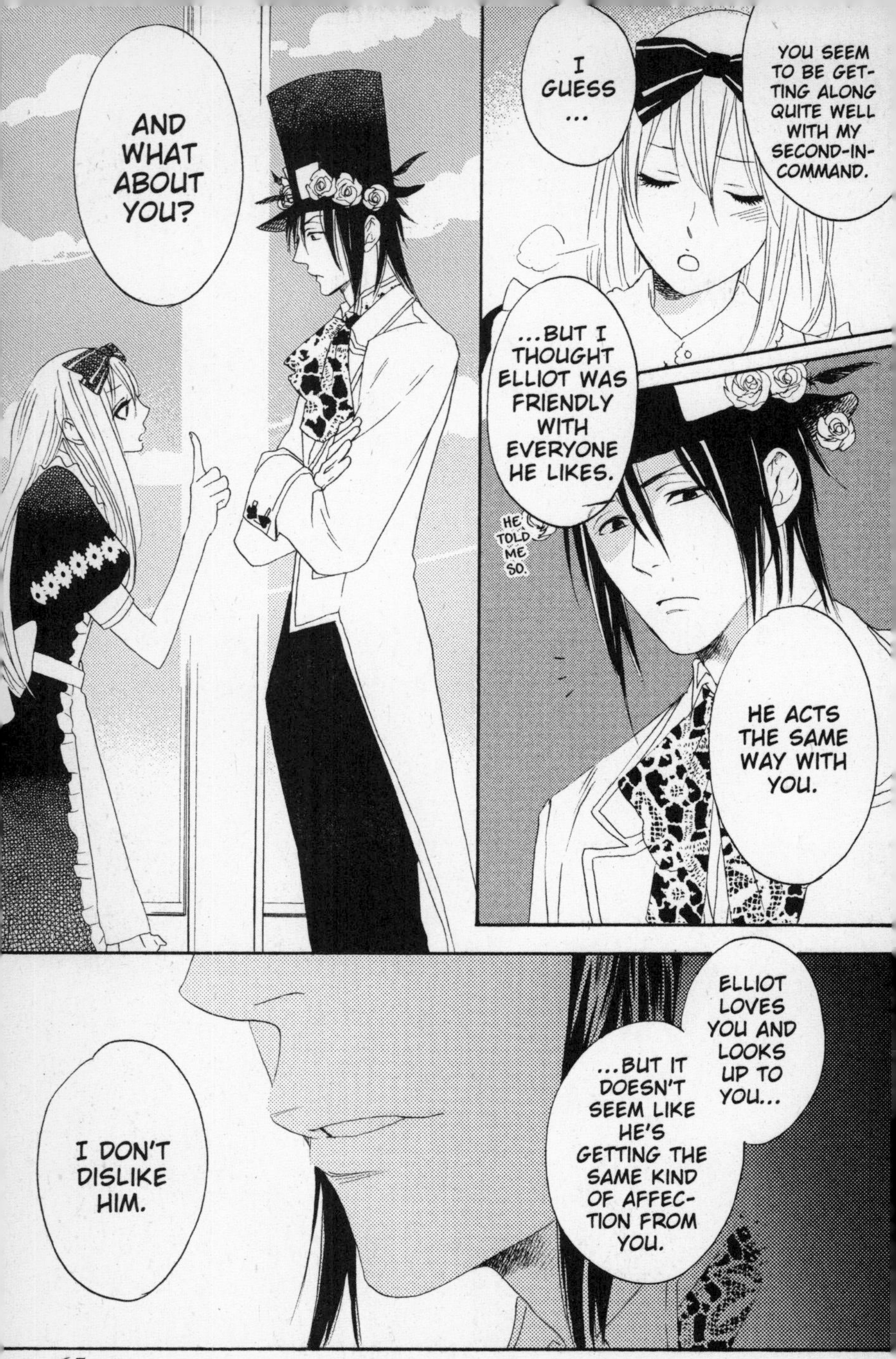
YOU SEEM TO BE GETTING ALONG QUITE WELL WITH MY SECOND-IN-COMMAND.
I GUESS...
...BUT I THOUGHT ELLIOT WAS FRIENDLY WITH EVERYONE HE LIKES.
HE TOLD ME SO.
HE ACTS THE SAME WAY WITH YOU.
AND WHAT ABOUT YOU?
ELLIOT LOVES YOU AND LOOKS UP TO YOU...
...BUT IT DOESN'T SEEM LIKE HE'S GETTING THE SAME KIND OF AFFECTION FROM YOU.
I DON'T DISLIKE HIM.

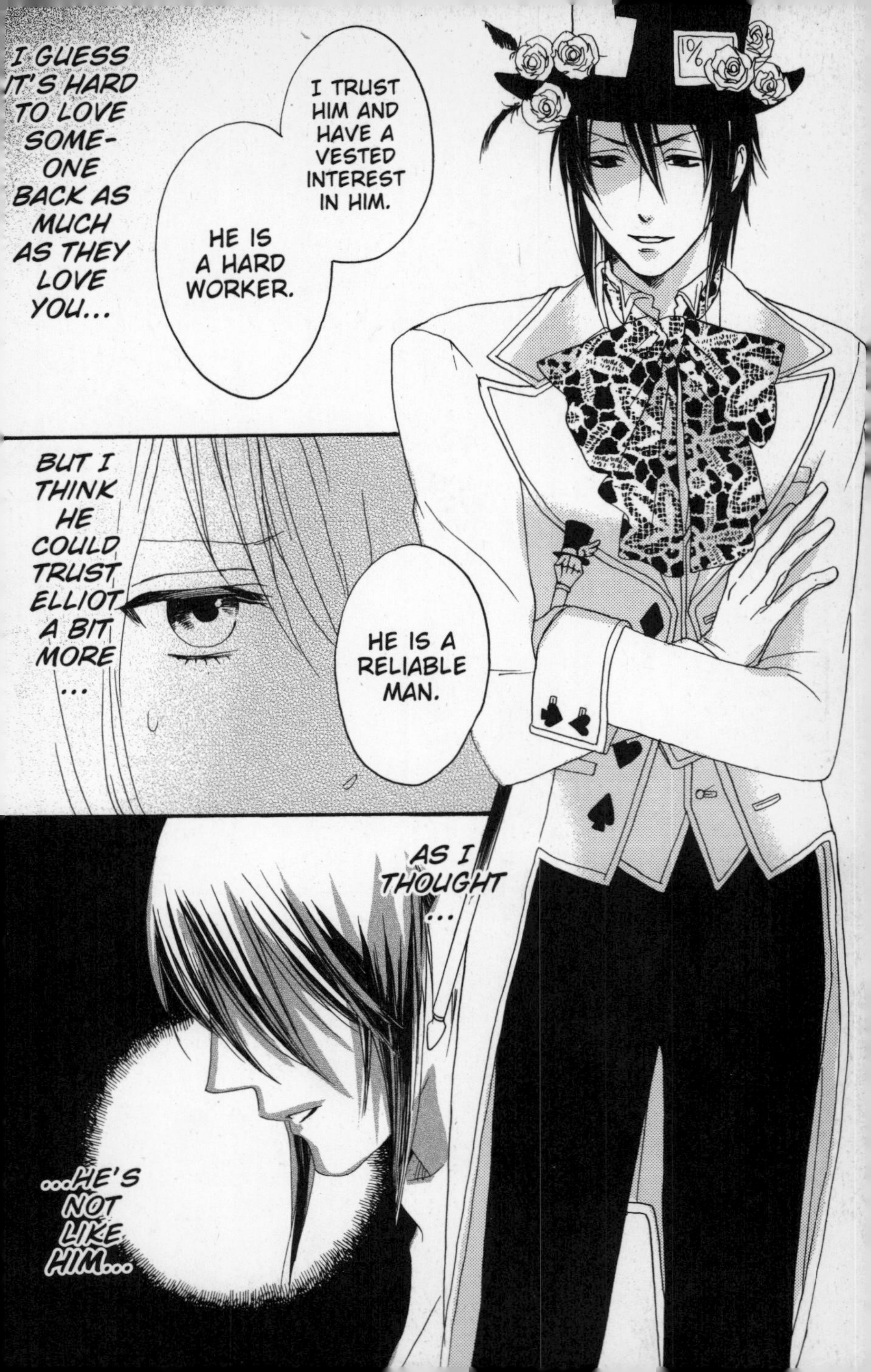
I TRUST HIM AND HAVE A VESTED INTEREST IN HIM.
HE IS A HARD WORKER.
I GUESS IT'S HARD TO LOVE SOME-ONE BACK AS MUCH AS THEY LOVE YOU...
HE IS A RELIABLE MAN.
BUT I THINK HE COULD TRUST ELLIOT A BIT MORE ...
AS I THOUGHT ...
...HE'S NOT LIKE HIM...

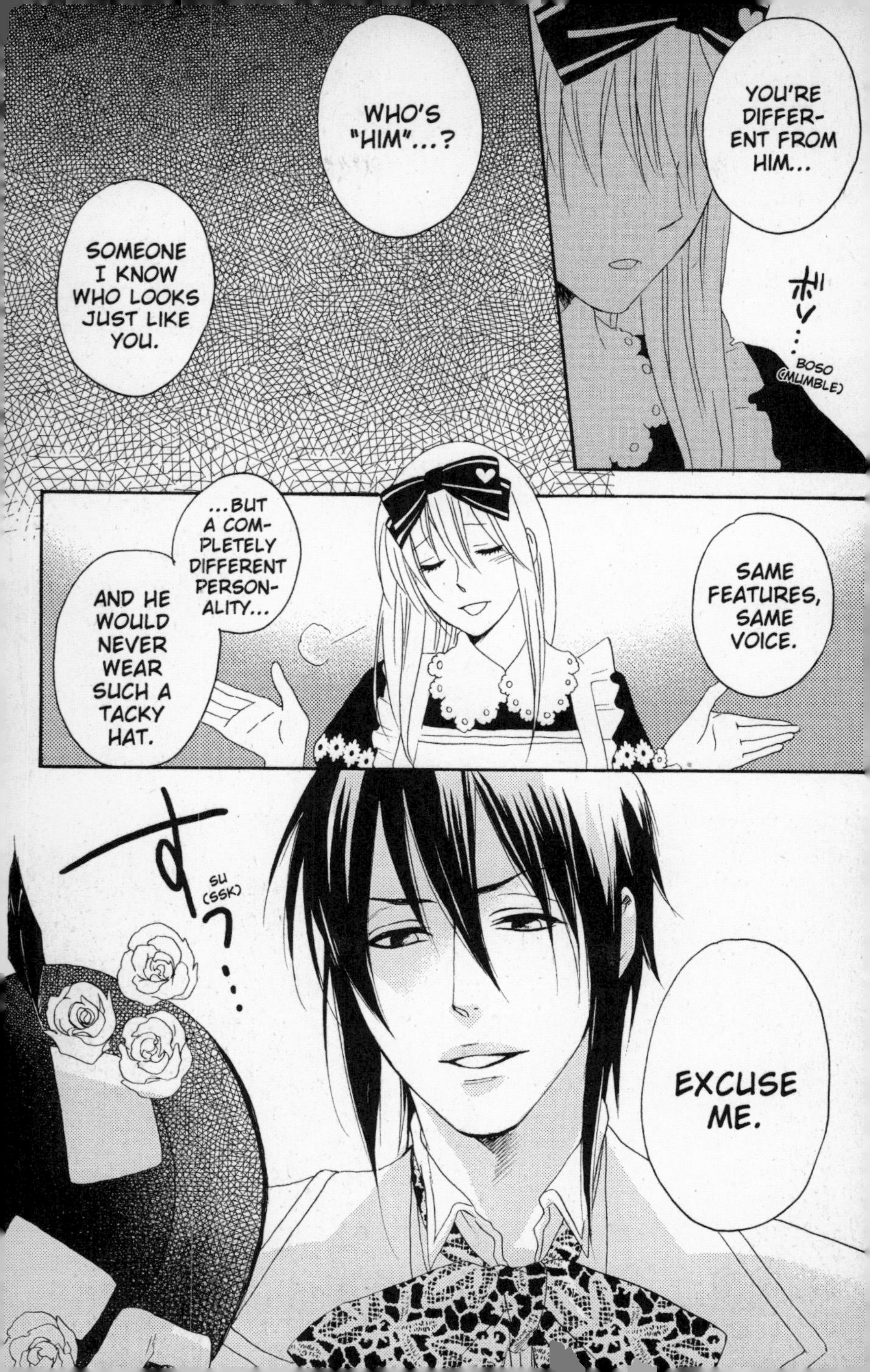
YOU'RE DIFFER-ENT FROM HIM...
BOSO (MUMBLE)
WHO'S "HIM"...?
SOMEONE I KNOW WHO LOOKS JUST LIKE YOU.
SAME FEATURES, SAME VOICE.
...BUT A COM-PLETELY DIFFERENT PERSON-ALITY...
AND HE WOULD NEVER WEAR SUCH A TACKY HAT.
SU (SSK)
EXCUSE ME.

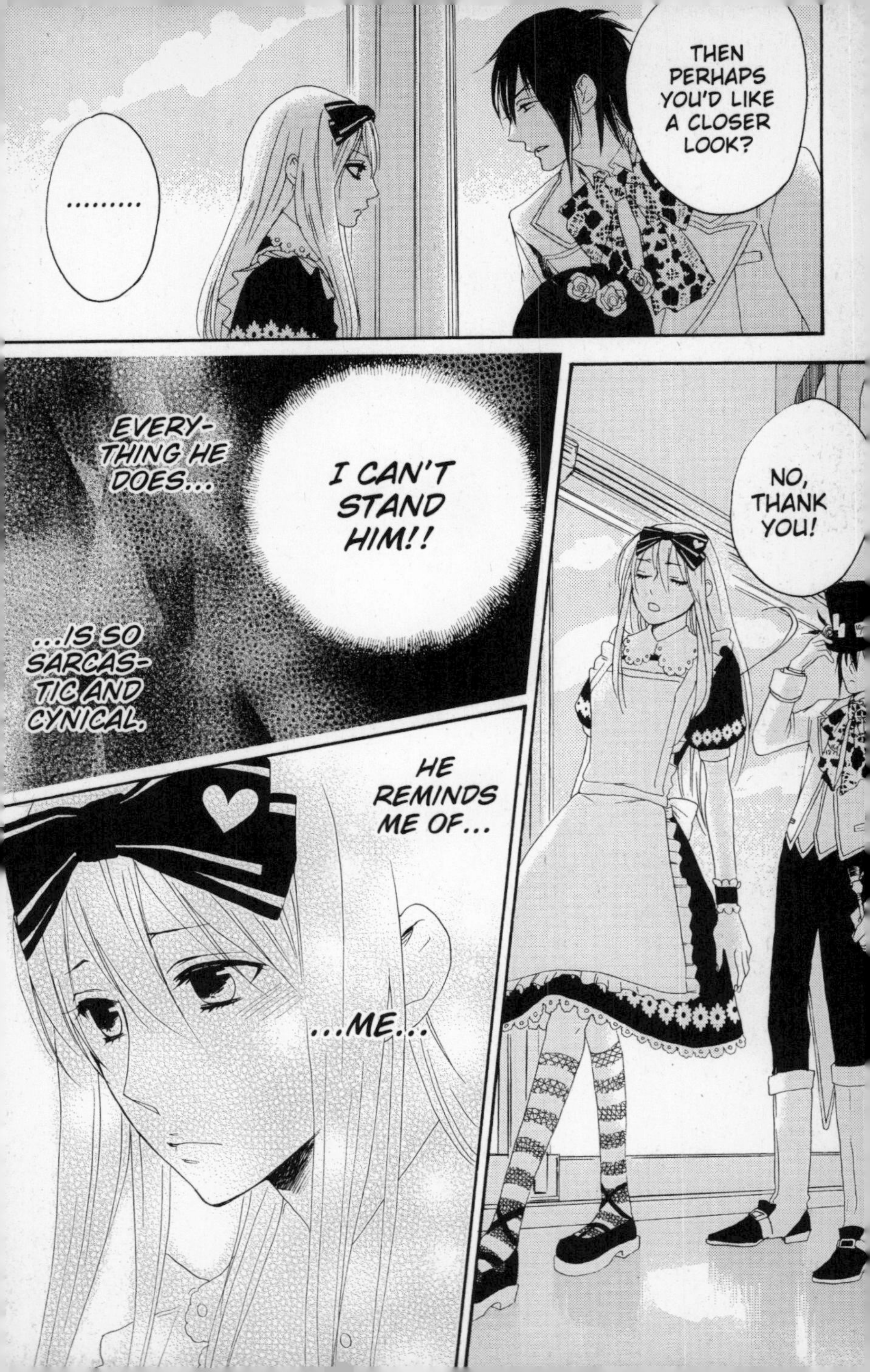
THEN PERHAPS YOU'D LIKE A CLOSER LOOK?
....
NO, THANK YOU!
I CAN'T STAND HIM!!
EVERY-THING HE DOES...
...IS SO SARCAS-TIC AND CYNICAL.
HE REMINDS ME OF...
...ME...

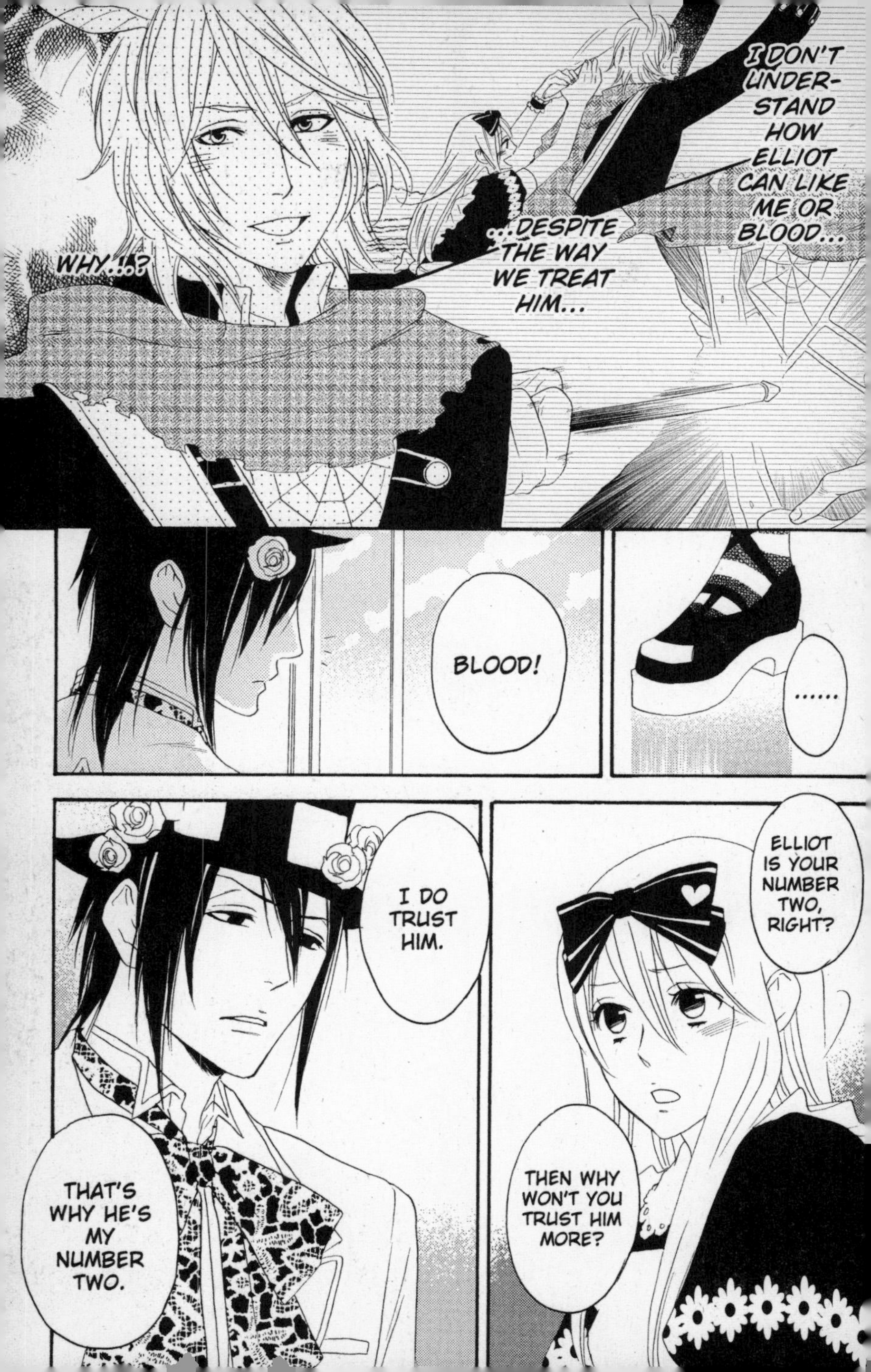
I DON'T UNDERSTAND HOW ELLIOT CAN LIKE ME OR BLOOD...
...DESPITE THE WAY WE TREAT HIM...
WHY..!?
......
BLOOD!
ELLIOT IS YOUR NUMBER TWO, RIGHT?
THEN WHY WON'T YOU TRUST HIM MORE?
I DO TRUST HIM.
THAT'S WHY HE'S MY NUMBER TWO.

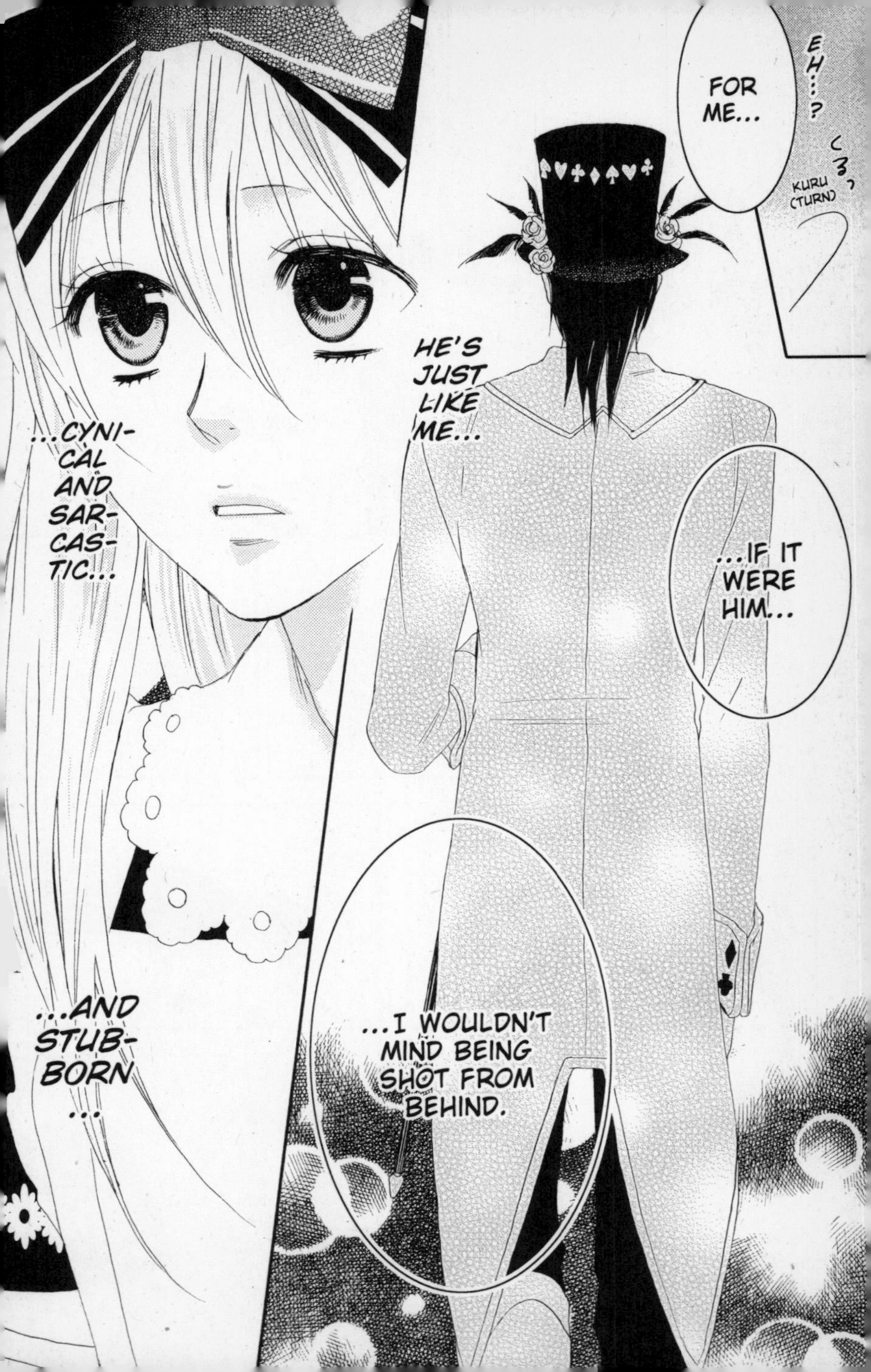
EH...?
FOR ME...
くるっ
KURU (TURN)
HE'S JUST LIKE ME...
...CYNICAL AND SARCASTIC...
...AND STUBBORN...
...IF IT WERE HIM...
...I WOULDN'T MIND BEING SHOT FROM BEHIND.

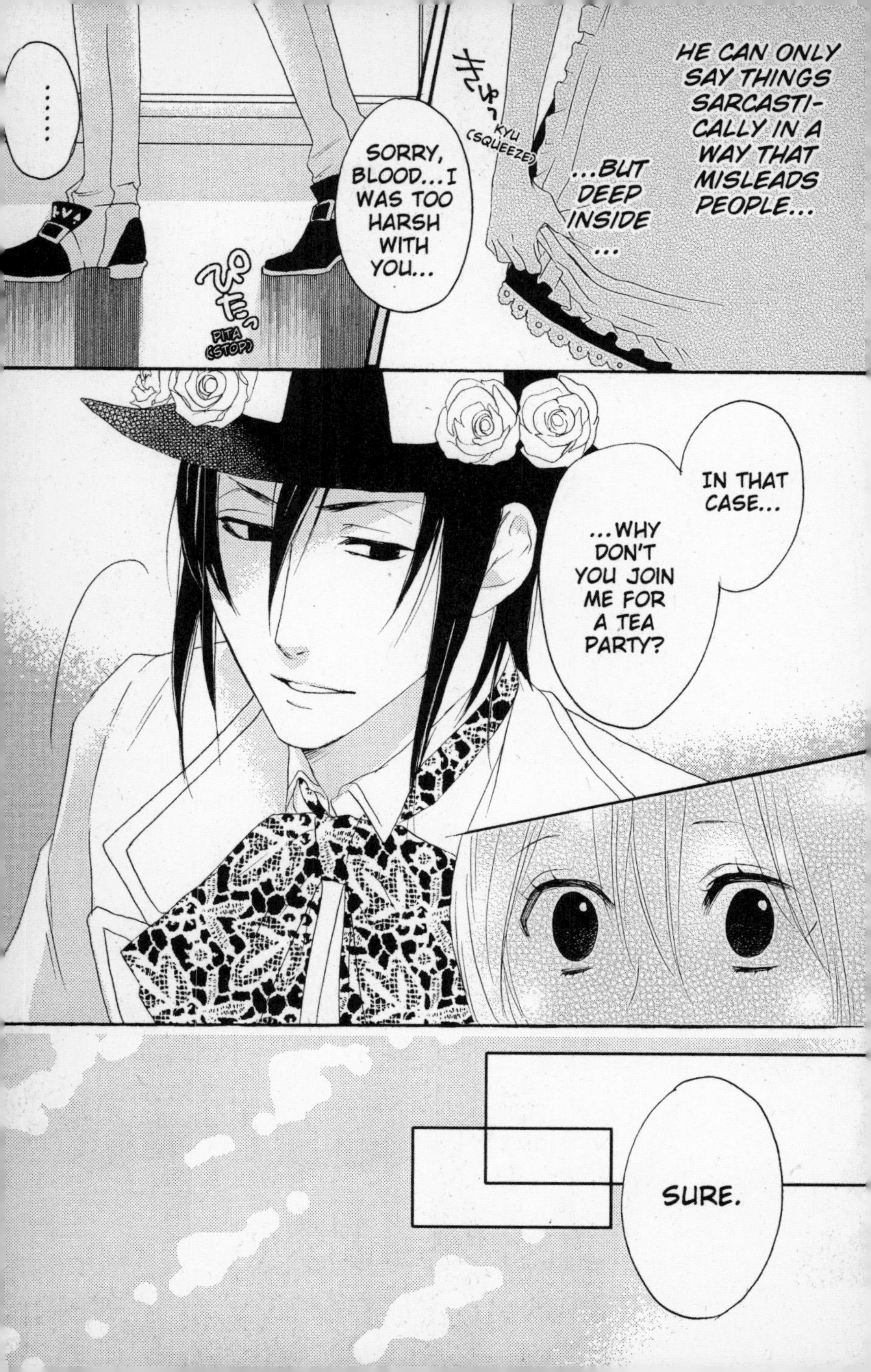
HE CAN ONLY SAY THINGS SARCASTICALLY IN A WAY THAT MISLEADS PEOPLE...
...BUT DEEP INSIDE...
きゅっ
KYU (SQUEEZE)
SORRY, BLOOD...I WAS TOO HARSH WITH YOU...
ぴたっ
PITA (STOP)
......
IN THAT CASE...
...WHY DON'T YOU JOIN ME FOR A TEA PARTY?
SURE.

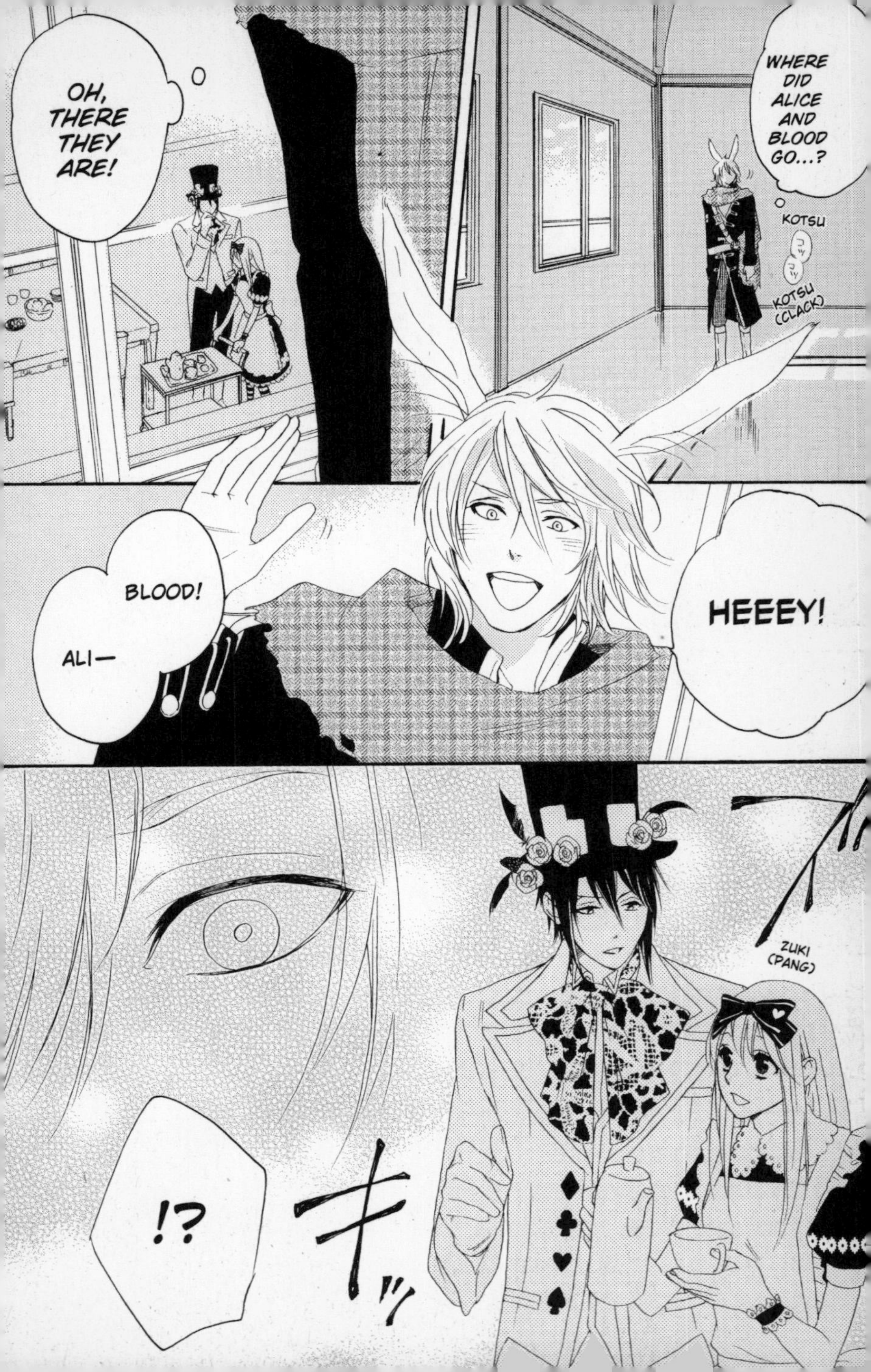
WHERE DID ALICE AND BLOOD GO...?
KOTSU
KOTSU (CLACK)
OH, THERE THEY ARE!
HEEEY!
BLOOD!
ALI—
ZUKI (PANG)
!?

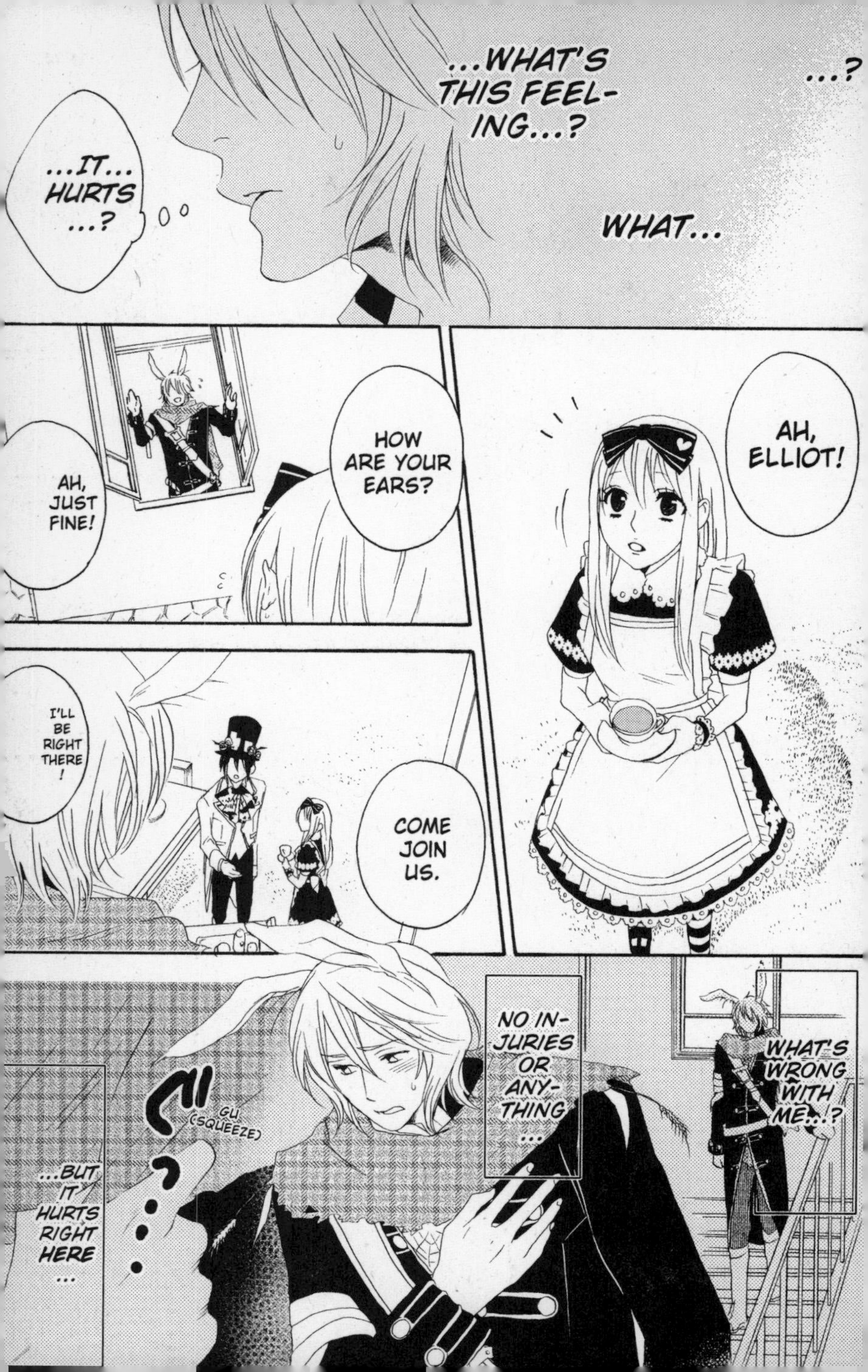
...?
...WHAT'S THIS FEEL-ING...?
WHAT...
...IT... HURTS ...?
AH, ELLIOT!
HOW ARE YOUR EARS?
AH, JUST FINE!
COME JOIN US.
I'LL BE RIGHT THERE!
WHAT'S WRONG WITH ME...?
NO IN-JURIES OR ANY-THING ...
GU (SQUEEZE)
...BUT IT HURTS RIGHT HERE ...

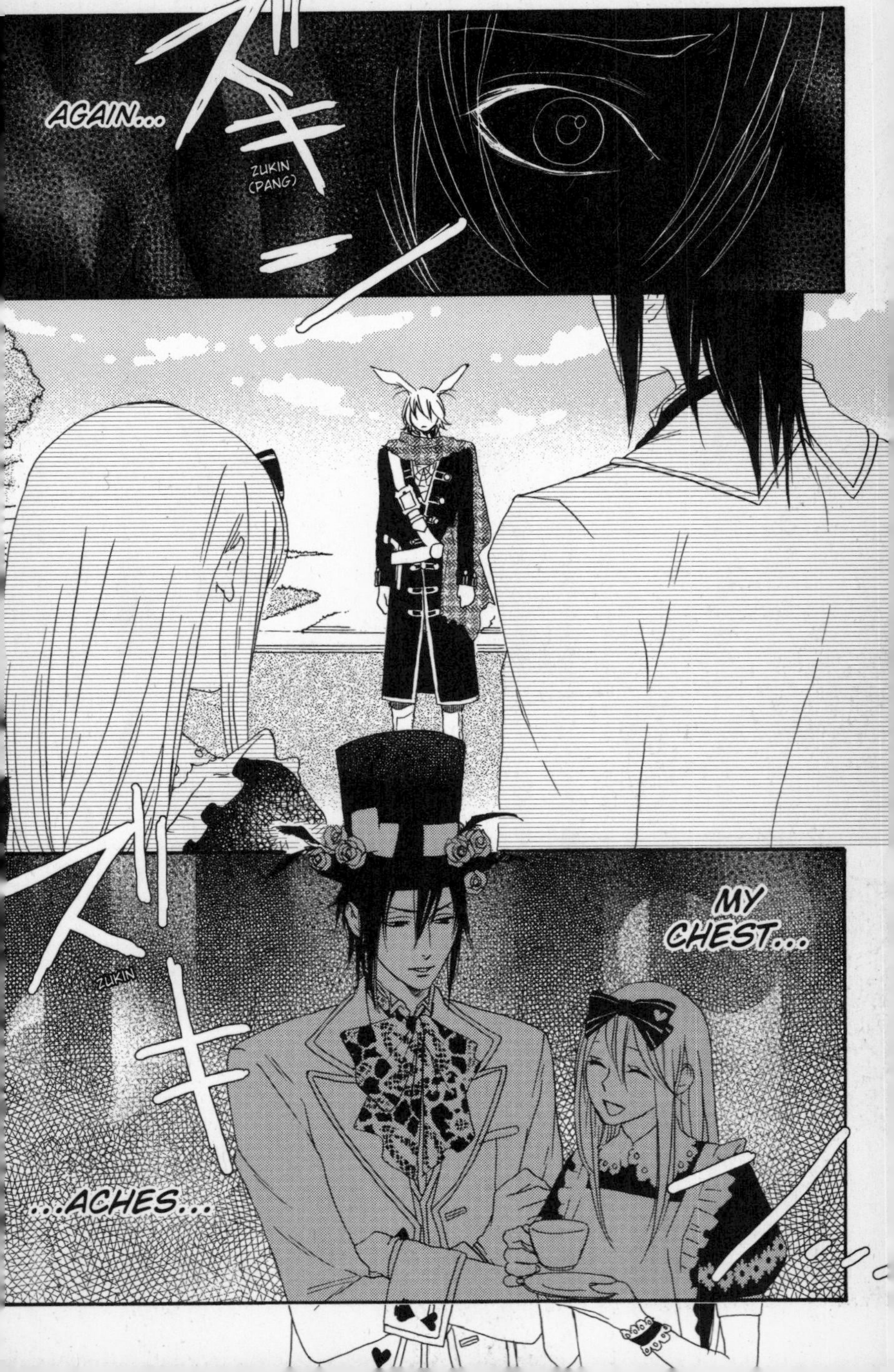
AGAIN...
ZUKIN (PANG)
MY CHEST...
ZUKIN
...ACHES...

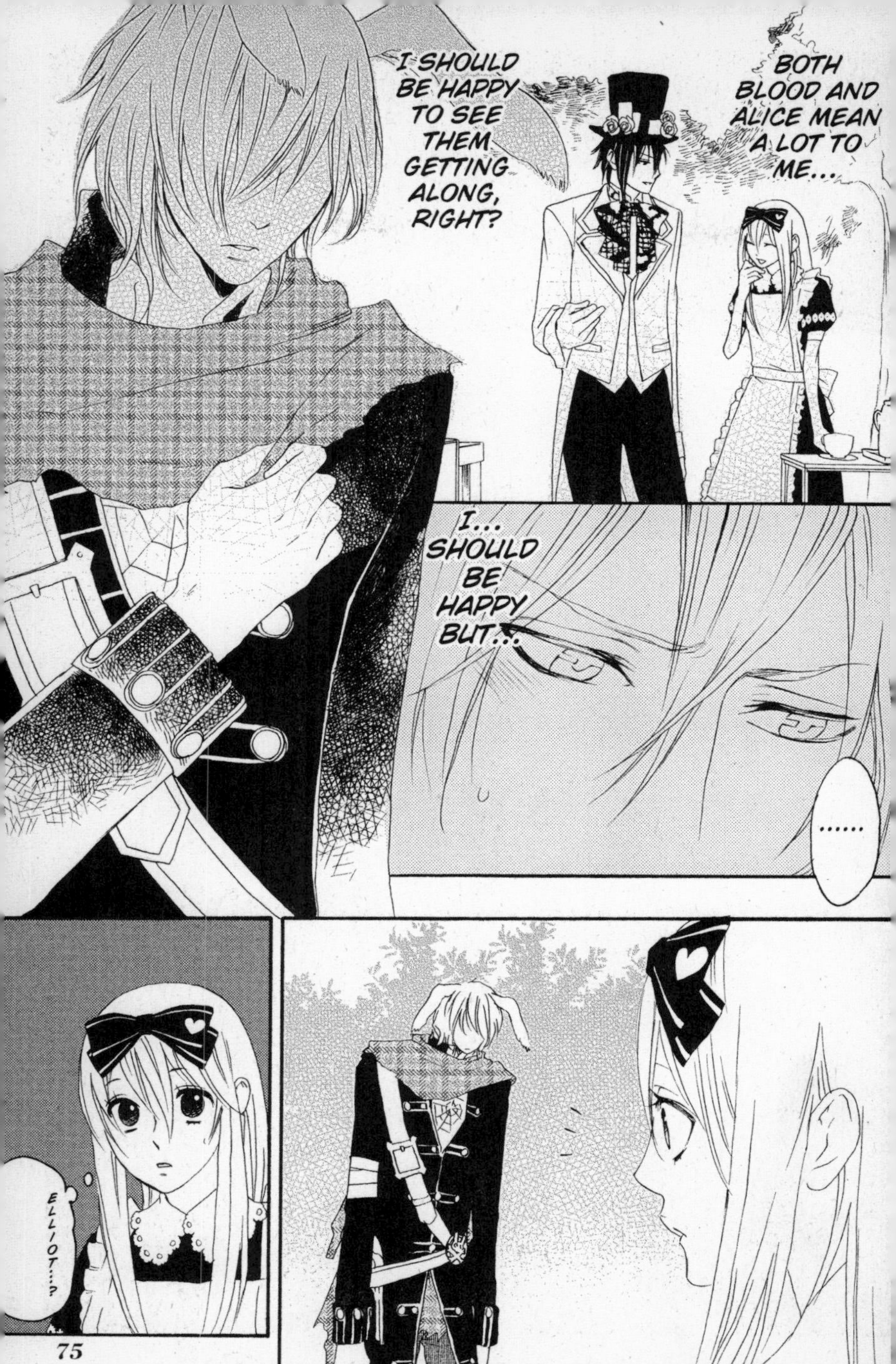
BOTH BLOOD AND ALICE MEAN A LOT TO ME...
I SHOULD BE HAPPY TO SEE THEM GETTING ALONG, RIGHT?
I... SHOULD BE HAPPY BUT...
......
ELLIOT...?

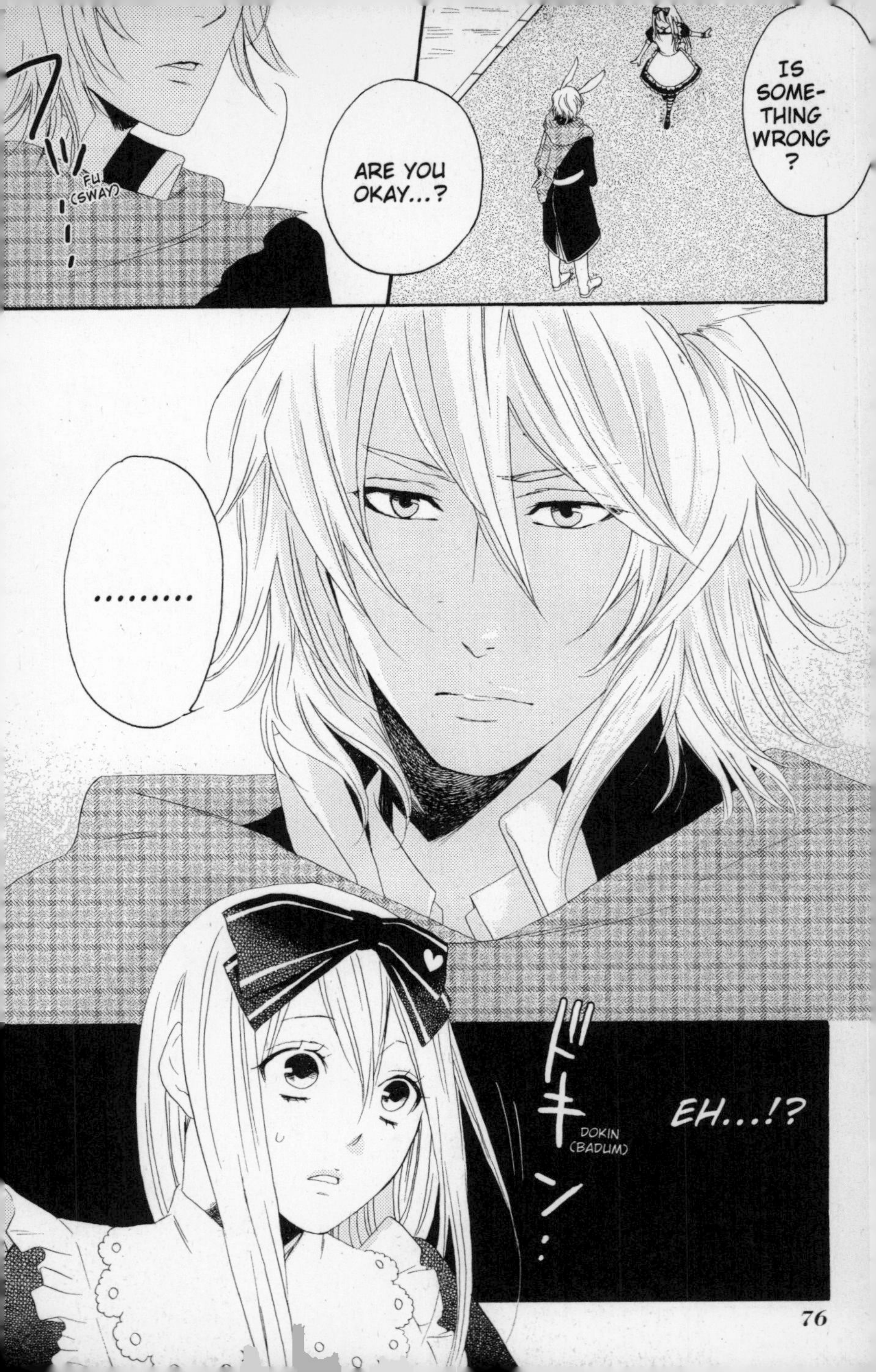
IS SOMETHING WRONG?
ARE YOU OKAY...?
FU (SWAY)
....
EH...!?
ドキン
DOKIN (BADUM)

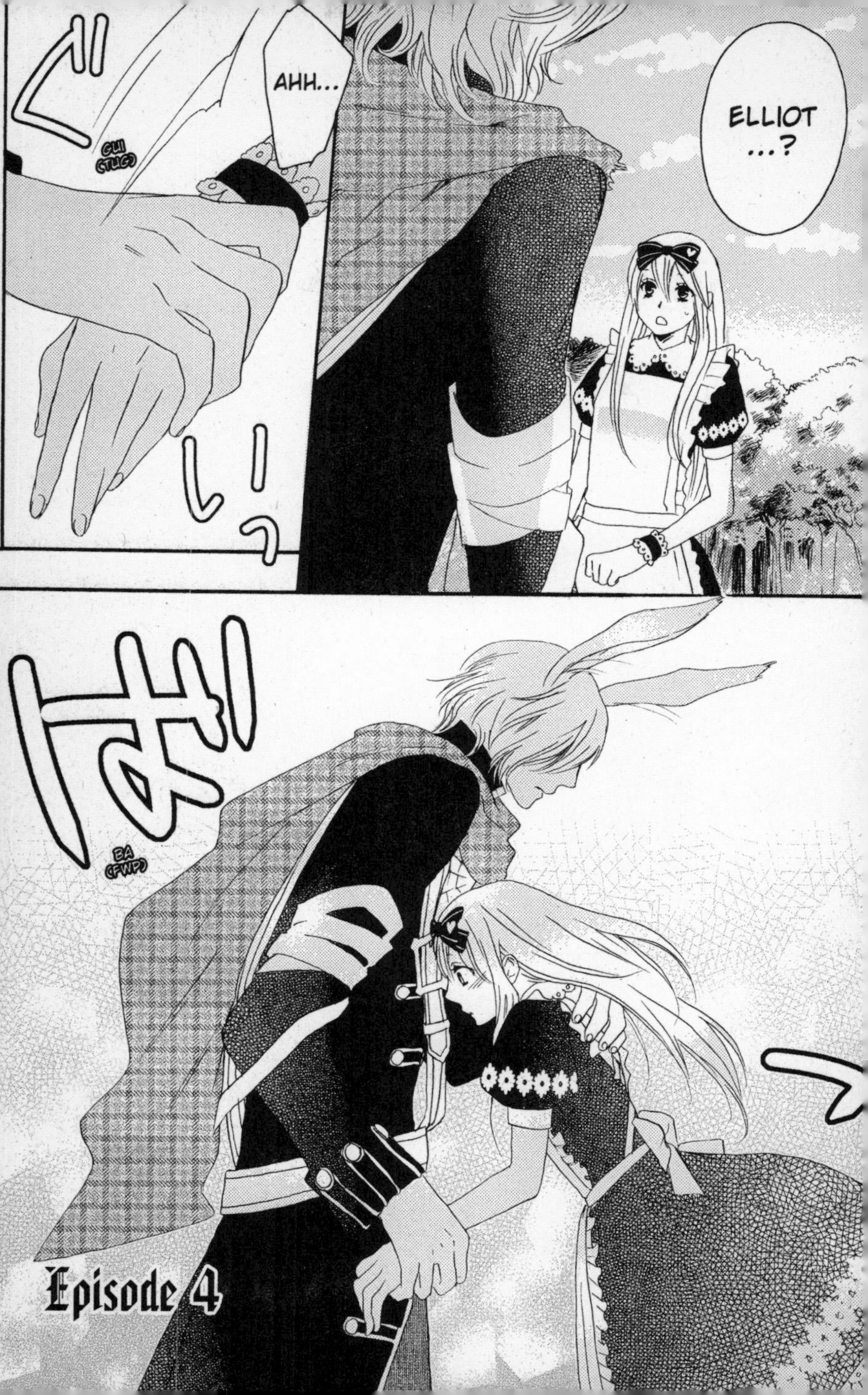
ELLIOT ...?
AHH...
GUI (TUG)
BA (FWP)
Episode 4

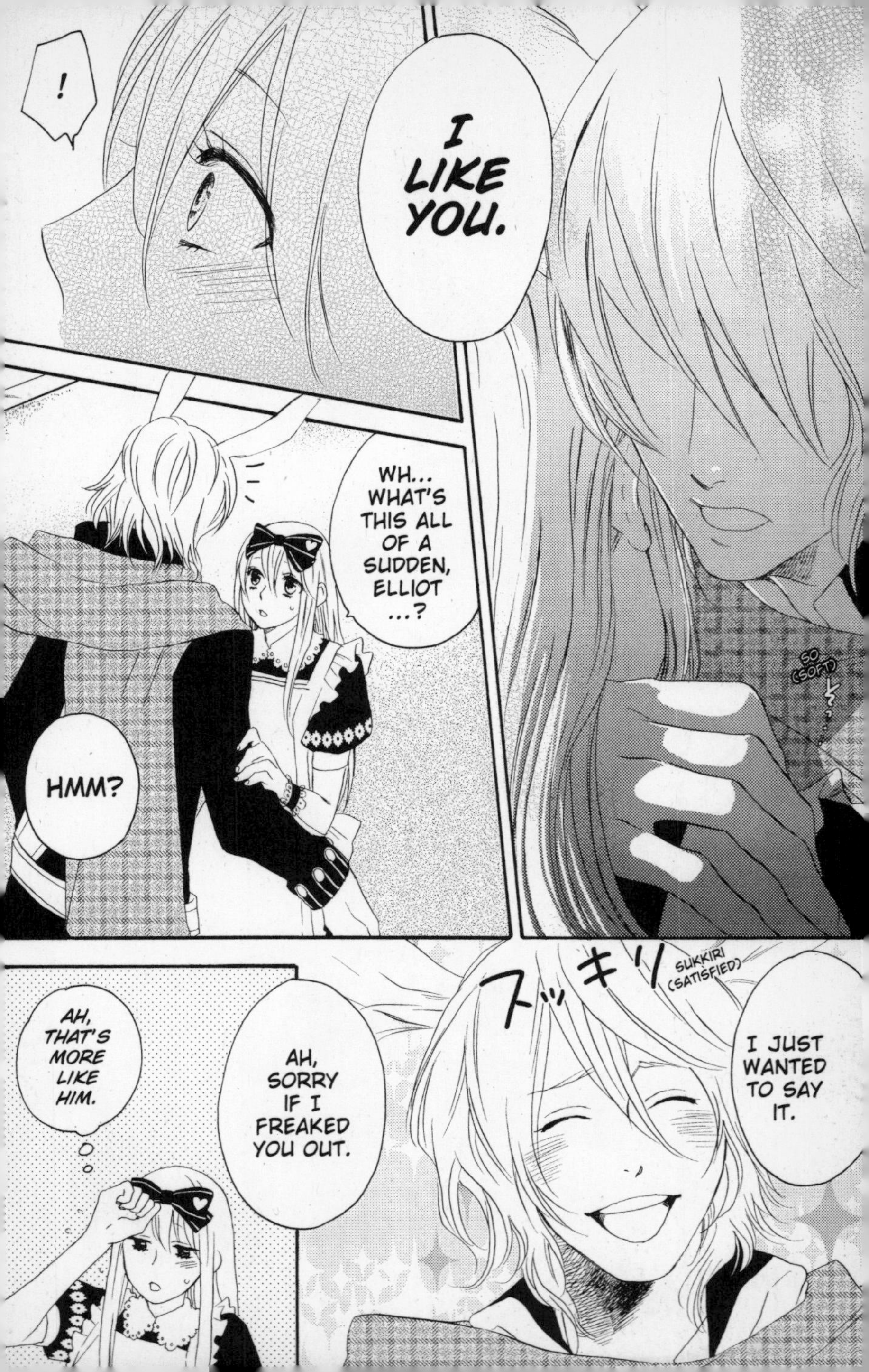
I LIKE YOU.
SO (SOFT)
!
WH... WHAT'S THIS ALL OF A SUDDEN, ELLIOT ...?
HMM?
スッキリ
SUKKIRI (SATISFIED)
I JUST WANTED TO SAY IT.
AH, SORRY IF I FREAKED YOU OUT.
AH, THAT'S MORE LIKE HIM.

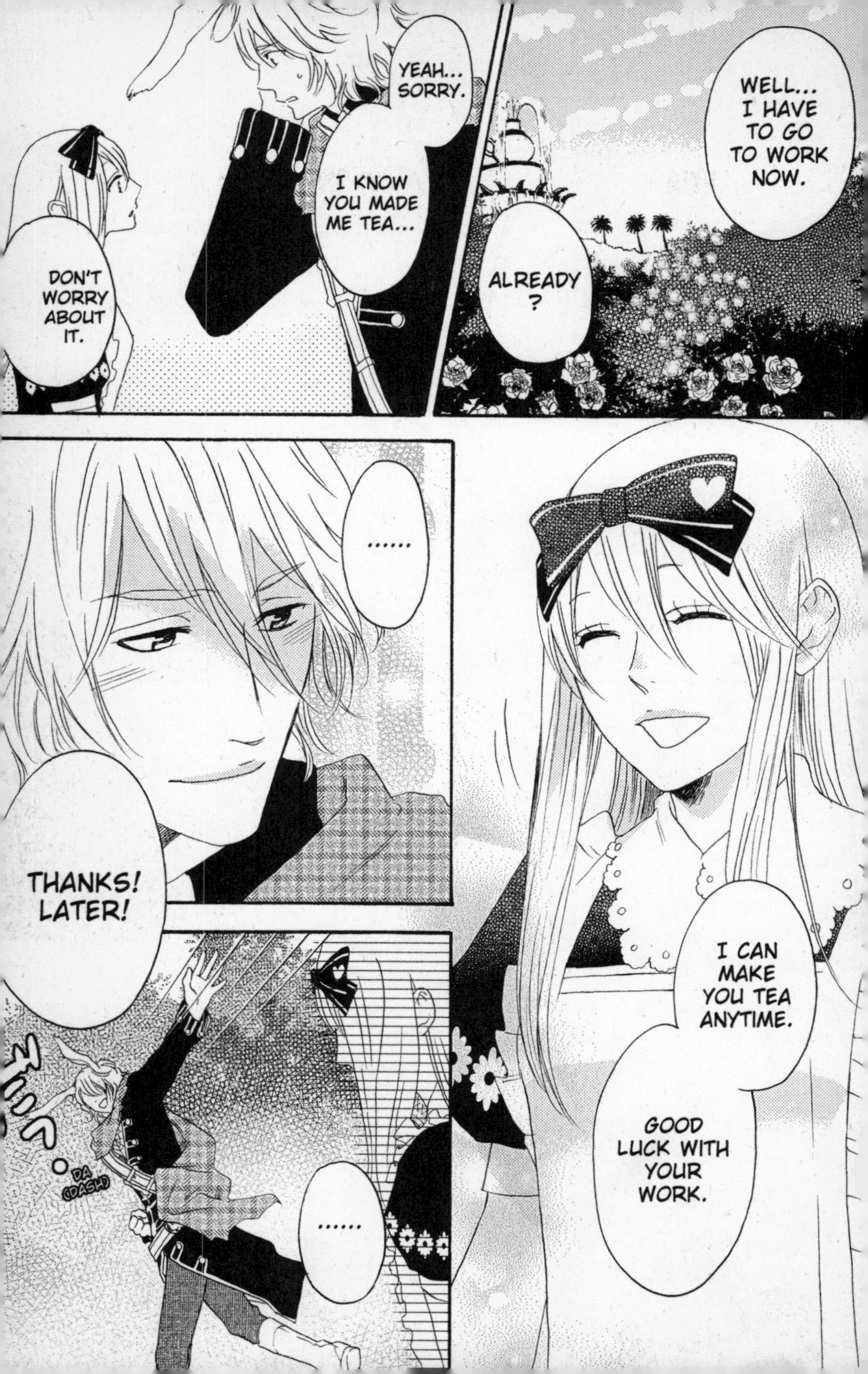
WELL... I HAVE TO GO TO WORK NOW.
ALREADY?
YEAH... SORRY.
I KNOW YOU MADE ME TEA...
DON'T WORRY ABOUT IT.
I CAN MAKE YOU TEA ANYTIME.
GOOD LUCK WITH YOUR WORK.
......
THANKS! LATER!
DA (DASH)
......

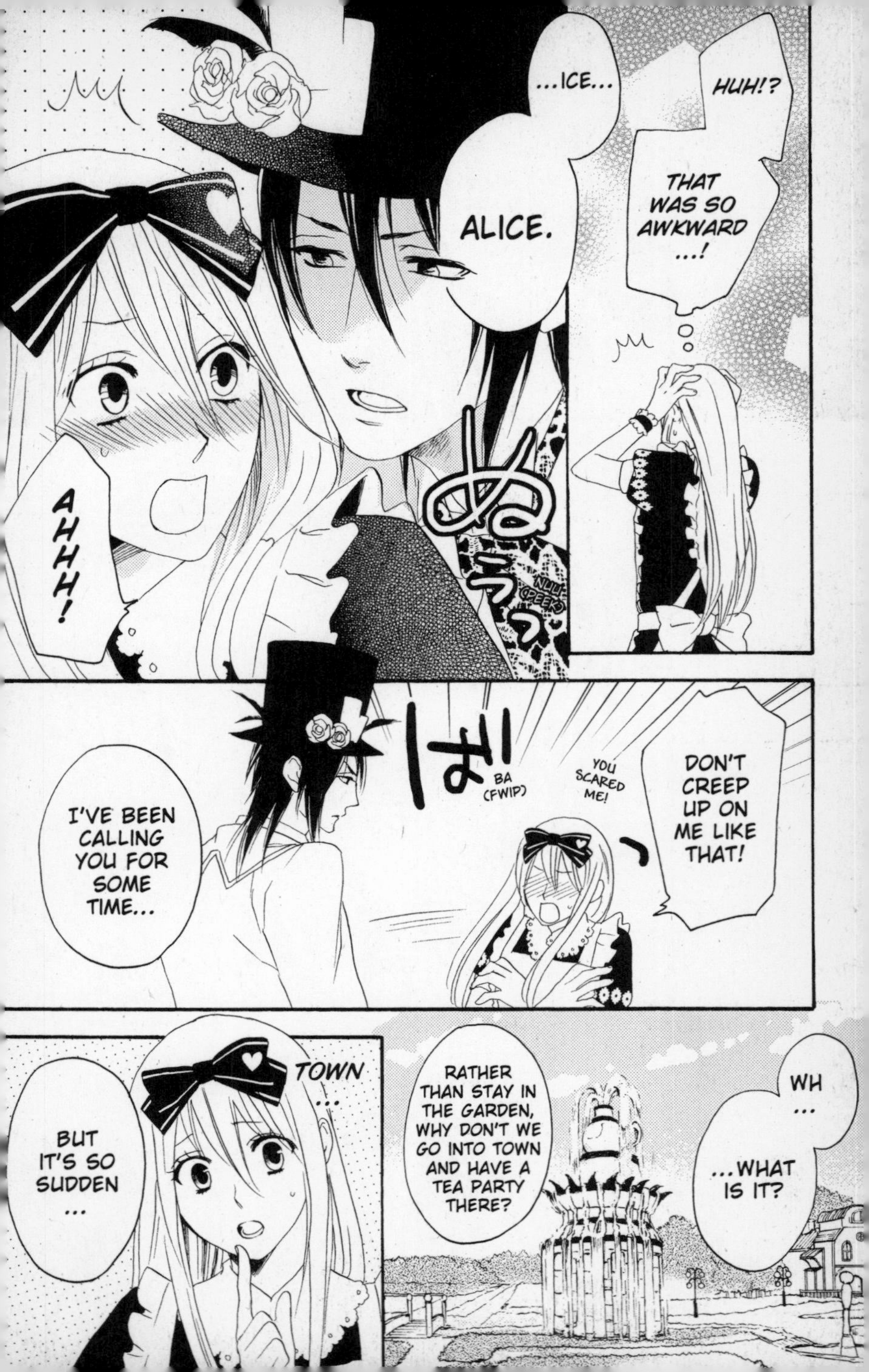
HUH!?
THAT WAS SO AWKWARD ...!
...ICE...
ALICE.
NUU (PEEK)
AHHH!
DON'T CREEP UP ON ME LIKE THAT!
YOU SCARED ME!
BA (FWIP)
I'VE BEEN CALLING YOU FOR SOME TIME...
WH ...
...WHAT IS IT?
RATHER THAN STAY IN THE GARDEN, WHY DON'T WE GO INTO TOWN AND HAVE A TEA PARTY THERE?
TOWN ...
BUT IT'S SO SUDDEN ...

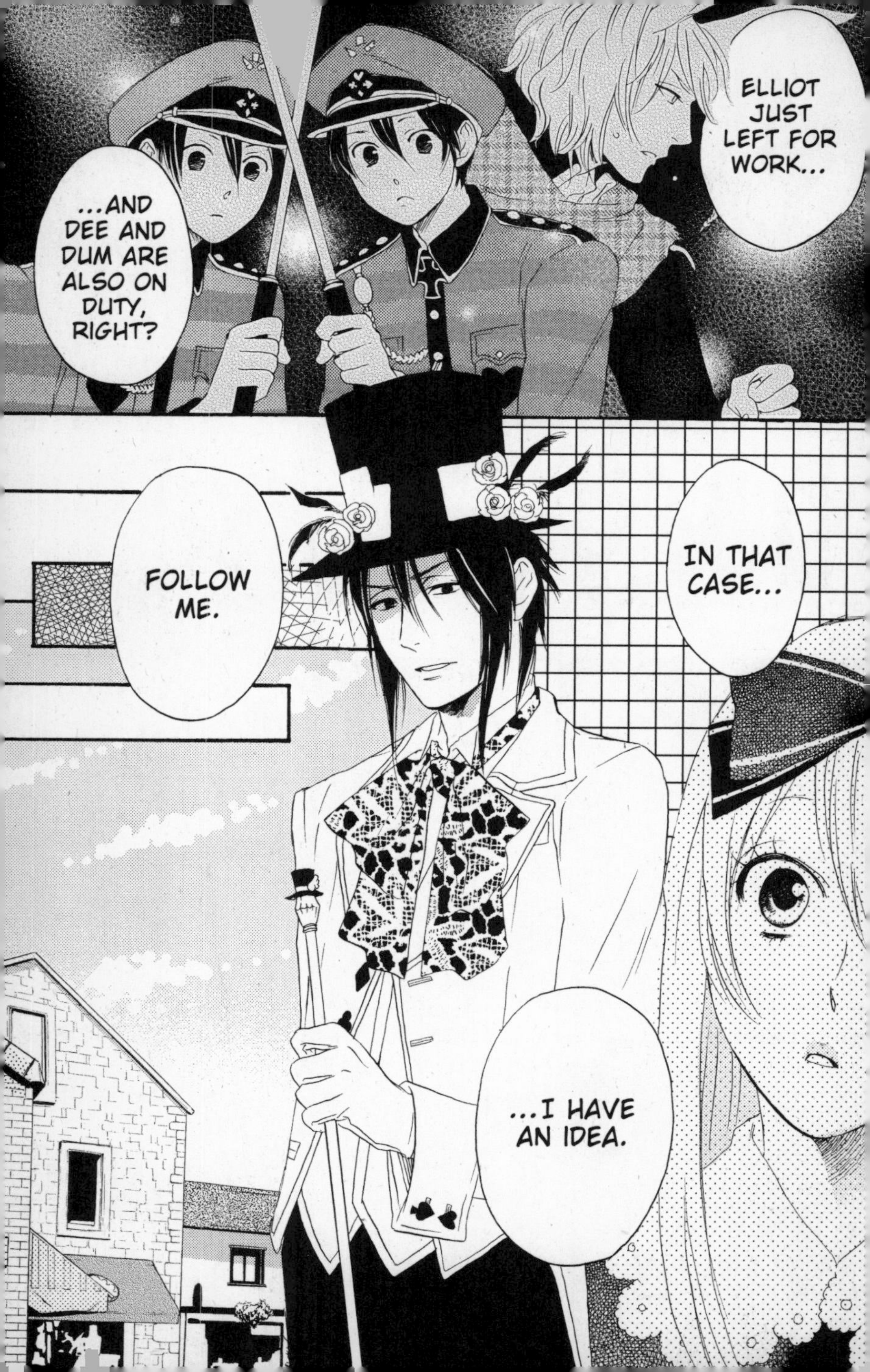
ELLIOT JUST LEFT FOR WORK...
...AND DEE AND DUM ARE ALSO ON DUTY, RIGHT?
IN THAT CASE...
...I HAVE AN IDEA.
FOLLOW ME.

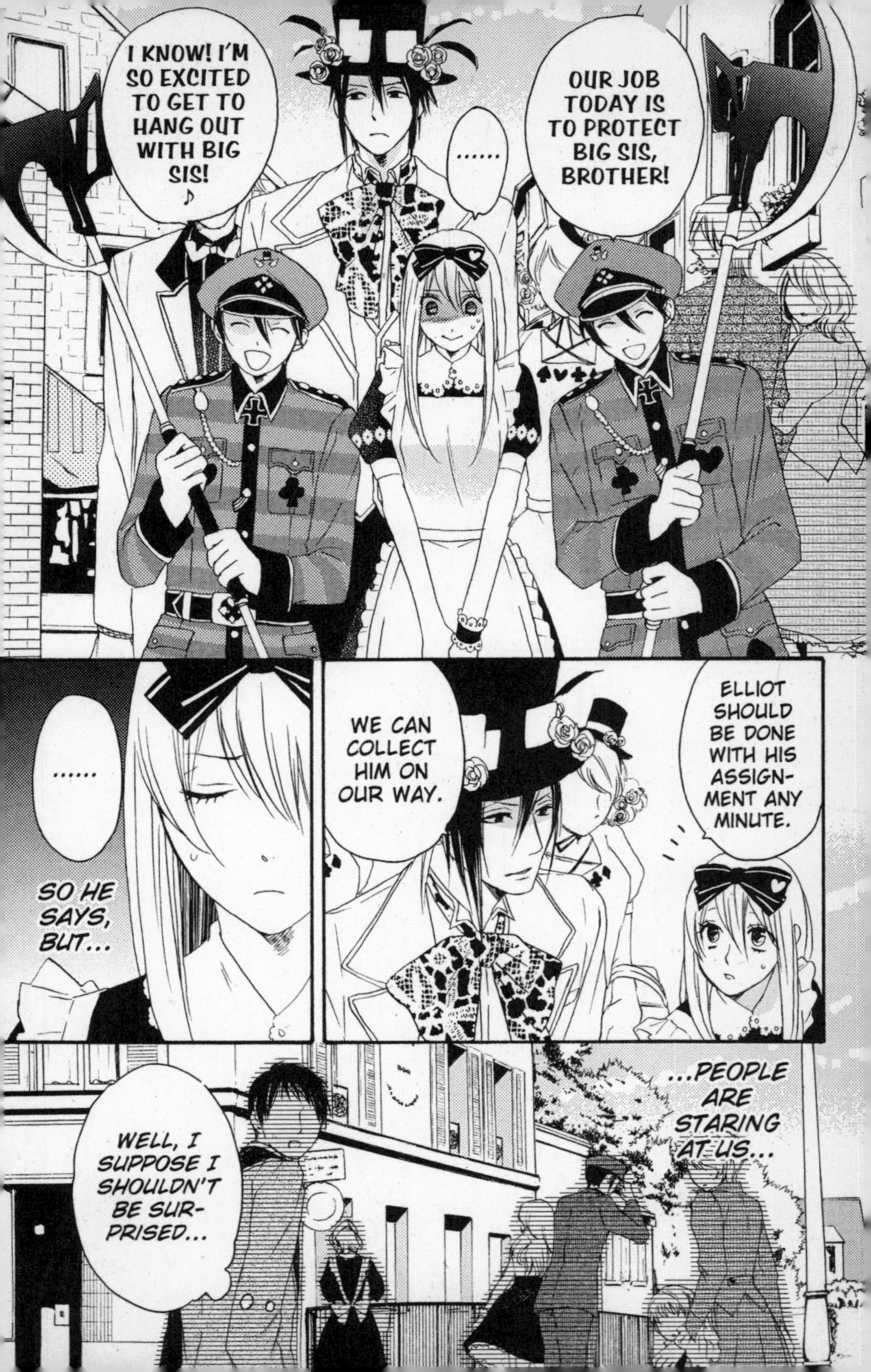
OUR JOB TODAY IS TO PROTECT BIG SIS, BROTHER!
I KNOW! I'M SO EXCITED TO GET TO HANG OUT WITH BIG SIS! ♪
......
ELLIOT SHOULD BE DONE WITH HIS ASSIGN-MENT ANY MINUTE.
WE CAN COLLECT HIM ON OUR WAY.
......
SO HE SAYS, BUT...
...PEOPLE ARE STARING AT US...
WELL, I SUPPOSE I SHOULDN'T BE SUR-PRISED...

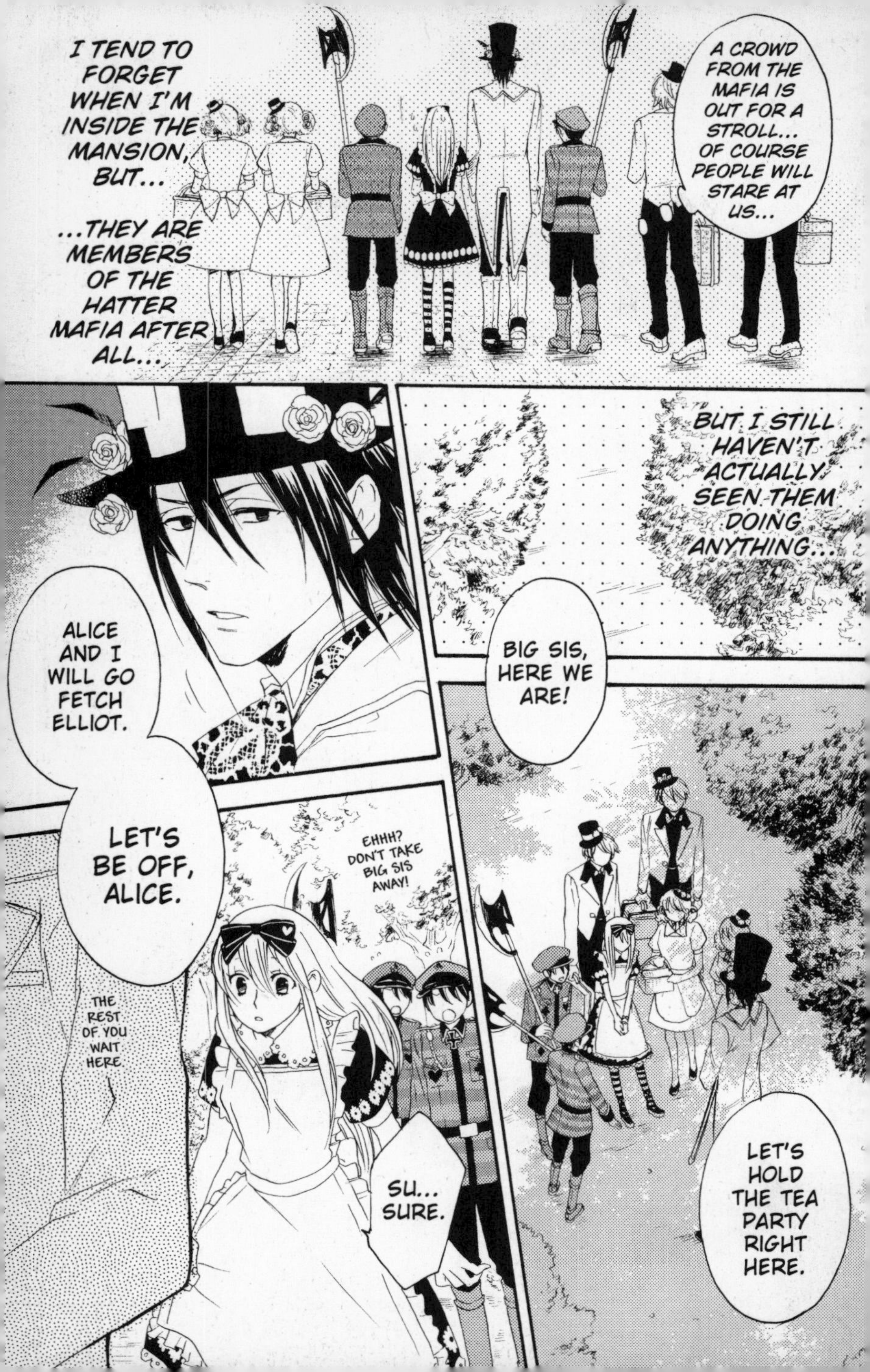
A CROWD FROM THE MAFIA IS OUT FOR A STROLL... OF COURSE PEOPLE WILL STARE AT US...
I TEND TO FORGET WHEN I'M INSIDE THE MANSION, BUT...
...THEY ARE MEMBERS OF THE HATTER MAFIA AFTER ALL...
BUT I STILL HAVEN'T ACTUALLY SEEN THEM DOING ANYTHING...
BIG SIS, HERE WE ARE!
LET'S HOLD THE TEA PARTY RIGHT HERE.
ALICE AND I WILL GO FETCH ELLIOT.
LET'S BE OFF, ALICE.
EHHH? DON'T TAKE BIG SIS AWAY!
THE REST OF YOU WAIT HERE.
SU... SURE.

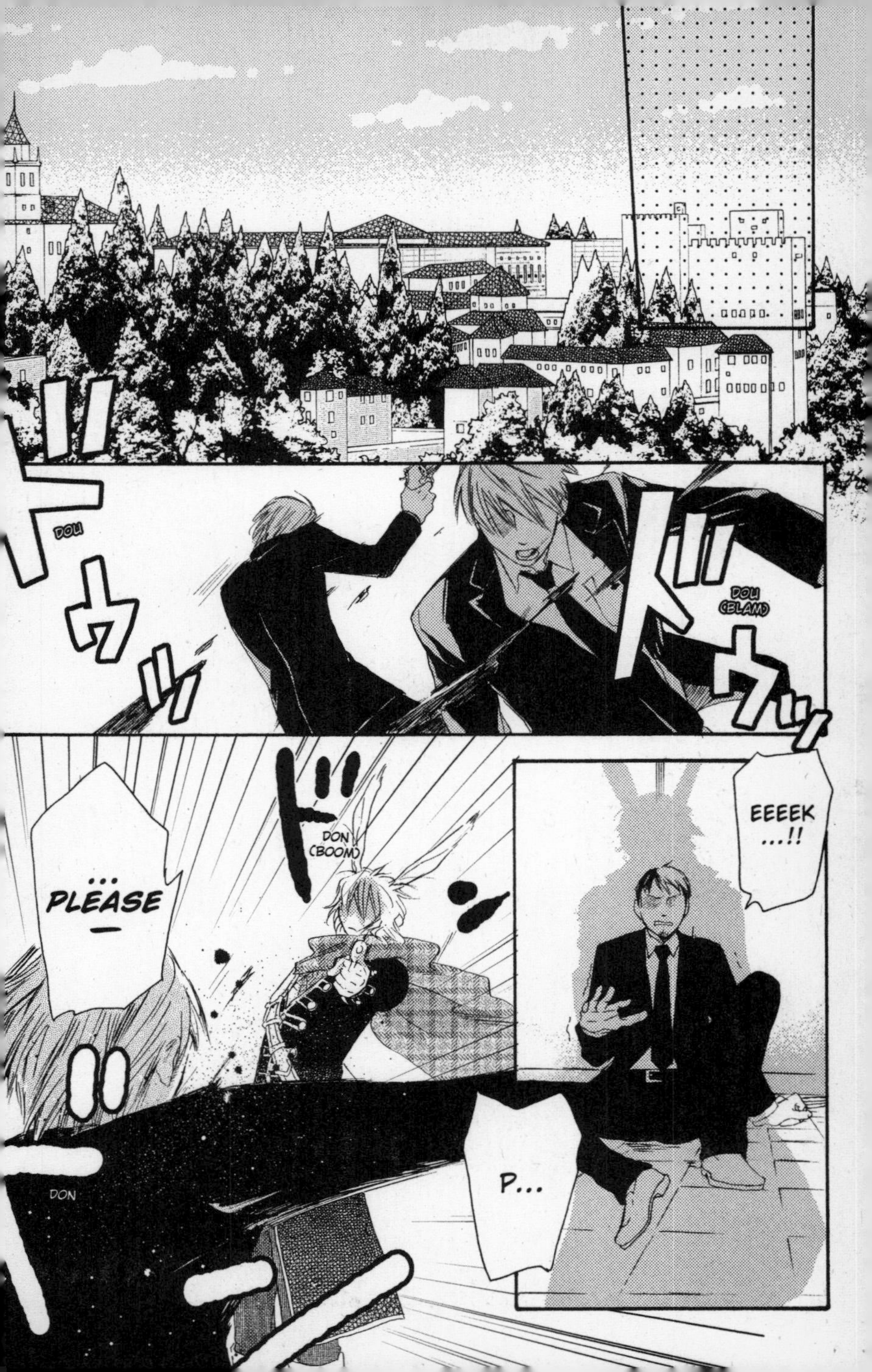
DOU (BLAM)
DOU
EEEEK ...!!
P...
DON (BOOM)
... PLEASE —
DON

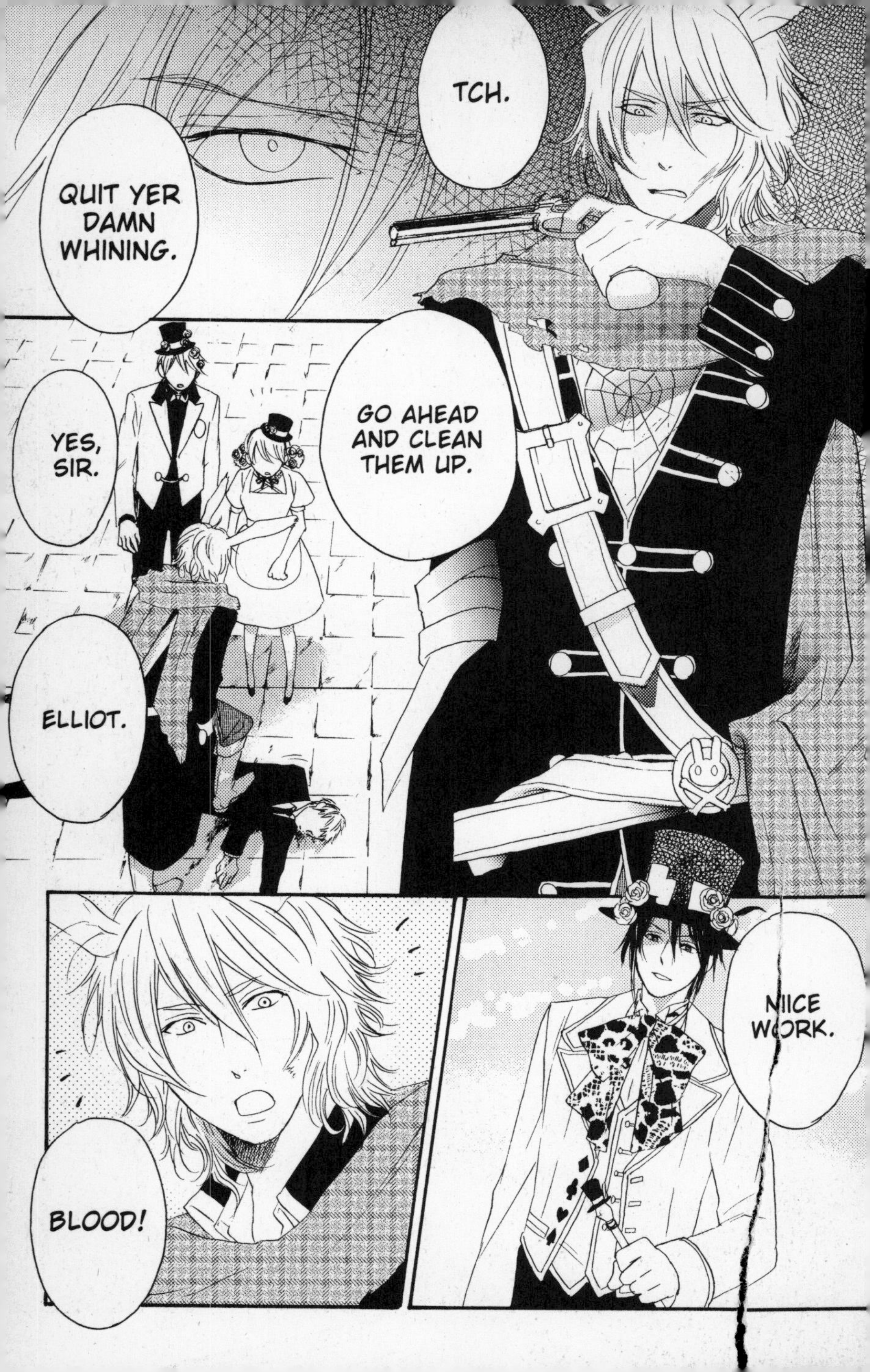
TCH.
QUIT YER DAMN WHINING.
GO AHEAD AND CLEAN THEM UP.
YES, SIR.
ELLIOT.
NICE WORK.
BLOOD!

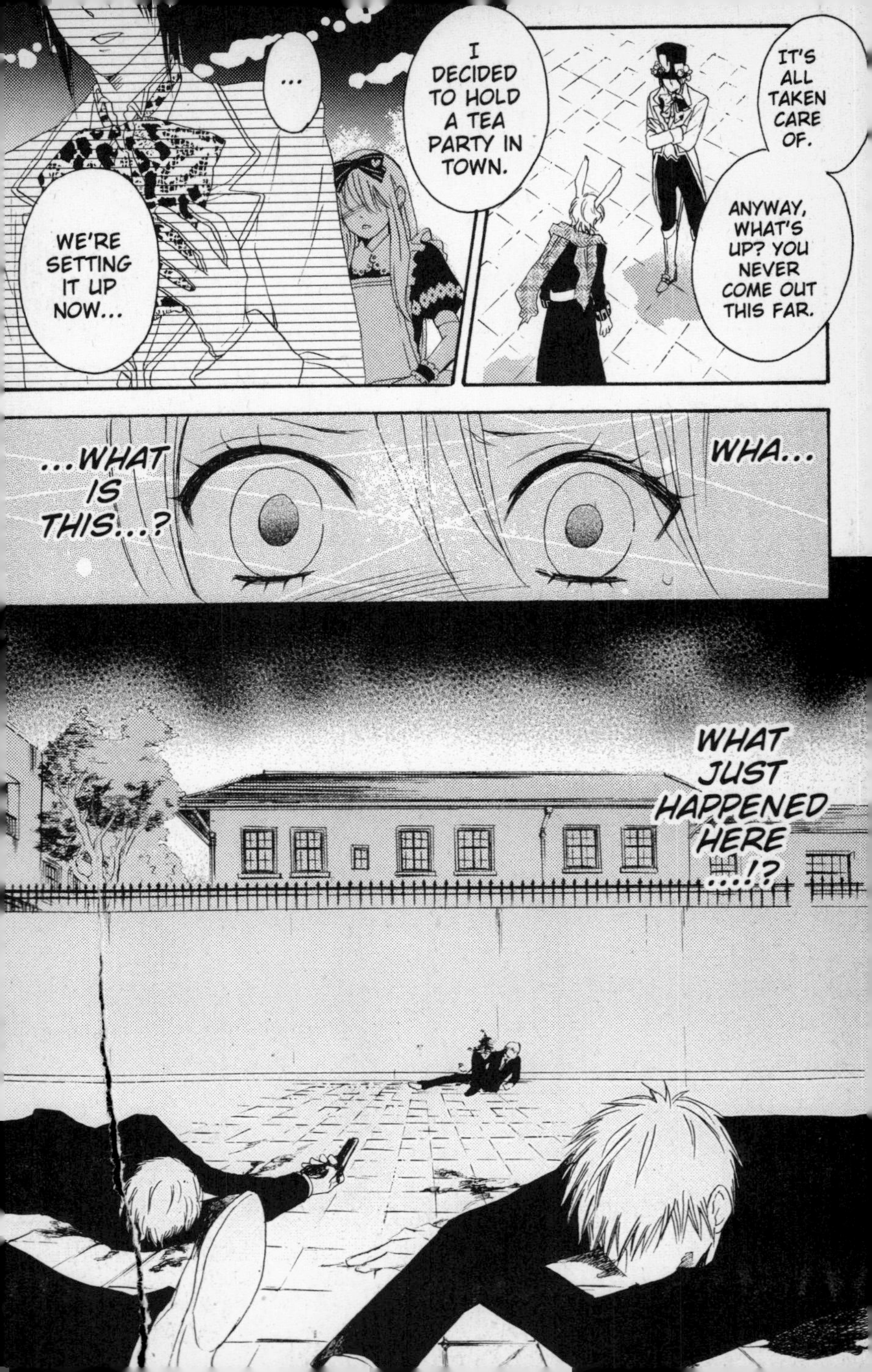
IT'S ALL TAKEN CARE OF.
ANYWAY, WHAT'S UP? YOU NEVER COME OUT THIS FAR.
I DECIDED TO HOLD A TEA PARTY IN TOWN.
...
WE'RE SETTING IT UP NOW...
WHA...
...WHAT IS THIS...?
WHAT JUST HAPPENED HERE...!?

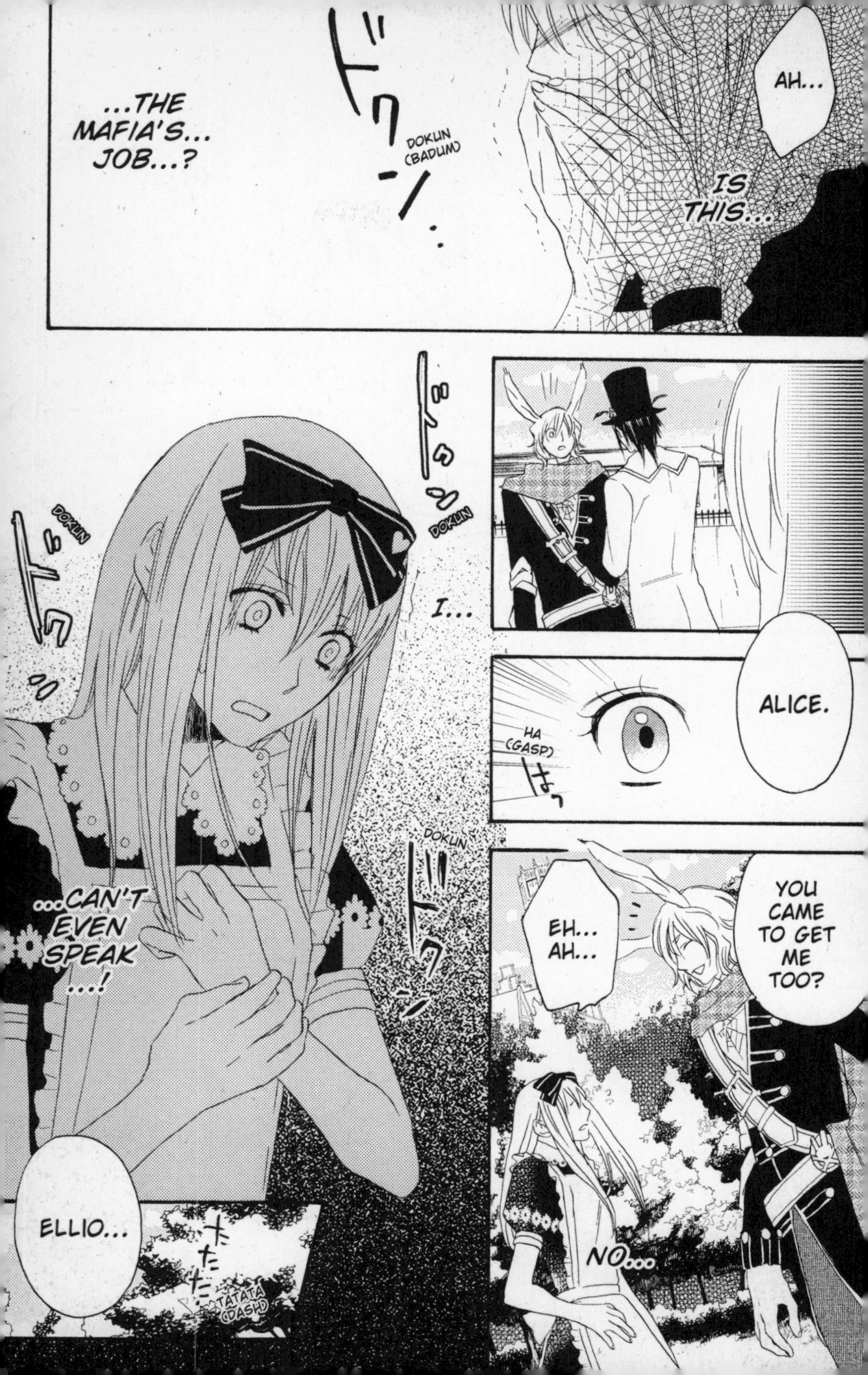
AH...
IS THIS...
DOKUN (BADUM)
...THE MAFIA'S... JOB...?
ALICE.
HA (GASP)
YOU CAME TO GET ME TOO?
EH... AH...
NO...
DOKUN
I...
DOKUN
...CAN'T EVEN SPEAK ...!
DOKUN
ELLIO...
TATATA (DASH)

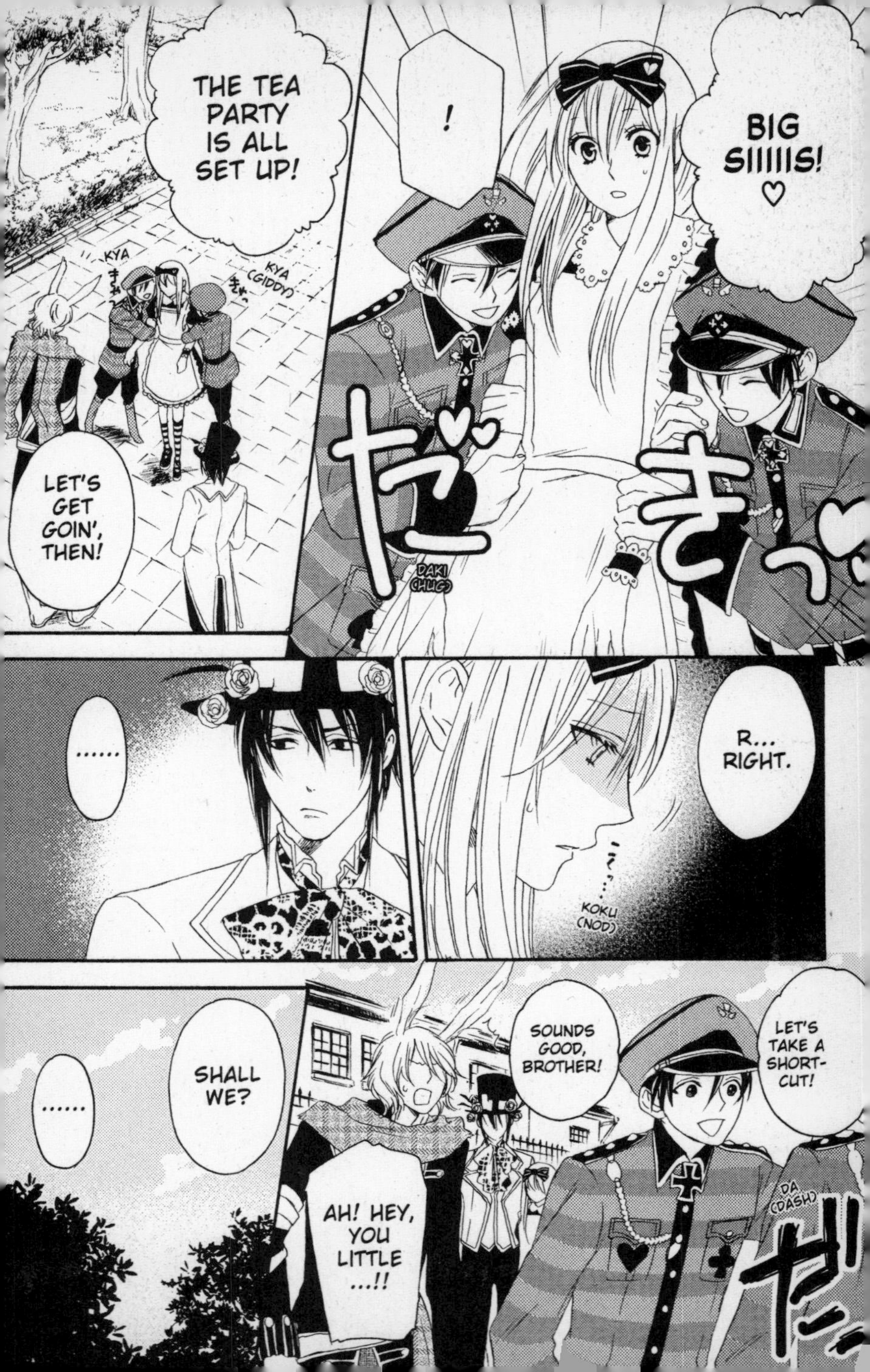
BIG SIIIIIS! ♡
!
DAKI (HUG)
THE TEA PARTY IS ALL SET UP!
KYA (GIDDY)
KYA
LET'S GET GOIN', THEN!
R... RIGHT.
KOKU (NOD)
......
LET'S TAKE A SHORT-CUT!
DA (DASH)
SOUNDS GOOD, BROTHER!
SHALL WE?
AH! HEY, YOU LITTLE ...!!
......

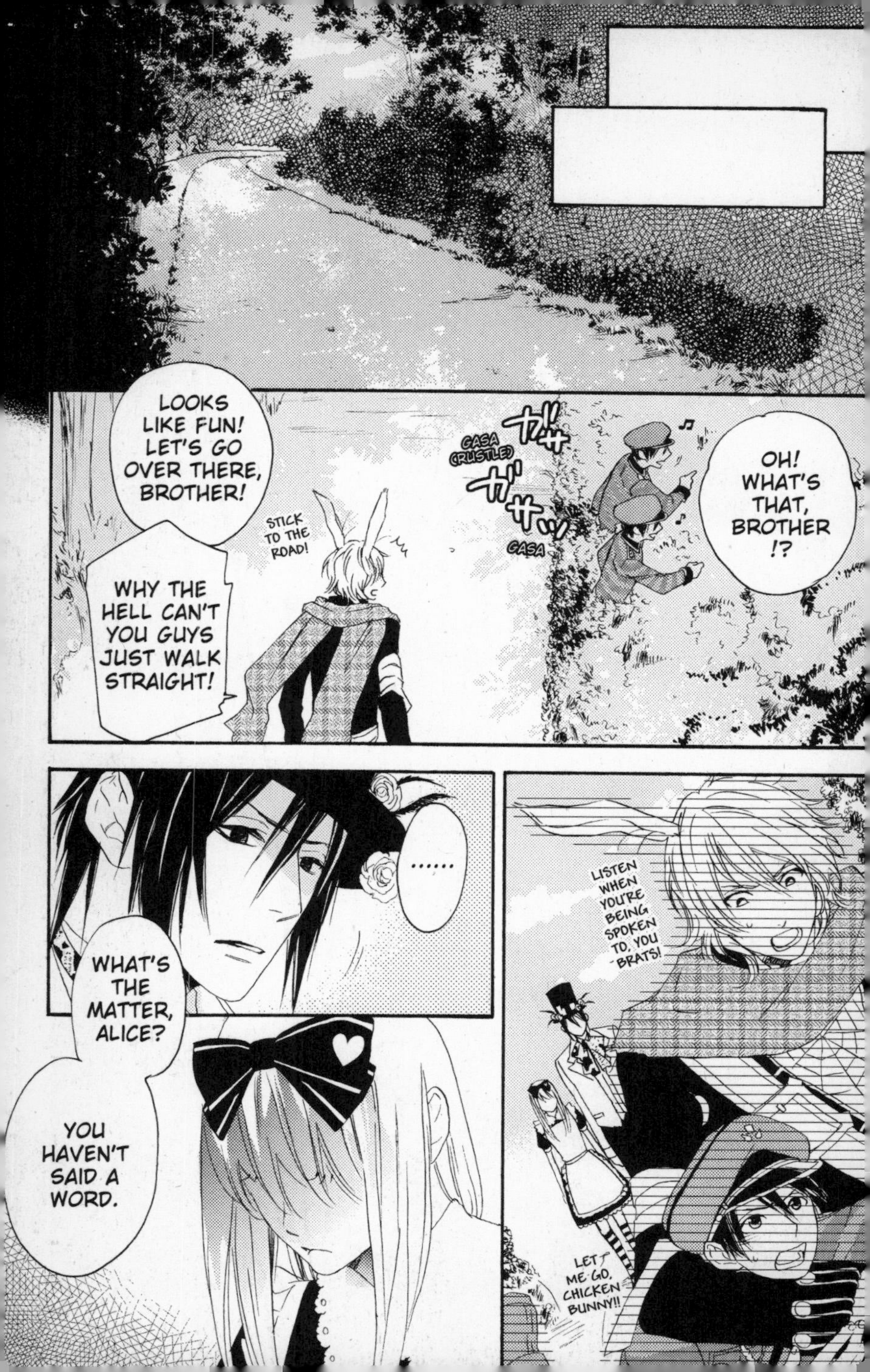
OH! WHAT'S THAT, BROTHER!?
GASA (RUSTLED)
GASA
STICK TO THE ROAD!
LOOKS LIKE FUN! LET'S GO OVER THERE, BROTHER!
WHY THE HELL CAN'T YOU GUYS JUST WALK STRAIGHT!
LISTEN WHEN YOU'RE BEING SPOKEN TO, YOU BRATS!
LET ME GO, CHICKEN BUNNY!!
......
WHAT'S THE MATTER, ALICE?
YOU HAVEN'T SAID A WORD.

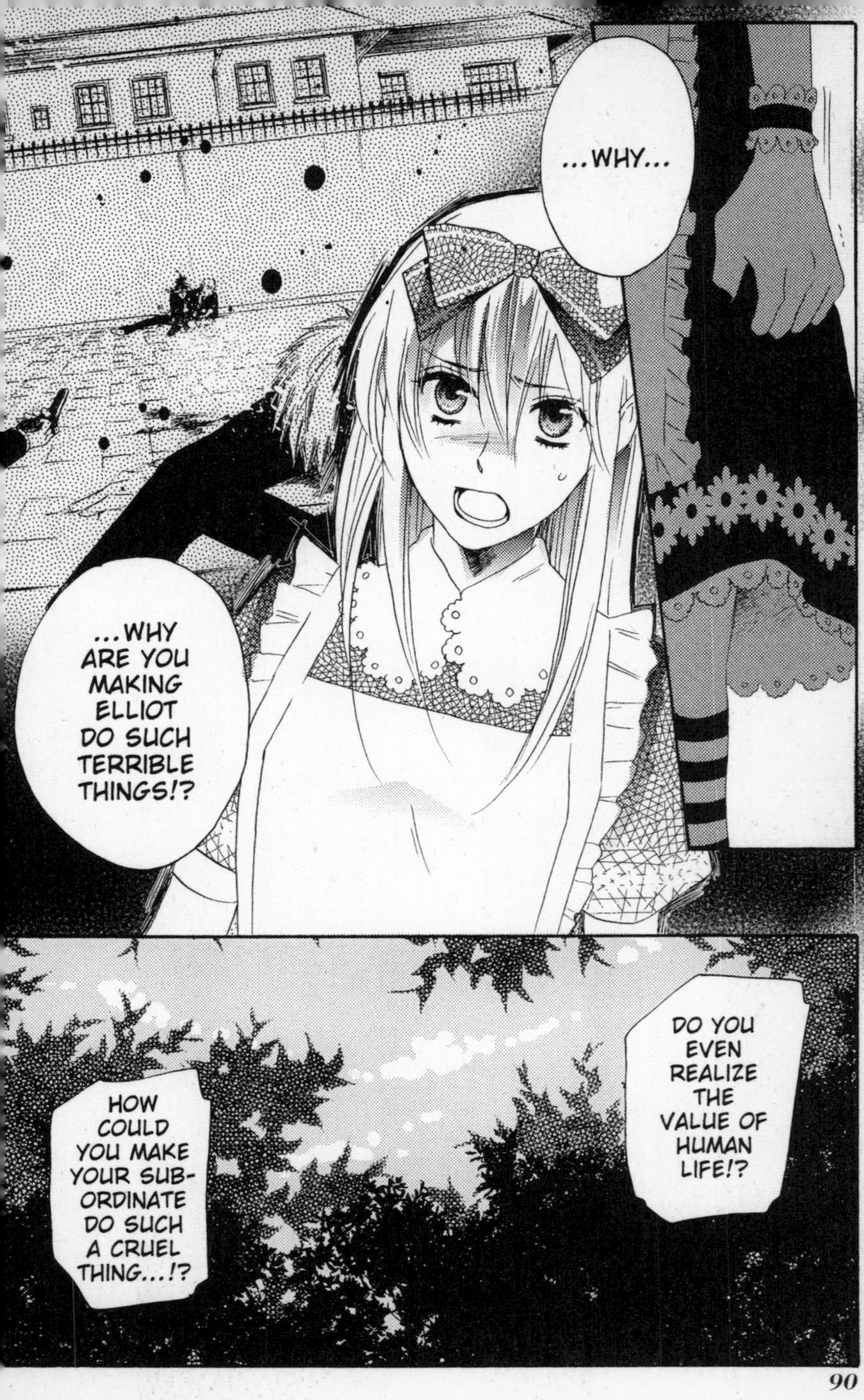
...WHY...
...WHY ARE YOU MAKING ELLIOT DO SUCH TERRIBLE THINGS!?
DO YOU EVEN REALIZE THE VALUE OF HUMAN LIFE!?
HOW COULD YOU MAKE YOUR SUB-ORDINATE DO SUCH A CRUEL THING...!?

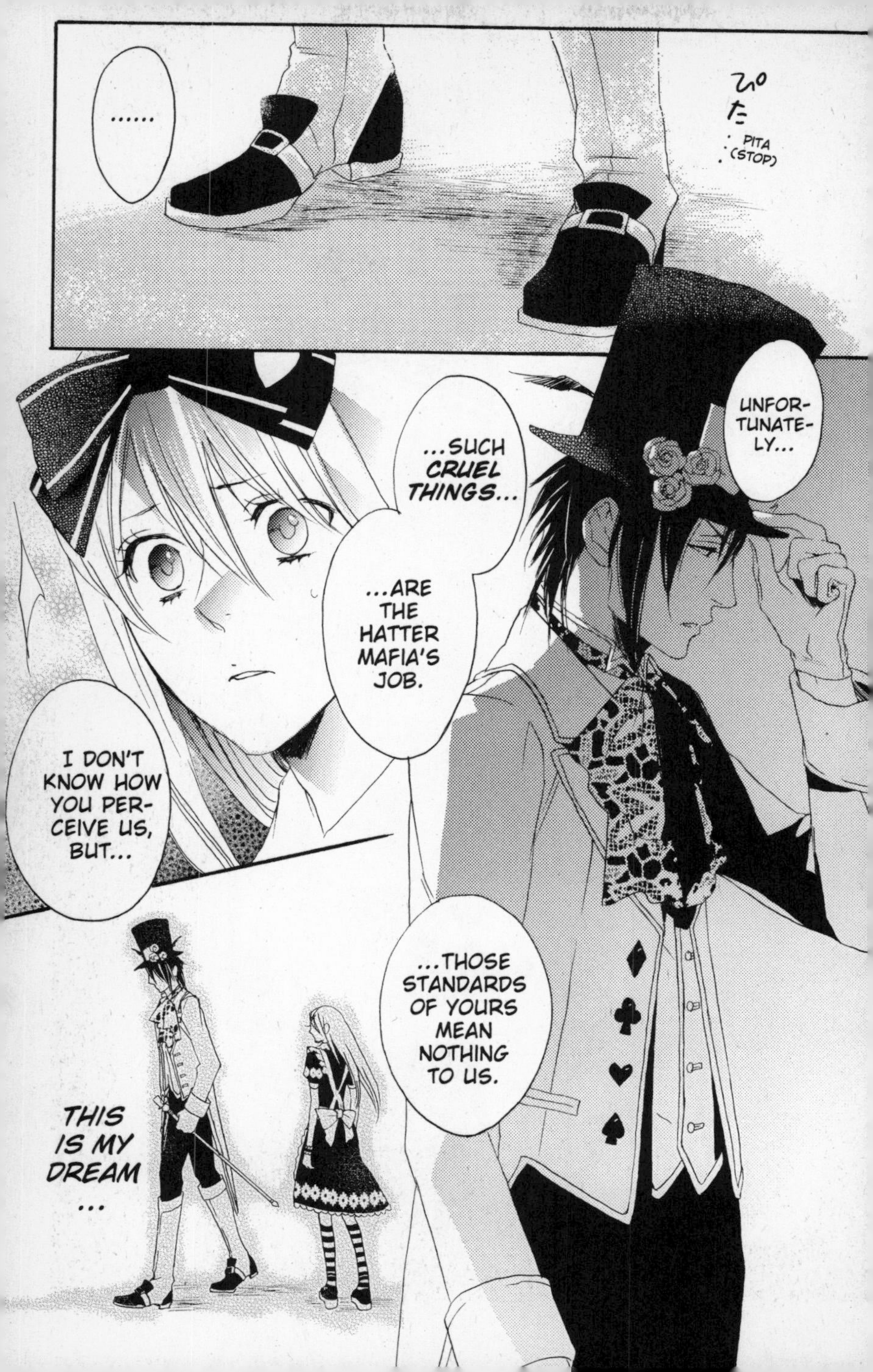
ぴた
PITA (STOP)
......
UNFOR-TUNATE-LY...
...SUCH CRUEL THINGS...
...ARE THE HATTER MAFIA'S JOB.
I DON'T KNOW HOW YOU PER-CEIVE US, BUT...
...THOSE STANDARDS OF YOURS MEAN NOTHING TO US.
THIS IS MY DREAM ...

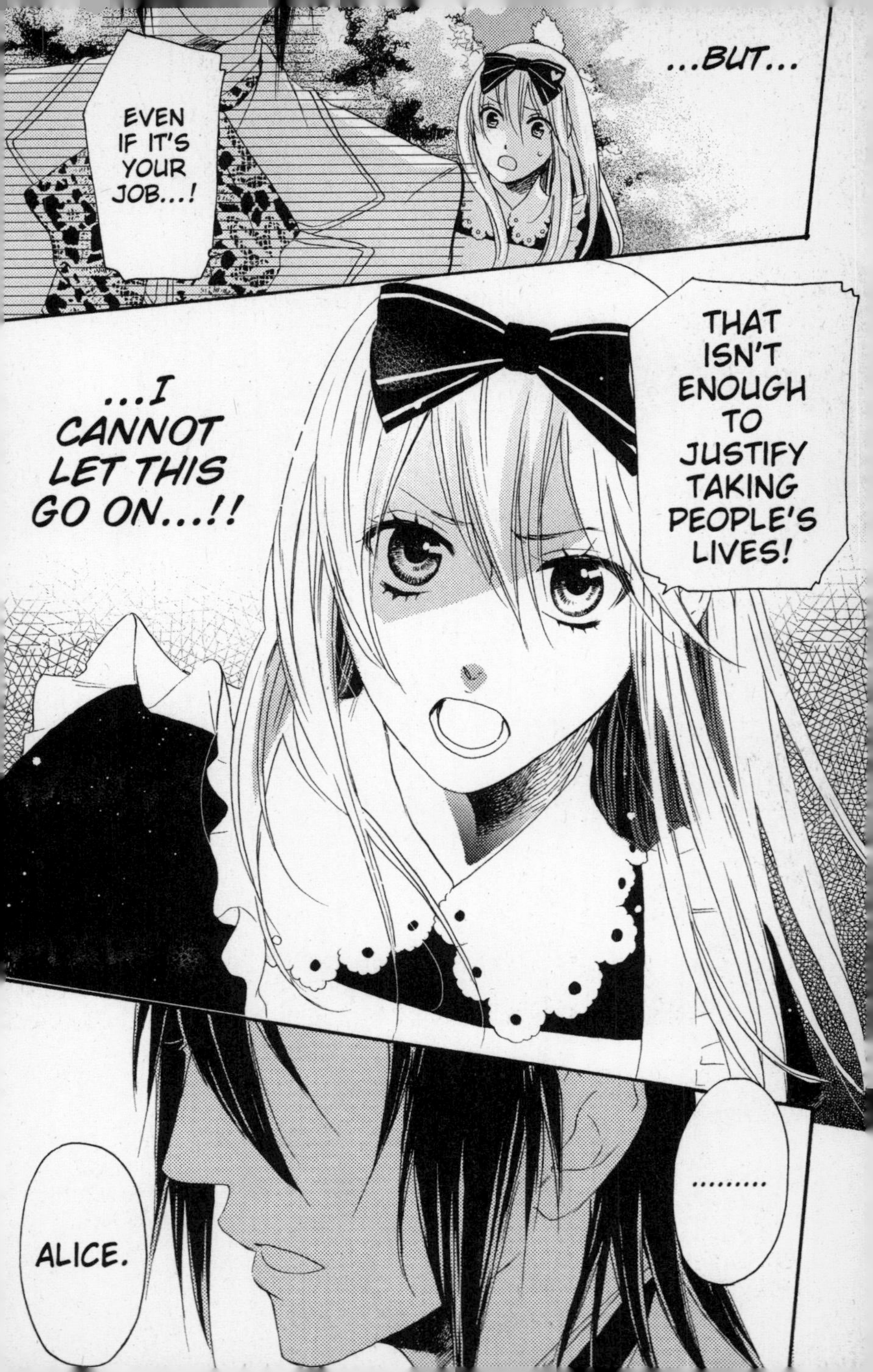
...BUT...
EVEN IF IT'S YOUR JOB...!
THAT ISN'T ENOUGH TO JUSTIFY TAKING PEOPLE'S LIVES!
...I CANNOT LET THIS GO ON...!!
....
ALICE.

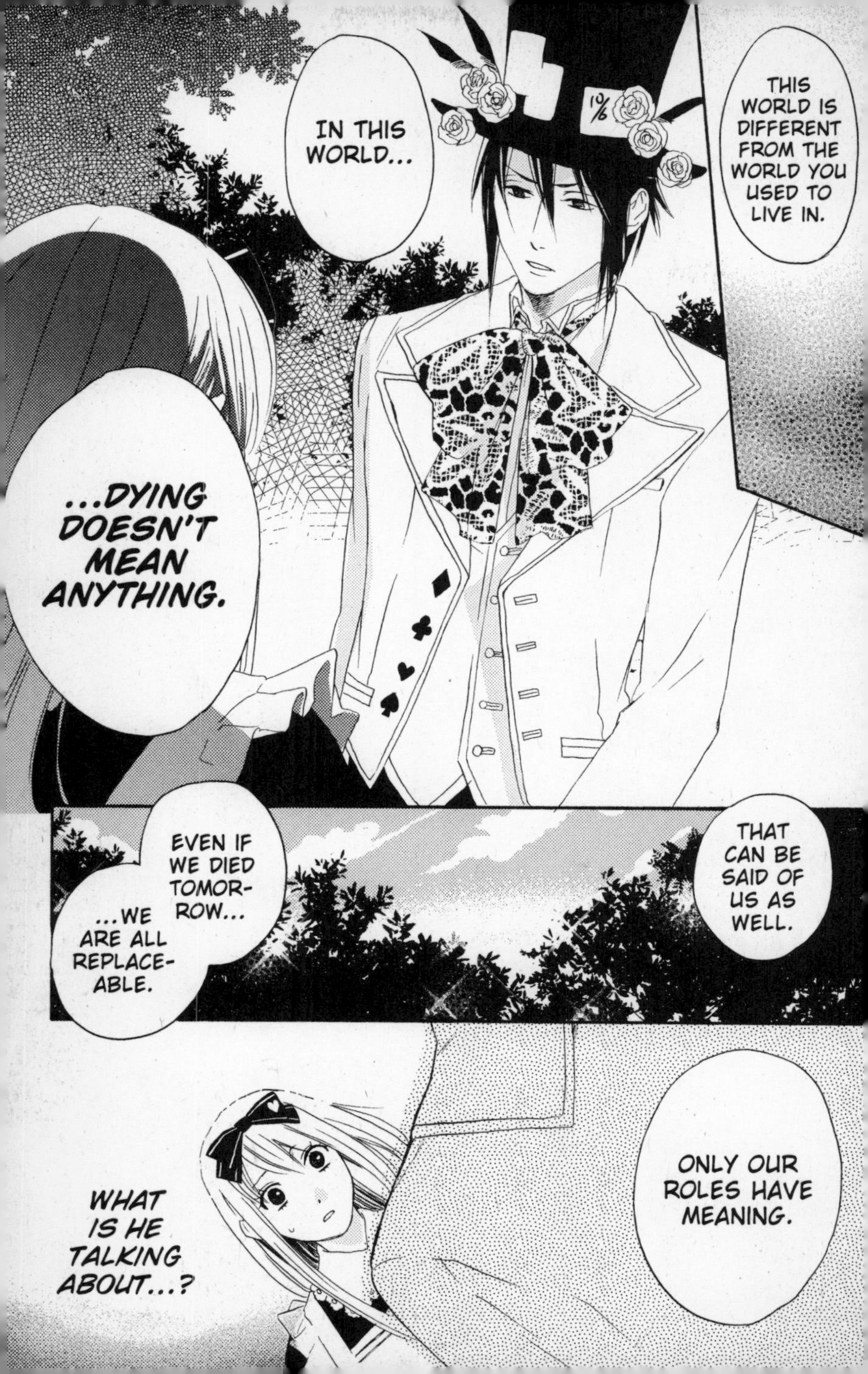
THIS WORLD IS DIFFERENT FROM THE WORLD YOU USED TO LIVE IN.
IN THIS WORLD...
...DYING DOESN'T MEAN ANYTHING.
THAT CAN BE SAID OF US AS WELL.
EVEN IF WE DIED TOMORROW...
...WE ARE ALL REPLACEABLE.
ONLY OUR ROLES HAVE MEANING.
WHAT IS HE TALKING ABOUT...?

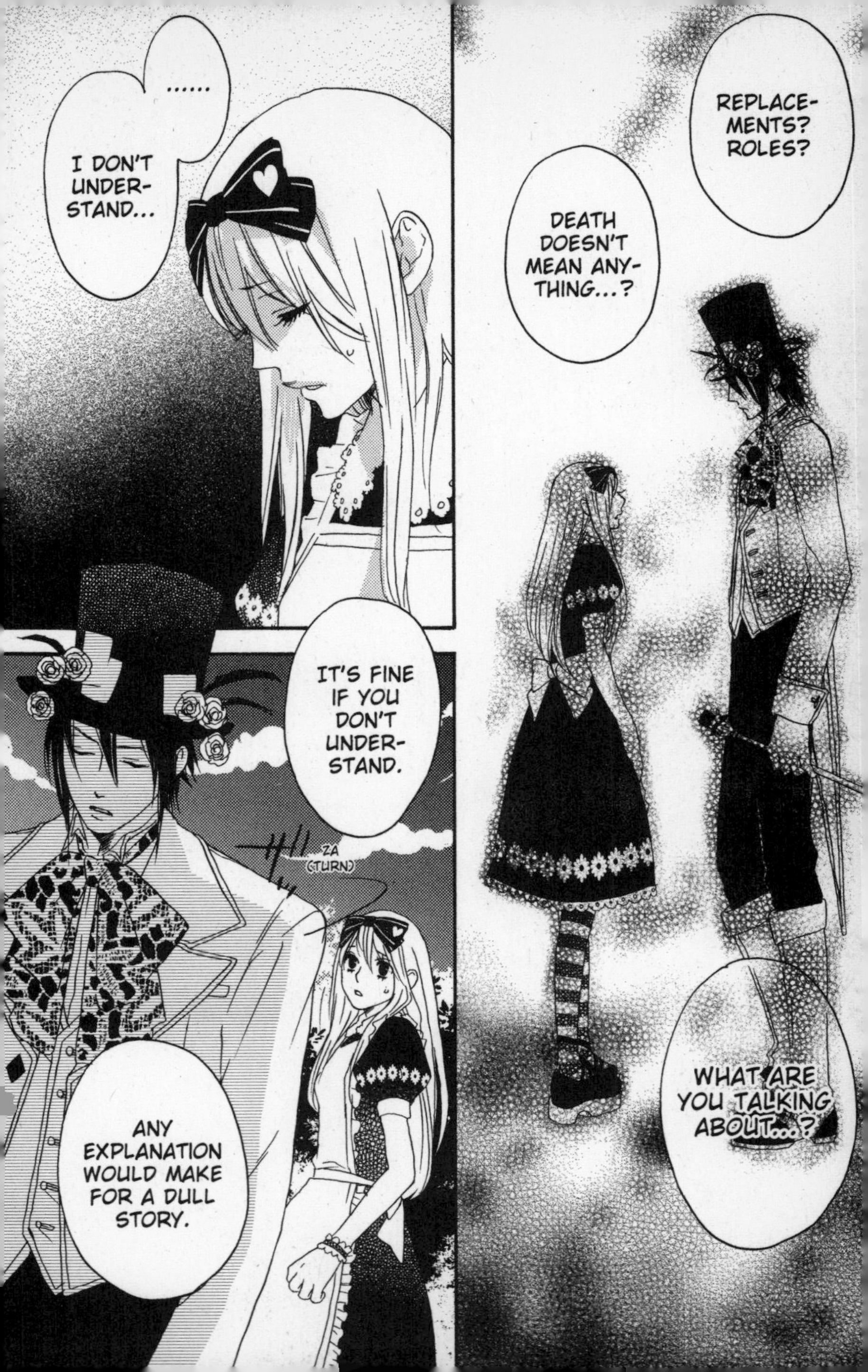
REPLACEMENTS? ROLES?
DEATH DOESN'T MEAN ANYTHING...?
WHAT ARE YOU TALKING ABOUT...?
......
I DON'T UNDERSTAND...
IT'S FINE IF YOU DON'T UNDERSTAND.
ZA (TURN)
ANY EXPLANATION WOULD MAKE FOR A DULL STORY.

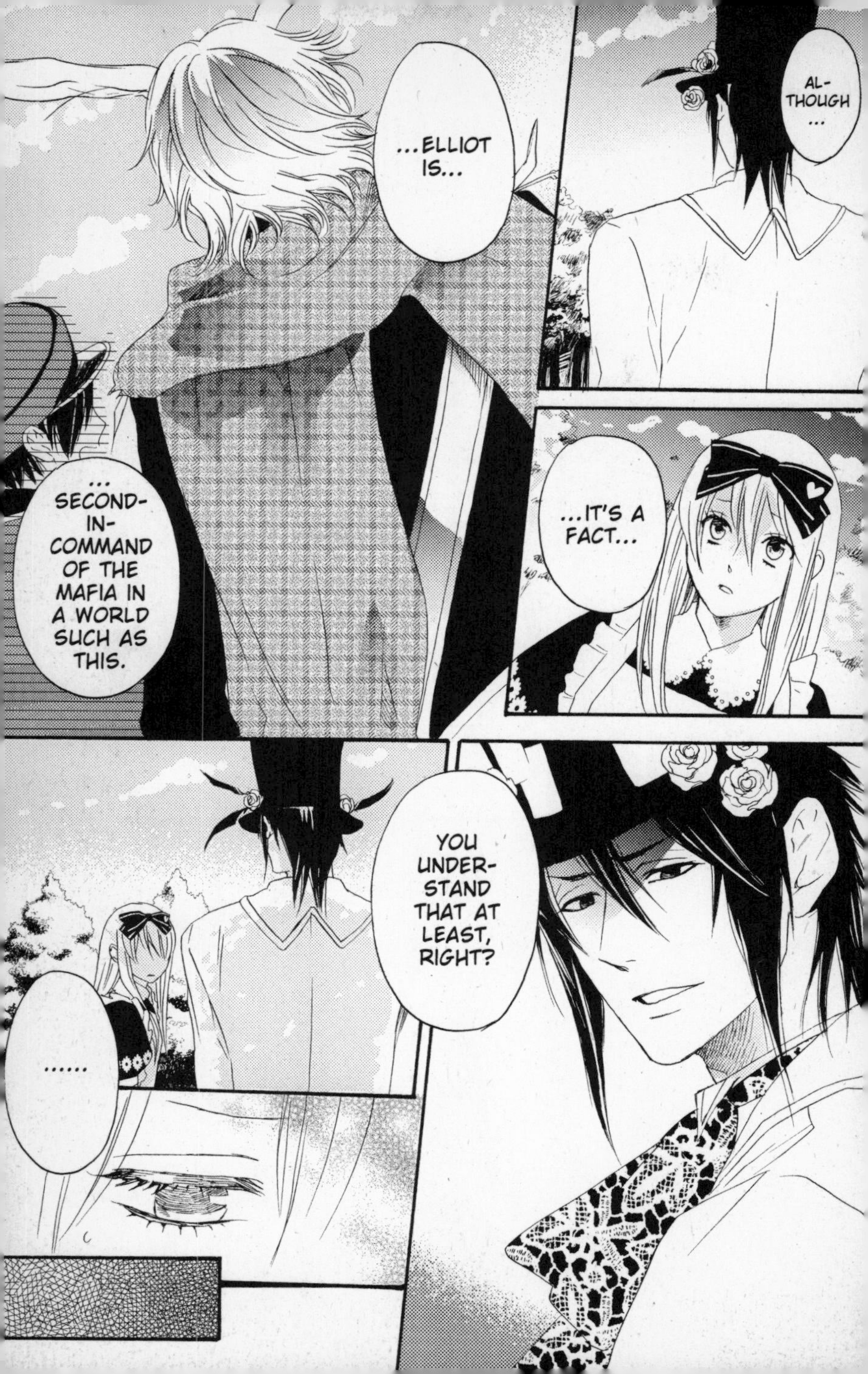
AL-THOUGH...
...IT'S A FACT...
...ELLIOT IS...
...SECOND-IN-COMMAND OF THE MAFIA IN A WORLD SUCH AS THIS.
YOU UNDER-STAND THAT AT LEAST, RIGHT?
......

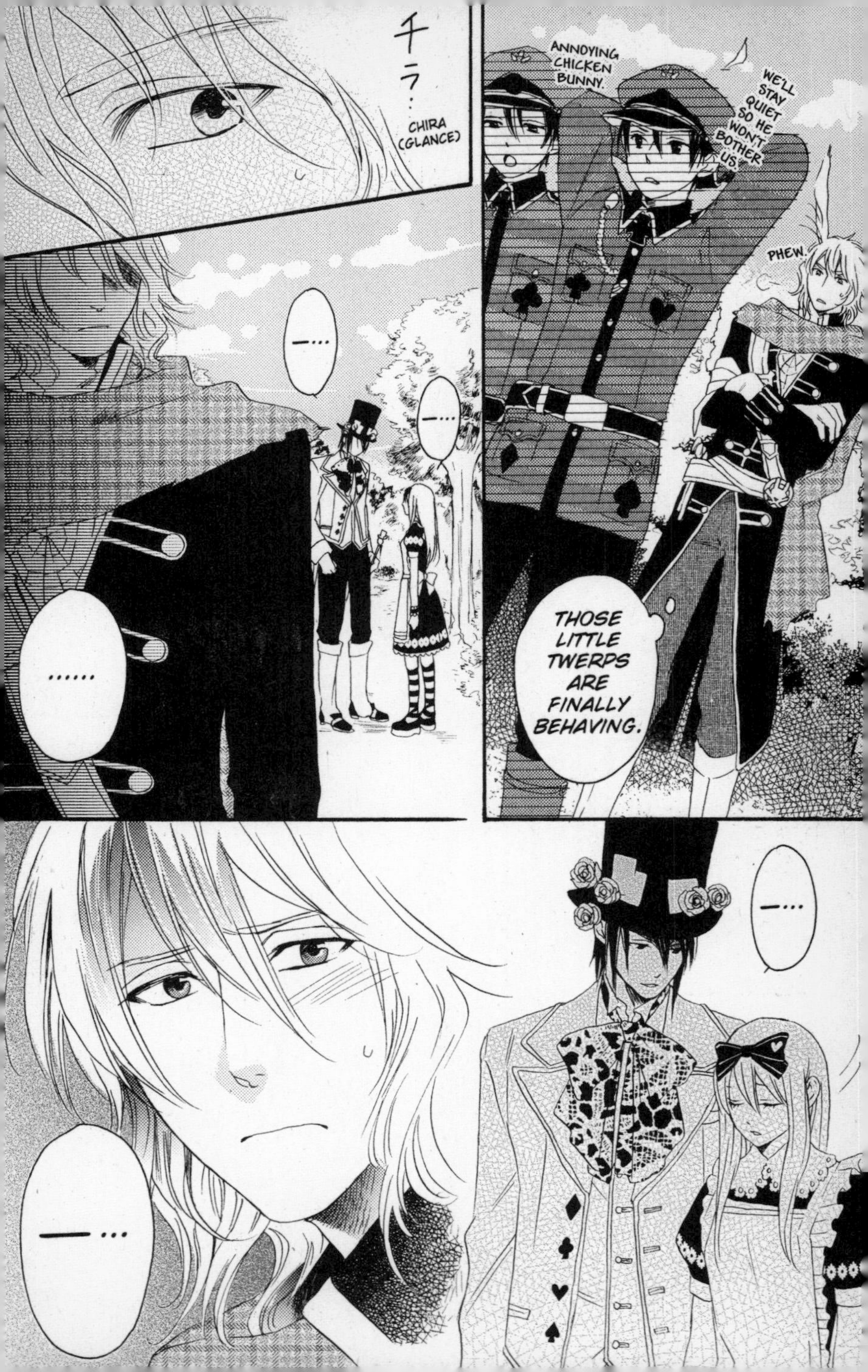
WE'LL STAY QUIET SO HE WON'T BOTHER US.
ANNOYING CHICKEN BUNNY.
PHEW.
THOSE LITTLE TWERPS ARE FINALLY BEHAVING.
チラ…
CHIRA (GLANCE)
—…
—…
……
—…
—…

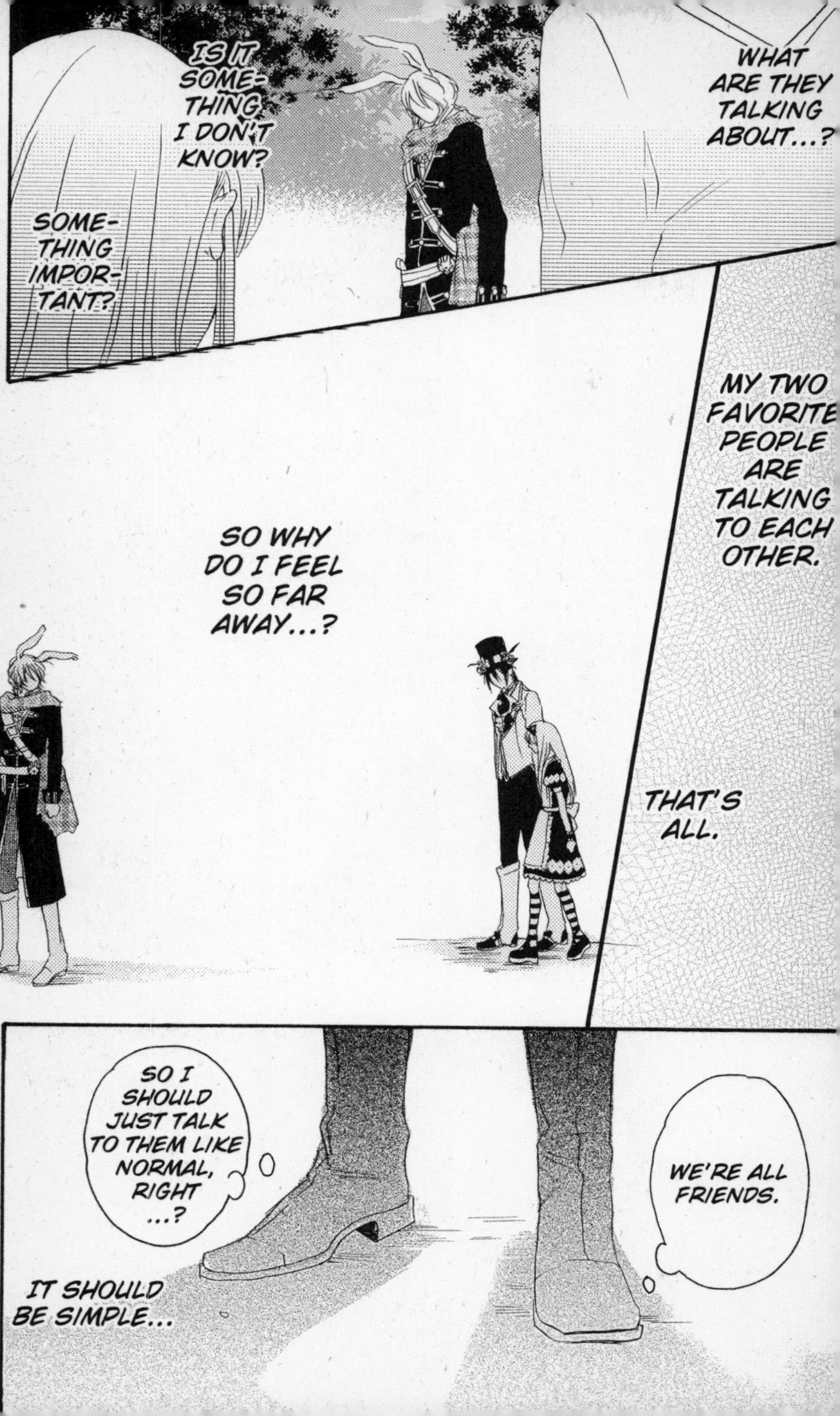
WHAT ARE THEY TALKING ABOUT...?
IS IT SOMETHING I DON'T KNOW?
SOMETHING IMPORTANT?
MY TWO FAVORITE PEOPLE ARE TALKING TO EACH OTHER.
THAT'S ALL.
SO WHY DO I FEEL SO FAR AWAY...?
WE'RE ALL FRIENDS.
SO I SHOULD JUST TALK TO THEM LIKE NORMAL, RIGHT...?
IT SHOULD BE SIMPLE...

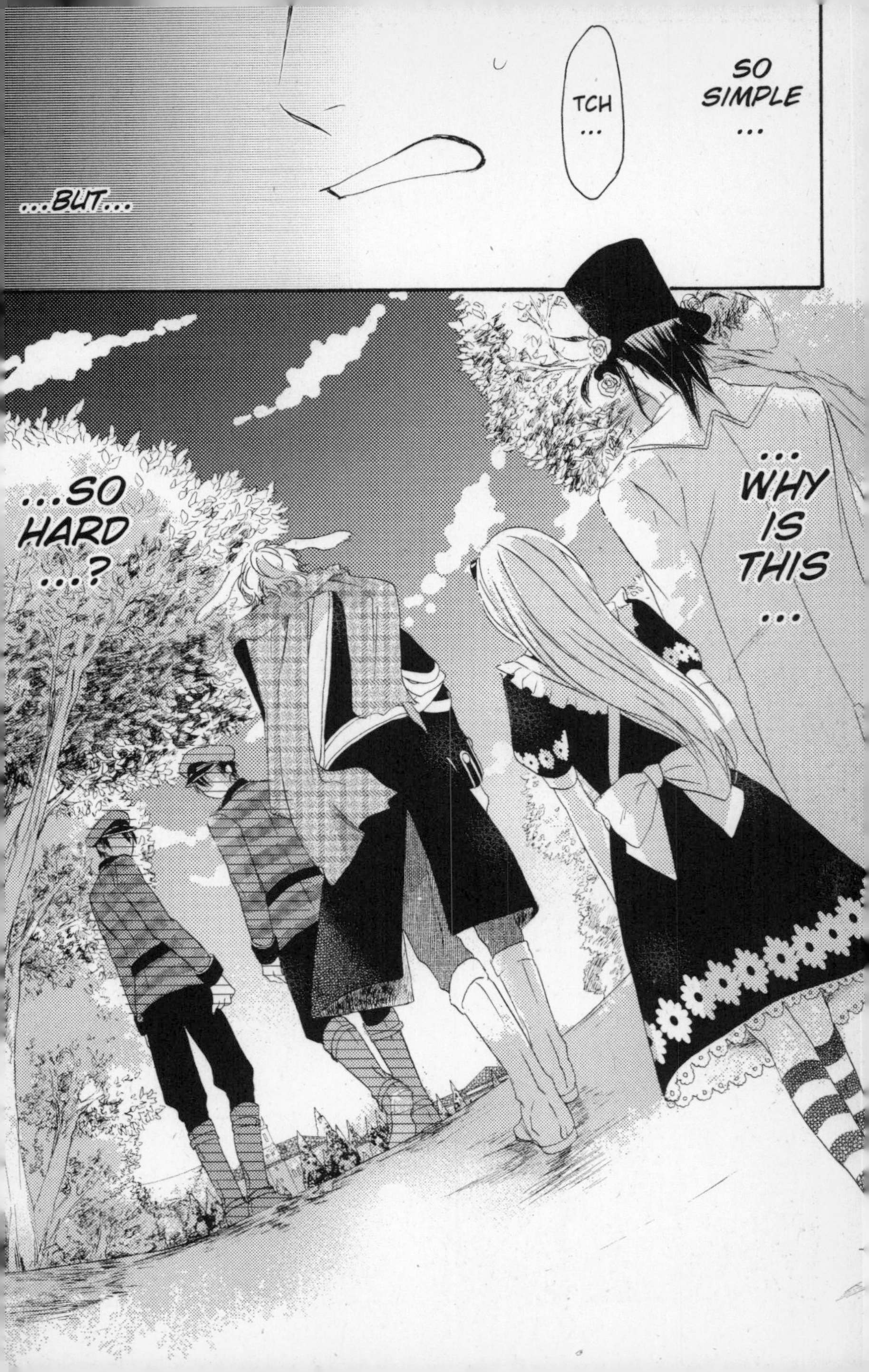
SO SIMPLE ...
TCH ...
...BUT...
... WHY IS THIS ...
...SO HARD ...?

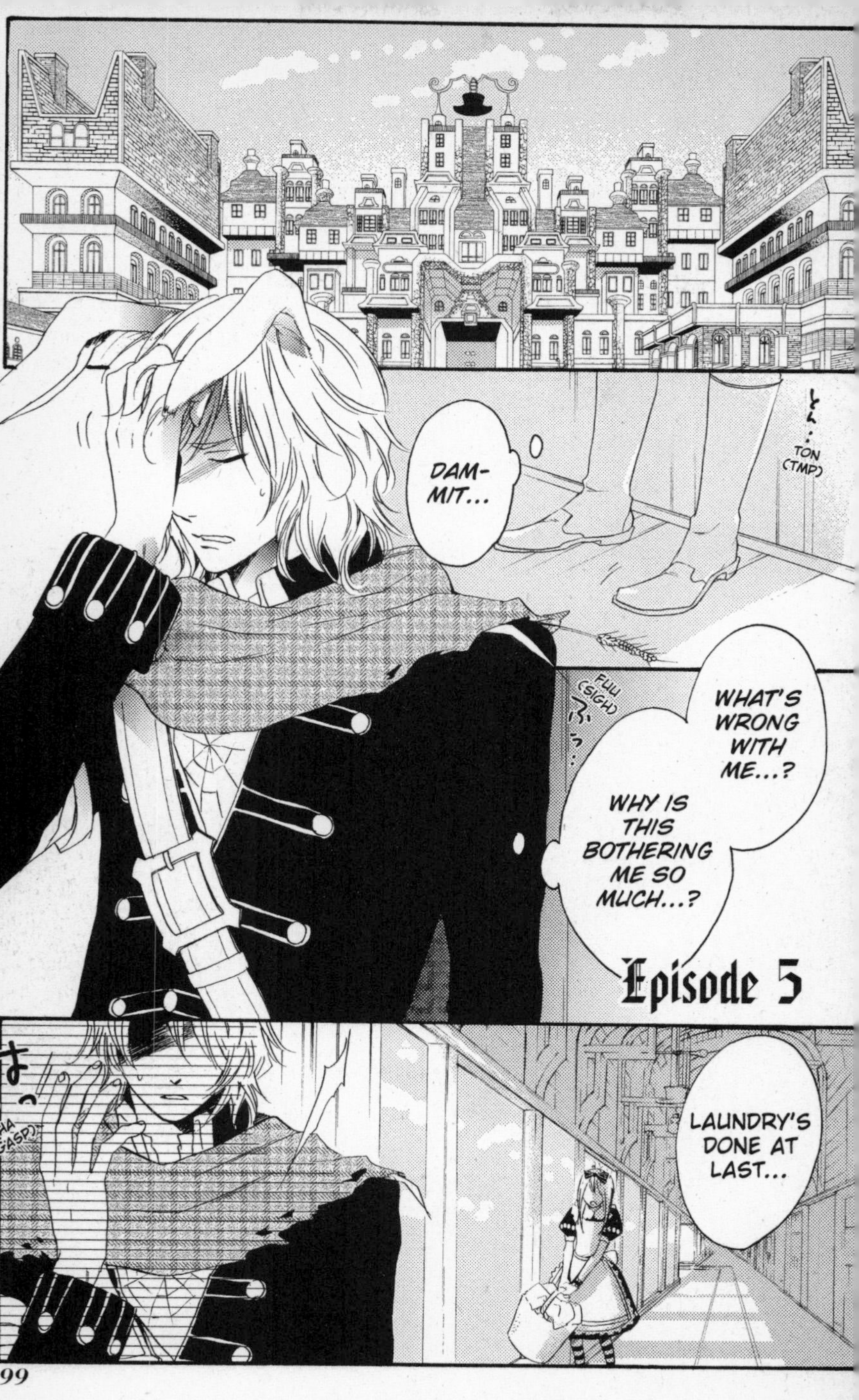

とん・・
TON (TMP)
DAM-MIT...
ふーっ・・・
FUU (SIGH)
WHAT'S WRONG WITH ME...?
WHY IS THIS BOTHERING ME SO MUCH...?
Episode 5
LAUNDRY'S DONE AT LAST...
はっ
HA (GASP)

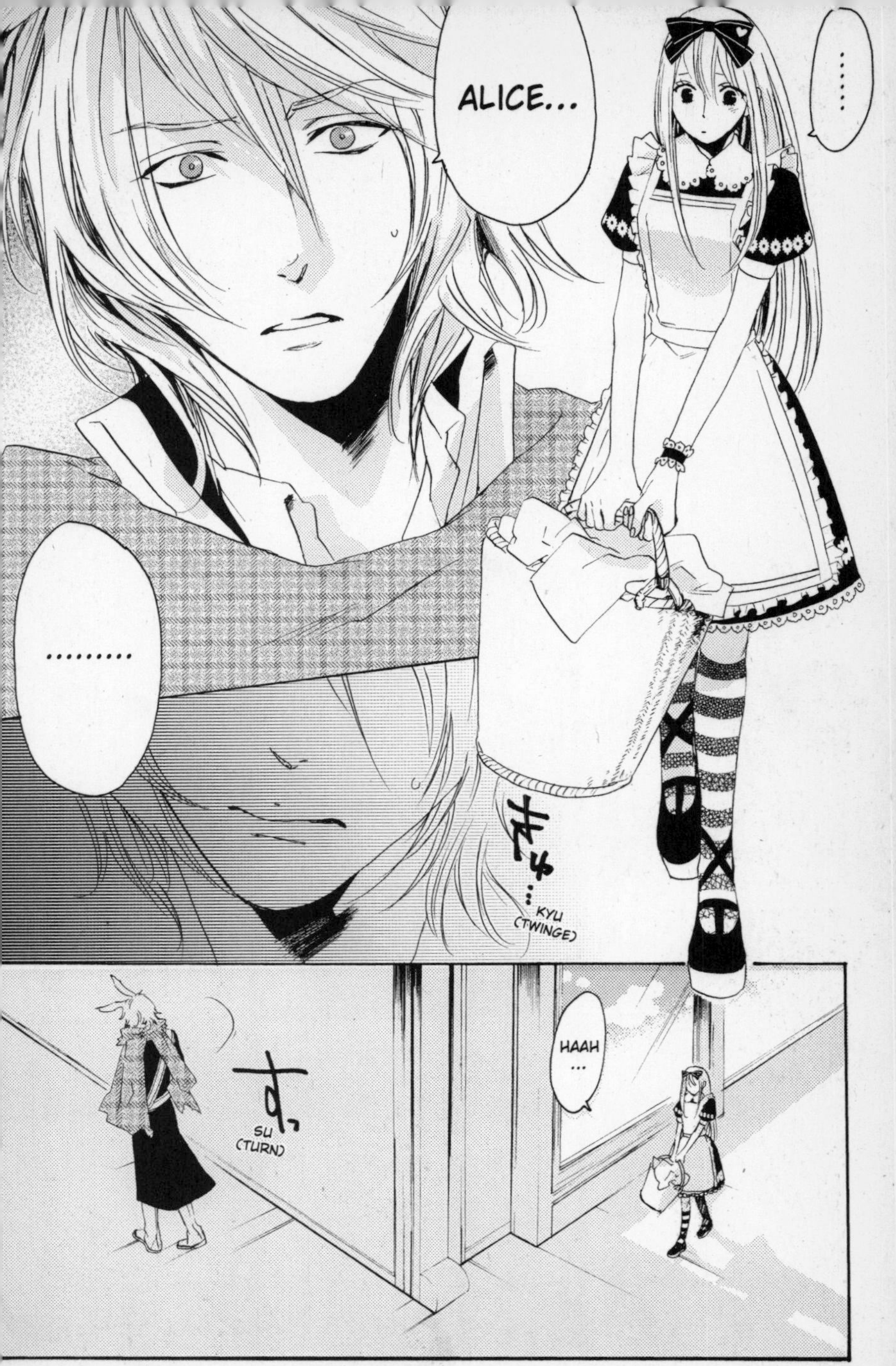
......
ALICE...
....
KYU
(TWINGE)
HAAH ...
SU
(TURN)

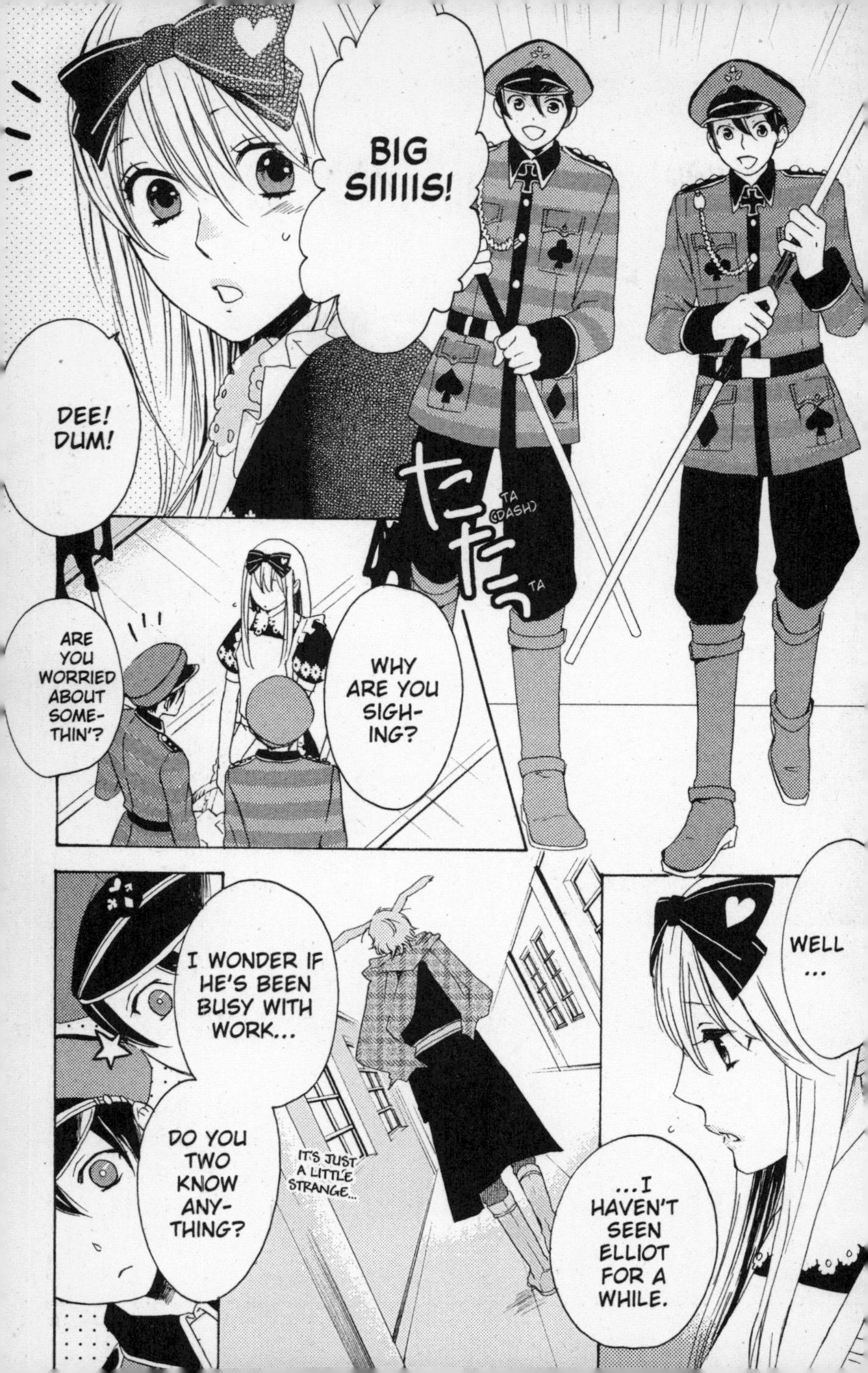
BIG SIIIIIS!
DEE! DUM!
TA (DASH)
TA
WHY ARE YOU SIGHING?
ARE YOU WORRIED ABOUT SOMETHIN'?
WELL...
...I HAVEN'T SEEN ELLIOT FOR A WHILE.
I WONDER IF HE'S BEEN BUSY WITH WORK...
IT'S JUST A LITTLE STRANGE...
DO YOU TWO KNOW ANYTHING?

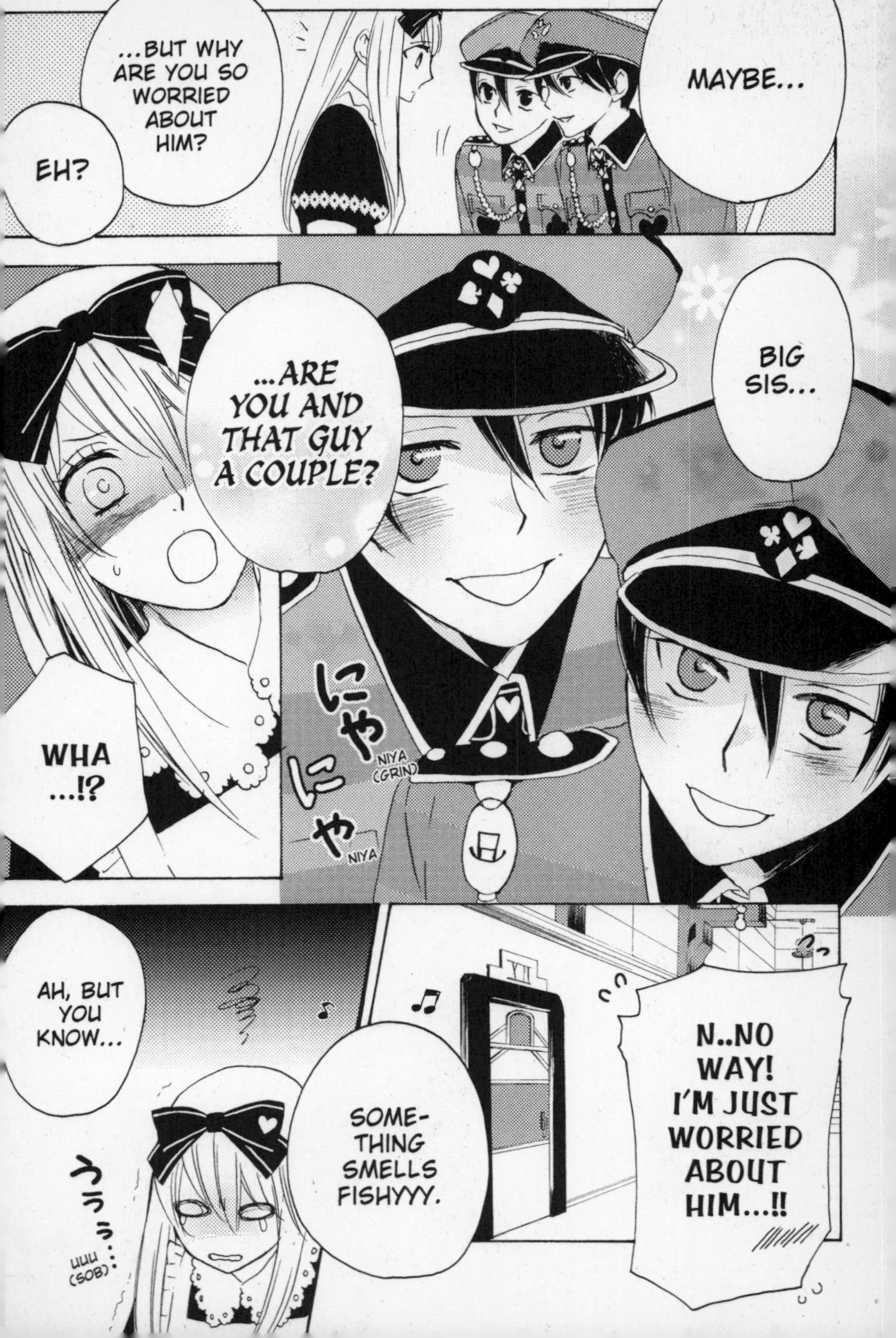
MAYBE...
...BUT WHY ARE YOU SO WORRIED ABOUT HIM?
EH?
BIG SIS...
...ARE YOU AND THAT GUY A COUPLE?
にや
NIYA (GRIN)
にや
NIYA
WHA ...!?
N..NO WAY! I'M JUST WORRIED ABOUT HIM...!!
AH, BUT YOU KNOW...
SOME-THING SMELLS FISHYYY.
うぅ...
UUU (SOB)

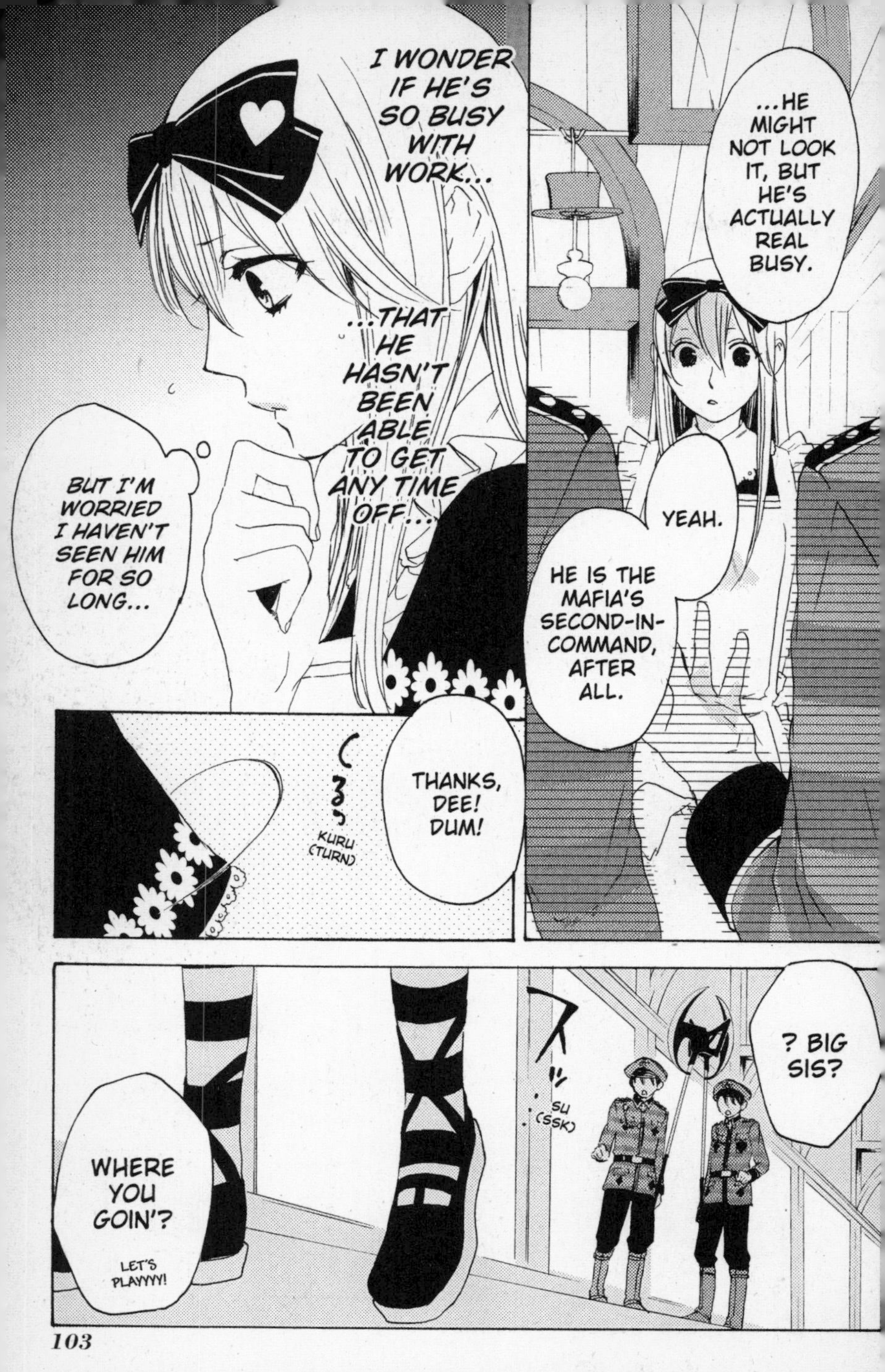
...HE MIGHT NOT LOOK IT, BUT HE'S ACTUALLY REAL BUSY.
YEAH.
HE IS THE MAFIA'S SECOND-IN-COMMAND, AFTER ALL.
I WONDER IF HE'S SO BUSY WITH WORK...
...THAT HE HASN'T BEEN ABLE TO GET ANY TIME OFF...
BUT I'M WORRIED I HAVEN'T SEEN HIM FOR SO LONG...
THANKS, DEE! DUM!
KURU (TURN)
? BIG SIS?
SU (SSK)
WHERE YOU GOIN'?
LET'S PLAYYYY!

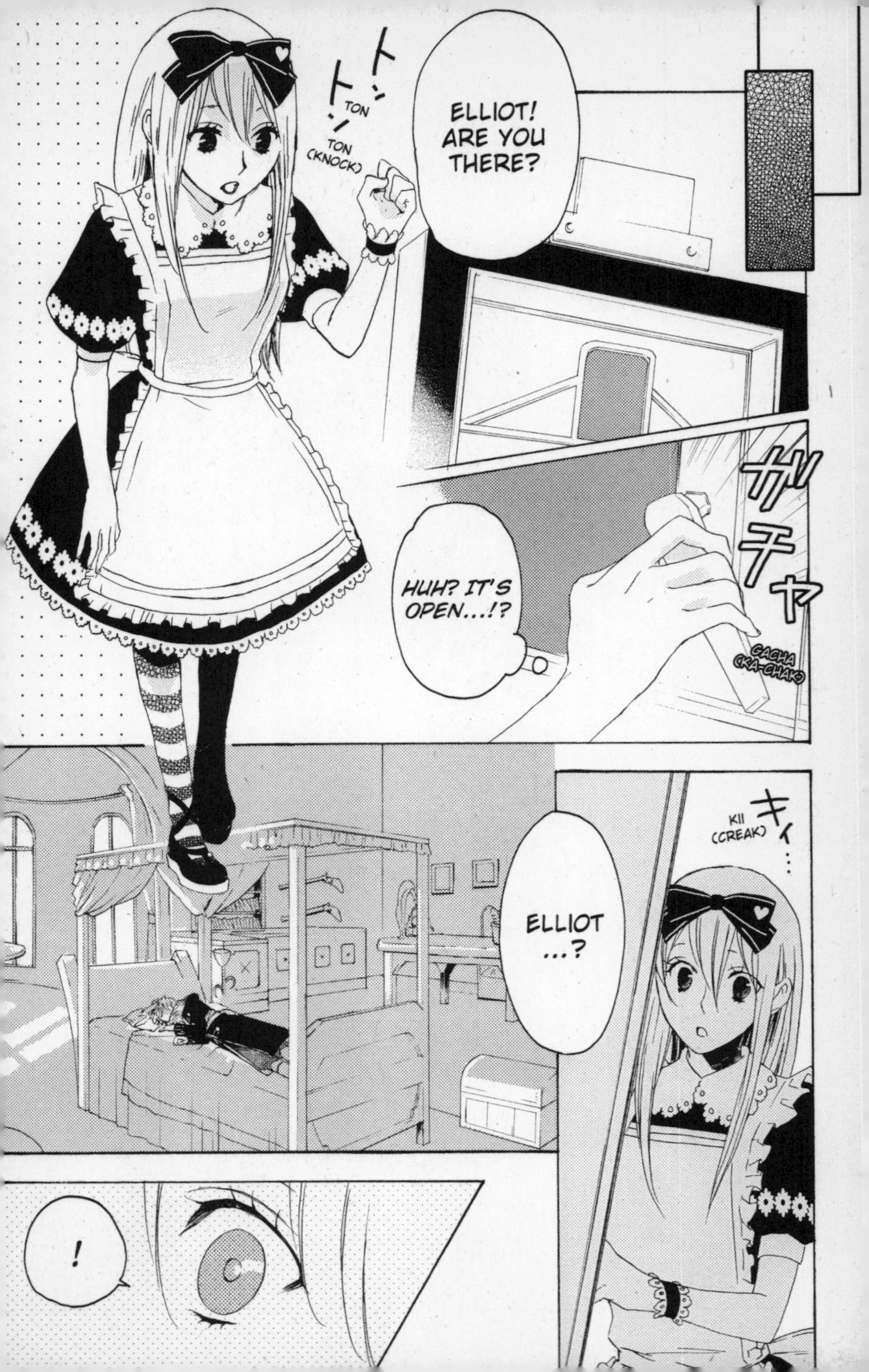
ELLIOT! ARE YOU THERE?
ガチャ
GACHA (KA-CHAK)
HUH? IT'S OPEN...!?
トントン
TON
TON (KNOCK)
キイ…
KII (CREAK)
ELLIOT ...?
!

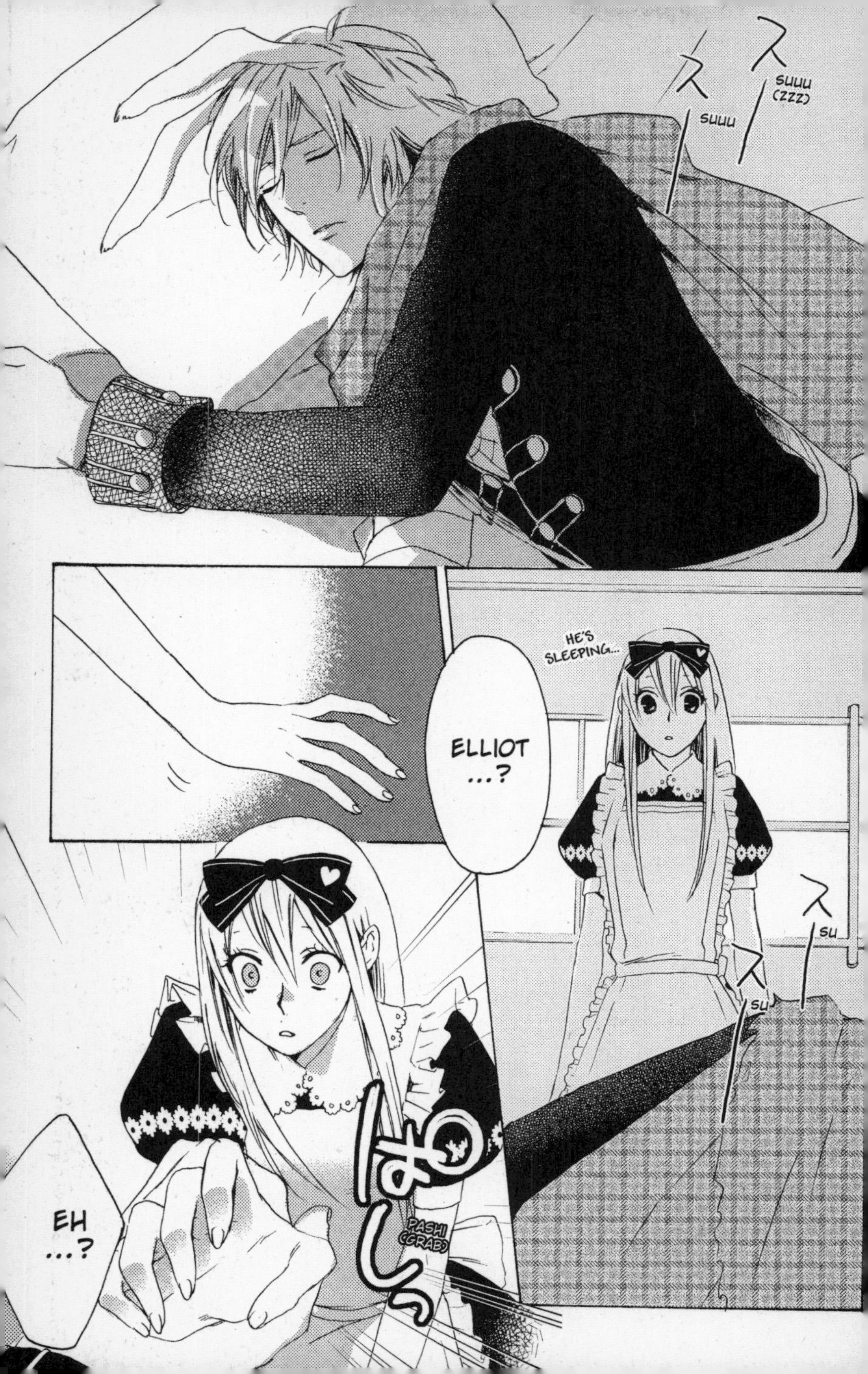
スー
SUUU (ZZZ)
スー
SUUU
HE'S SLEEPING...
スー
SU
スー
SU
ELLIOT ...?
ぱしっ
PASHI (GRAB)
EH ...?

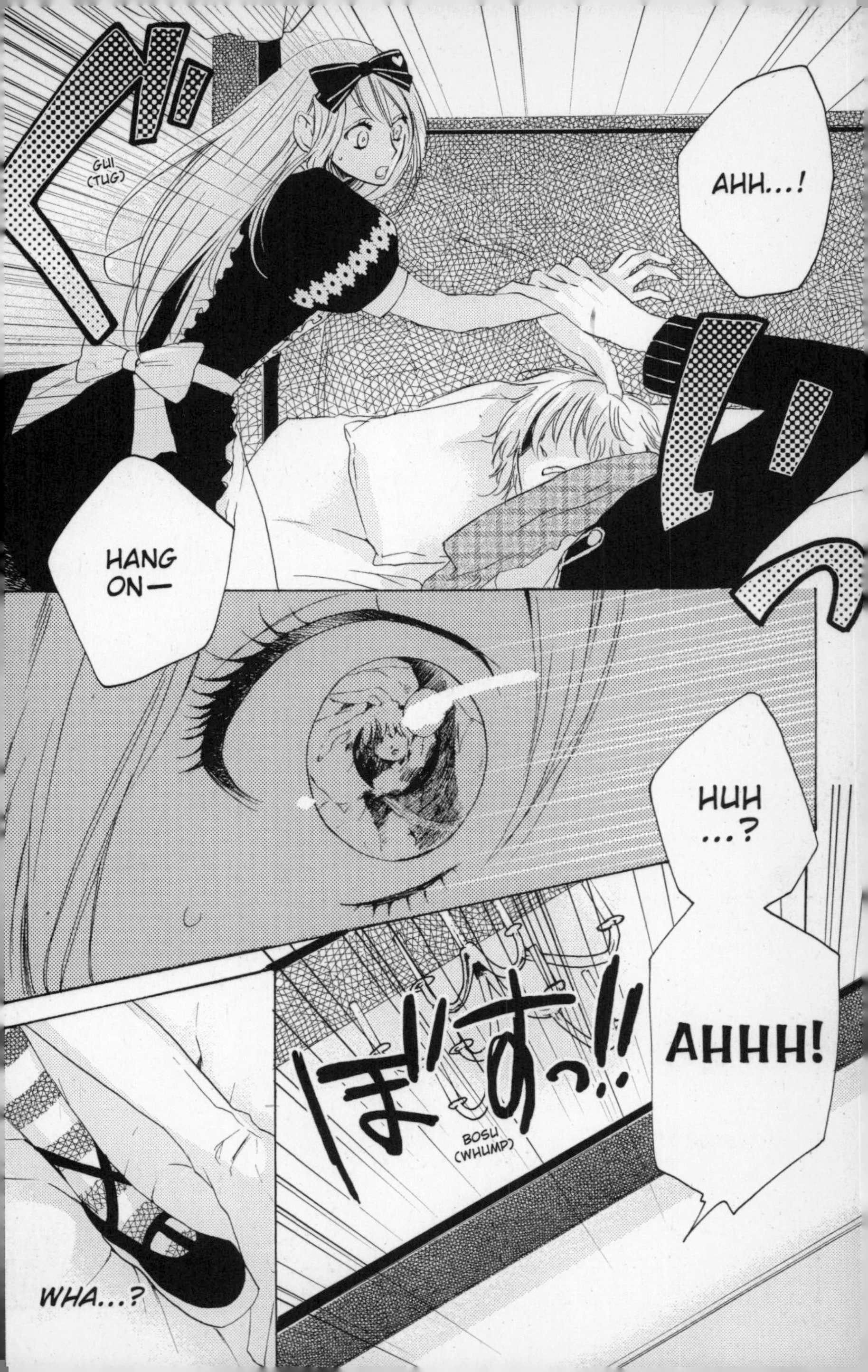
AHH...!
GUI
(TUG)
HANG ON—
HUH
...?
AHHH!
ぼすっ!!
BOSU
(WHUMP)
WHA...?

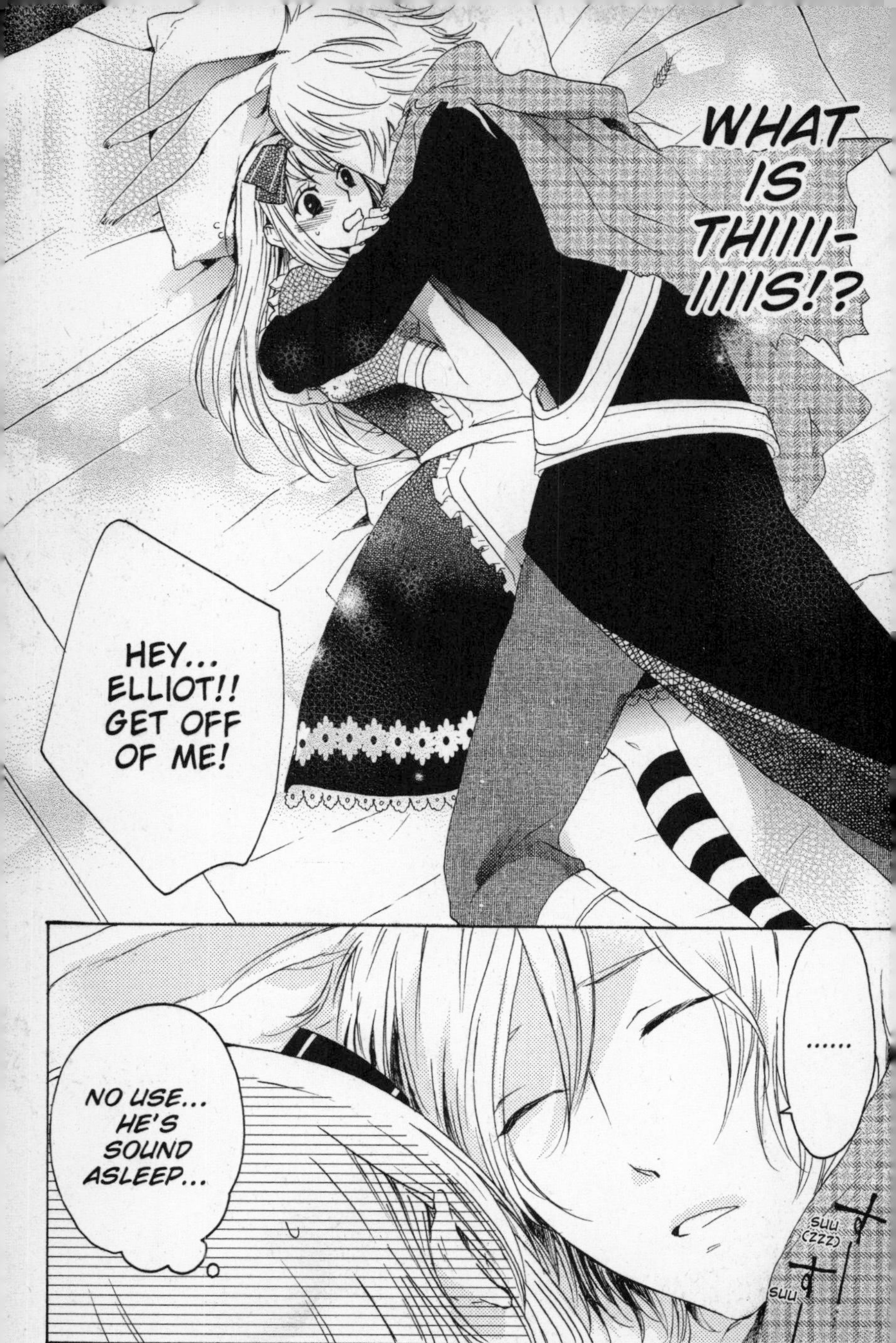
WHAT IS THIIII-IIIIS!?
HEY... ELLIOT!! GET OFF OF ME!
......
SUU (ZZZ)
SUU
NO USE... HE'S SOUND ASLEEP...

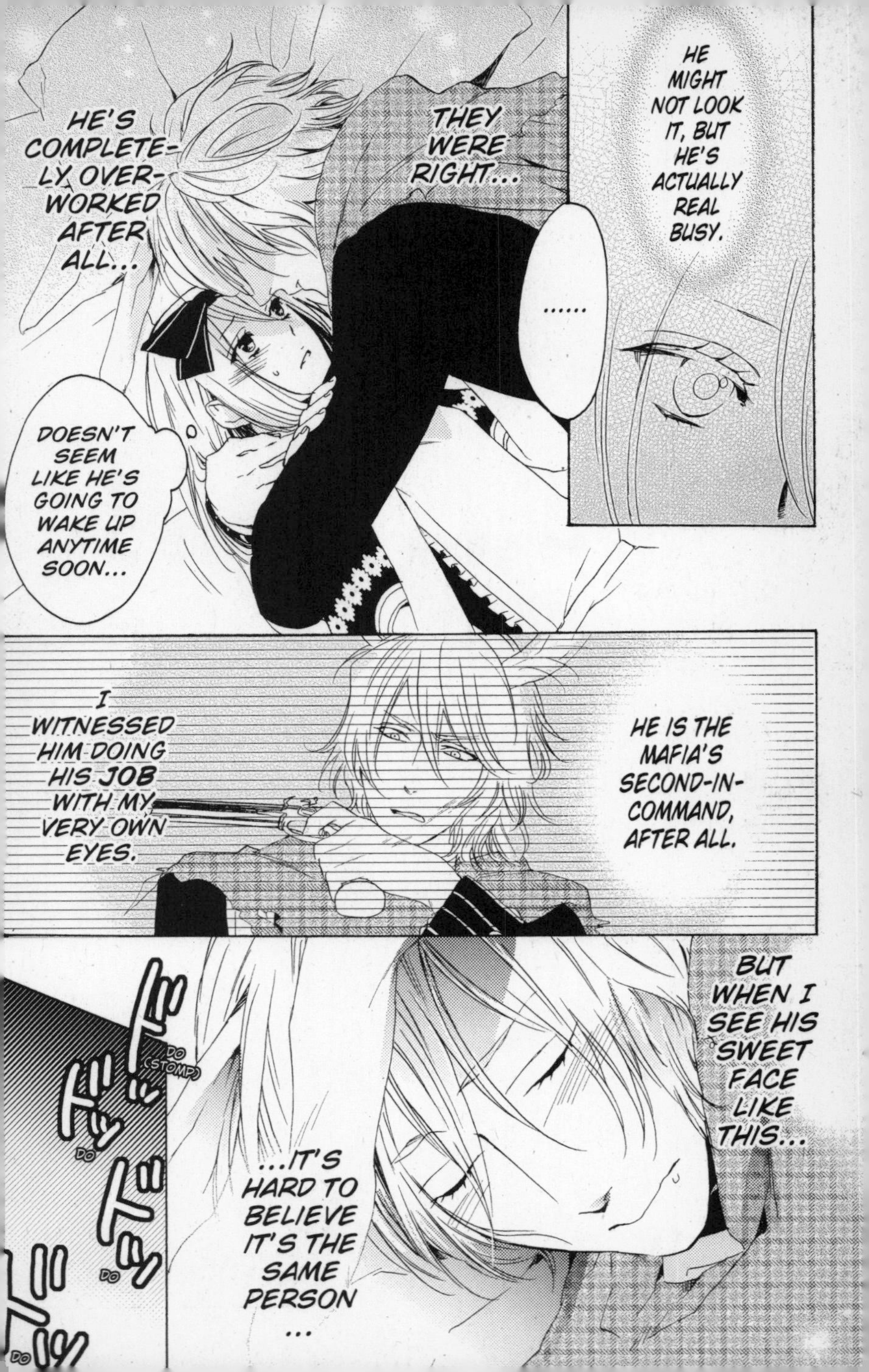
HE MIGHT NOT LOOK IT, BUT HE'S ACTUALLY REAL BUSY.
......
THEY WERE RIGHT...
HE'S COMPLETELY OVERWORKED AFTER ALL...
DOESN'T SEEM LIKE HE'S GOING TO WAKE UP ANYTIME SOON...
HE IS THE MAFIA'S SECOND-IN-COMMAND, AFTER ALL.
I WITNESSED HIM DOING HIS JOB WITH MY VERY OWN EYES.
BUT WHEN I SEE HIS SWEET FACE LIKE THIS...
...IT'S HARD TO BELIEVE IT'S THE SAME PERSON...
DO (STOMP)
DO
DO
DO

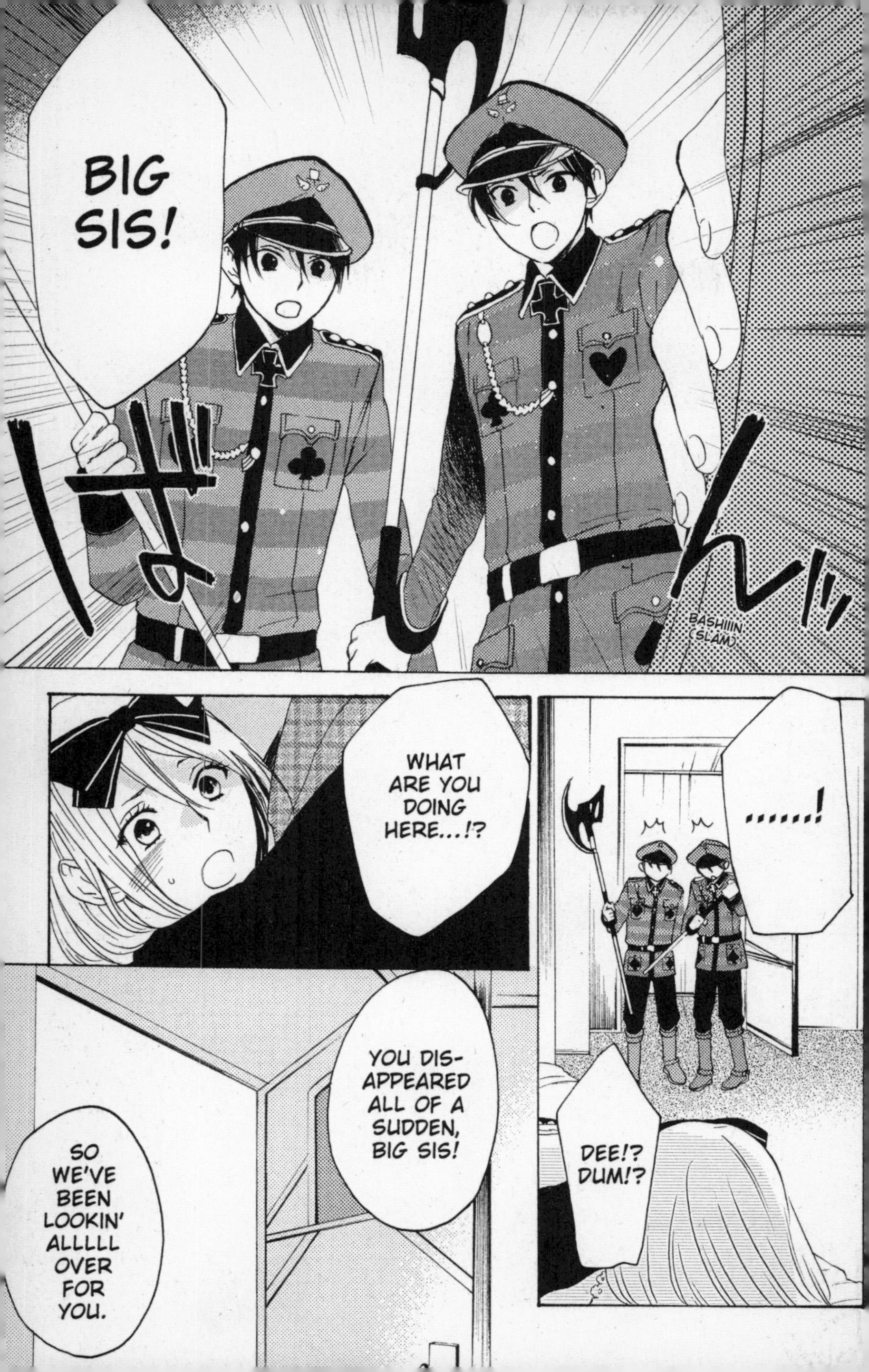
BIG SIS!
ばん
BASHIIIN (SLAM)
......!
DEE!? DUM!?
WHAT ARE YOU DOING HERE...!?
YOU DIS-APPEARED ALL OF A SUDDEN, BIG SIS!
SO WE'VE BEEN LOOKIN' ALLLLL OVER FOR YOU.

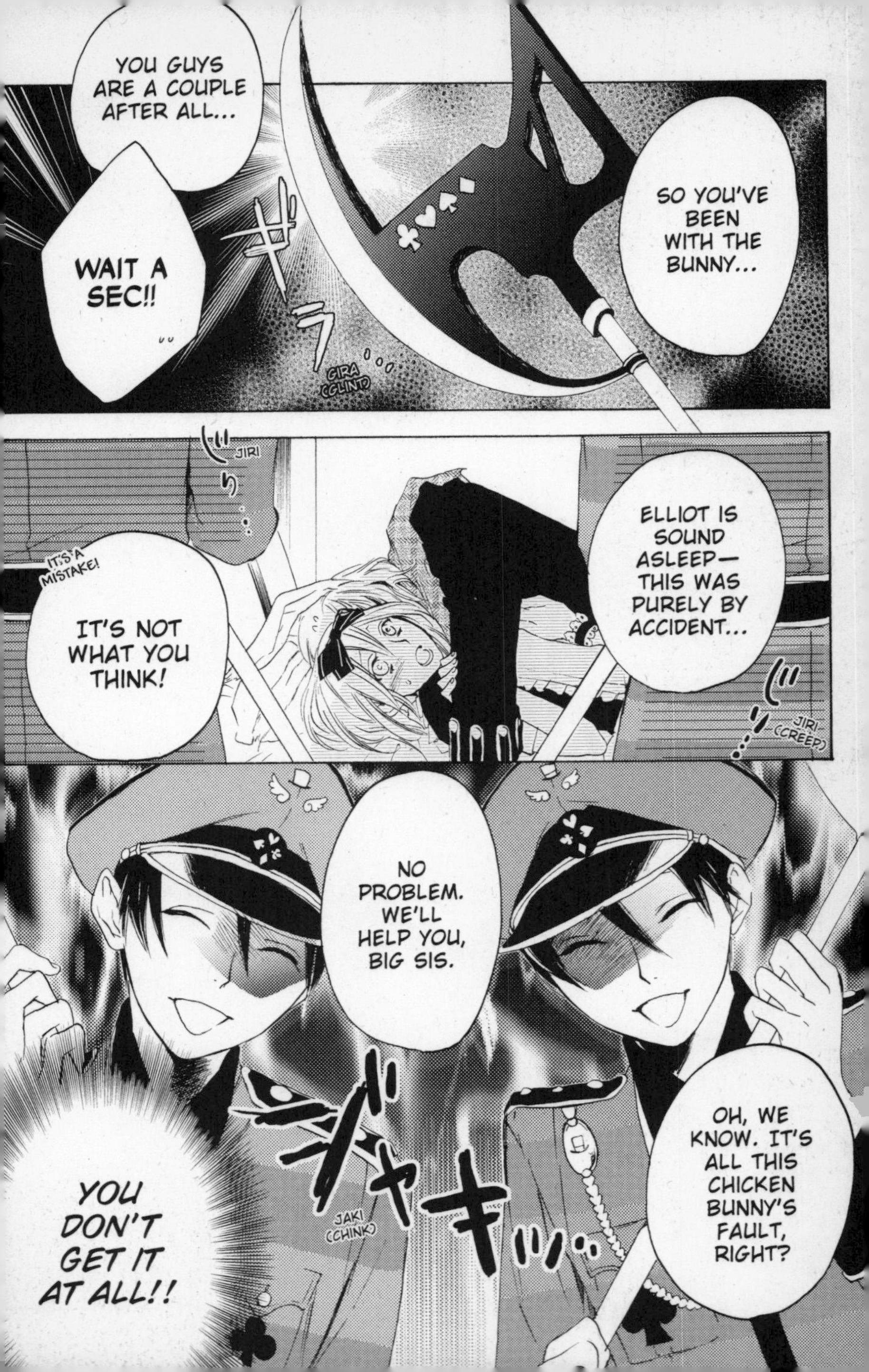
SO YOU'VE BEEN WITH THE BUNNY...
YOU GUYS ARE A COUPLE AFTER ALL...
WAIT A SEC!!
GIRA (GLINT)
ELLIOT IS SOUND ASLEEP—THIS WAS PURELY BY ACCIDENT...
JIRI (CREEP)
JIRI
IT'S A MISTAKE!
IT'S NOT WHAT YOU THINK!
NO PROBLEM. WE'LL HELP YOU, BIG SIS.
OH, WE KNOW. IT'S ALL THIS CHICKEN BUNNY'S FAULT, RIGHT?
JAKI (CHINK)
YOU DON'T GET IT AT ALL!!

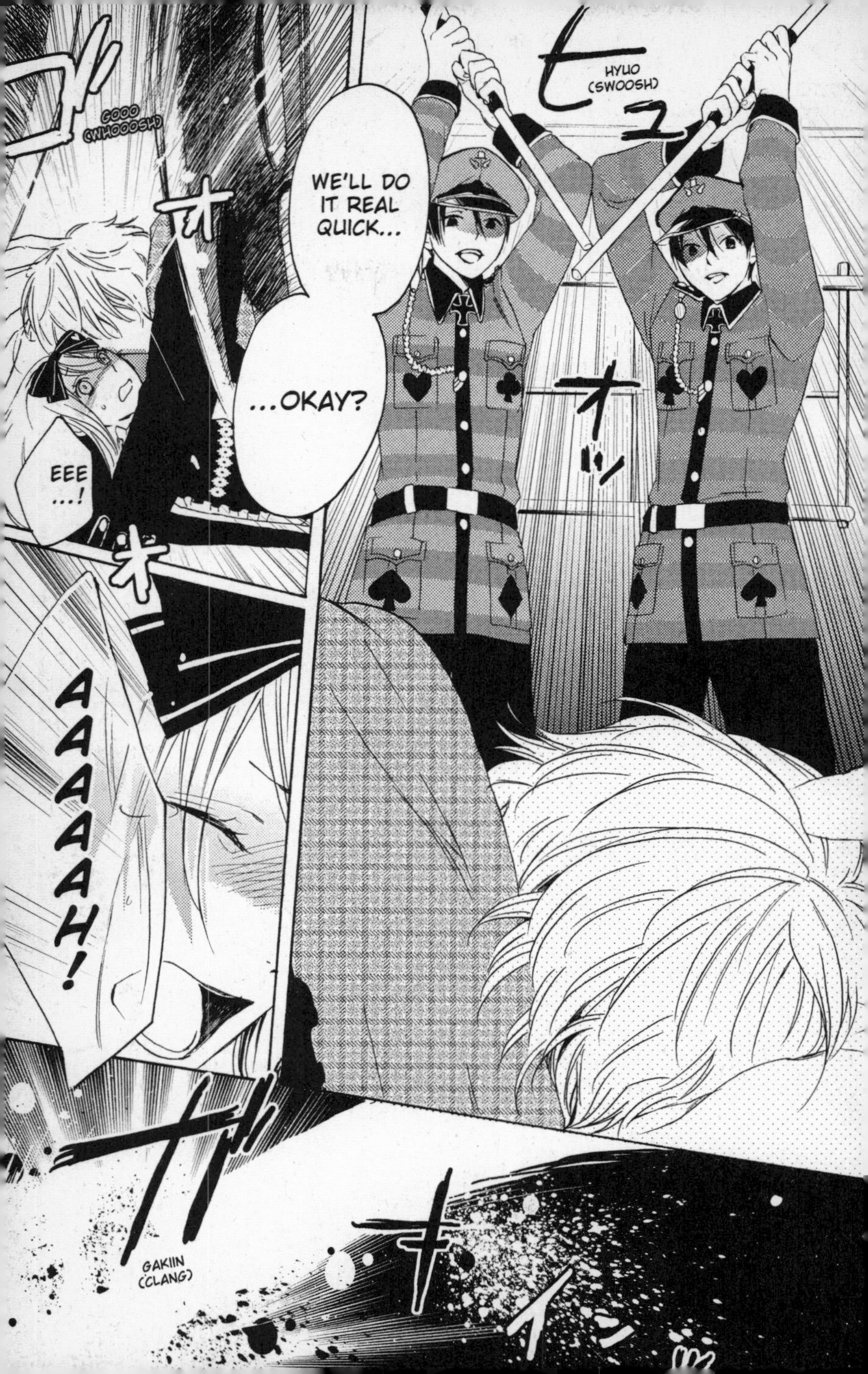
HYUO (SWOOSH)
WE'LL DO IT REAL QUICK...
...OKAY?
GOOO (WHOOOSH)
EEE ...!
AAAAAAH!
GAKIIN (CLANG)

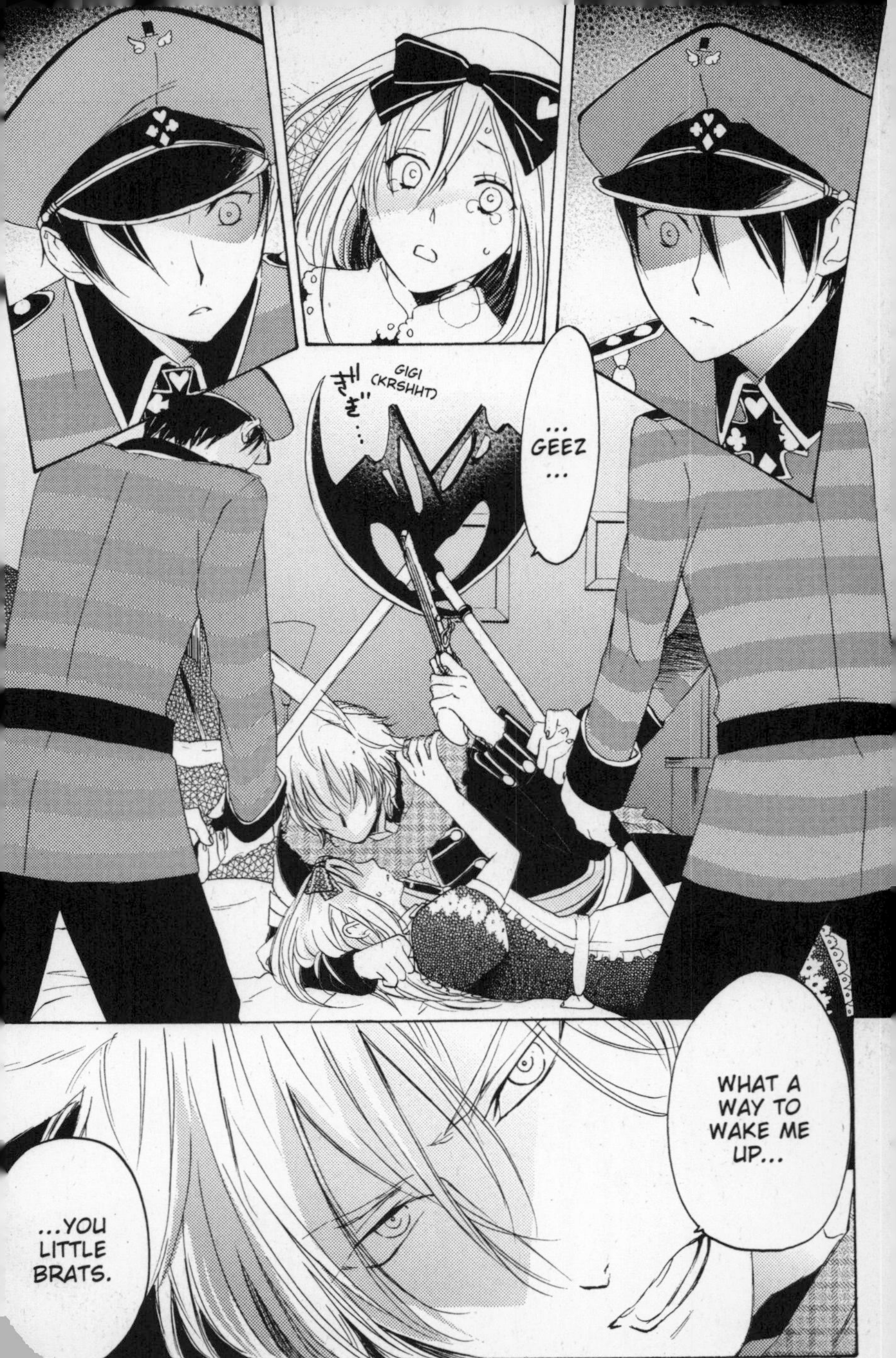
...GEEZ...
ぎぎ…
GIGI (KRSHHT)
WHAT A WAY TO WAKE ME UP...
...YOU LITTLE BRATS.

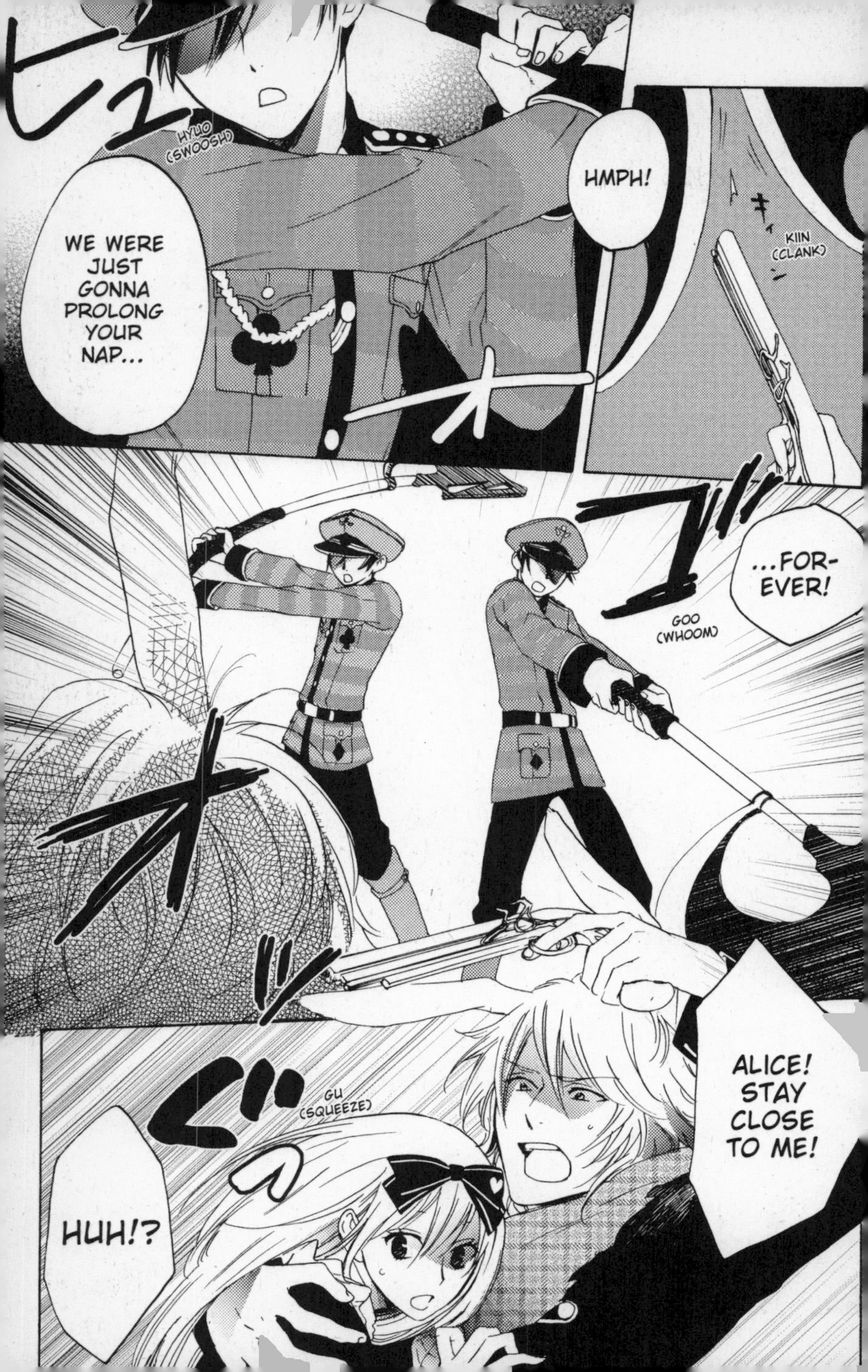
HMPH!
KIIN (CLANK)
HYUO (SWOOSH)
WE WERE JUST GONNA PROLONG YOUR NAP...
...FOR-EVER!
GOO (WHOOM)
ALICE! STAY CLOSE TO ME!
GU (SQUEEZE)
HUH!?

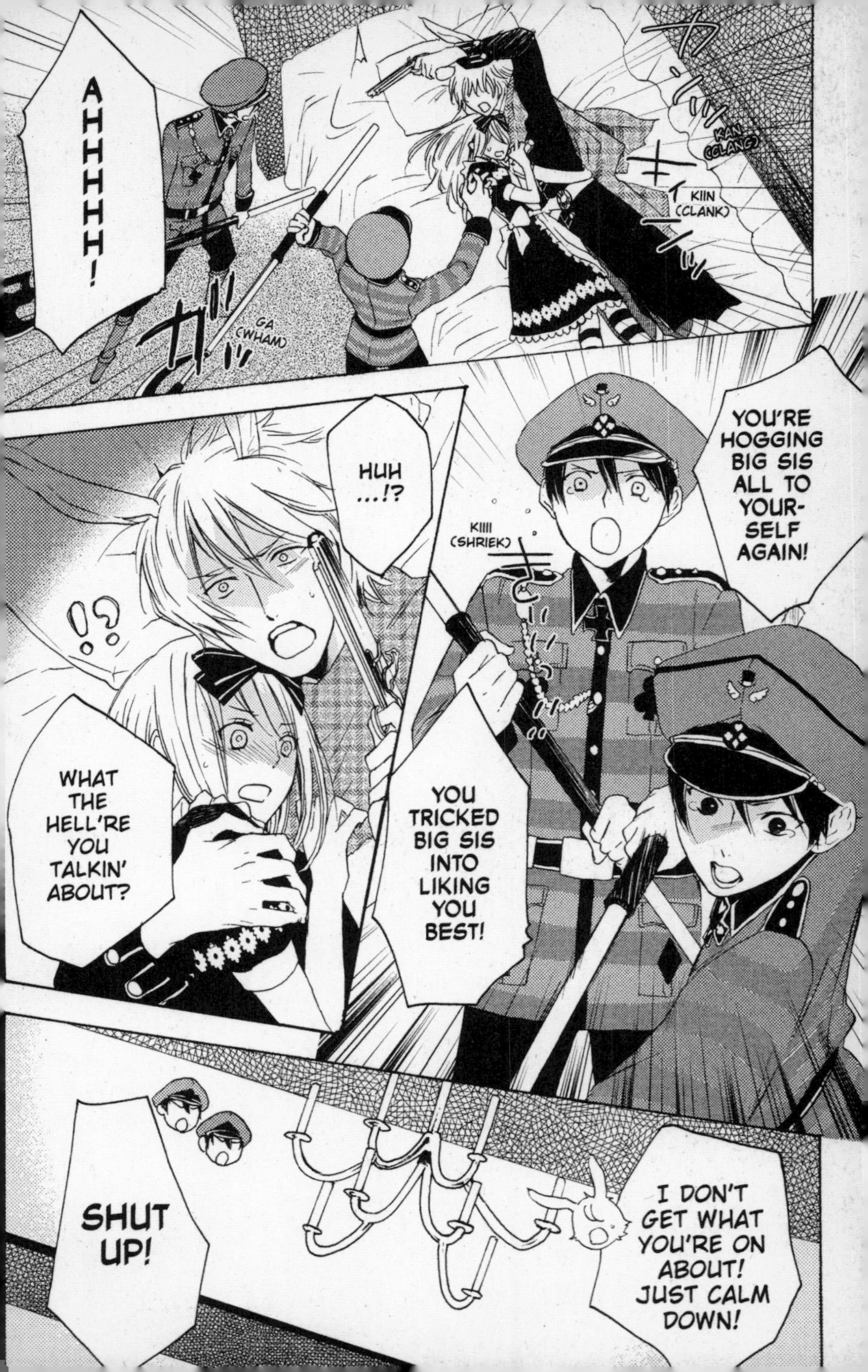
KAN (CLANG)
KIIN (CLANK)
AHHHHH!
GA (WHAM)
YOU'RE HOGGING BIG SIS ALL TO YOURSELF AGAIN!
KIIII (SHRIEK)
YOU TRICKED BIG SIS INTO LIKING YOU BEST!
HUH ...!?
!?
WHAT THE HELL'RE YOU TALKIN' ABOUT?
I DON'T GET WHAT YOU'RE ON ABOUT! JUST CALM DOWN!
SHUT UP!

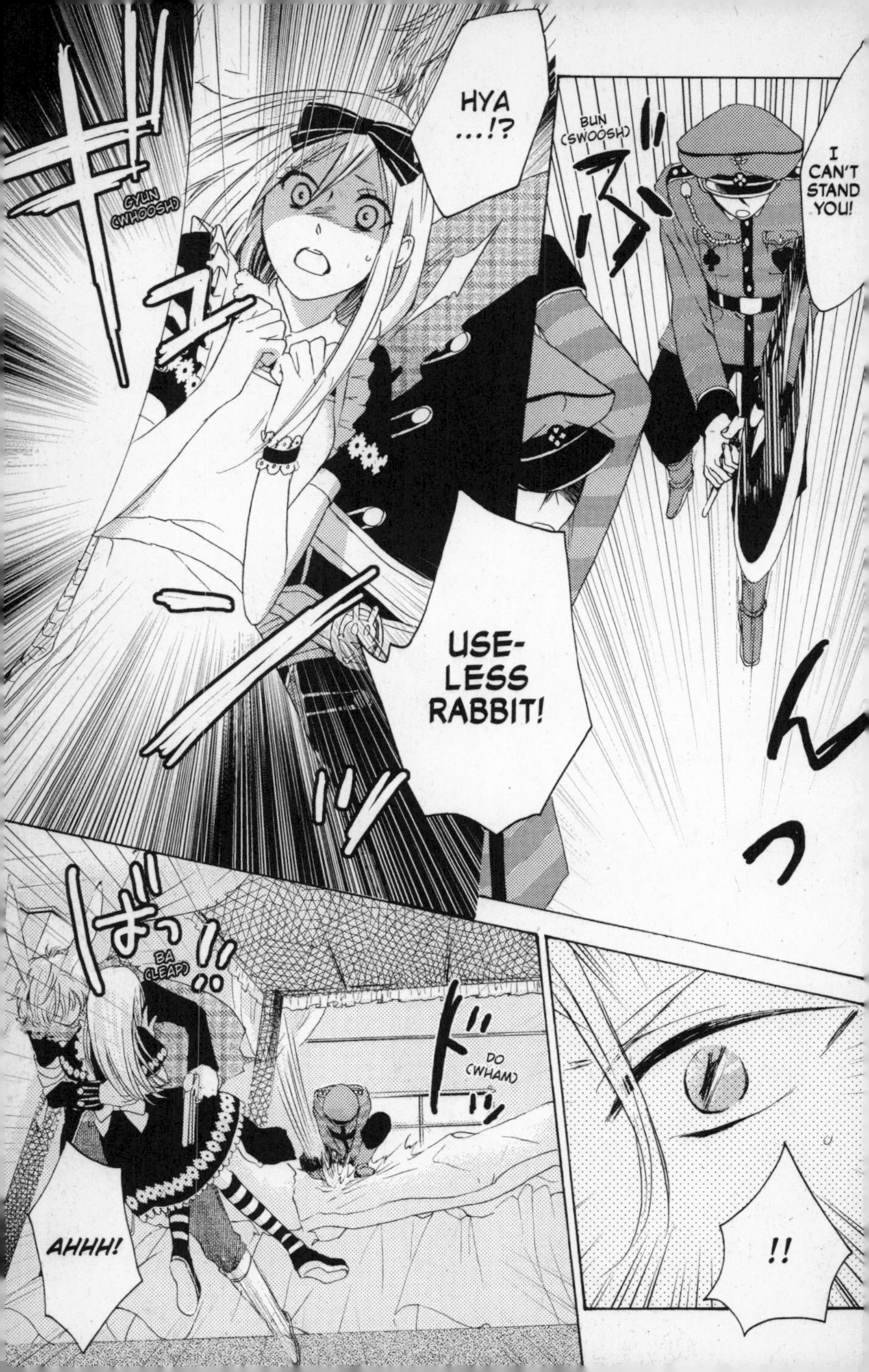
BUN (SWOOSH)
I CAN'T STAND YOU!
HYA ...!?
GYUN (WHOOSH)
USE-LESS RABBIT!
!!
BA (LEAP)
DO (WHAM)
AHHH!

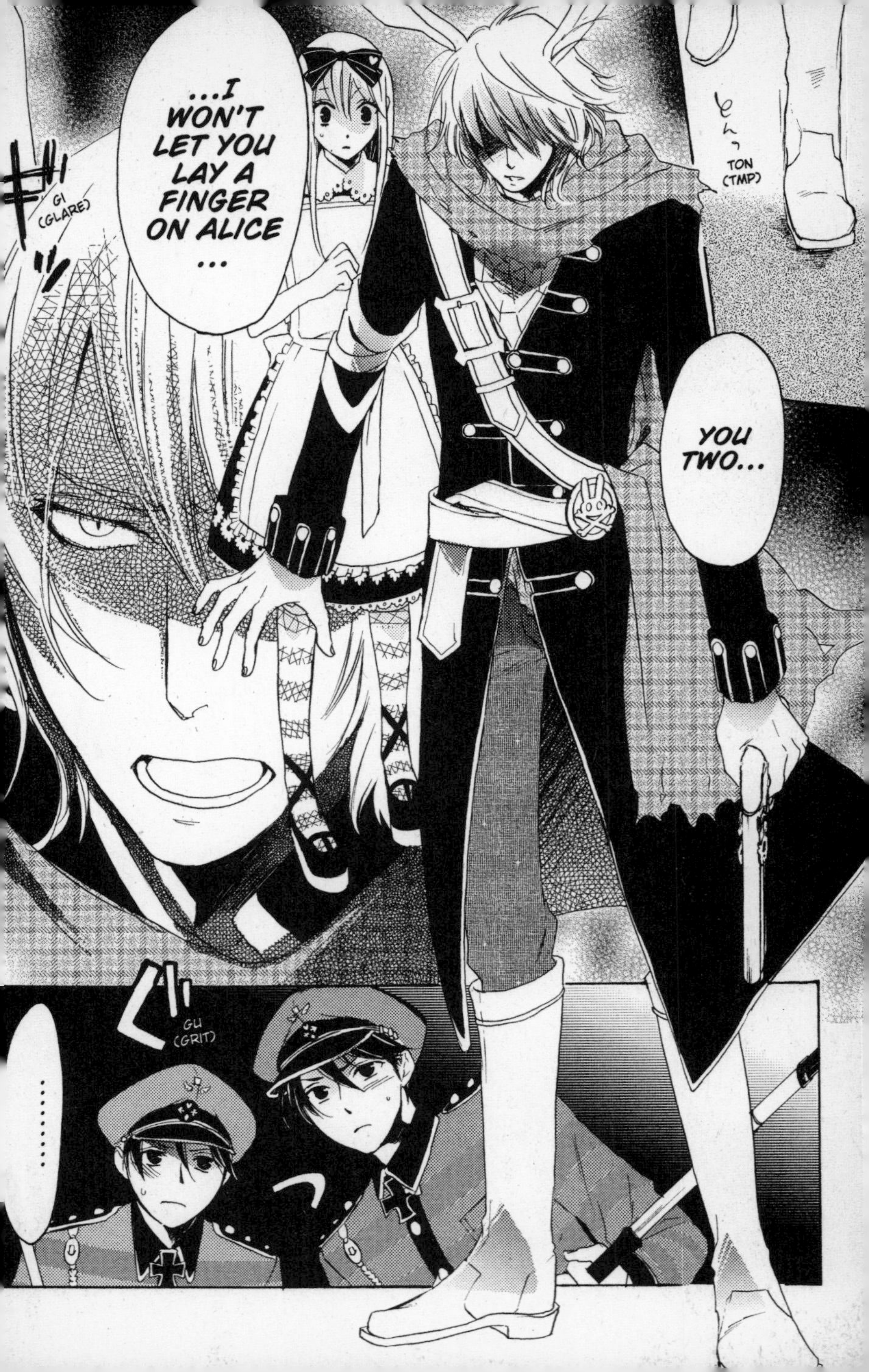
とんっ
TON (TMP)
...I WON'T LET YOU LAY A FINGER ON ALICE ...
GI (GLARE)
YOU TWO...
GU (GRIT)
......

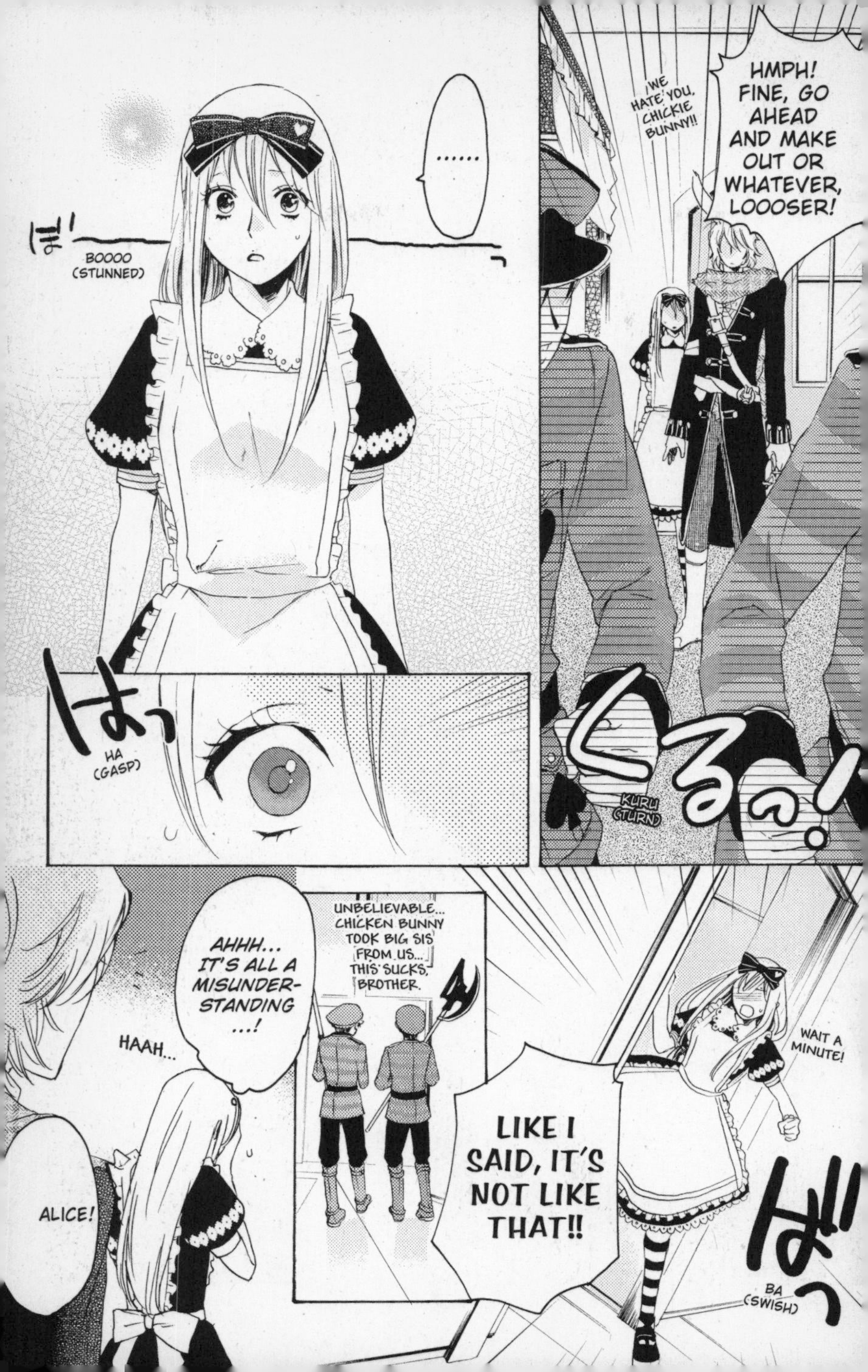
HMPH! FINE, GO AHEAD AND MAKE OUT OR WHATEVER, LOOOSER!
WE HATE YOU, CHICKIE BUNNY!!
くるっ!
KURU (TURN)
......
ぼー
BOOOO (STUNNED)
はっ
HA (GASP)
WAIT A MINUTE!
ばっ
BA (SWISH)
UNBELIEVABLE... CHICKEN BUNNY TOOK BIG SIS FROM US... THIS SUCKS, BROTHER.
LIKE I SAID, IT'S NOT LIKE THAT!!
AHHH... IT'S ALL A MISUNDER-STANDING ...!
HAAH...
ALICE!

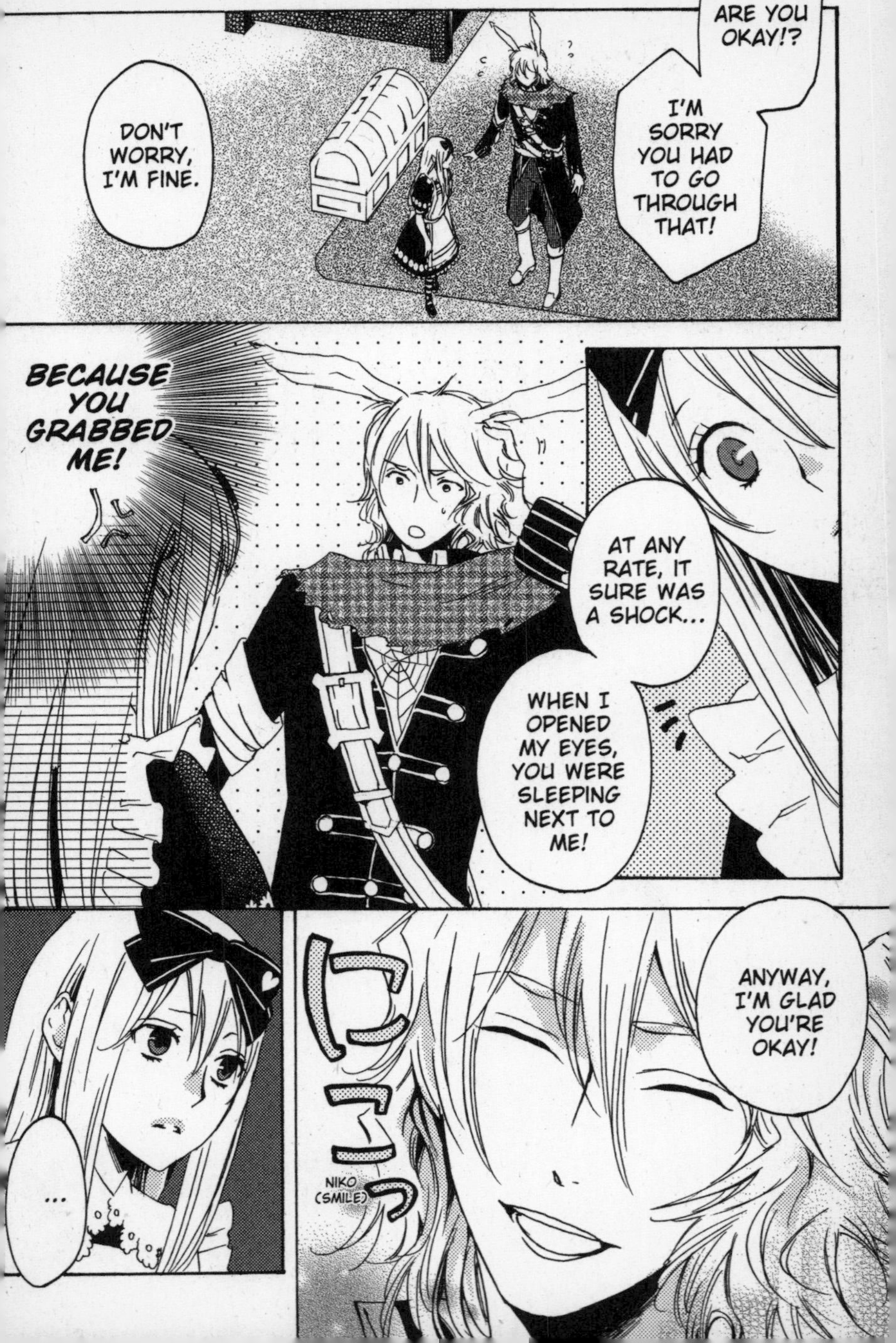
ARE YOU OKAY!?
I'M SORRY YOU HAD TO GO THROUGH THAT!
DON'T WORRY, I'M FINE.
AT ANY RATE, IT SURE WAS A SHOCK...
WHEN I OPENED MY EYES, YOU WERE SLEEPING NEXT TO ME!
BECAUSE YOU GRABBED ME!
ANYWAY, I'M GLAD YOU'RE OKAY!
NIKO (SMILE)
...

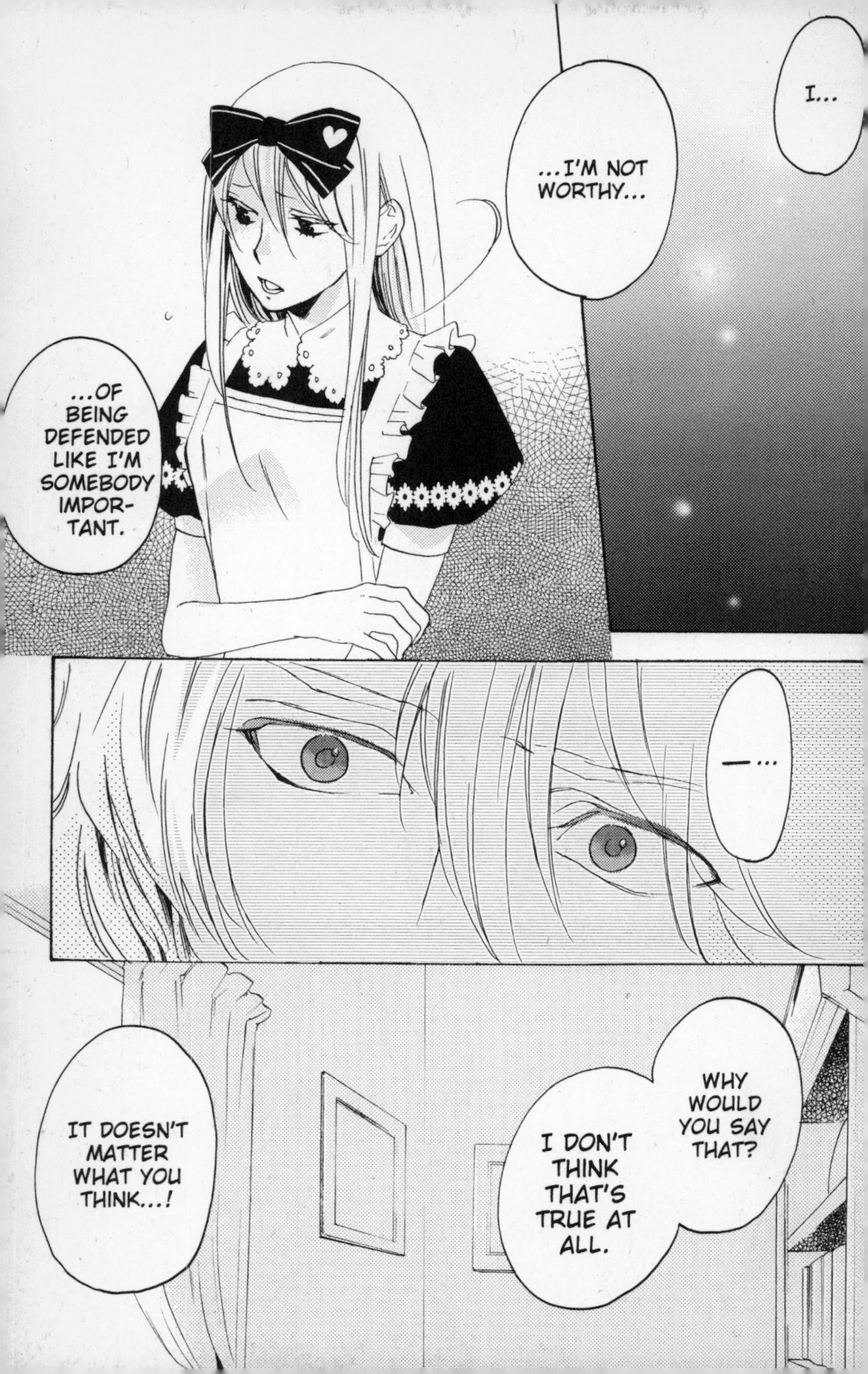
I...
...I'M NOT WORTHY...
...OF BEING DEFENDED LIKE I'M SOMEBODY IMPORTANT.
—...
WHY WOULD YOU SAY THAT?
I DON'T THINK THAT'S TRUE AT ALL.
IT DOESN'T MATTER WHAT YOU THINK...!

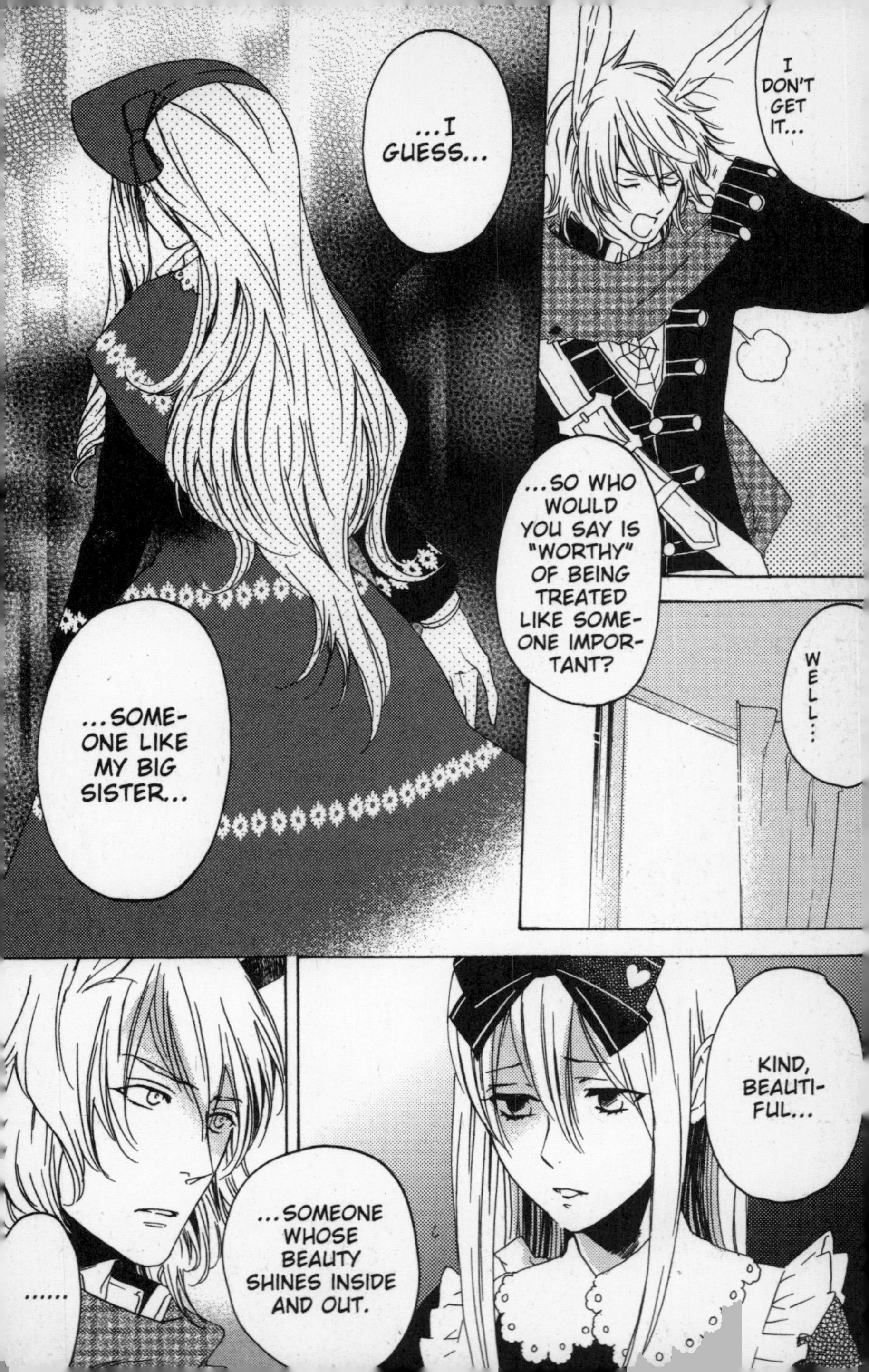
I DON'T GET IT...
...SO WHO WOULD YOU SAY IS "WORTHY" OF BEING TREATED LIKE SOME-ONE IMPOR-TANT?
WELL...
...I GUESS...
...SOME-ONE LIKE MY BIG SISTER...
KIND, BEAUTI-FUL...
...SOMEONE WHOSE BEAUTY SHINES INSIDE AND OUT.
......

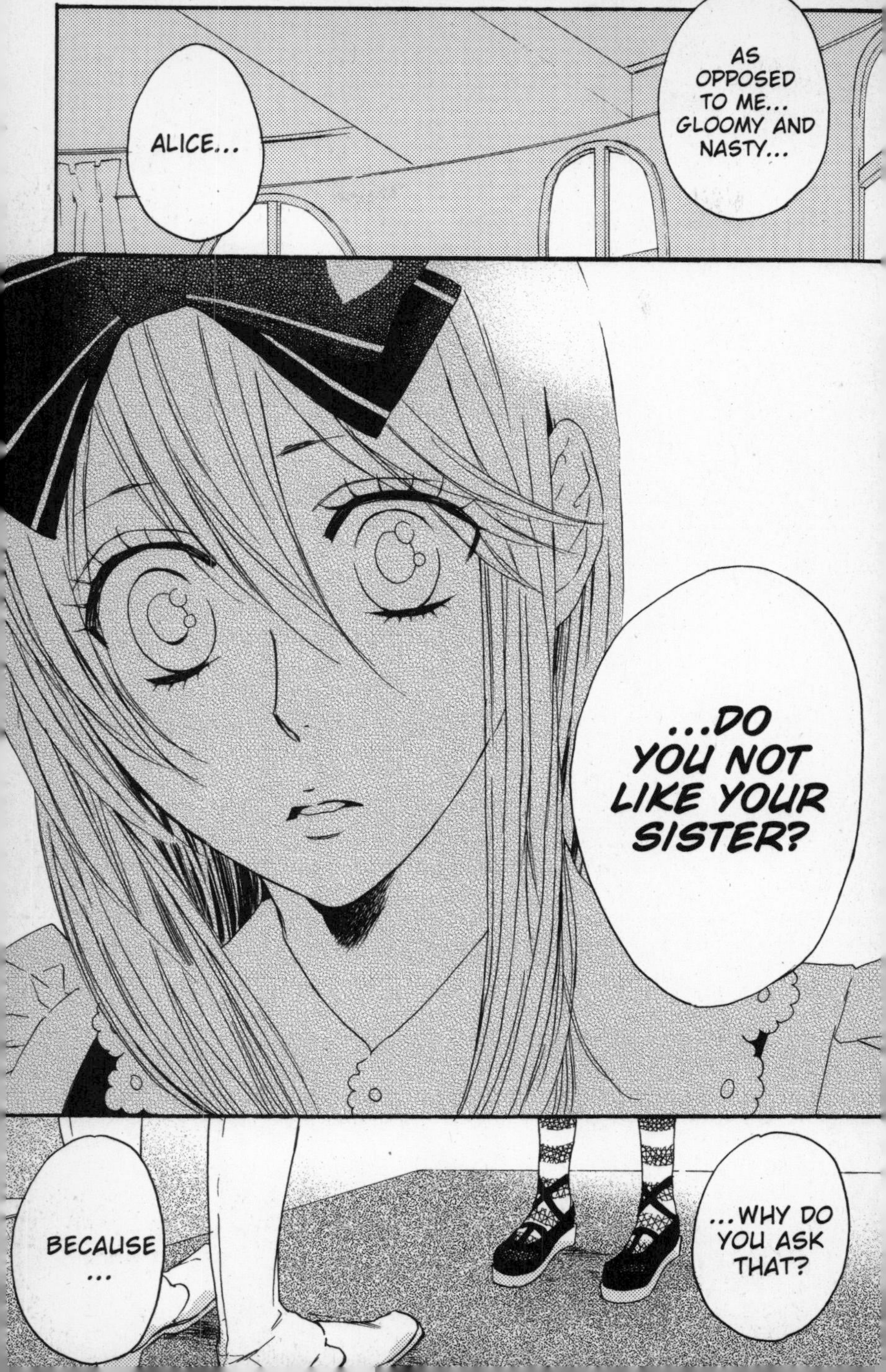
AS OPPOSED TO ME... GLOOMY AND NASTY...
ALICE...
...DO YOU NOT LIKE YOUR SISTER?
...WHY DO YOU ASK THAT?
BECAUSE ...

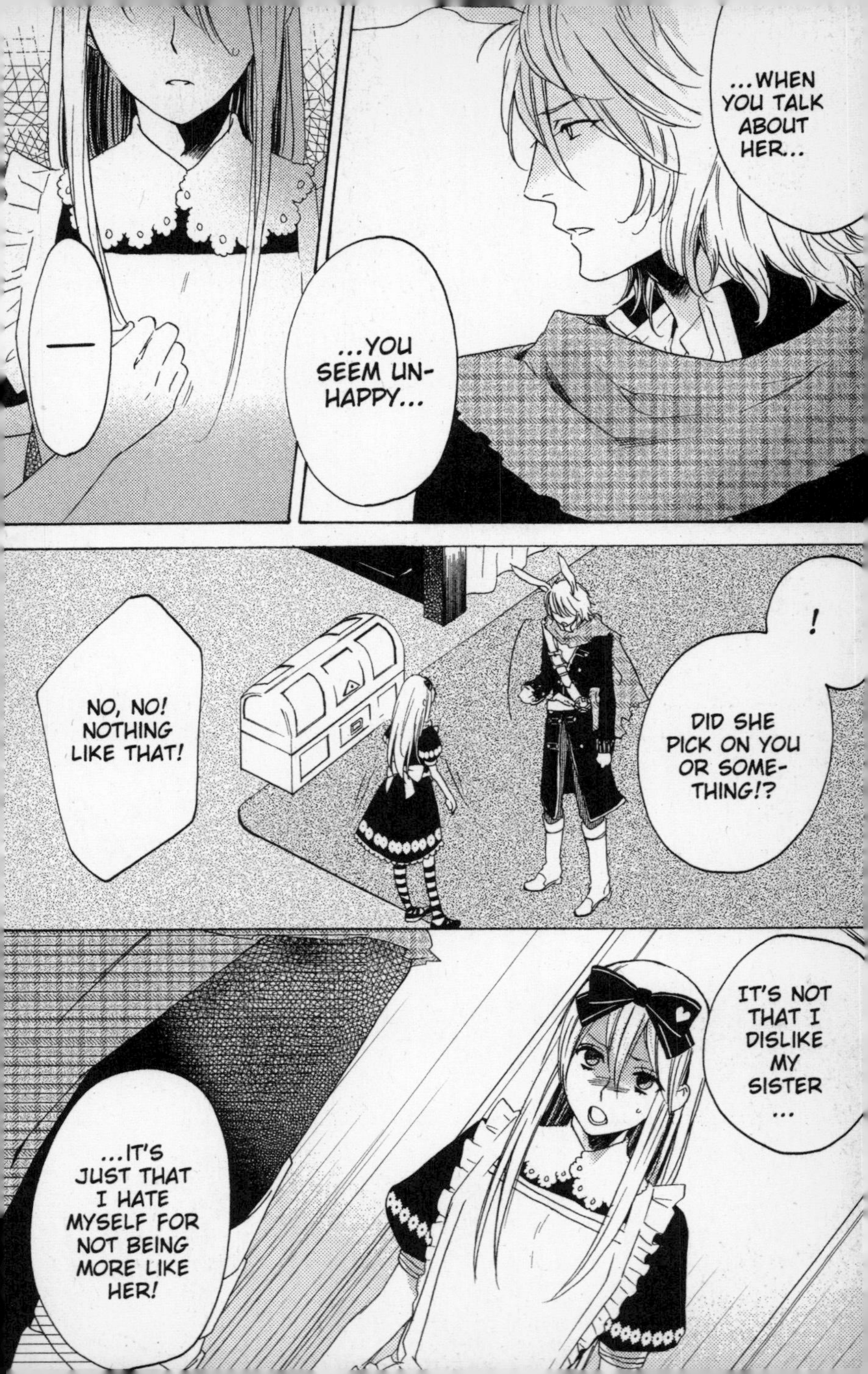
...WHEN YOU TALK ABOUT HER...
...YOU SEEM UN-HAPPY...
—
!
DID SHE PICK ON YOU OR SOME-THING!?
NO, NO! NOTHING LIKE THAT!
IT'S NOT THAT I DISLIKE MY SISTER ...
...IT'S JUST THAT I HATE MYSELF FOR NOT BEING MORE LIKE HER!

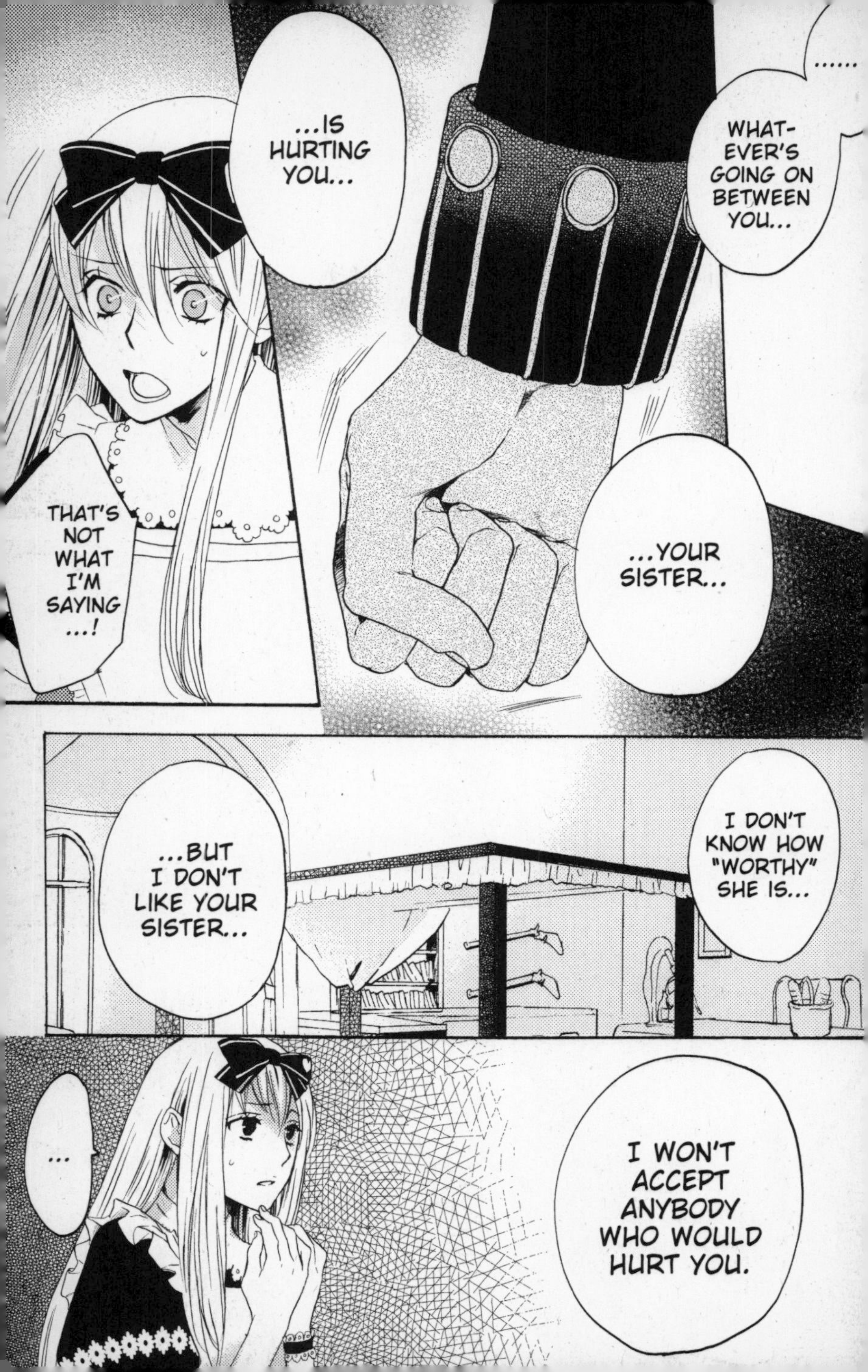
......
WHAT-EVER'S GOING ON BETWEEN YOU...
...IS HURTING YOU...
...YOUR SISTER...
THAT'S NOT WHAT I'M SAYING...!
I DON'T KNOW HOW "WORTHY" SHE IS...
...BUT I DON'T LIKE YOUR SISTER...
I WON'T ACCEPT ANYBODY WHO WOULD HURT YOU.
...

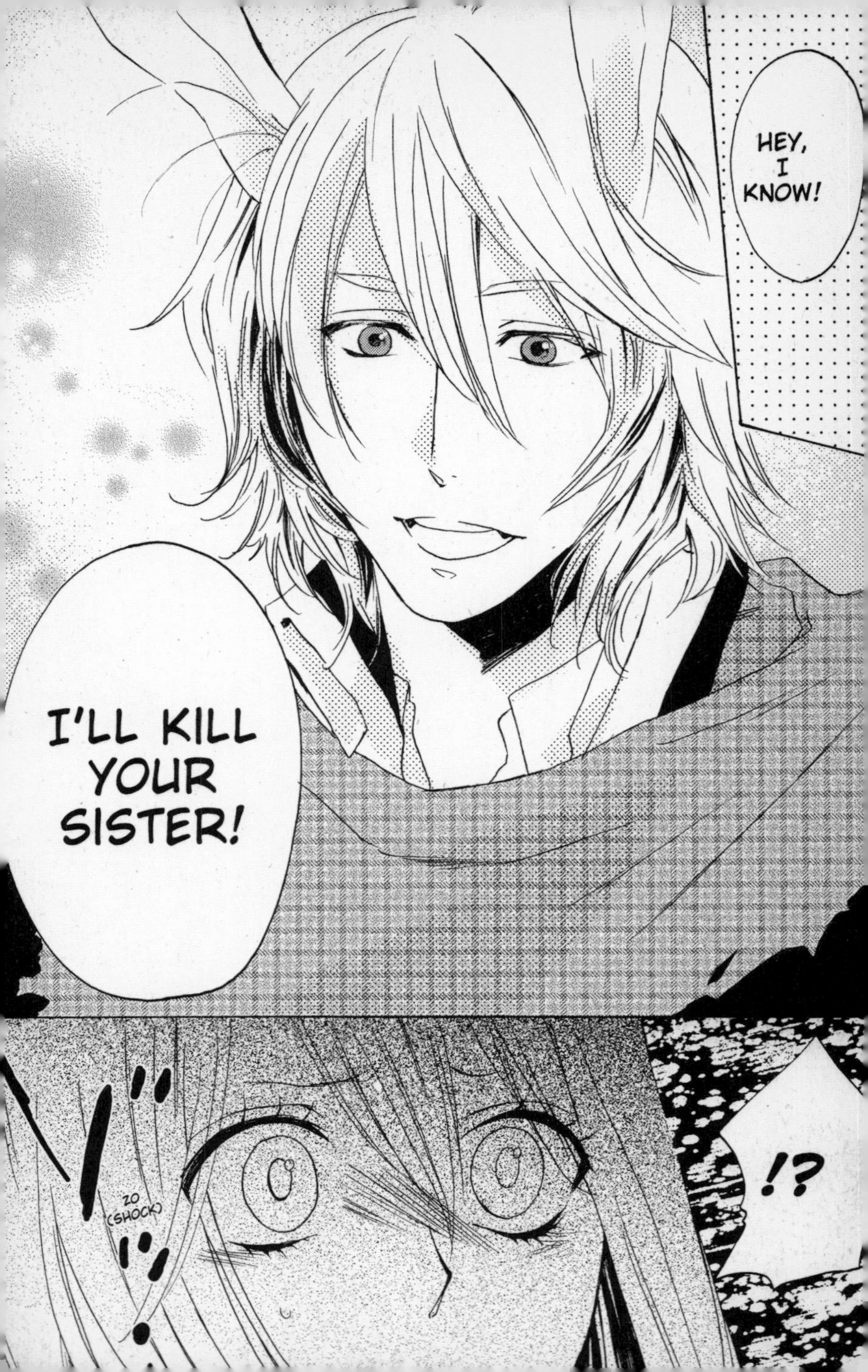
HEY, I KNOW!
I'LL KILL YOUR SISTER!
!?
ZO (SHOCK)

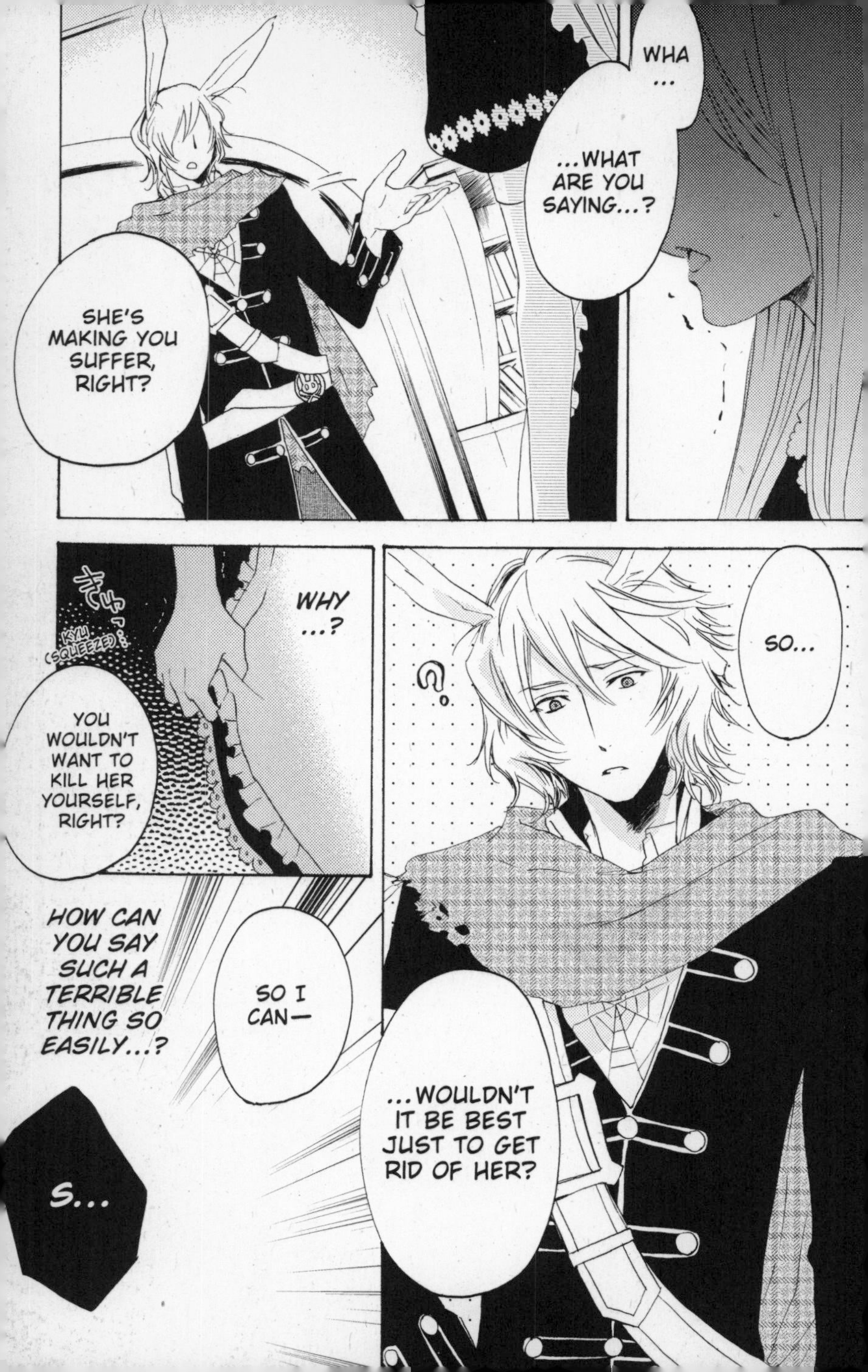
WHA ...
...WHAT ARE YOU SAYING...?
SHE'S MAKING YOU SUFFER, RIGHT?
SO...
...WOULDN'T IT BE BEST JUST TO GET RID OF HER?
WHY ...?
きゅっ...
KYU (SQUEEZED)
YOU WOULDN'T WANT TO KILL HER YOURSELF, RIGHT?
SO I CAN—
HOW CAN YOU SAY SUCH A TERRIBLE THING SO EASILY...?
S...

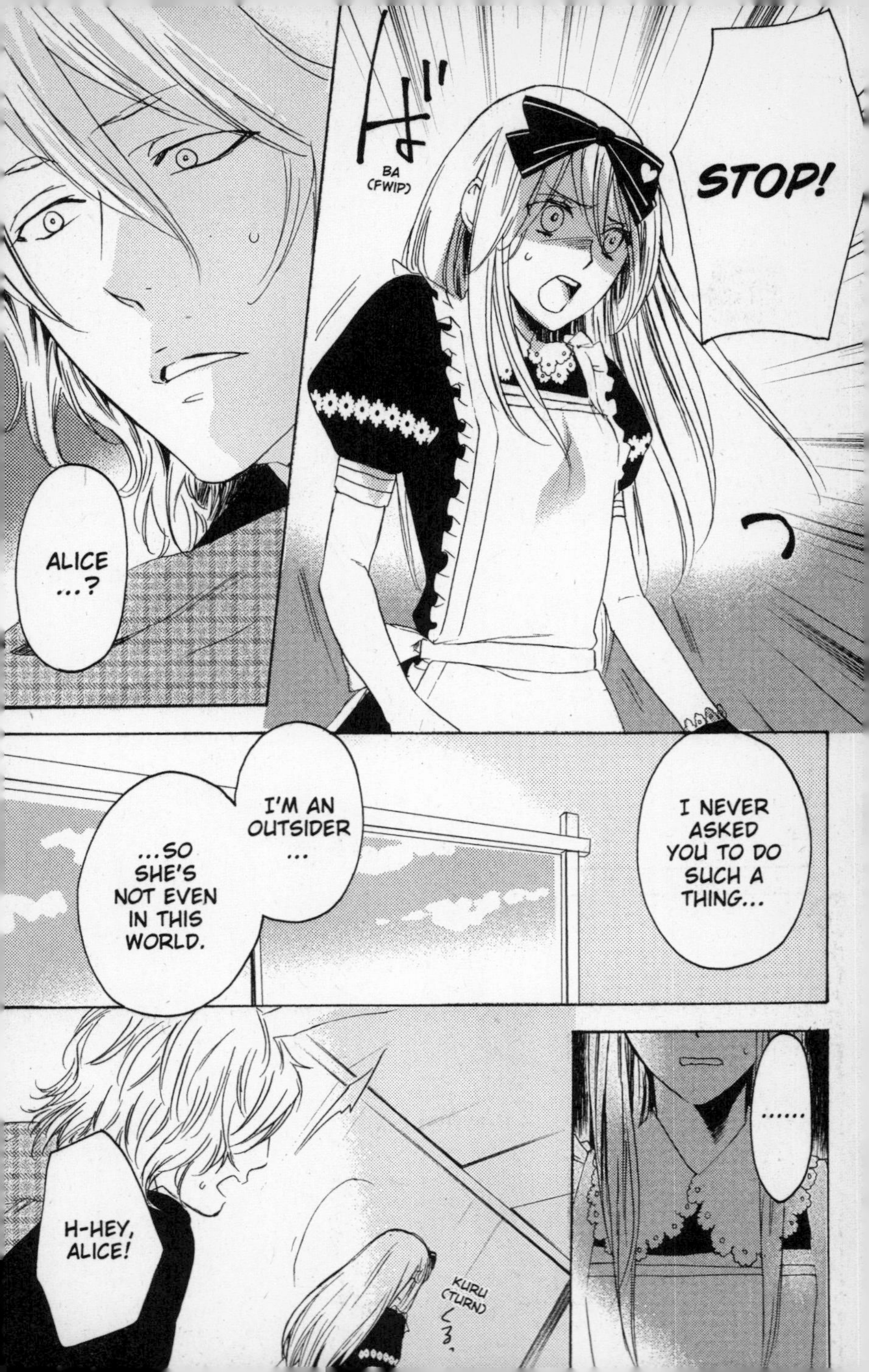
STOP!
ば
BA (FWIP)
ALICE ...?
I NEVER ASKED YOU TO DO SUCH A THING...
I'M AN OUTSIDER ...
...SO SHE'S NOT EVEN IN THIS WORLD.
......
くる
KURU (TURN)
H-HEY, ALICE!

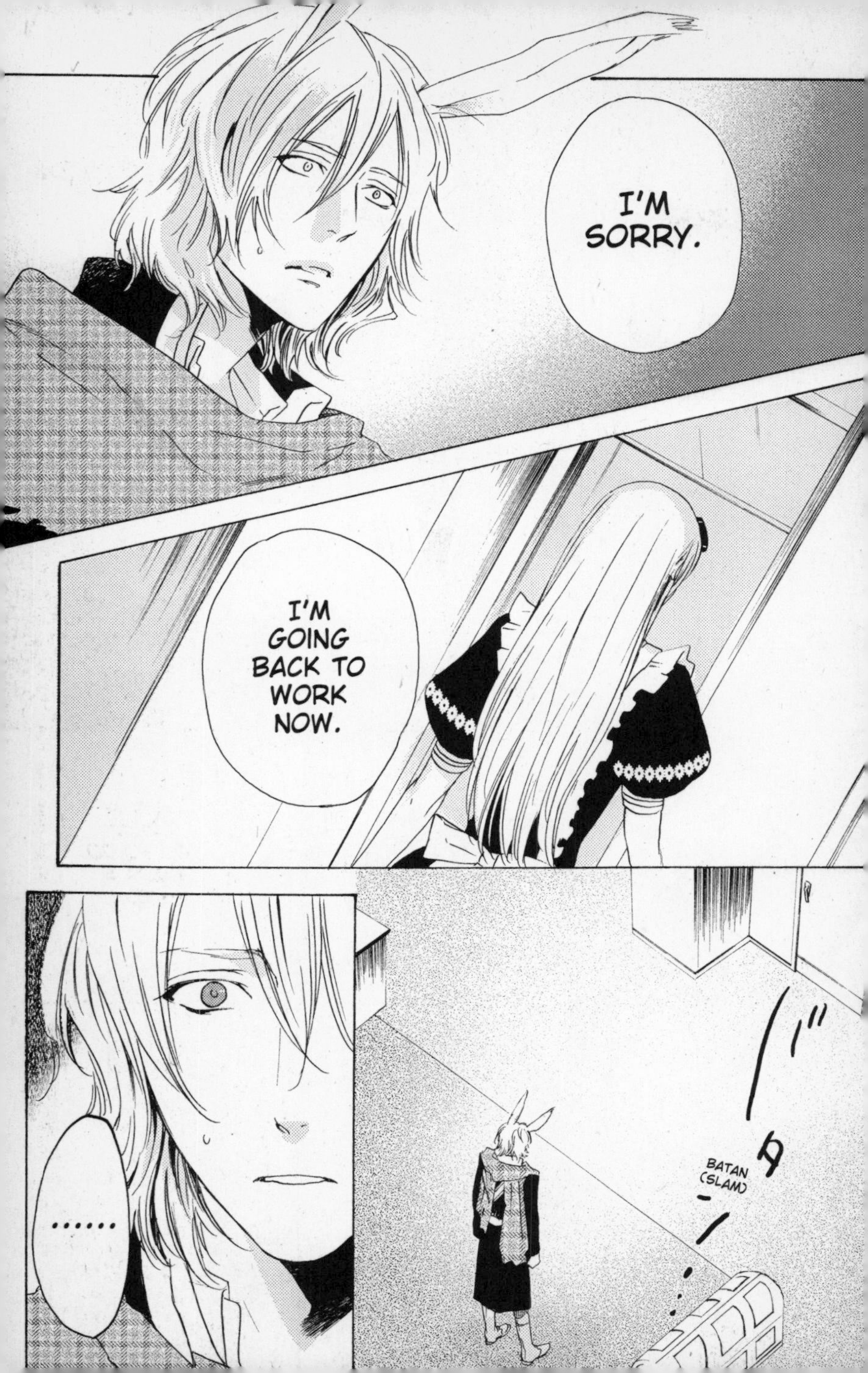
I'M SORRY.
I'M GOING BACK TO WORK NOW.
BATAN (SLAM)
......

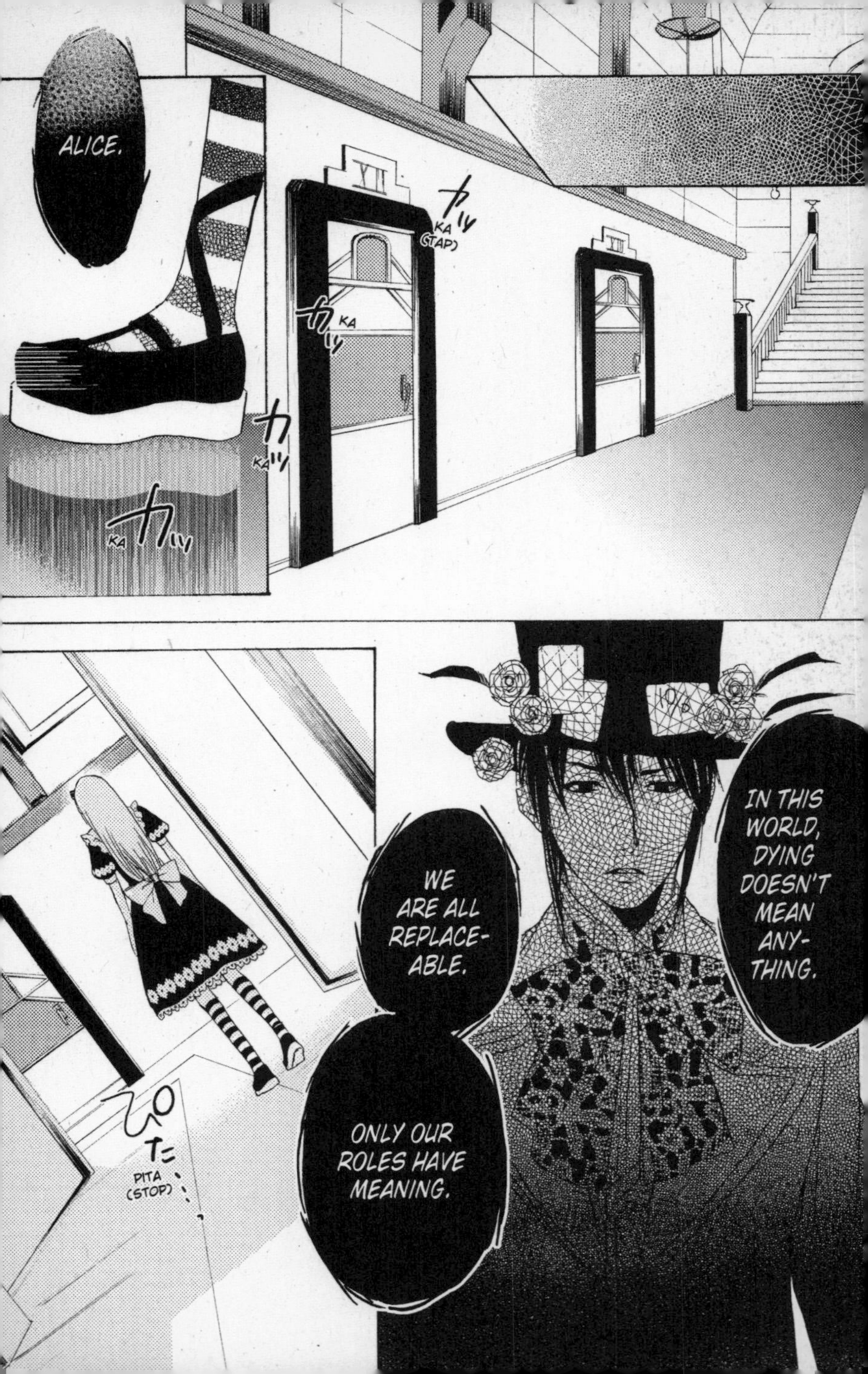
KA (TAP)
KA
KA
ALICE.
KA
IN THIS WORLD, DYING DOESN'T MEAN ANY-THING.
WE ARE ALL REPLACE-ABLE.
ONLY OUR ROLES HAVE MEANING.
PITA (STOP)

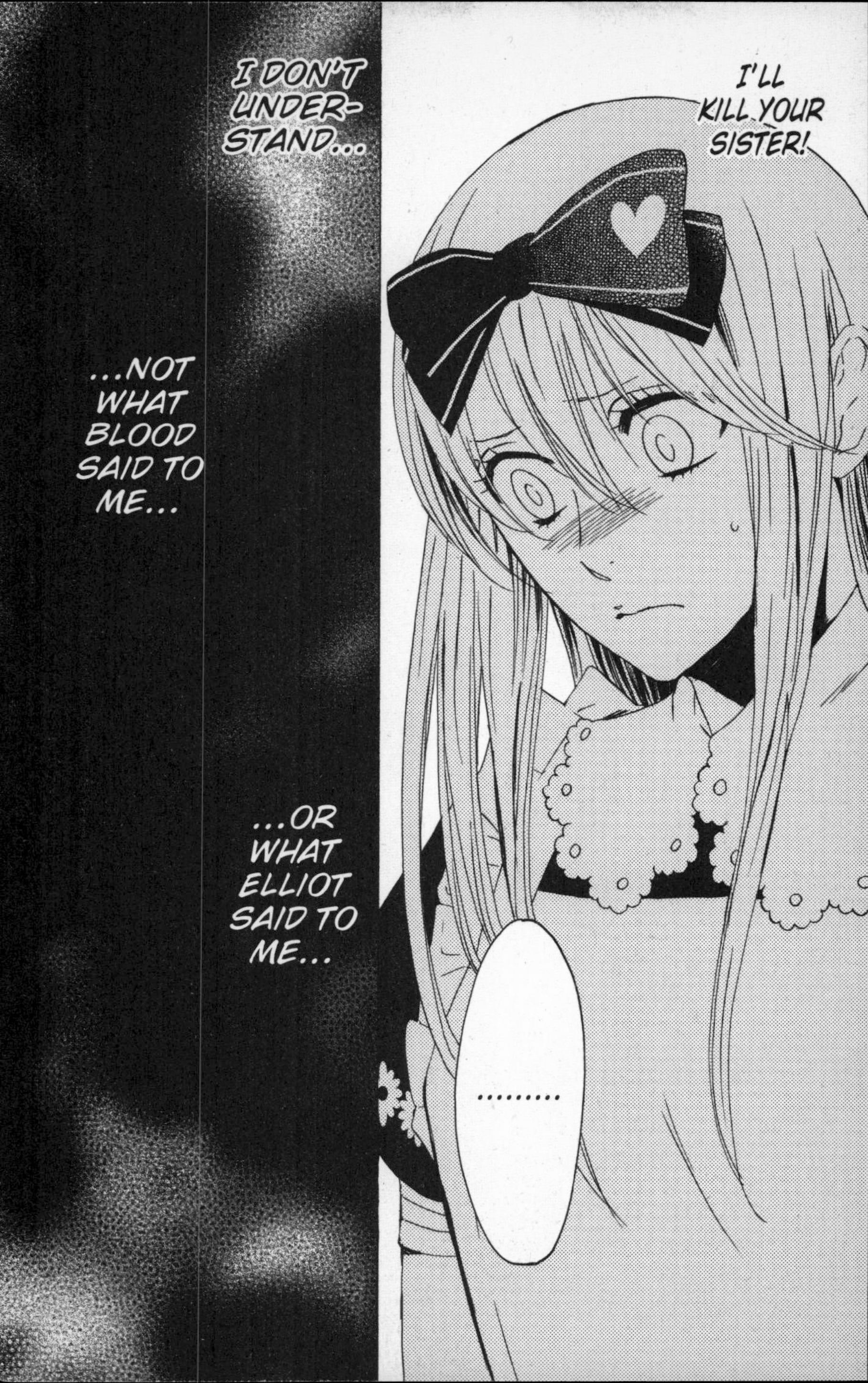
I'LL KILL YOUR SISTER!
....
I DON'T UNDER-STAND...
...OR WHAT ELLIOT SAID TO ME...
...NOT WHAT BLOOD SAID TO ME...

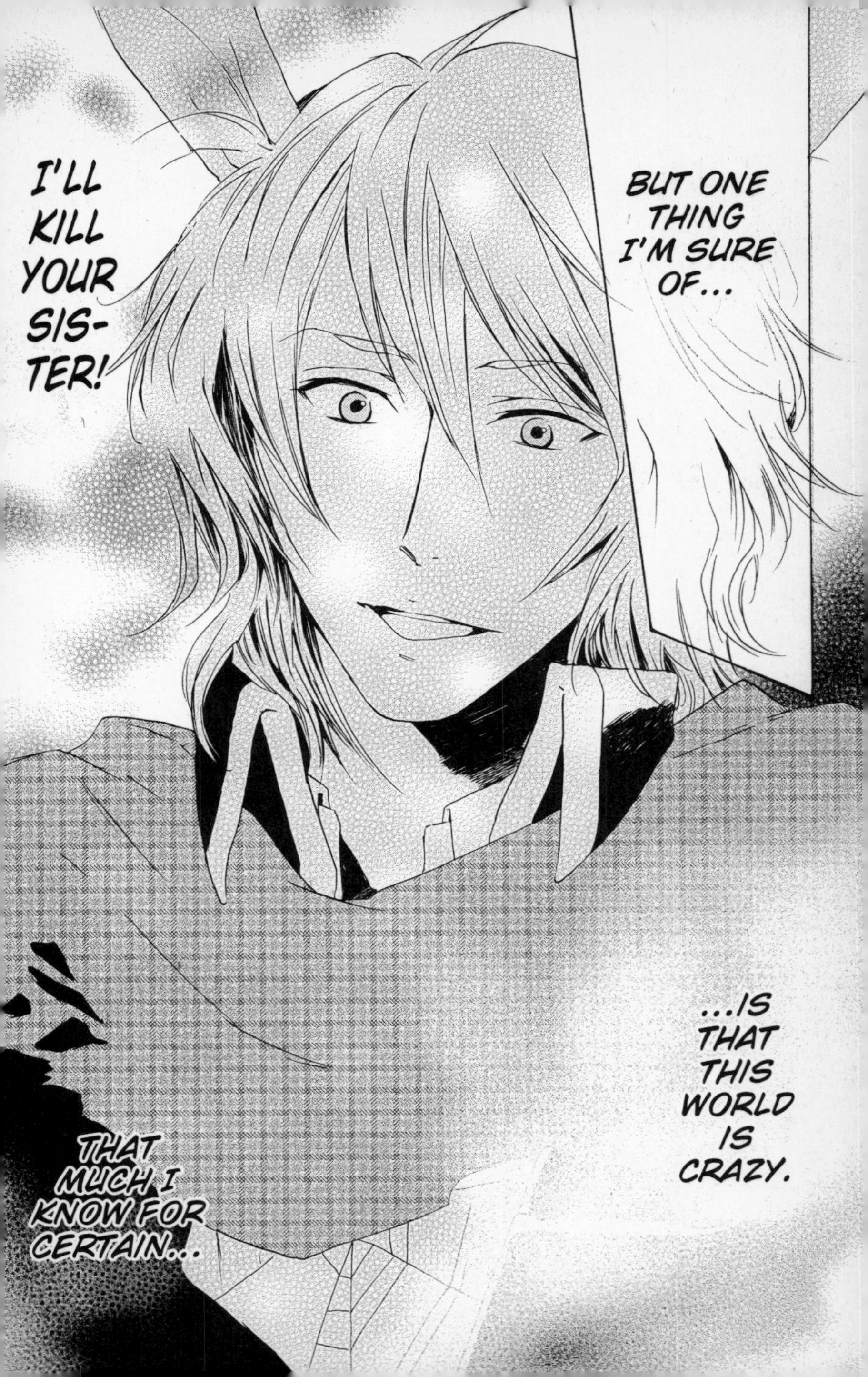
BUT ONE THING I'M SURE OF...
I'LL KILL YOUR SIS-TER!
...IS THAT THIS WORLD IS CRAZY.
THAT MUCH I KNOW FOR CERTAIN...

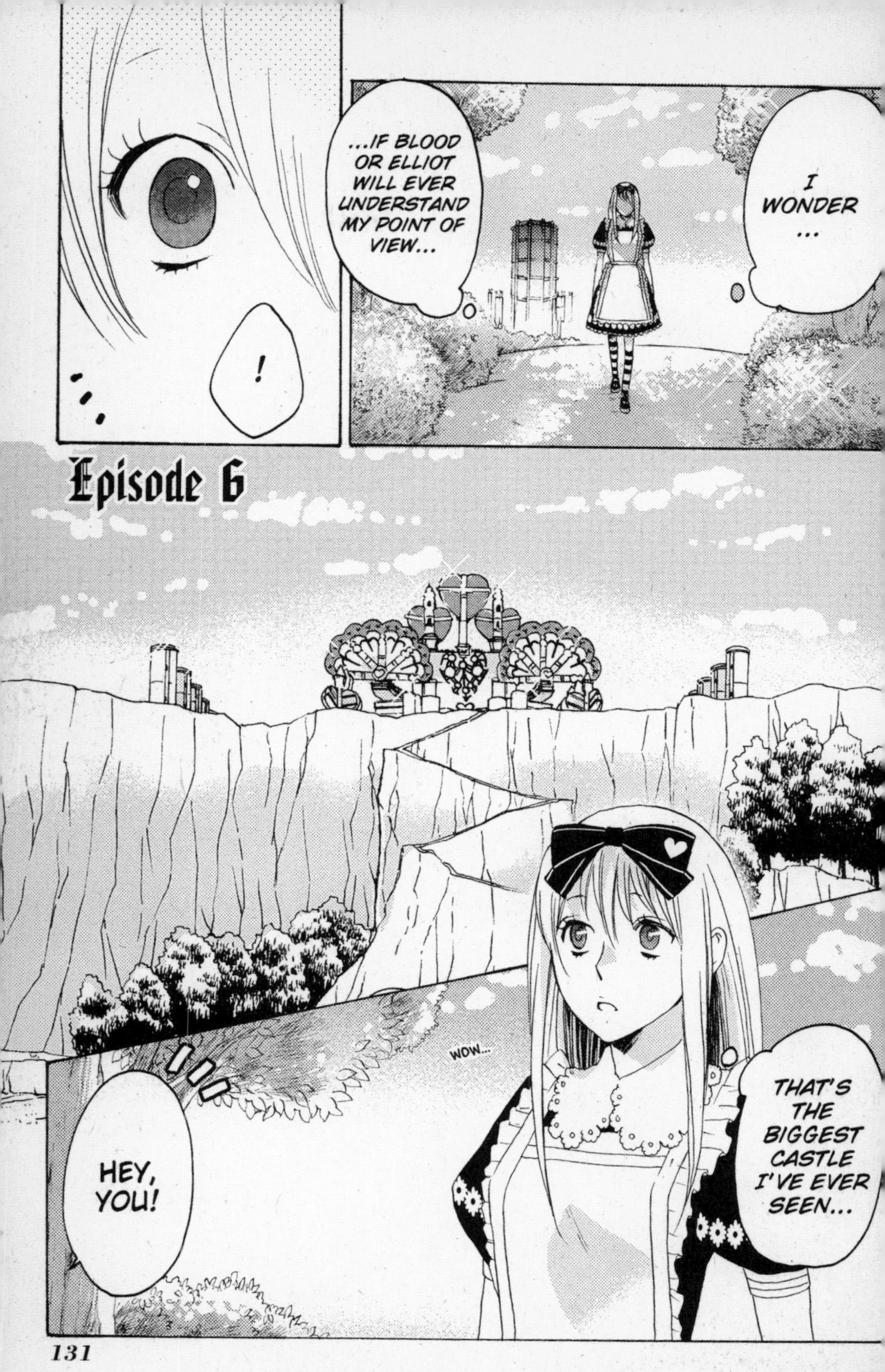
I WONDER...
...IF BLOOD OR ELLIOT WILL EVER UNDERSTAND MY POINT OF VIEW...
!
Episode 6
WOW...
THAT'S THE BIGGEST CASTLE I'VE EVER SEEN...
HEY, YOU!

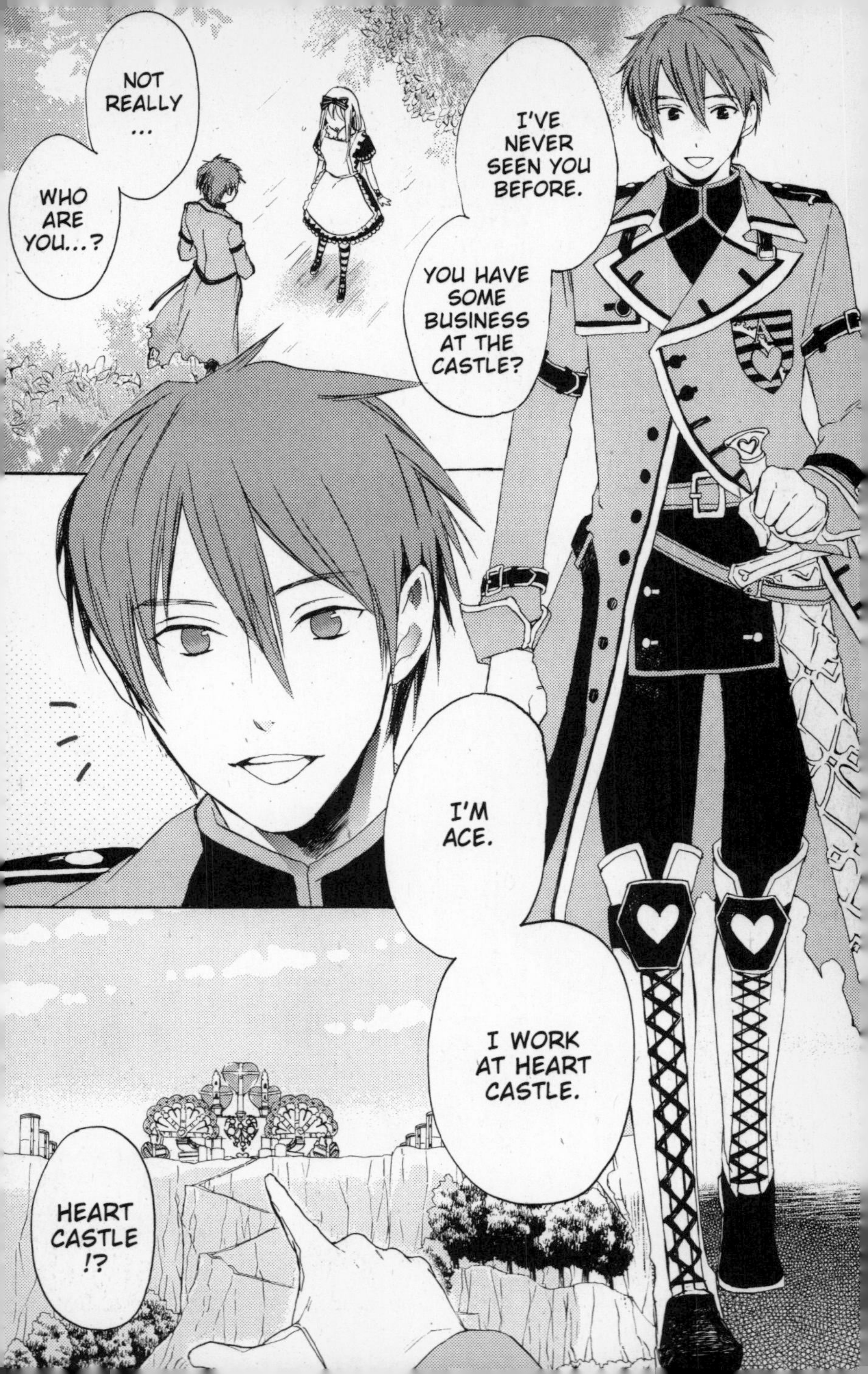
I'VE NEVER SEEN YOU BEFORE.
YOU HAVE SOME BUSINESS AT THE CASTLE?
NOT REALLY ...
WHO ARE YOU...?
I'M ACE.
I WORK AT HEART CASTLE.
HEART CASTLE !?

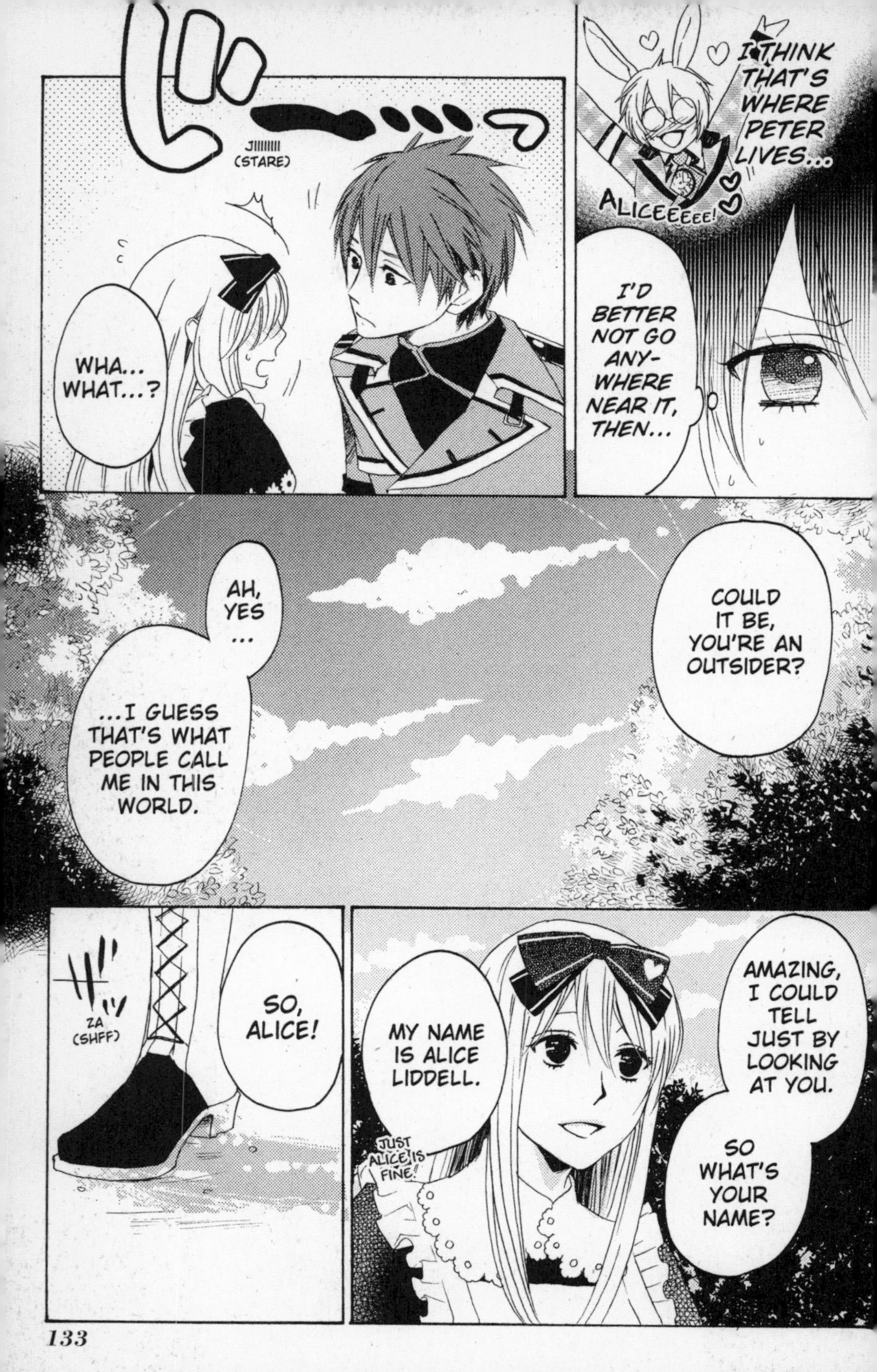

I THINK THAT'S WHERE PETER LIVES...
ALICEEEEEE!
I'D BETTER NOT GO ANY-WHERE NEAR IT, THEN...
JIIIIIIII (STARE)
WHA... WHAT...?
COULD IT BE, YOU'RE AN OUTSIDER?
AH, YES...
...I GUESS THAT'S WHAT PEOPLE CALL ME IN THIS WORLD.
AMAZING, I COULD TELL JUST BY LOOKING AT YOU.
SO WHAT'S YOUR NAME?
MY NAME IS ALICE LIDDELL.
JUST ALICE IS FINE!
SO, ALICE!
ZA (SHFF)

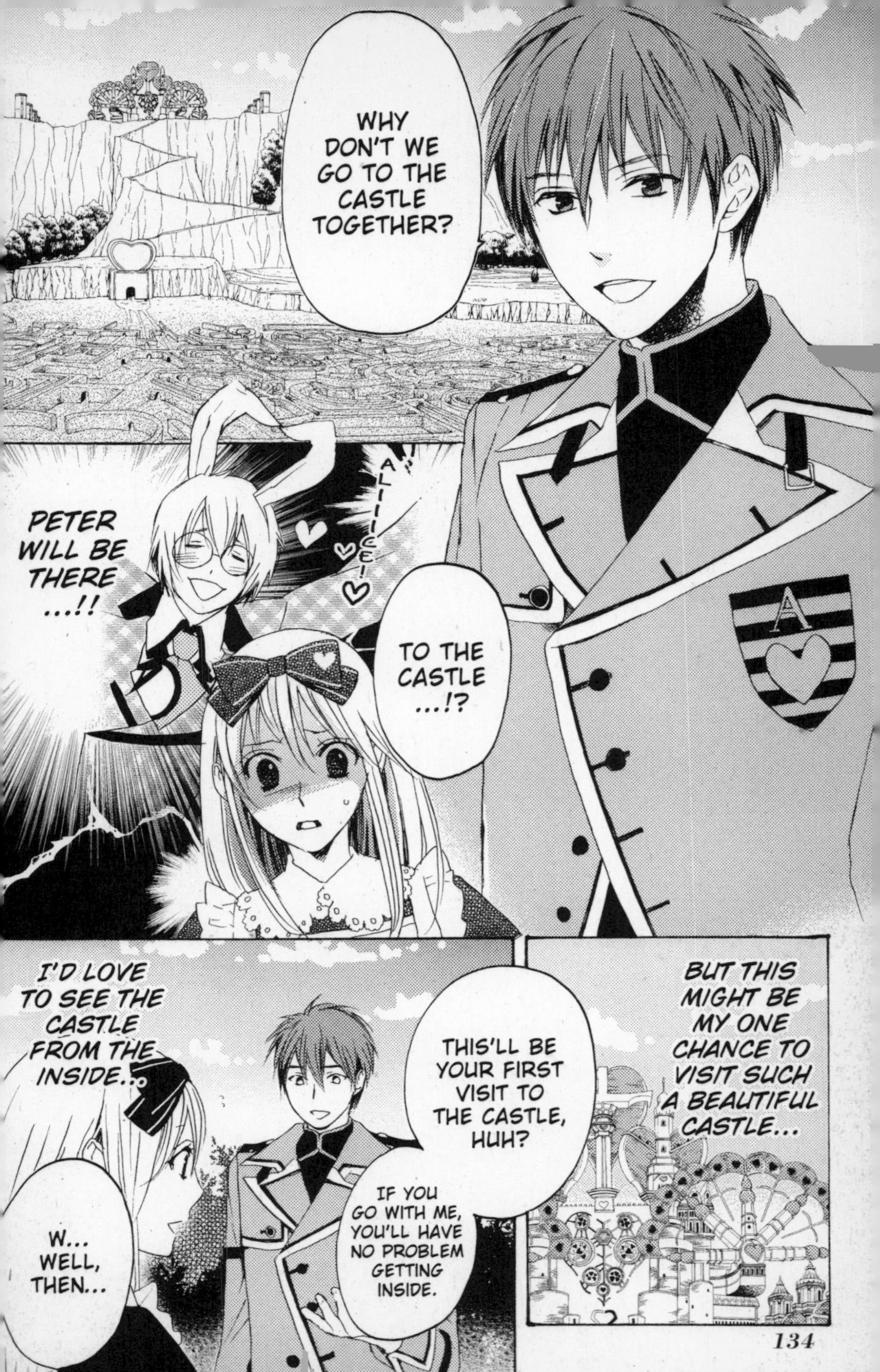
WHY DON'T WE GO TO THE CASTLE TOGETHER?
TO THE CASTLE ...!?
ALIIICE!
PETER WILL BE THERE ...!!
BUT THIS MIGHT BE MY ONE CHANCE TO VISIT SUCH A BEAUTIFUL CASTLE...
THIS'LL BE YOUR FIRST VISIT TO THE CASTLE, HUH?
IF YOU GO WITH ME, YOU'LL HAVE NO PROBLEM GETTING INSIDE.
I'D LOVE TO SEE THE CASTLE FROM THE INSIDE...
W... WELL, THEN...

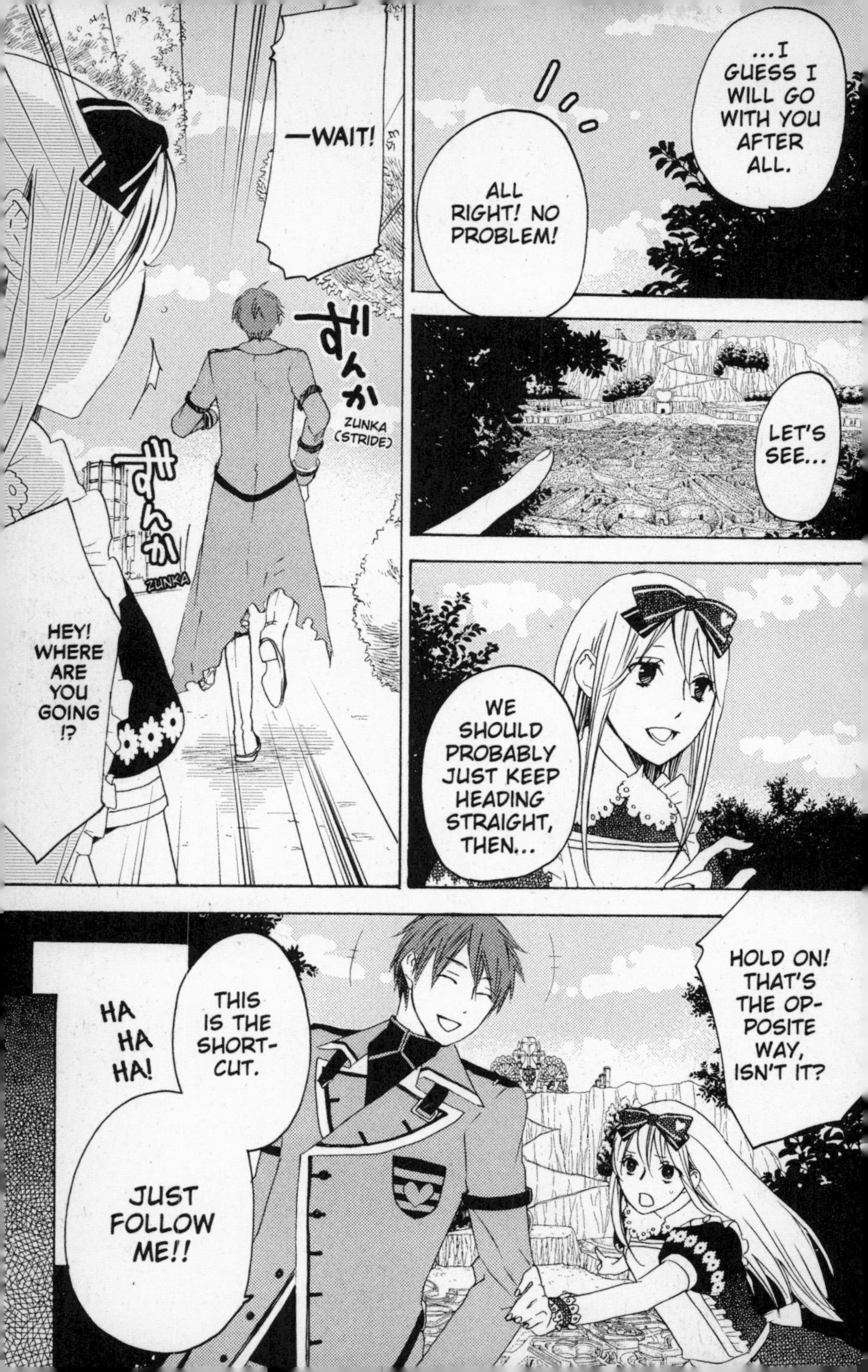
...I GUESS I WILL GO WITH YOU AFTER ALL.
ALL RIGHT! NO PROBLEM!
LET'S SEE...
WE SHOULD PROBABLY JUST KEEP HEADING STRAIGHT, THEN...
—WAIT!
ずんか
ZUNKA (STRIDE)
ずんか
ZUNKA
HEY! WHERE ARE YOU GOING!?
HOLD ON! THAT'S THE OP-POSITE WAY, ISN'T IT?
THIS IS THE SHORT-CUT.
HA HA HA!
JUST FOLLOW ME!!

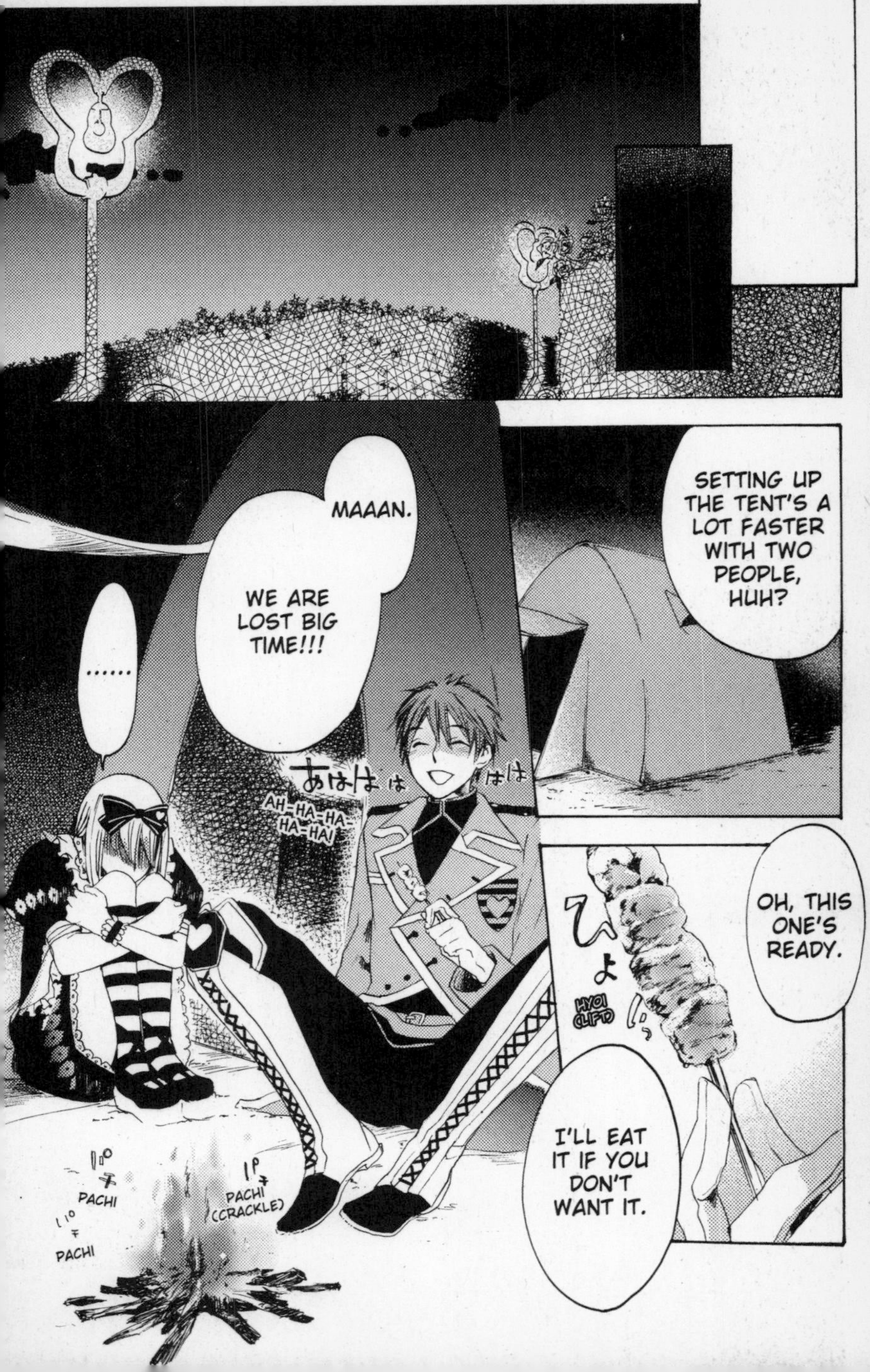
SETTING UP THE TENT'S A LOT FASTER WITH TWO PEOPLE, HUH?
OH, THIS ONE'S READY.
HYOI (LIFT)
I'LL EAT IT IF YOU DON'T WANT IT.
MAAAN.
WE ARE LOST BIG TIME!!!
AH-HA-HA-HA-HA!
......
PACHI (CRACKLE)
PACHI
PACHI

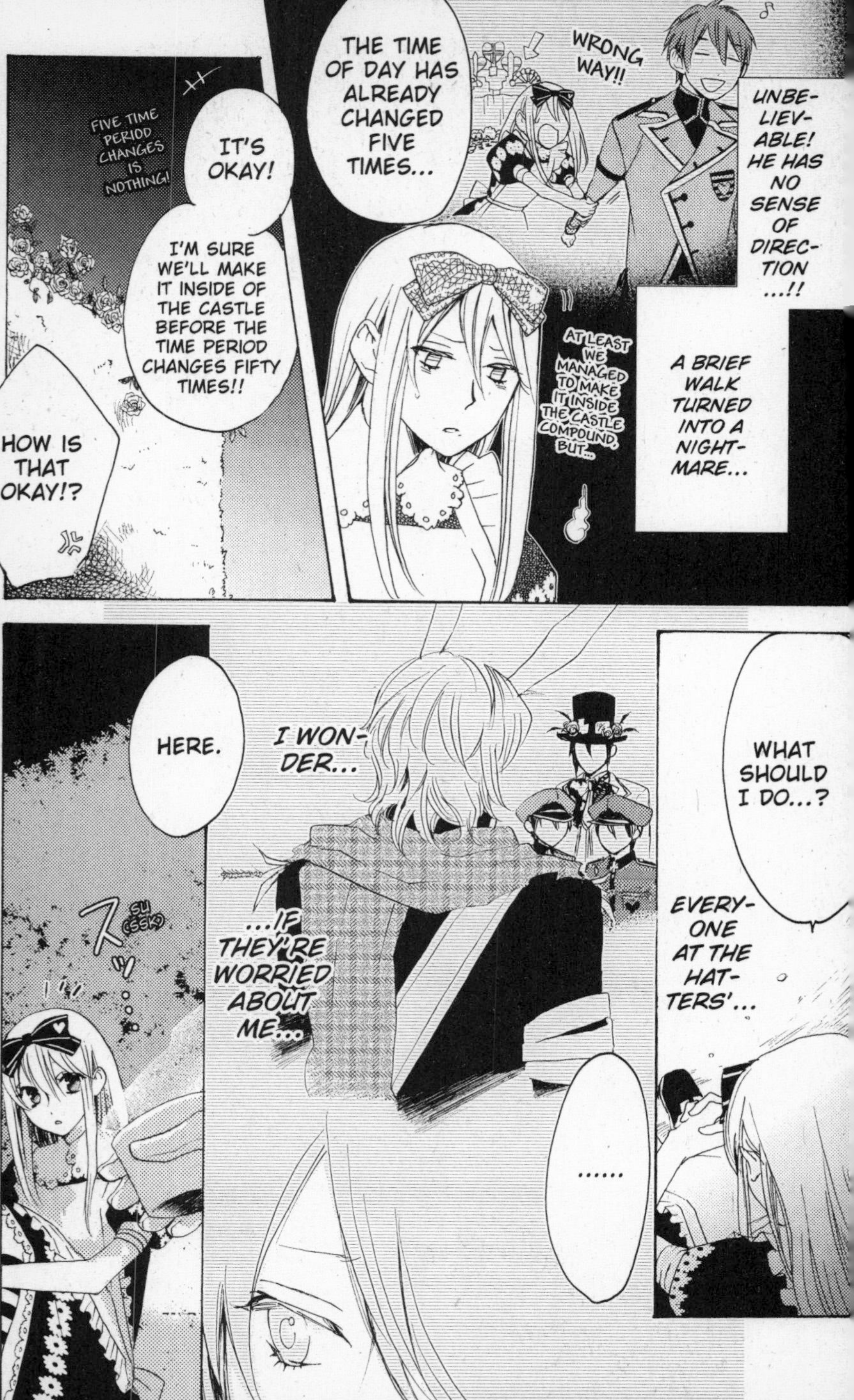
WRONG WAY!!
UNBELIEVABLE! HE HAS NO SENSE OF DIRECTION...!!
THE TIME OF DAY HAS ALREADY CHANGED FIVE TIMES...
A BRIEF WALK TURNED INTO A NIGHTMARE...
AT LEAST WE MANAGED TO MAKE IT INSIDE THE CASTLE COMPOUND, BUT...
IT'S OKAY!
FIVE TIME PERIOD CHANGES IS NOTHING!
I'M SURE WE'LL MAKE IT INSIDE OF THE CASTLE BEFORE THE TIME PERIOD CHANGES FIFTY TIMES!!
HOW IS THAT OKAY!?
WHAT SHOULD I DO...?
EVERYONE AT THE HATTERS'...
I WONDER...
...IF THEY'RE WORRIED ABOUT ME...
......
HERE.
SU (SSK)

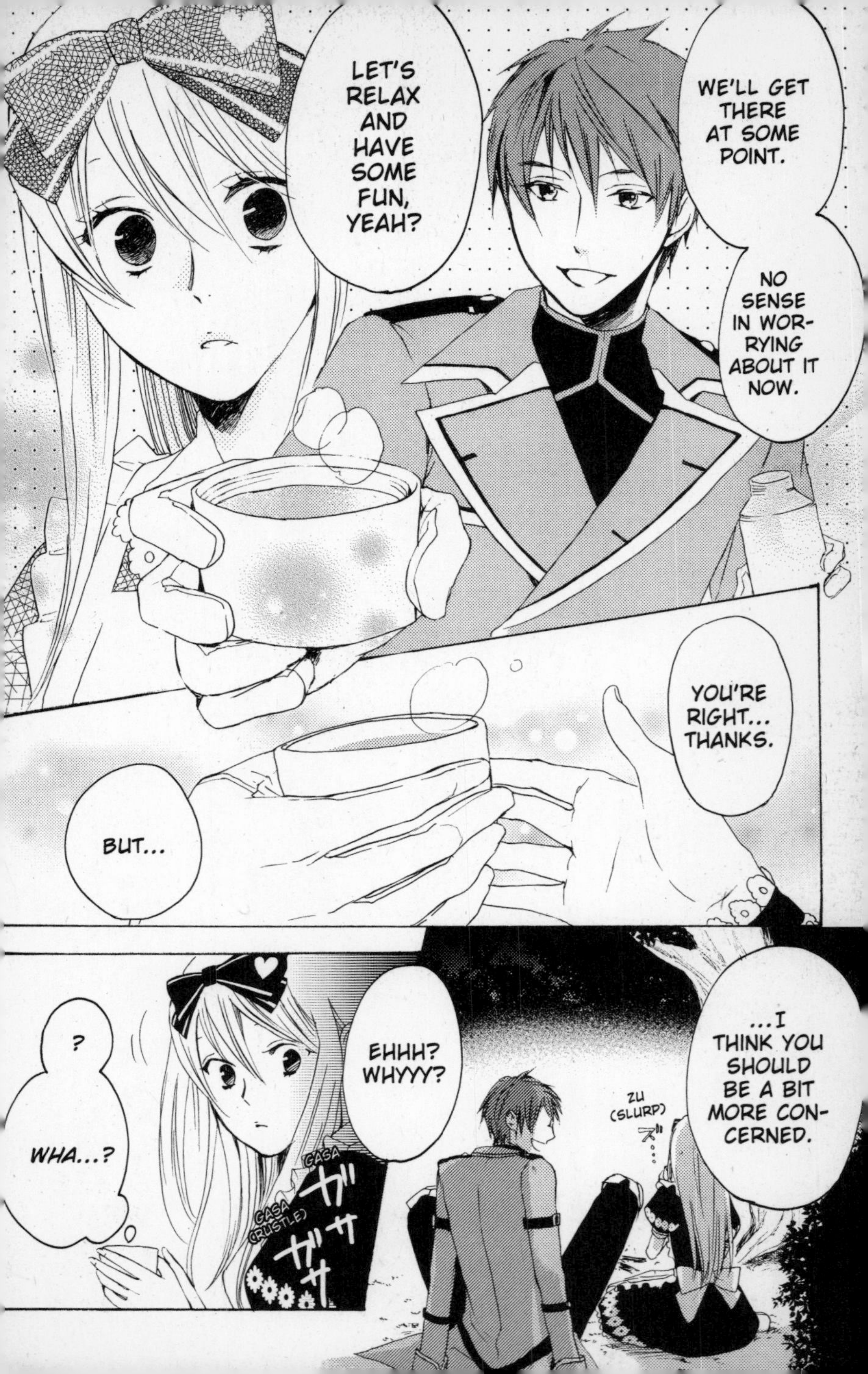
WE'LL GET THERE AT SOME POINT.
NO SENSE IN WORRYING ABOUT IT NOW.
LET'S RELAX AND HAVE SOME FUN, YEAH?
YOU'RE RIGHT... THANKS.
BUT...
...I THINK YOU SHOULD BE A BIT MORE CONCERNED.
ZU (SLURP)
EHHH? WHYYY?
GASA GASA (RUSTLE)
?
WHA...?

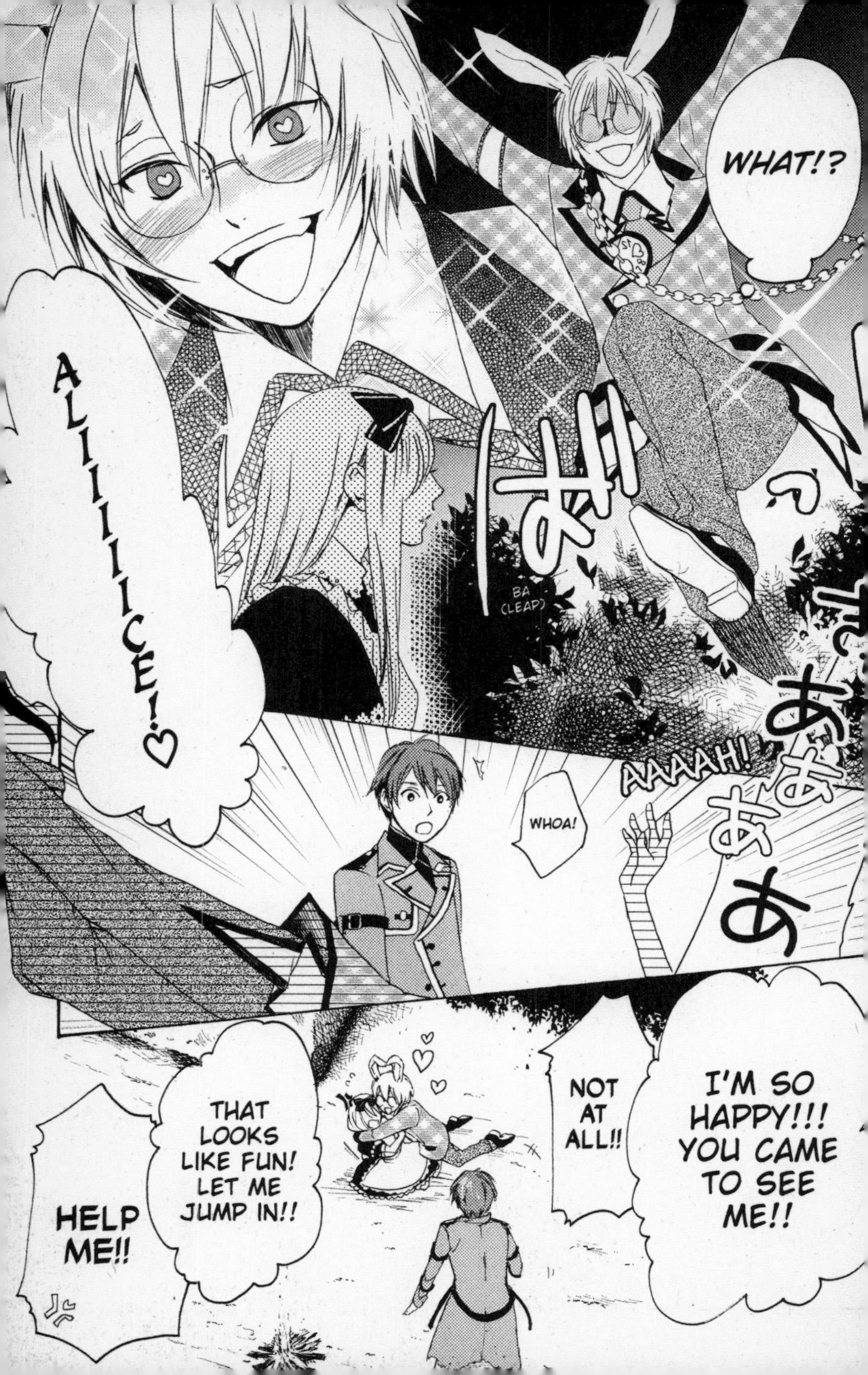

WHAT!?
ALIIIIICE!♡
ば
BA (LEAP)
あああ
AAAAH!
WHOA!
I'M SO HAPPY!!! YOU CAME TO SEE ME!!
NOT AT ALL!!
THAT LOOKS LIKE FUN! LET ME JUMP IN!!
HELP ME!!

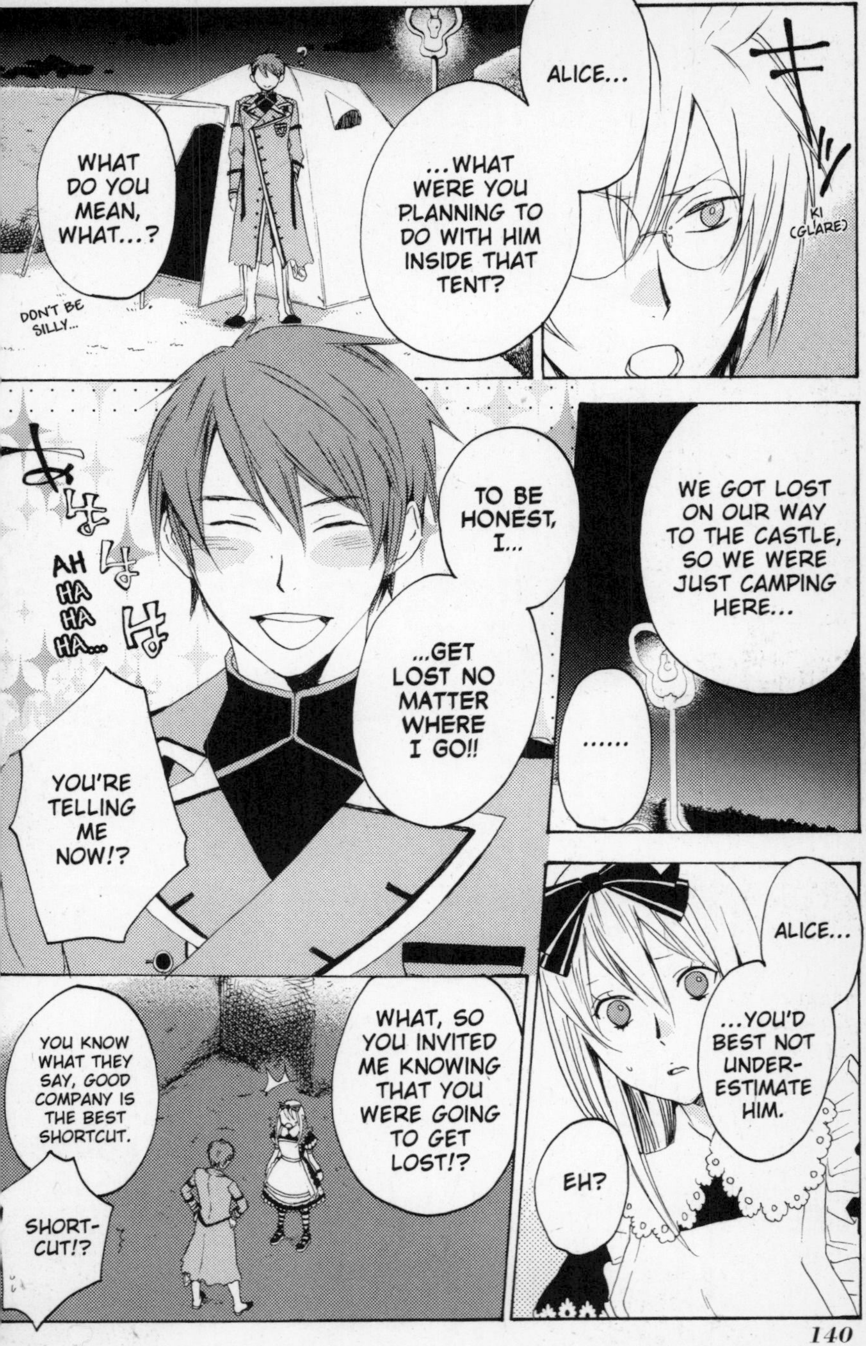
ALICE...
...WHAT WERE YOU PLANNING TO DO WITH HIM INSIDE THAT TENT?
KI (GLARE)
WHAT DO YOU MEAN, WHAT...?
DON'T BE SILLY...
WE GOT LOST ON OUR WAY TO THE CASTLE, SO WE WERE JUST CAMPING HERE...
......
TO BE HONEST, I...
...GET LOST NO MATTER WHERE I GO!!
AH HA HA HA...
YOU'RE TELLING ME NOW!?
ALICE...
...YOU'D BEST NOT UNDER-ESTIMATE HIM.
EH?
WHAT, SO YOU INVITED ME KNOWING THAT YOU WERE GOING TO GET LOST!?
YOU KNOW WHAT THEY SAY, GOOD COMPANY IS THE BEST SHORTCUT.
SHORT-CUT!?

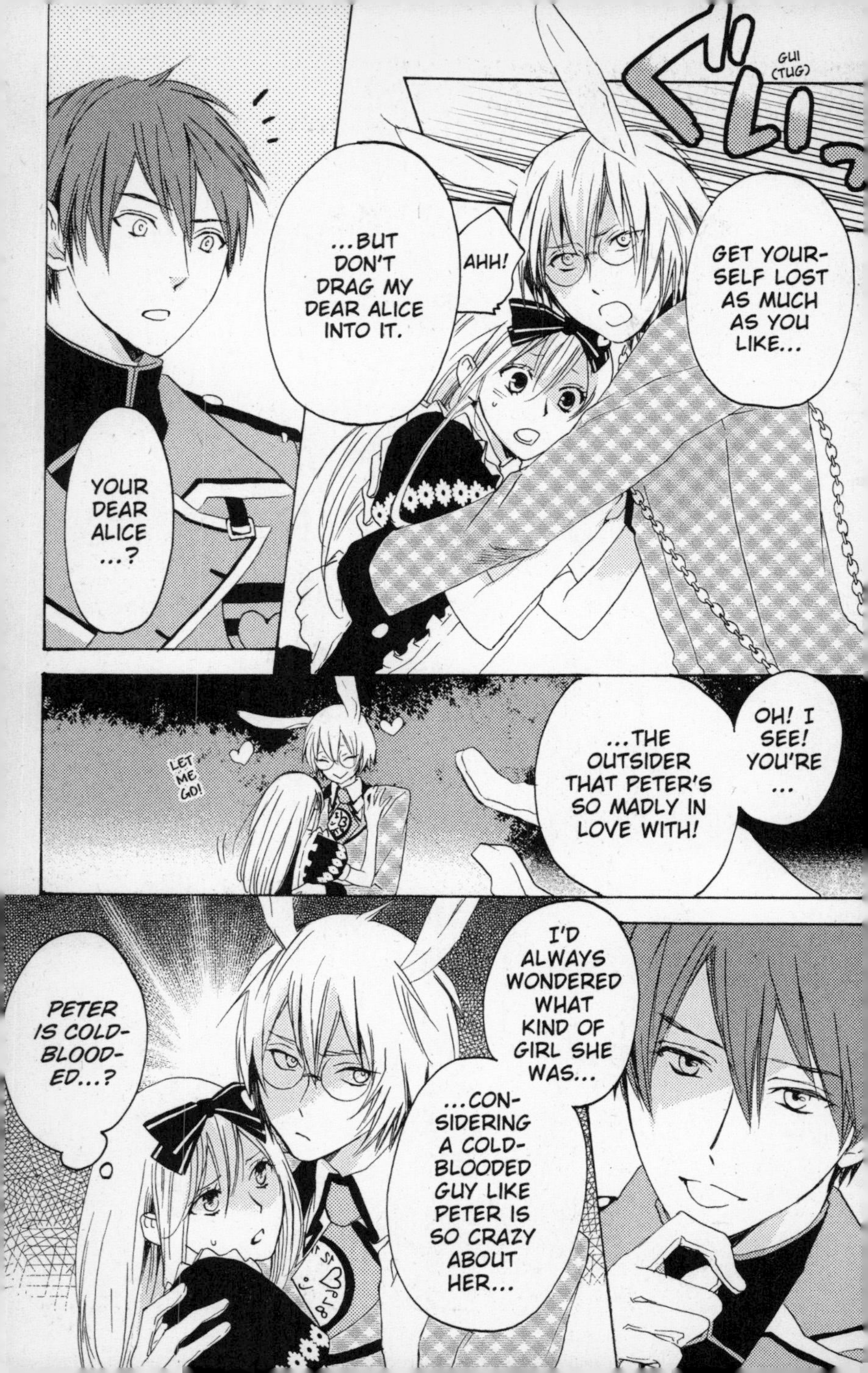
GUI (TUG)
GET YOUR-SELF LOST AS MUCH AS YOU LIKE...
AHH!
...BUT DON'T DRAG MY DEAR ALICE INTO IT.
YOUR DEAR ALICE ...?
OH! I SEE! YOU'RE ...
...THE OUTSIDER THAT PETER'S SO MADLY IN LOVE WITH!
LET ME GO!
I'D ALWAYS WONDERED WHAT KIND OF GIRL SHE WAS...
...CON-SIDERING A COLD-BLOODED GUY LIKE PETER IS SO CRAZY ABOUT HER...
PETER IS COLD-BLOOD-ED...?

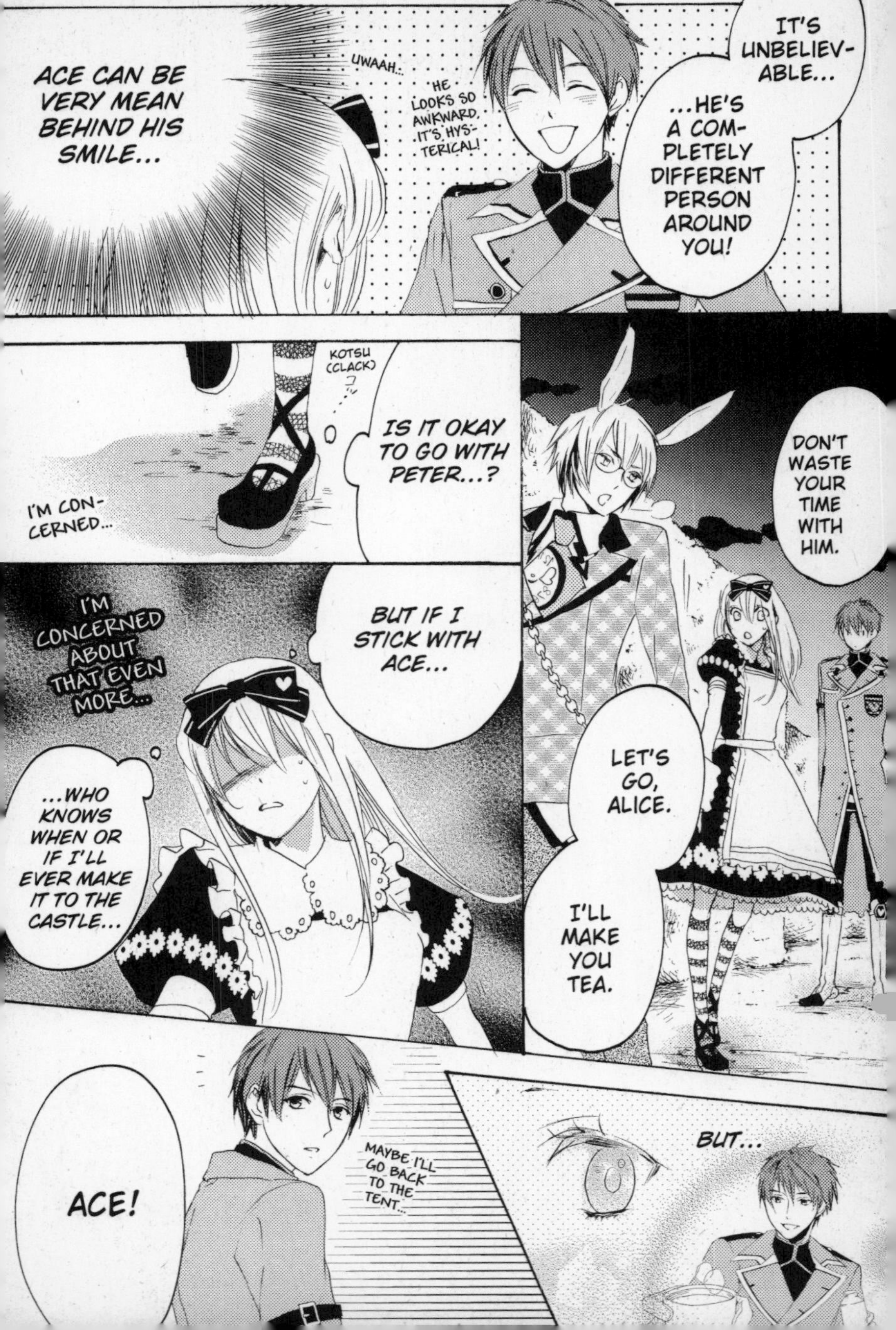
IT'S UNBELIEV-ABLE...
...HE'S A COMPLETELY DIFFERENT PERSON AROUND YOU!
HE LOOKS SO AWKWARD. IT'S HYSTERICAL!
UWAAH...
ACE CAN BE VERY MEAN BEHIND HIS SMILE...
DON'T WASTE YOUR TIME WITH HIM.
LET'S GO, ALICE.
I'LL MAKE YOU TEA.
KOTSU (CLACK)
IS IT OKAY TO GO WITH PETER...?
I'M CONCERNED...
BUT IF I STICK WITH ACE...
I'M CONCERNED ABOUT THAT EVEN MORE...
...WHO KNOWS WHEN OR IF I'LL EVER MAKE IT TO THE CASTLE...
BUT...
MAYBE I'LL GO BACK TO THE TENT...
ACE!

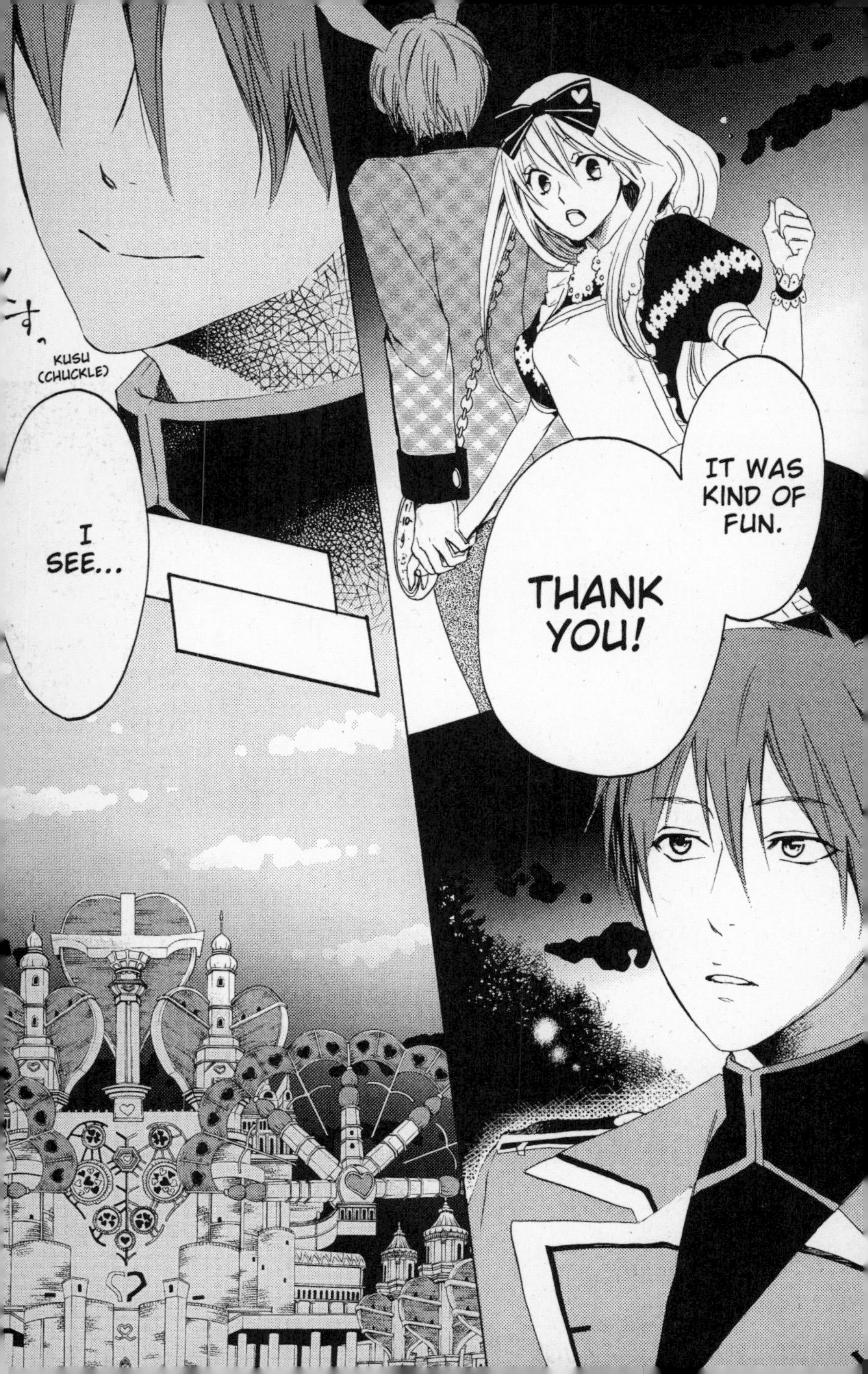
IT WAS KIND OF FUN.
THANK YOU!
くす、
KUSU (CHUCKLE)
I SEE...

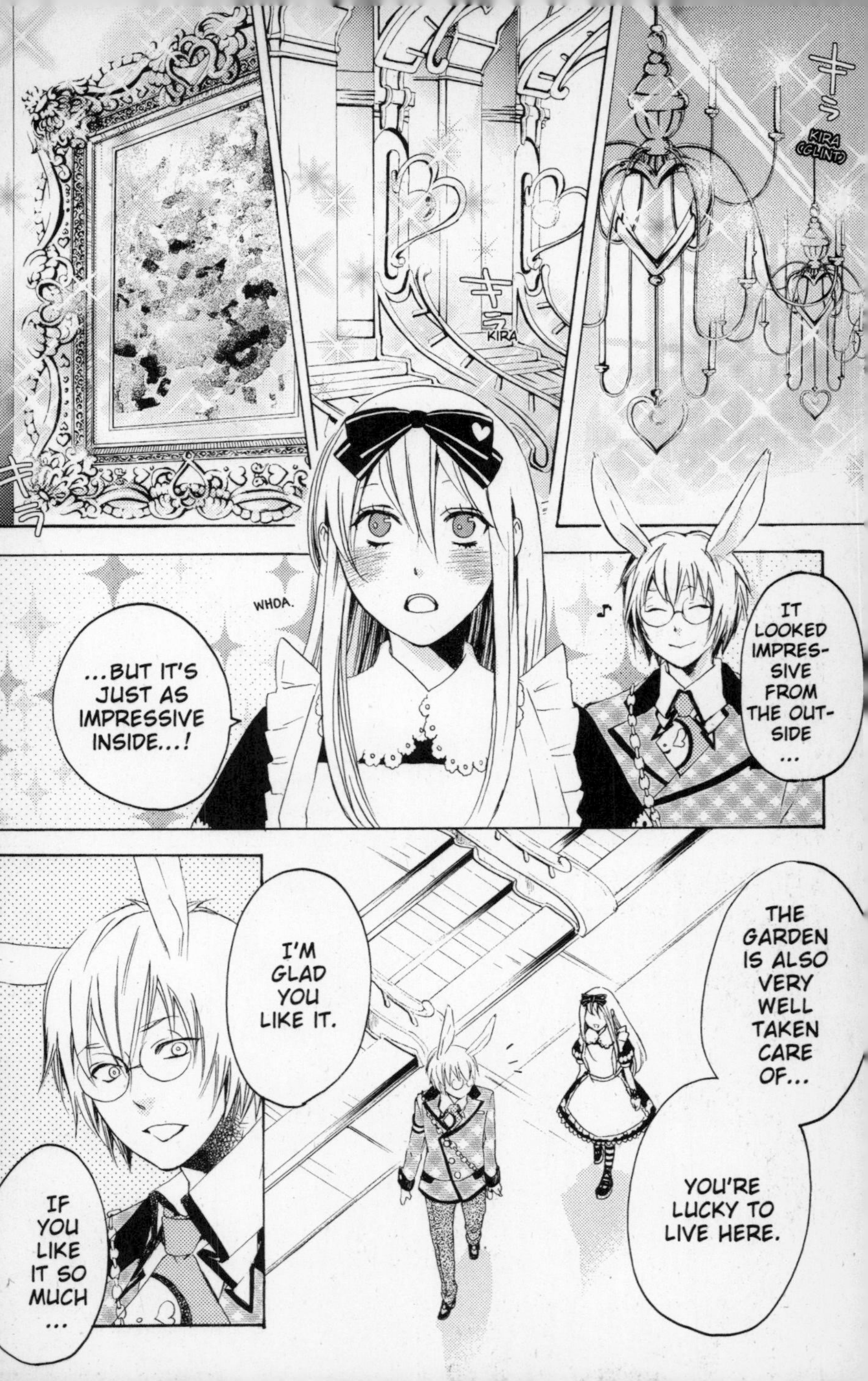
キラ
KIRA (GLINT)
キラ
KIRA
キラ
IT LOOKED IMPRESSIVE FROM THE OUTSIDE ...
WHOA.
...BUT IT'S JUST AS IMPRESSIVE INSIDE...!
THE GARDEN IS ALSO VERY WELL TAKEN CARE OF...
YOU'RE LUCKY TO LIVE HERE.
I'M GLAD YOU LIKE IT.
IF YOU LIKE IT SO MUCH ...

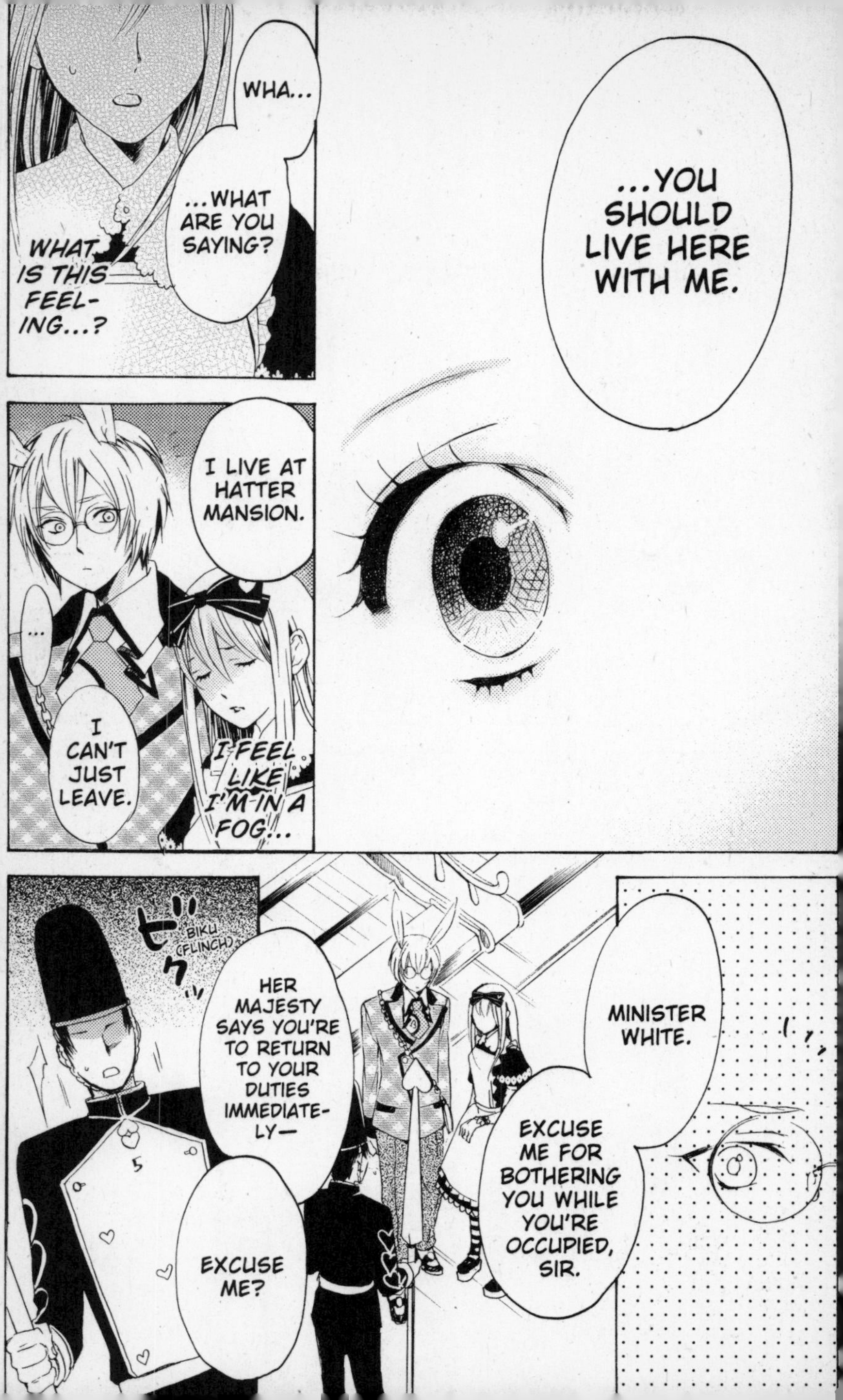
...YOU SHOULD LIVE HERE WITH ME.
WHA...
...WHAT ARE YOU SAYING?
WHAT IS THIS FEELING...?
I LIVE AT HATTER MANSION.
...
I CAN'T JUST LEAVE.
I FEEL LIKE I'M IN A FOG...
MINISTER WHITE.
EXCUSE ME FOR BOTHERING YOU WHILE YOU'RE OCCUPIED, SIR.
HER MAJESTY SAYS YOU'RE TO RETURN TO YOUR DUTIES IMMEDIATELY—
BIKU (FLINCH)
EXCUSE ME?

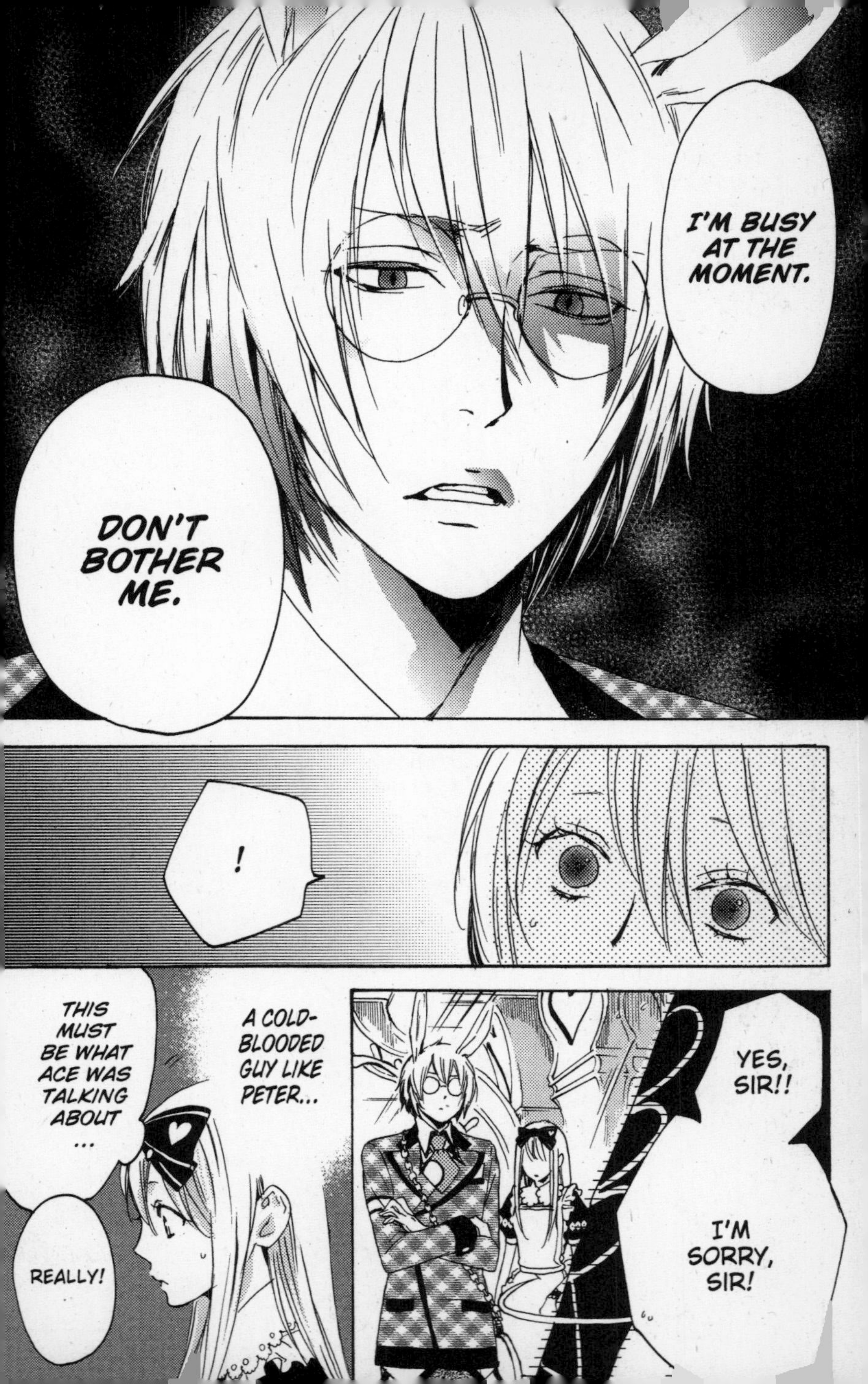
I'M BUSY AT THE MOMENT.
DON'T BOTHER ME.
!
YES, SIR!!
I'M SORRY, SIR!
A COLD-BLOODED GUY LIKE PETER...
THIS MUST BE WHAT ACE WAS TALKING ABOUT...
REALLY!

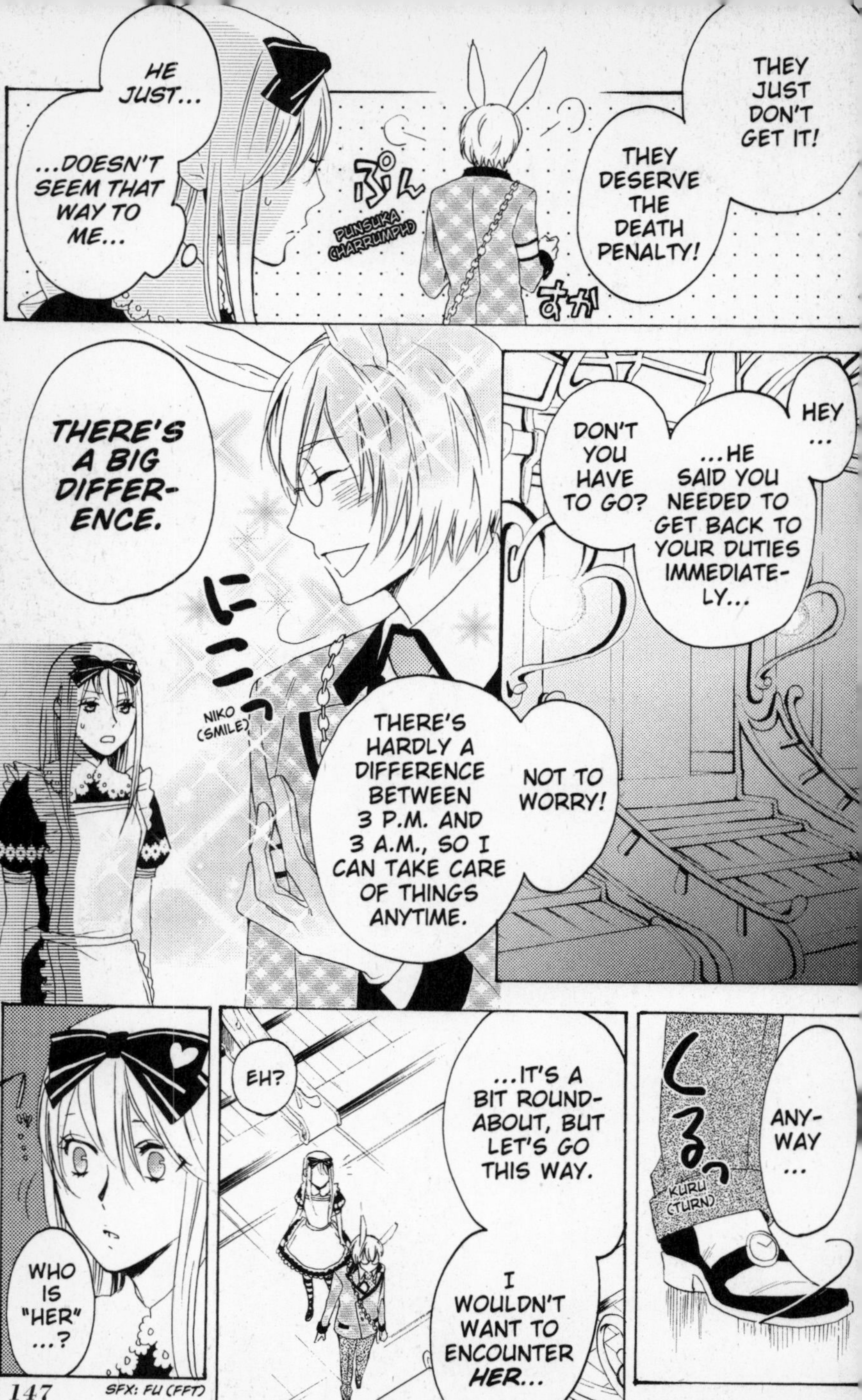
THEY JUST DON'T GET IT!
THEY DESERVE THE DEATH PENALTY!
PUNSUKA (HARRUMPH)
HE JUST...
...DOESN'T SEEM THAT WAY TO ME...
HEY ...
...HE SAID YOU NEEDED TO GET BACK TO YOUR DUTIES IMMEDIATE-LY...
DON'T YOU HAVE TO GO?
NOT TO WORRY!
THERE'S HARDLY A DIFFERENCE BETWEEN 3 P.M. AND 3 A.M., SO I CAN TAKE CARE OF THINGS ANYTIME.
THERE'S A BIG DIFFER-ENCE.
NIKO (SMILE)
ANY-WAY ...
KURU (TURN)
...IT'S A BIT ROUND-ABOUT, BUT LET'S GO THIS WAY.
I WOULDN'T WANT TO ENCOUNTER *HER*...
EH?
WHO IS "HER" ...?
SFX: FU (FFT)

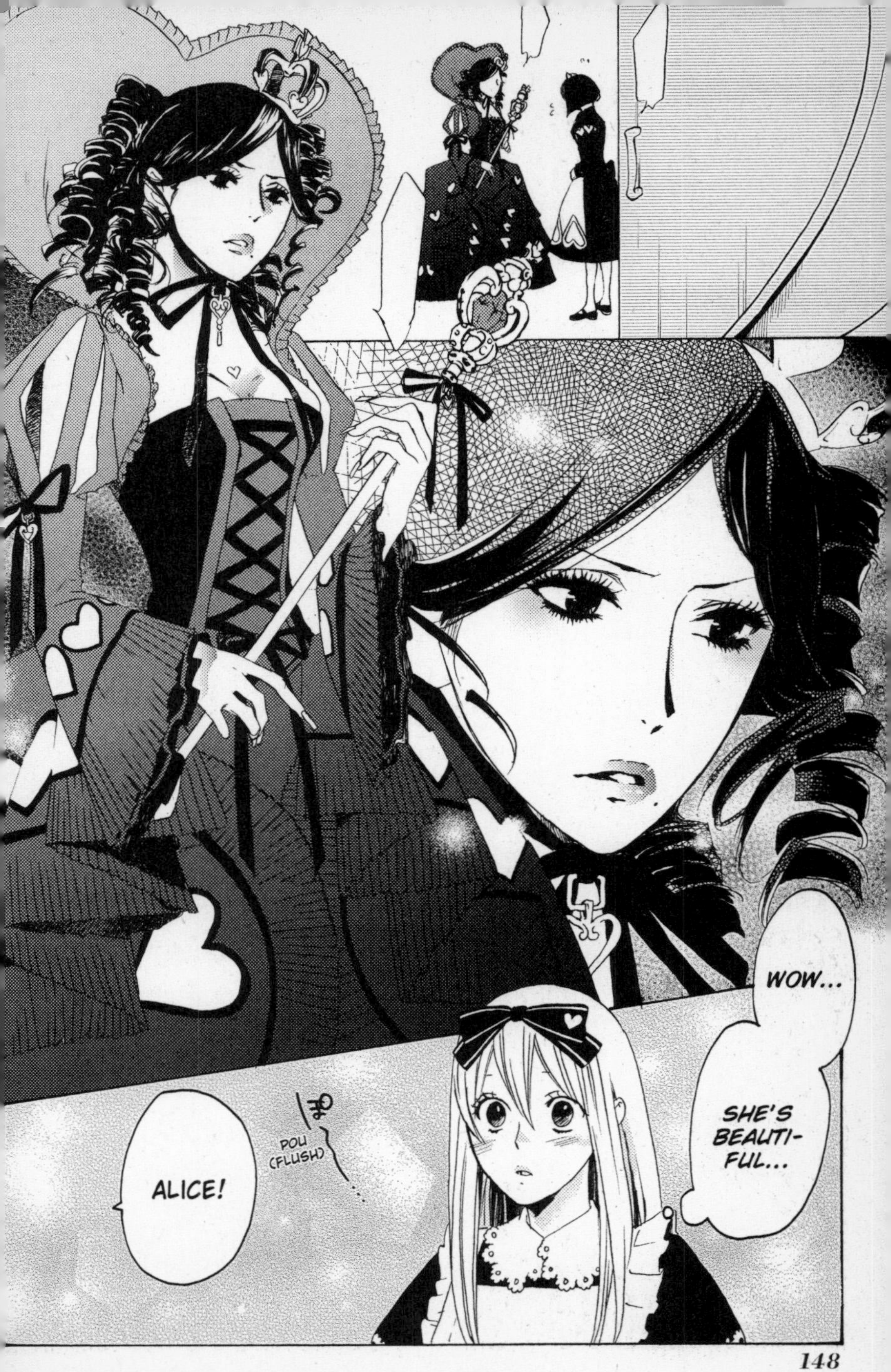
WOW...
SHE'S BEAUTI-FUL...
POU (FLUSH)
ALICE!

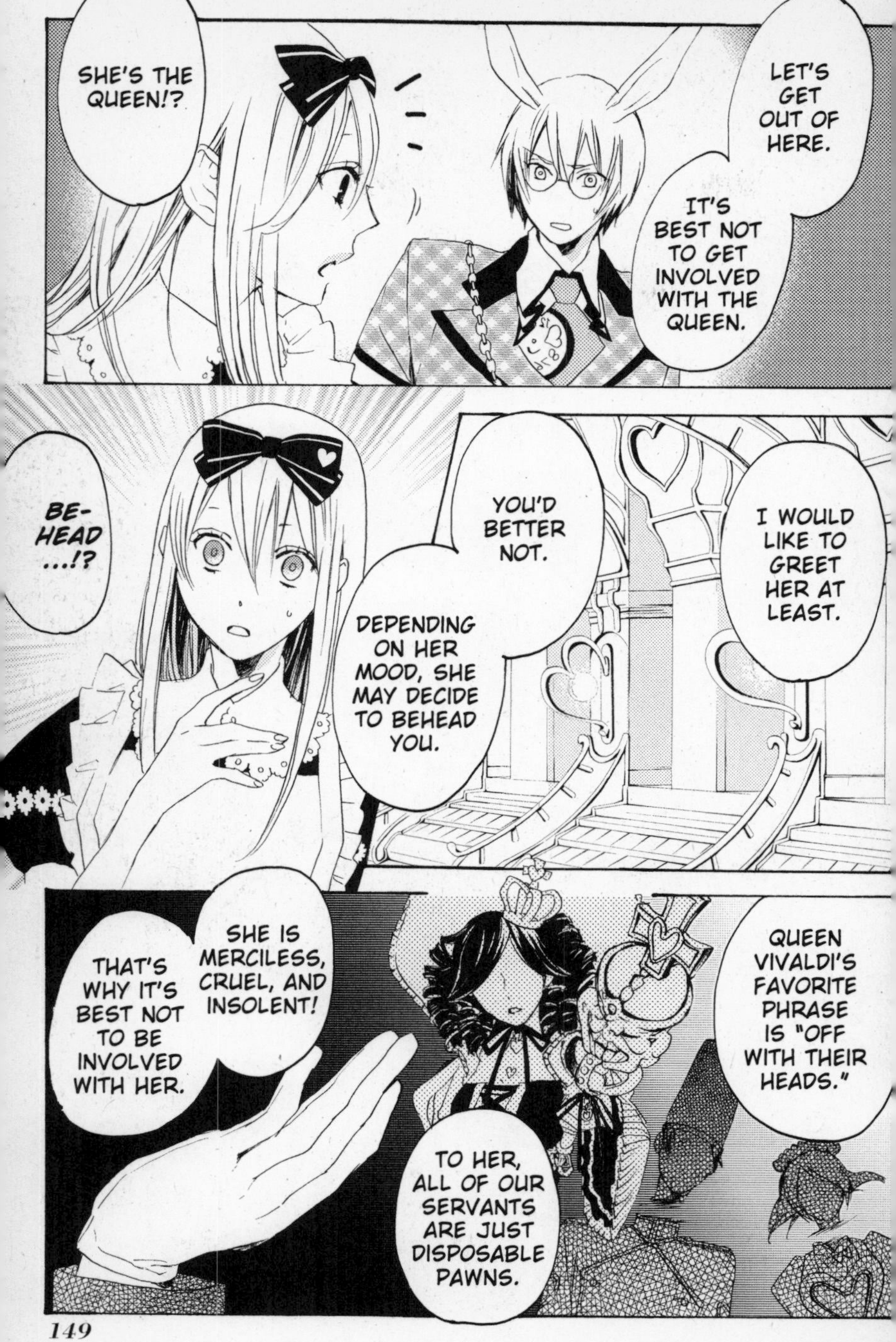
LET'S GET OUT OF HERE.
IT'S BEST NOT TO GET INVOLVED WITH THE QUEEN.
SHE'S THE QUEEN!?
I WOULD LIKE TO GREET HER AT LEAST.
YOU'D BETTER NOT.
DEPENDING ON HER MOOD, SHE MAY DECIDE TO BEHEAD YOU.
BE-HEAD...!?
QUEEN VIVALDI'S FAVORITE PHRASE IS "OFF WITH THEIR HEADS."
TO HER, ALL OF OUR SERVANTS ARE JUST DISPOSABLE PAWNS.
SHE IS MERCILESS, CRUEL, AND INSOLENT!
THAT'S WHY IT'S BEST NOT TO BE INVOLVED WITH HER.

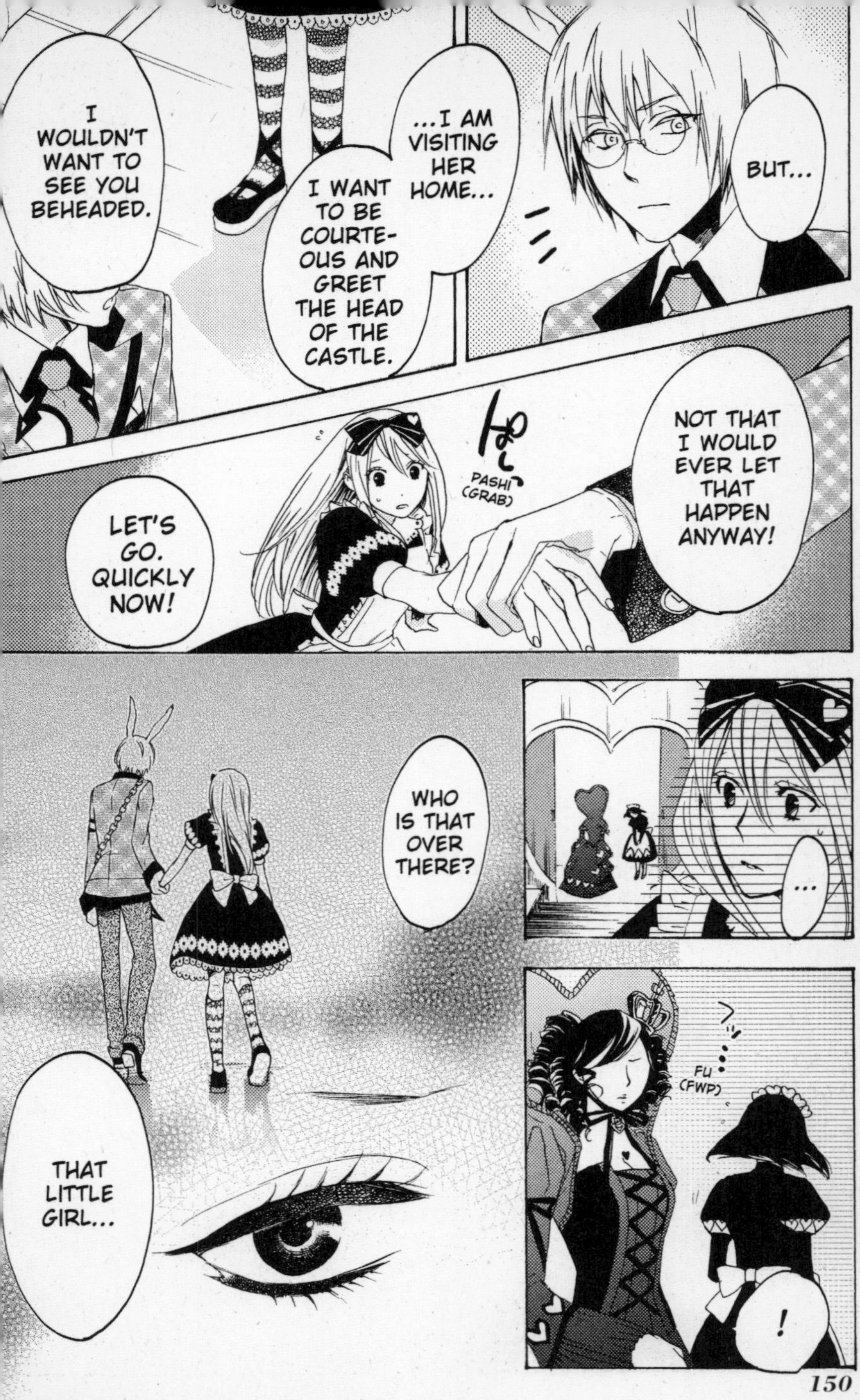
BUT...
...I AM VISITING HER HOME...
I WANT TO BE COURTEOUS AND GREET THE HEAD OF THE CASTLE.
I WOULDN'T WANT TO SEE YOU BEHEADED.
NOT THAT I WOULD EVER LET THAT HAPPEN ANYWAY!
PASHI (GRAB)
LET'S GO. QUICKLY NOW!
...
FU (FWP)
!
WHO IS THAT OVER THERE?
THAT LITTLE GIRL...

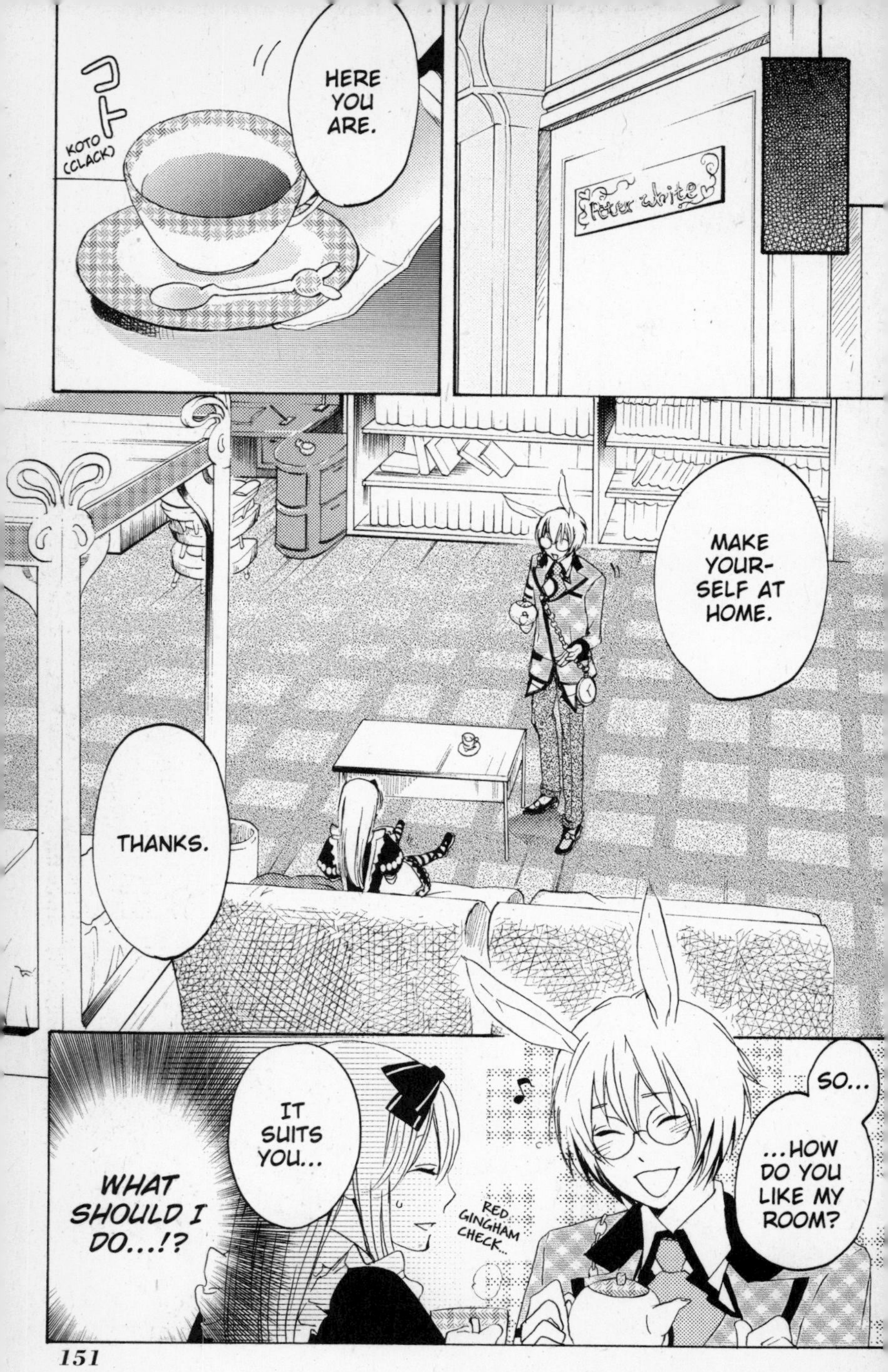
Peter white
HERE YOU ARE.
コト
KOTO (CLACK)
MAKE YOUR-SELF AT HOME.
THANKS.
SO...
...HOW DO YOU LIKE MY ROOM?
RED GINGHAM CHECK...
IT SUITS YOU...
WHAT SHOULD I DO...!?

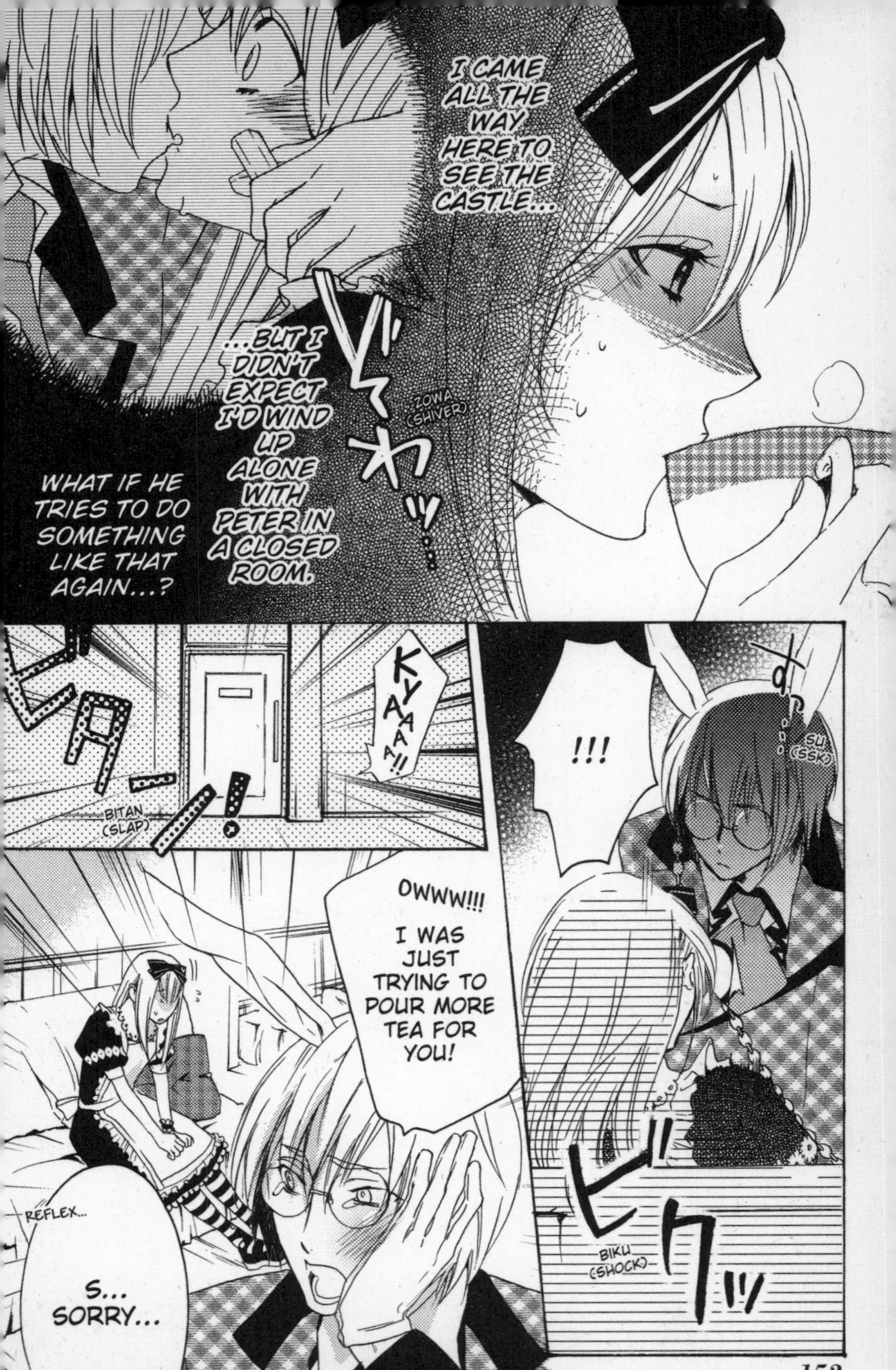
I CAME ALL THE WAY HERE TO SEE THE CASTLE...
...BUT I DIDN'T EXPECT I'D WIND UP ALONE WITH PETER IN A CLOSED ROOM.
ZOWA (SHIVER)
WHAT IF HE TRIES TO DO SOMETHING LIKE THAT AGAIN...?
SU (SSK)
!!!
BIKU (SHOCK)
KYAAAAA!!
BITAN (SLAP)
OWWW!!!
I WAS JUST TRYING TO POUR MORE TEA FOR YOU!
REFLEX...
S... SORRY...

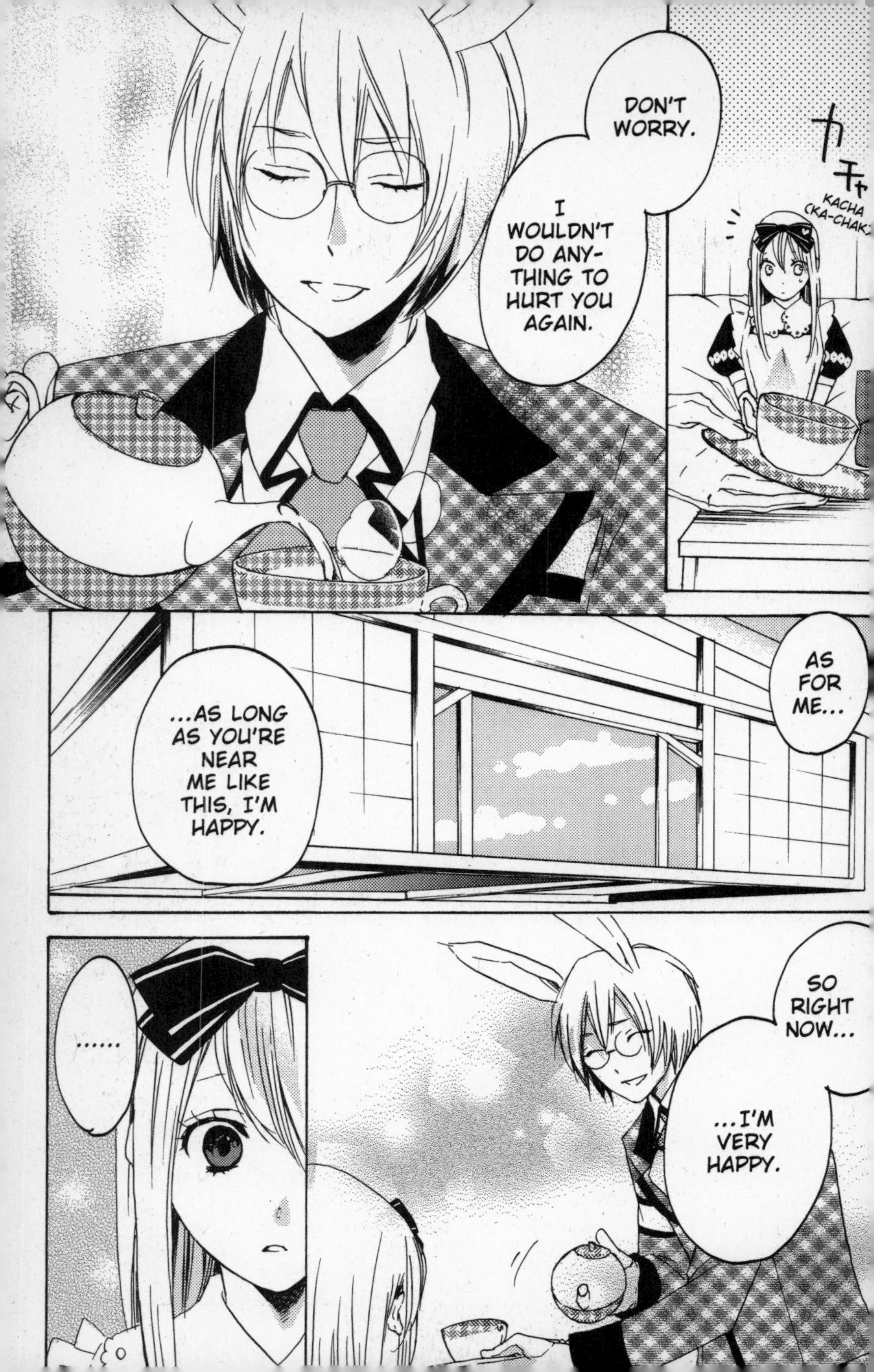
カチャ
KACHA (KA-CHAK)
DON'T WORRY.
I WOULDN'T DO ANY-THING TO HURT YOU AGAIN.
AS FOR ME...
...AS LONG AS YOU'RE NEAR ME LIKE THIS, I'M HAPPY.
SO RIGHT NOW...
...I'M VERY HAPPY.
......

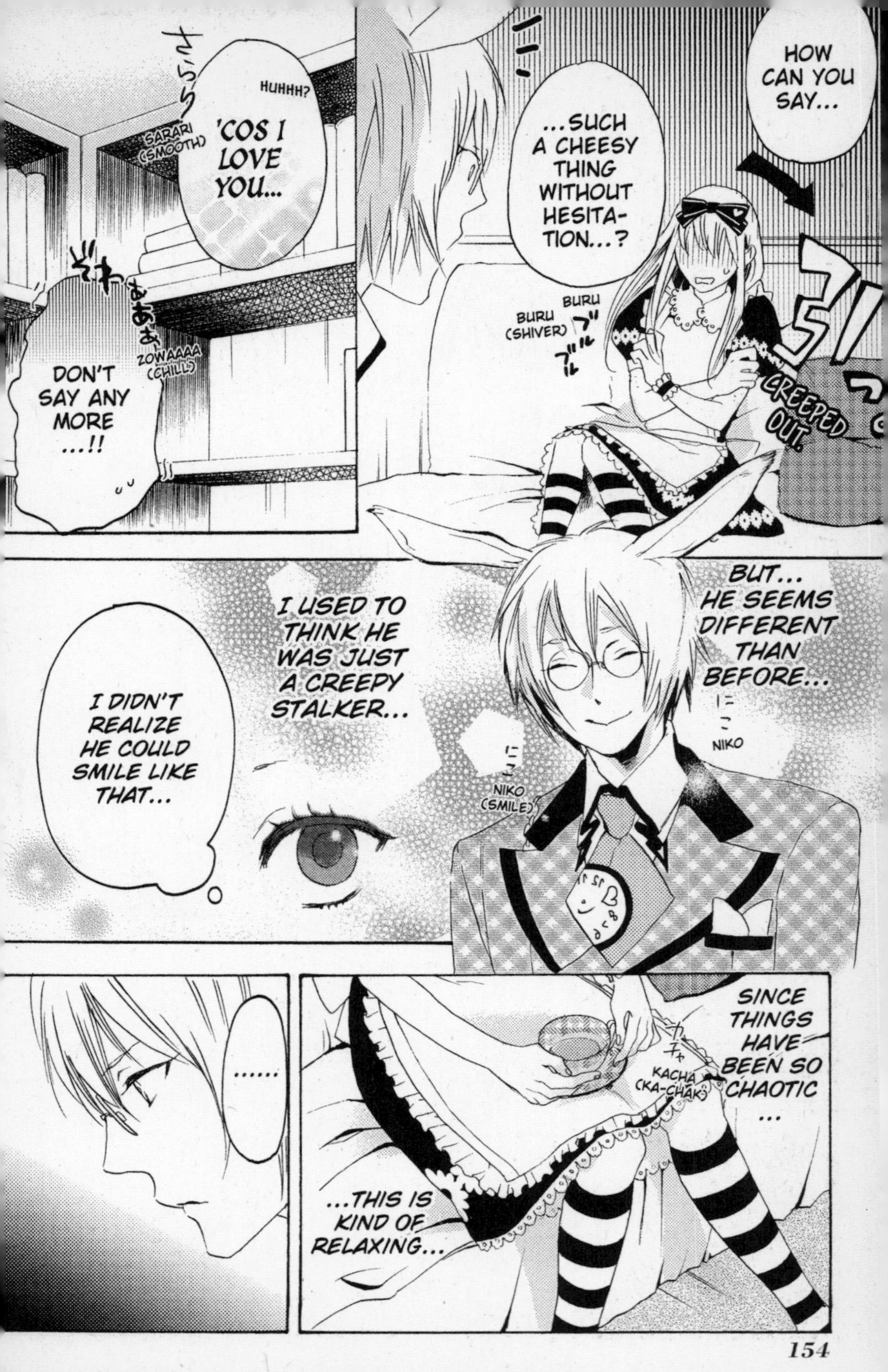
HOW CAN YOU SAY...
...SUCH A CHEESY THING WITHOUT HESITATION...?
BURU BURU (SHIVER)
CREEPED OUT.
HUHHH?
'COS I LOVE YOU...
SARARI (SMOOTH)
ZOWAAAA (CHILL)
DON'T SAY ANY MORE ...!!
BUT... HE SEEMS DIFFERENT THAN BEFORE...
NIKO
NIKO (SMILE)
I USED TO THINK HE WAS JUST A CREEPY STALKER...
I DIDN'T REALIZE HE COULD SMILE LIKE THAT...
SINCE THINGS HAVE BEEN SO CHAOTIC ...
KACHA (KA-CHAK)
...THIS IS KIND OF RELAXING...
......

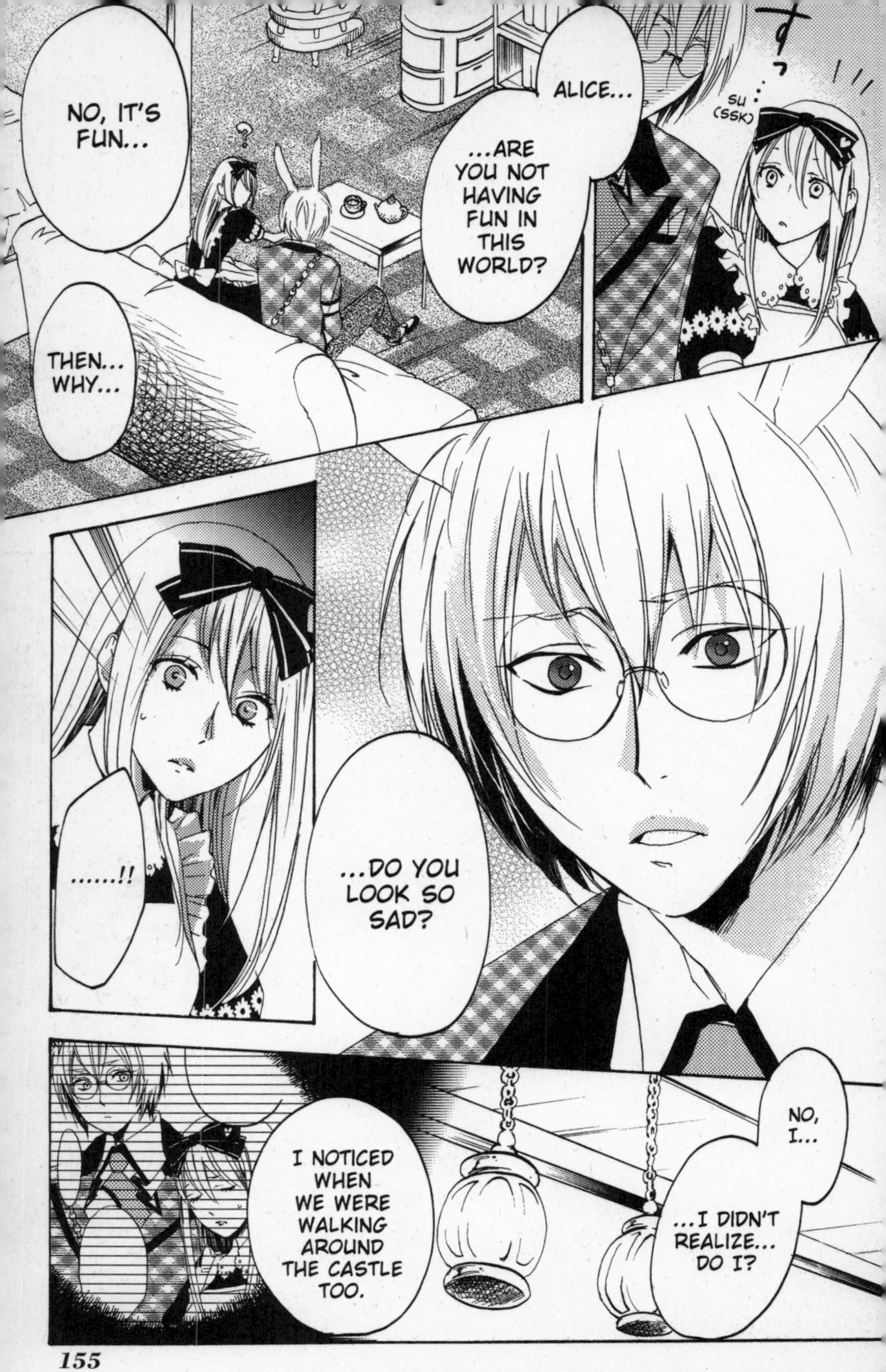
すっ
SU (SSK)
ALICE...
...ARE YOU NOT HAVING FUN IN THIS WORLD?
NO, IT'S FUN...
THEN... WHY...
...DO YOU LOOK SO SAD?
......!!
NO, I...
...I DIDN'T REALIZE... DO I?
I NOTICED WHEN WE WERE WALKING AROUND THE CASTLE TOO.

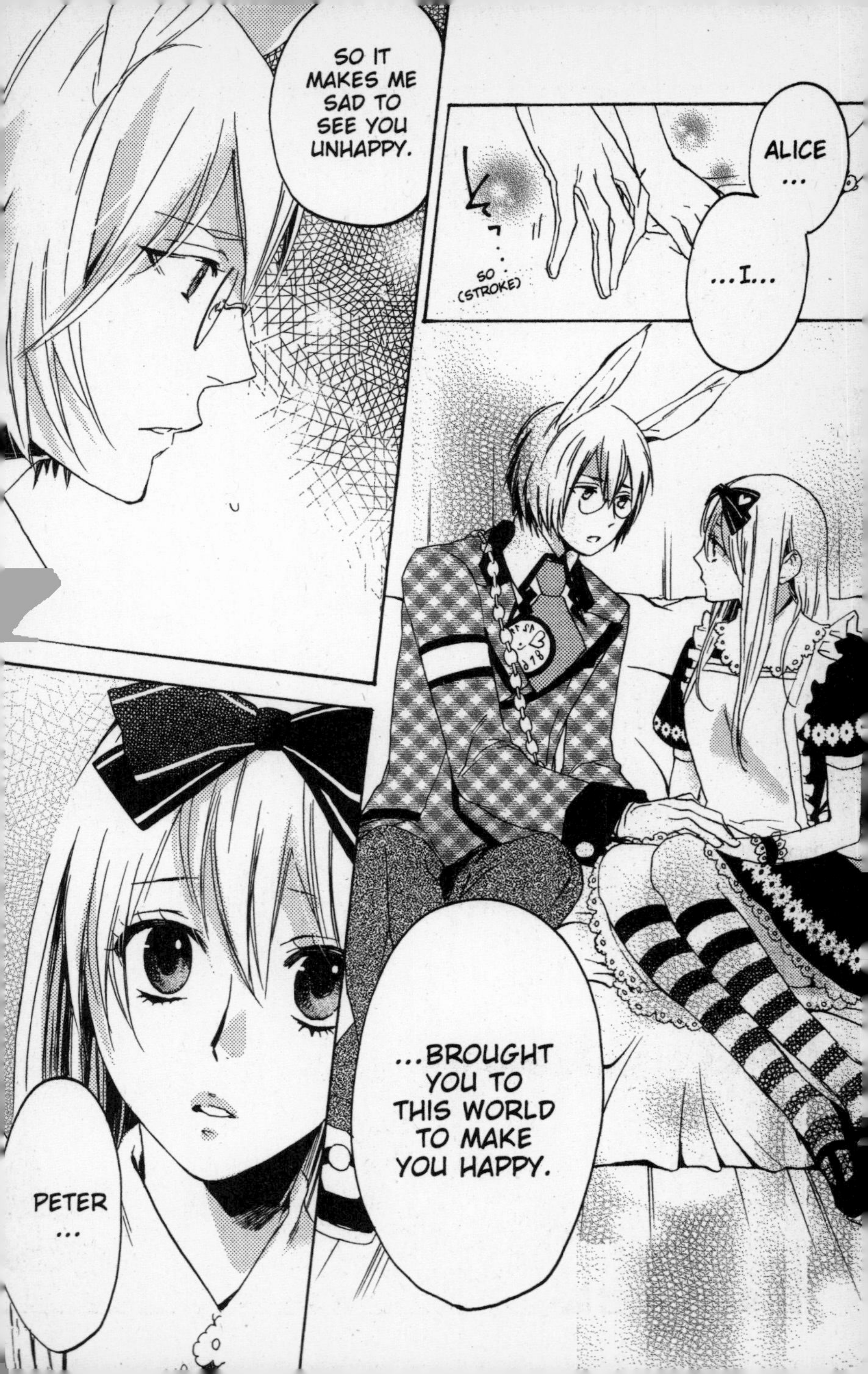
ALICE ...
...I...
SO (STROKE)
...BROUGHT YOU TO THIS WORLD TO MAKE YOU HAPPY.
SO IT MAKES ME SAD TO SEE YOU UNHAPPY.
PETER ...

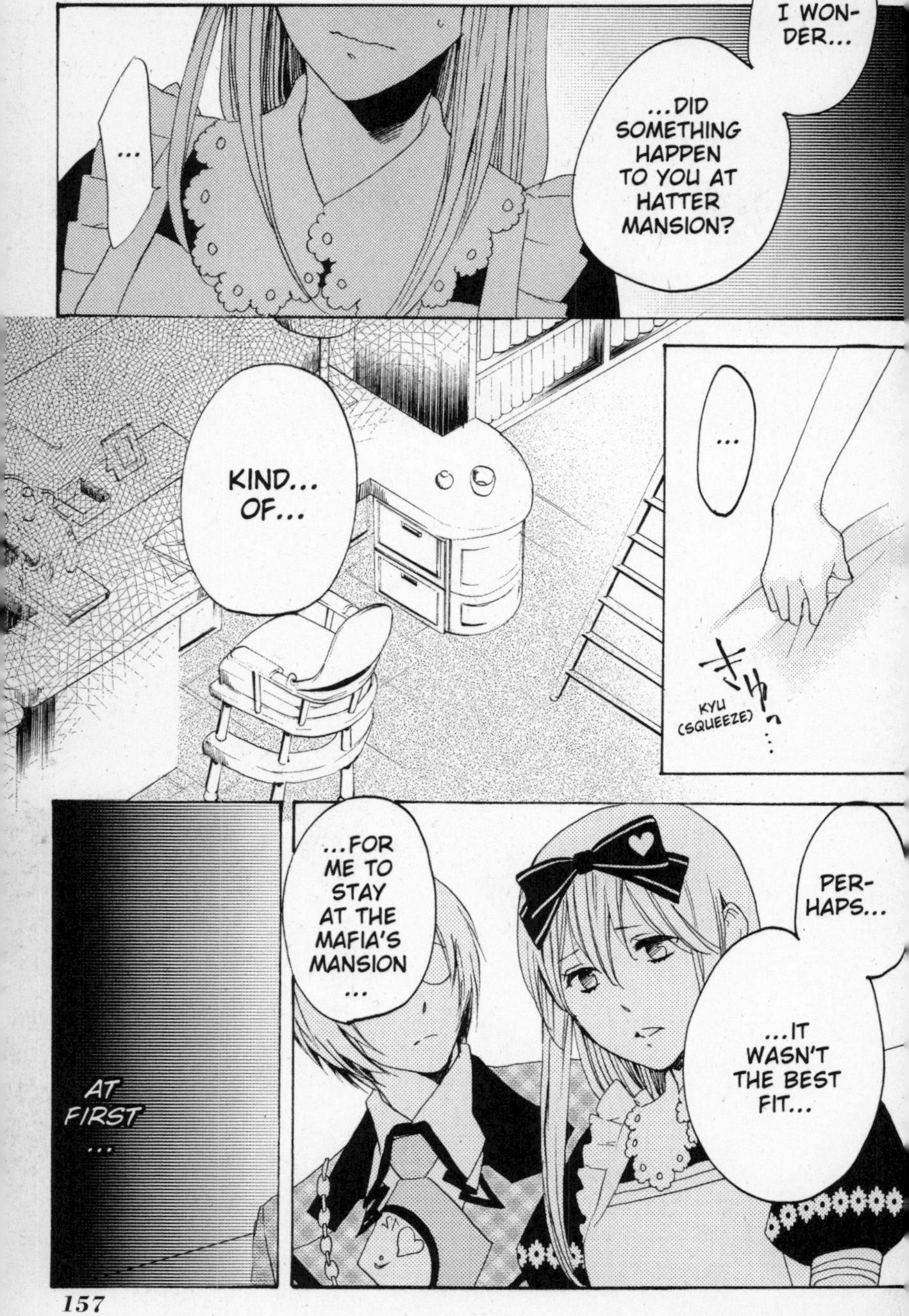
I WONDER...
...DID SOMETHING HAPPEN TO YOU AT HATTER MANSION?
...
...
KYU (SQUEEZE)
KIND... OF...
PERHAPS...
...IT WASN'T THE BEST FIT...
...FOR ME TO STAY AT THE MAFIA'S MANSION...
AT FIRST...

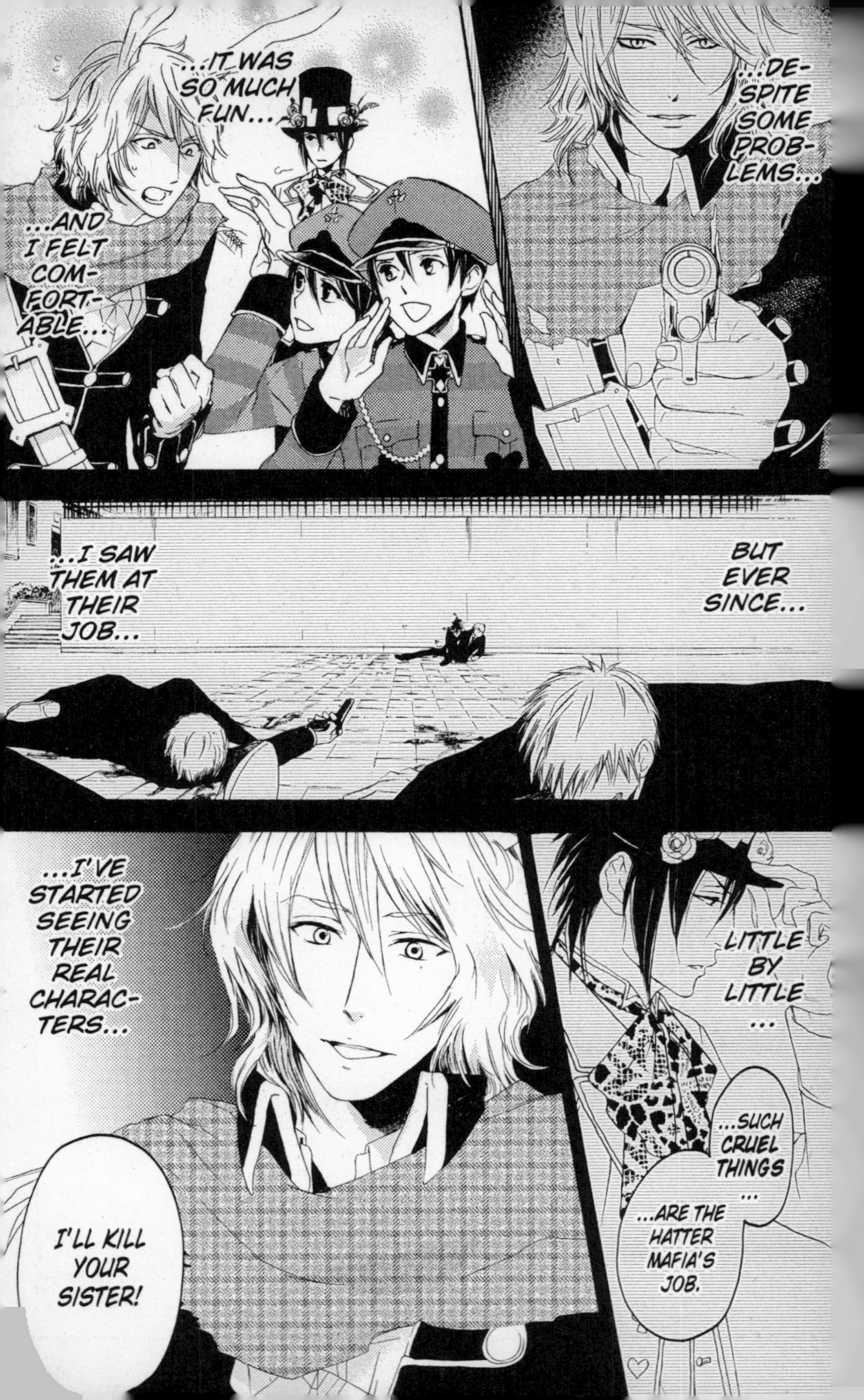
...DE-SPITE SOME PROB-LEMS...
...IT WAS SO MUCH FUN...
...AND I FELT COM-FORT-ABLE...
BUT EVER SINCE...
...I SAW THEM AT THEIR JOB...
LITTLE BY LITTLE...
...SUCH CRUEL THINGS...
...ARE THE HATTER MAFIA'S JOB.
...I'VE STARTED SEEING THEIR REAL CHARAC-TERS...
I'LL KILL YOUR SISTER!

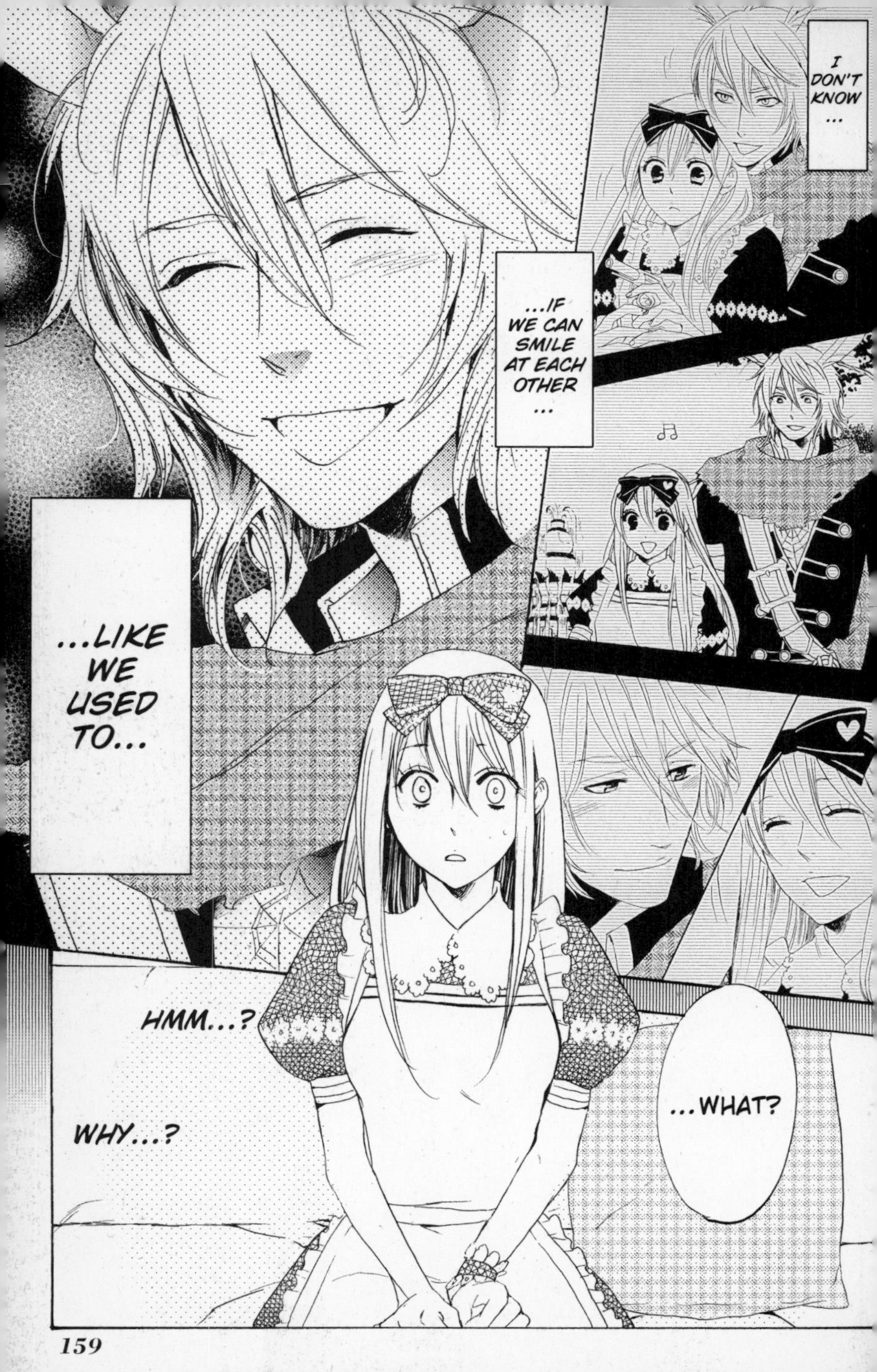
I DON'T KNOW...
...IF WE CAN SMILE AT EACH OTHER...
...LIKE WE USED TO...
...WHAT?
HMM...?
WHY...?

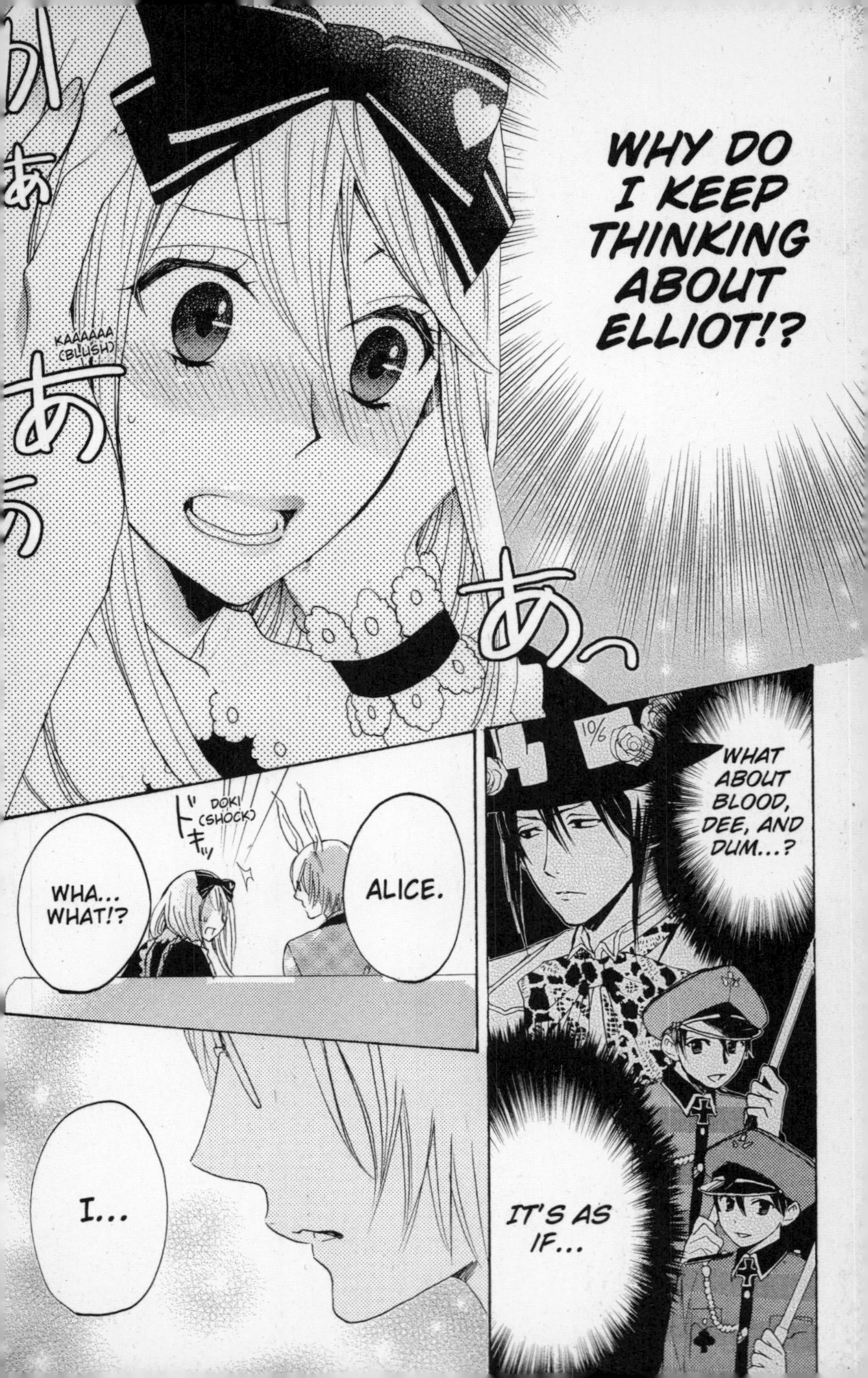
WHY DO I KEEP THINKING ABOUT ELLIOT!?
KAAAAAA (BLUSH)
WHAT ABOUT BLOOD, DEE, AND DUM...?
IT'S AS IF...
ALICE.
DOKI (SHOCK)
WHA... WHAT!?
I...

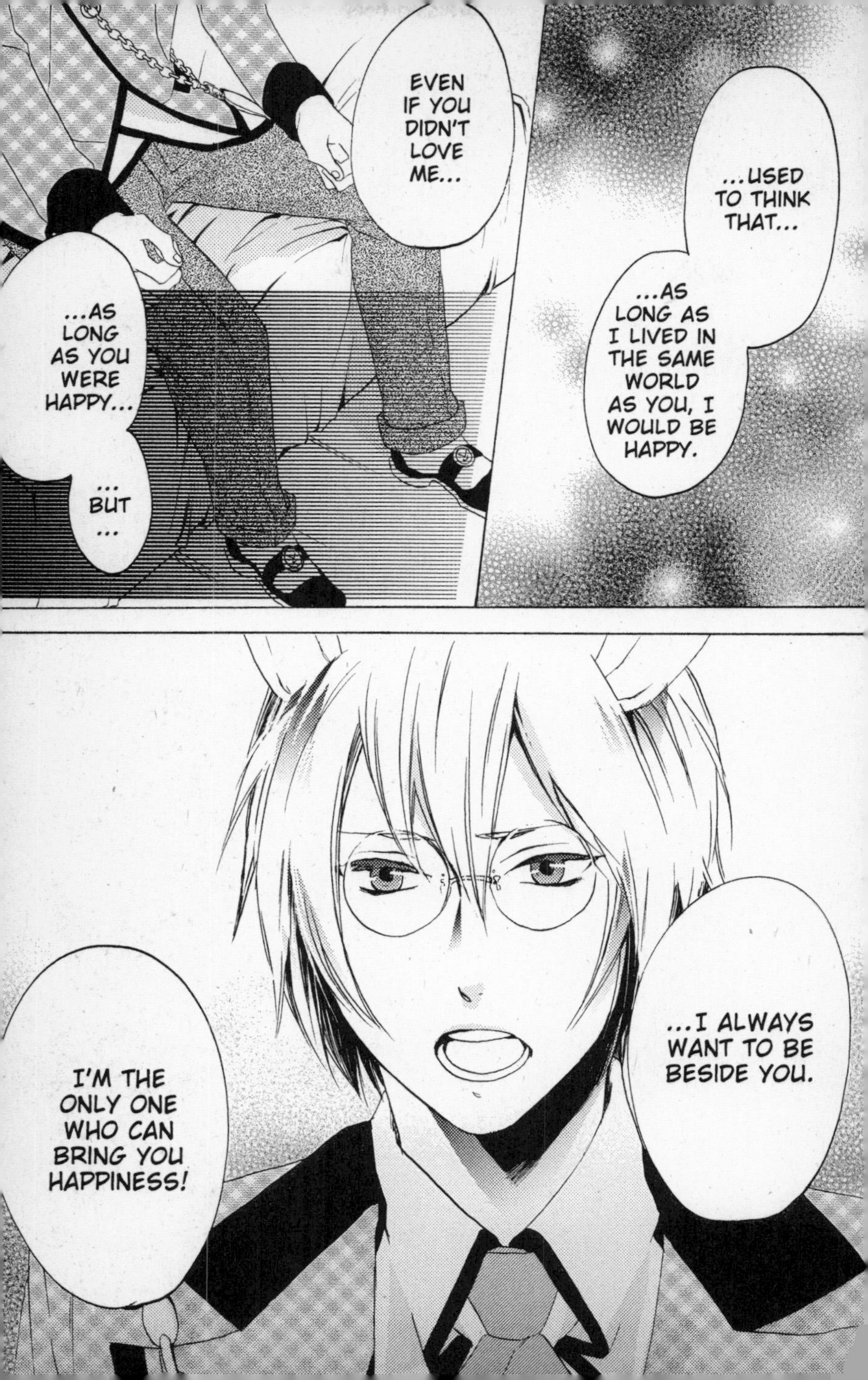
...USED TO THINK THAT...
...AS LONG AS I LIVED IN THE SAME WORLD AS YOU, I WOULD BE HAPPY.
EVEN IF YOU DIDN'T LOVE ME...
...AS LONG AS YOU WERE HAPPY...
...BUT...
...I ALWAYS WANT TO BE BESIDE YOU.
I'M THE ONLY ONE WHO CAN BRING YOU HAPPINESS!

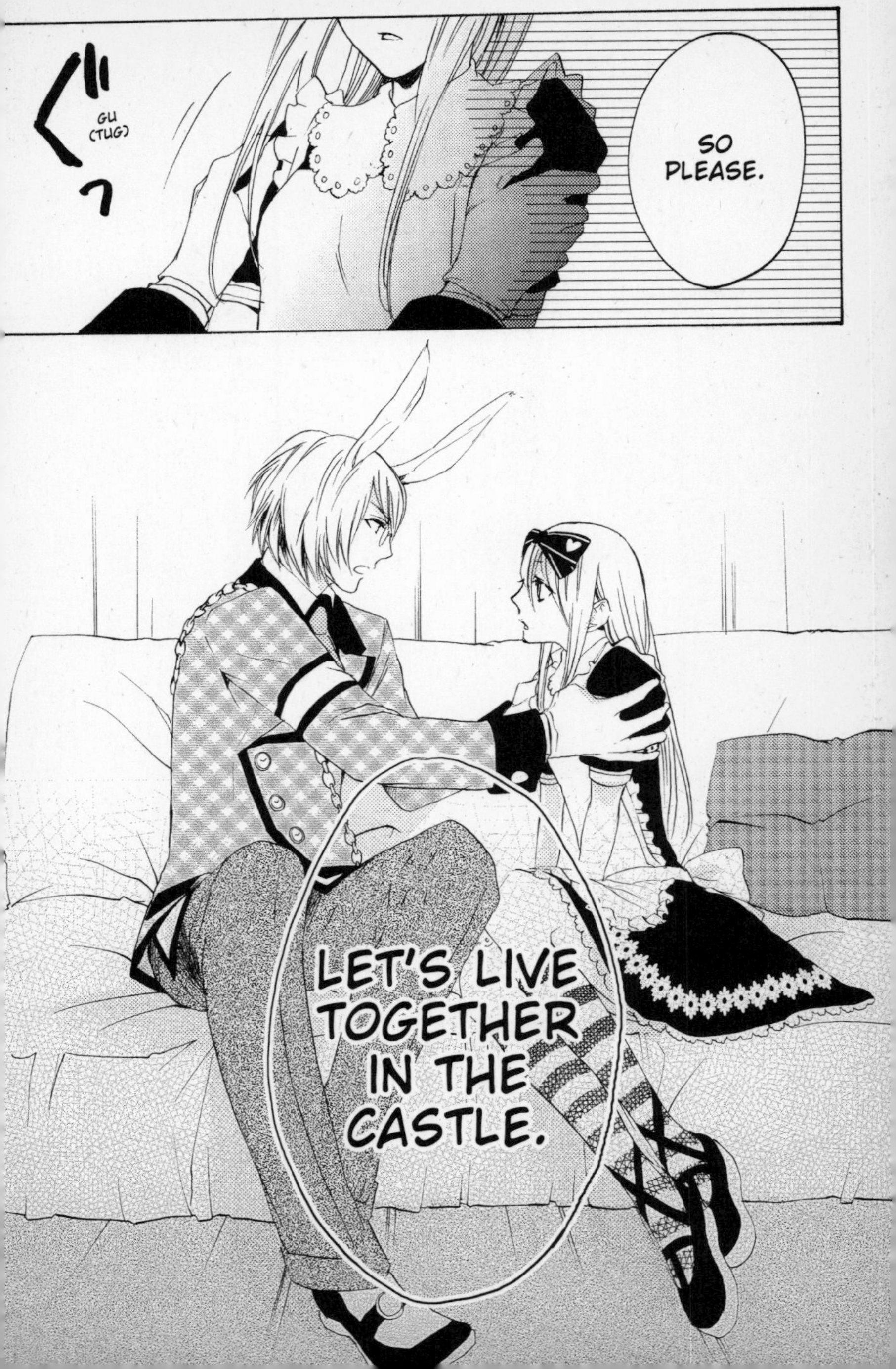
SO PLEASE.
GU (TUG)
LET'S LIVE TOGETHER IN THE CASTLE.

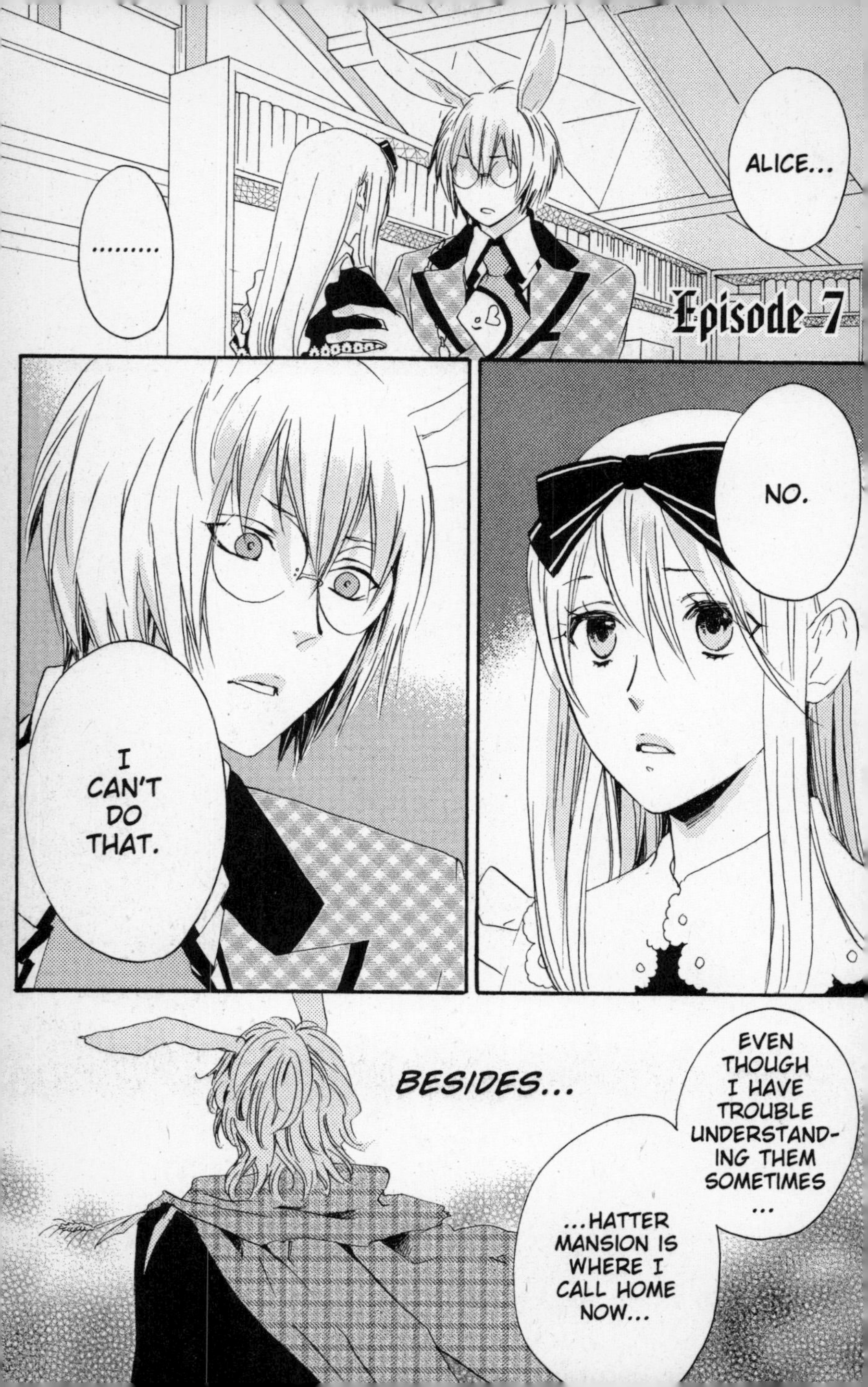
ALICE...
....
Episode 7
NO.
I CAN'T DO THAT.
BESIDES...
EVEN THOUGH I HAVE TROUBLE UNDERSTANDING THEM SOMETIMES ...
...HATTER MANSION IS WHERE I CALL HOME NOW...

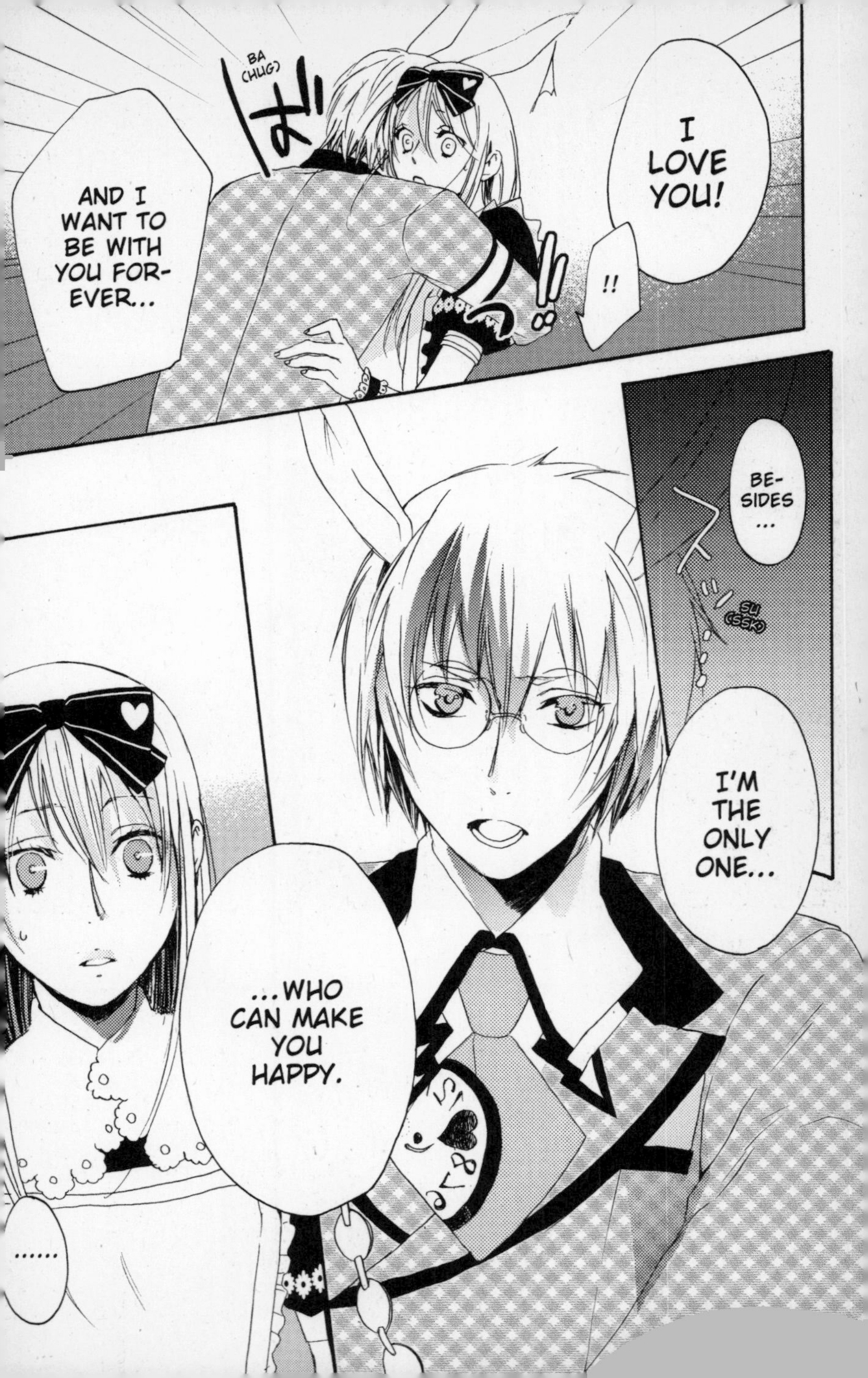
I LOVE YOU!
!!
BA (HUG)
AND I WANT TO BE WITH YOU FOR-EVER...
BE-SIDES...
SU (SSK)
I'M THE ONLY ONE...
...WHO CAN MAKE YOU HAPPY.
......

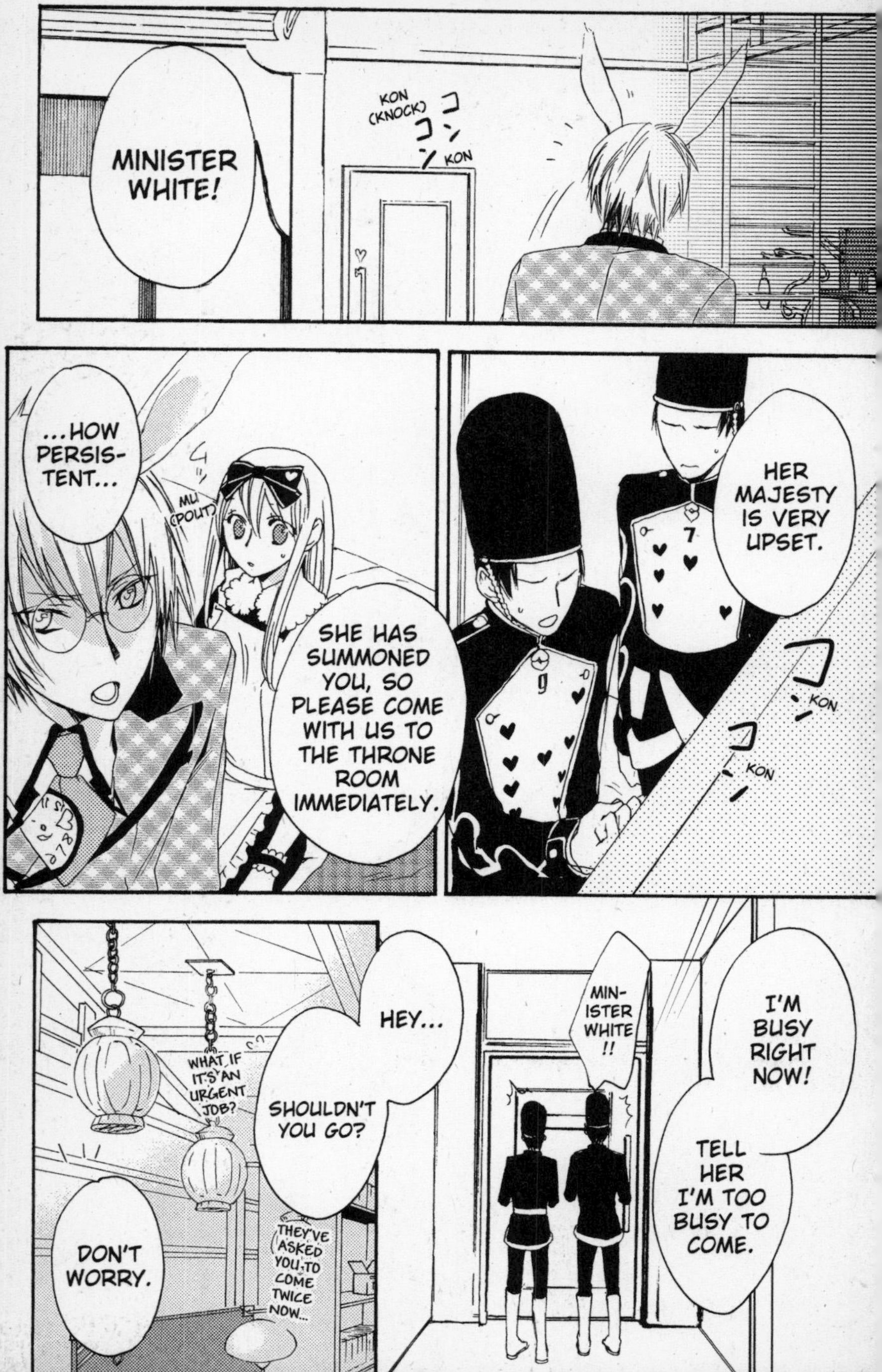
KON (KNOCK)
KON
MINISTER WHITE!
HER MAJESTY IS VERY UPSET.
SHE HAS SUMMONED YOU, SO PLEASE COME WITH US TO THE THRONE ROOM IMMEDIATELY.
KON
KON
MU (POUT)
...HOW PERSIS-TENT...
I'M BUSY RIGHT NOW!
TELL HER I'M TOO BUSY TO COME.
MIN-ISTER WHITE !!
HEY...
SHOULDN'T YOU GO?
WHAT IF IT'S AN URGENT JOB?
THEY'VE ASKED YOU TO COME TWICE NOW...
DON'T WORRY.

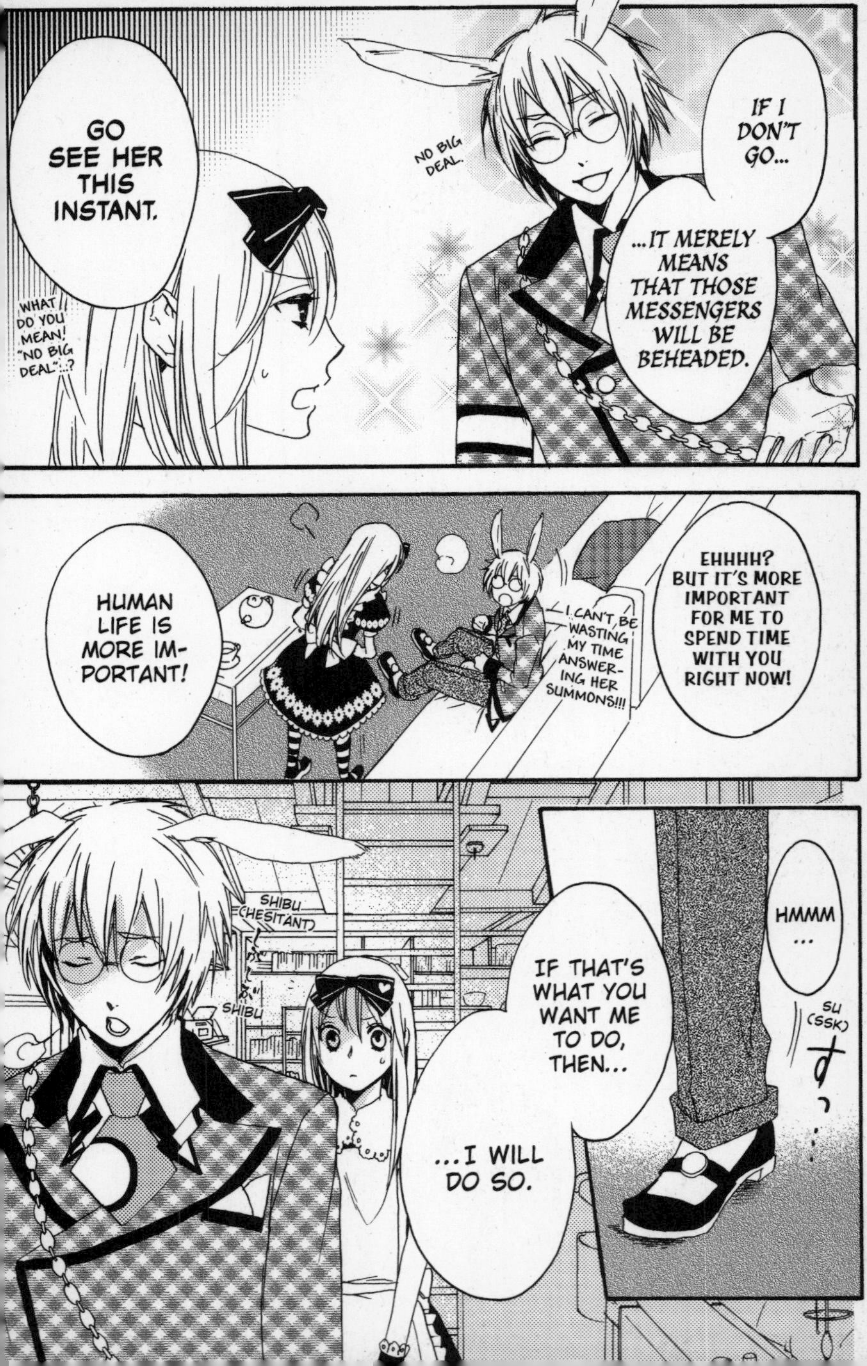
IF I DON'T GO...
...IT MERELY MEANS THAT THOSE MESSENGERS WILL BE BEHEADED.
NO BIG DEAL.
GO SEE HER THIS INSTANT.
WHAT DO YOU MEAN! "NO BIG DEAL"...?
EHHHH? BUT IT'S MORE IMPORTANT FOR ME TO SPEND TIME WITH YOU RIGHT NOW!
I CAN'T BE WASTING MY TIME ANSWERING HER SUMMONS!!!
HUMAN LIFE IS MORE IMPORTANT!
HMMM...
SU (SSK)
IF THAT'S WHAT YOU WANT ME TO DO, THEN...
SHIBU (HESITANT)
SHIBU
...I WILL DO SO.

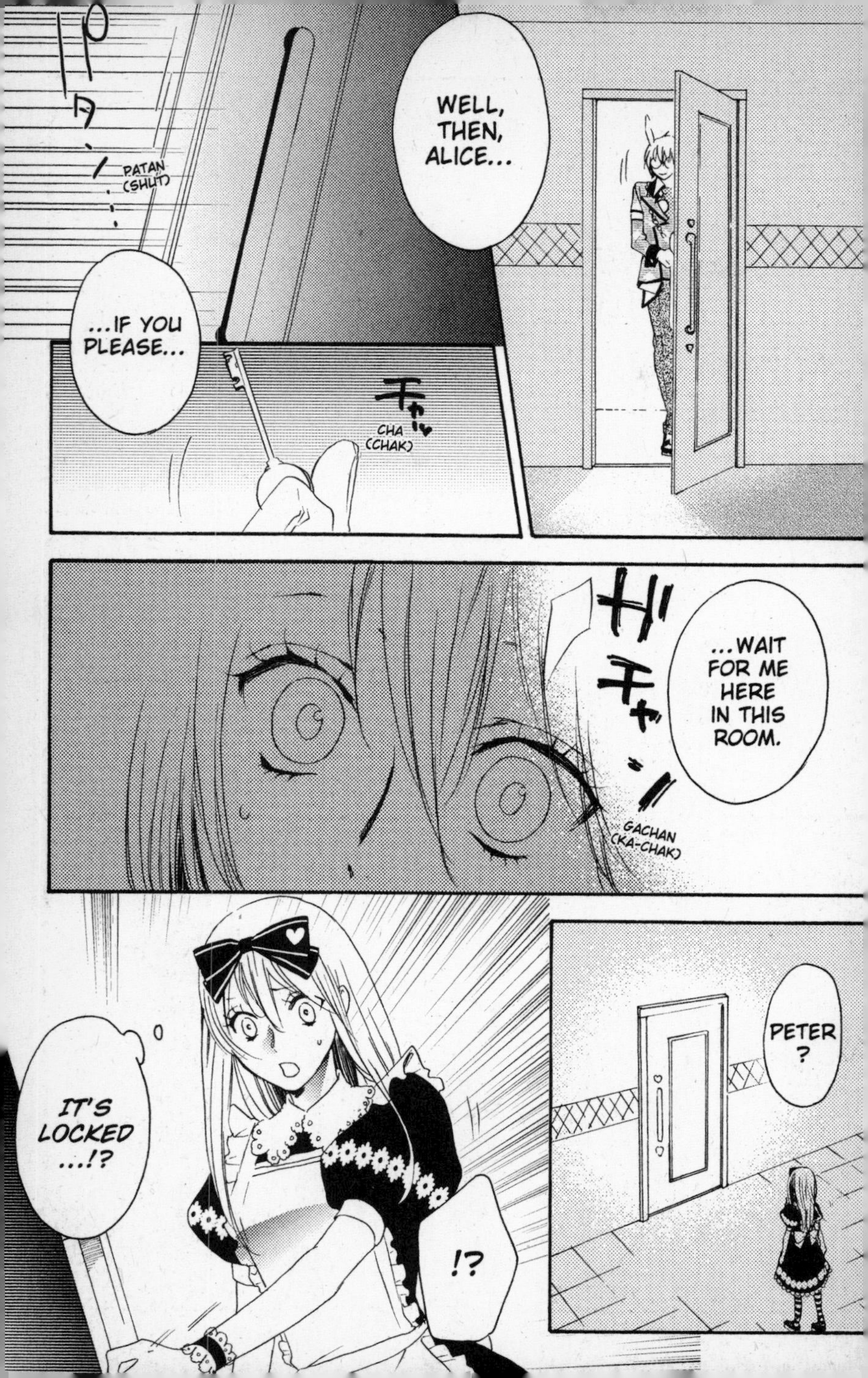
WELL, THEN, ALICE...
パタン…
PATAN (SHUT)
...IF YOU PLEASE...
チャ
CHA (CHAK)
...WAIT FOR ME HERE IN THIS ROOM.
ガチャン
GACHAN (KA-CHAK)
PETER?
!?
IT'S LOCKED ...!?

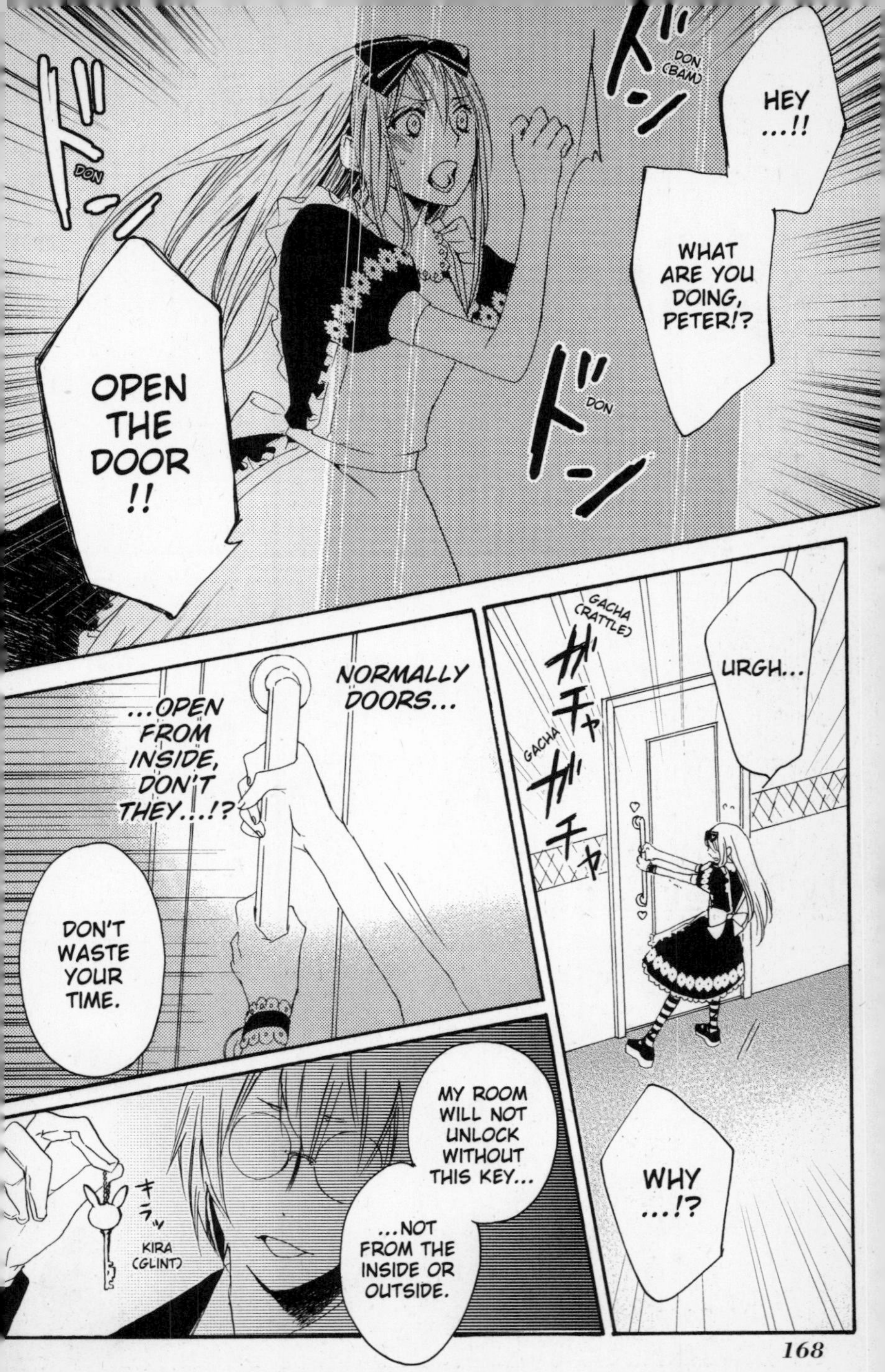
DON (BAM)
HEY ...!!
WHAT ARE YOU DOING, PETER!?
DON
DON
OPEN THE DOOR!!
GACHA (RATTLE)
URGH...
GACHA
WHY ...!?
NORMALLY DOORS...
...OPEN FROM INSIDE, DON'T THEY...!?
DON'T WASTE YOUR TIME.
MY ROOM WILL NOT UNLOCK WITHOUT THIS KEY...
...NOT FROM THE INSIDE OR OUTSIDE.
KIRA (GLINT)

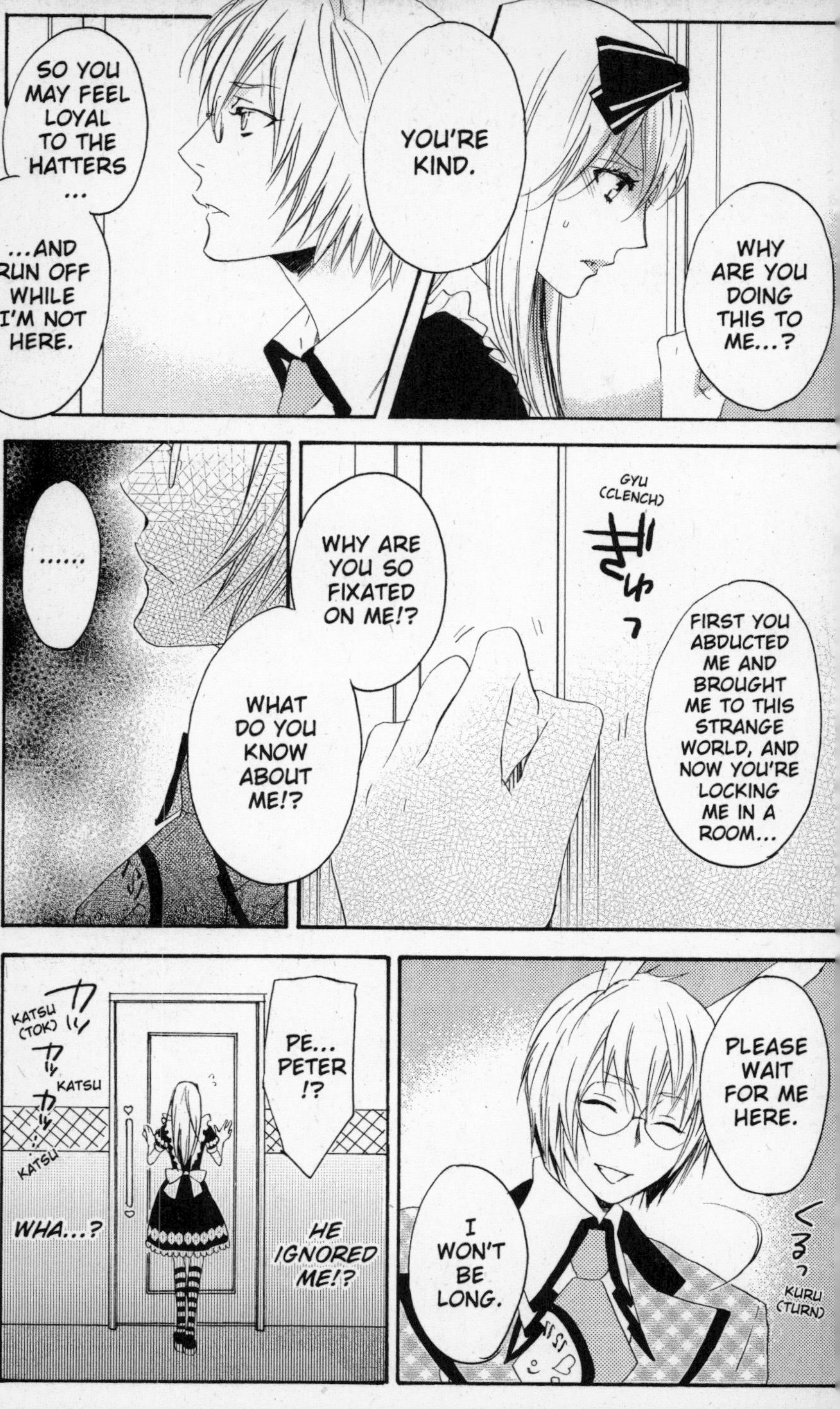
WHY ARE YOU DOING THIS TO ME...?
YOU'RE KIND.
SO YOU MAY FEEL LOYAL TO THE HATTERS...
...AND RUN OFF WHILE I'M NOT HERE.
GYU (CLENCH)
ぎゅっ
FIRST YOU ABDUCTED ME AND BROUGHT ME TO THIS STRANGE WORLD, AND NOW YOU'RE LOCKING ME IN A ROOM...
WHY ARE YOU SO FIXATED ON ME!?
WHAT DO YOU KNOW ABOUT ME!?
......
PLEASE WAIT FOR ME HERE.
くるっ
KURU (TURN)
I WON'T BE LONG.
PE... PETER!?
KATSU (TOK)
KATSU
KATSU
HE IGNORED ME!?
WHA...?

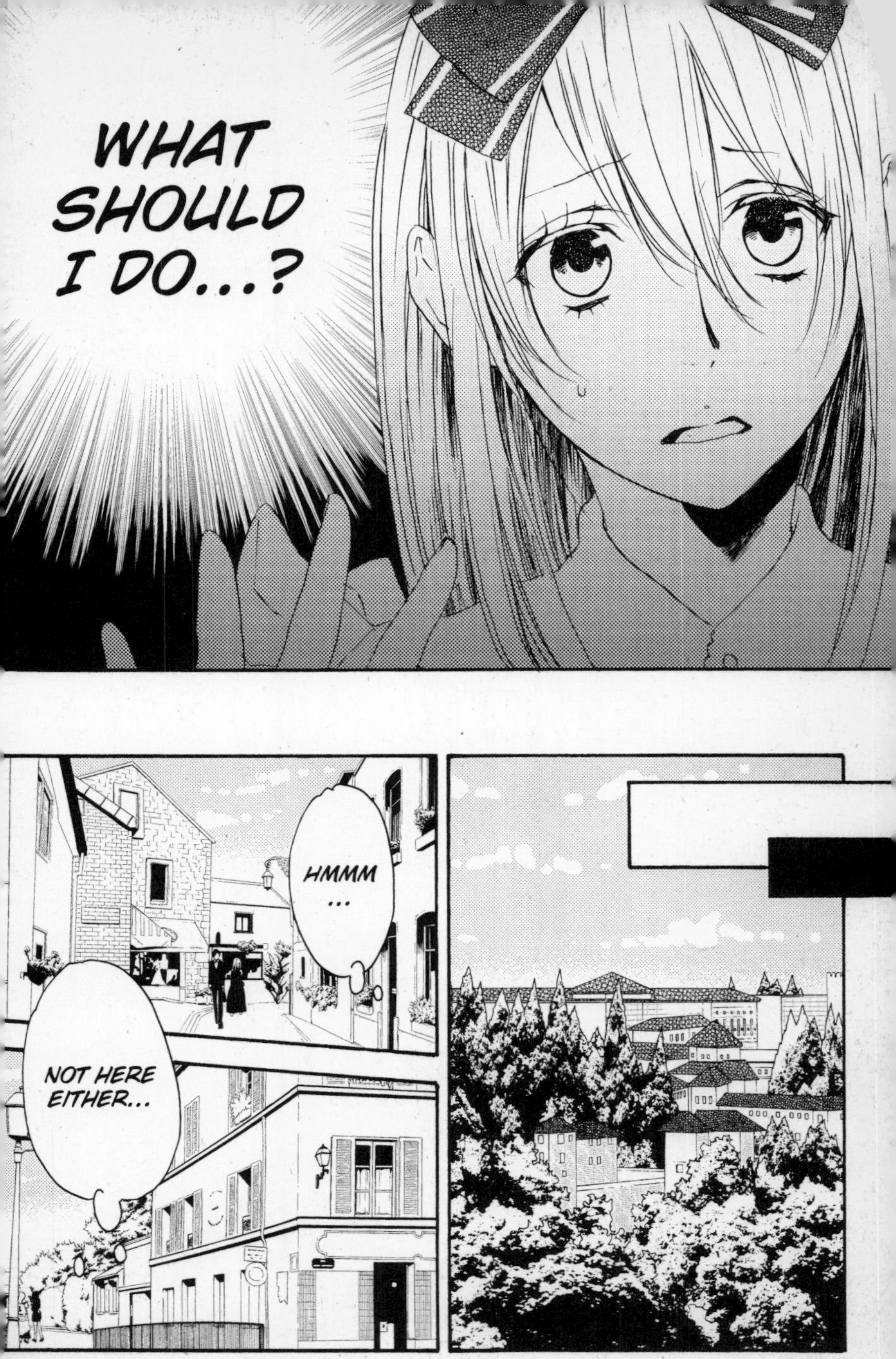
WHAT SHOULD I DO...?
HMMM ...
NOT HERE EITHER...

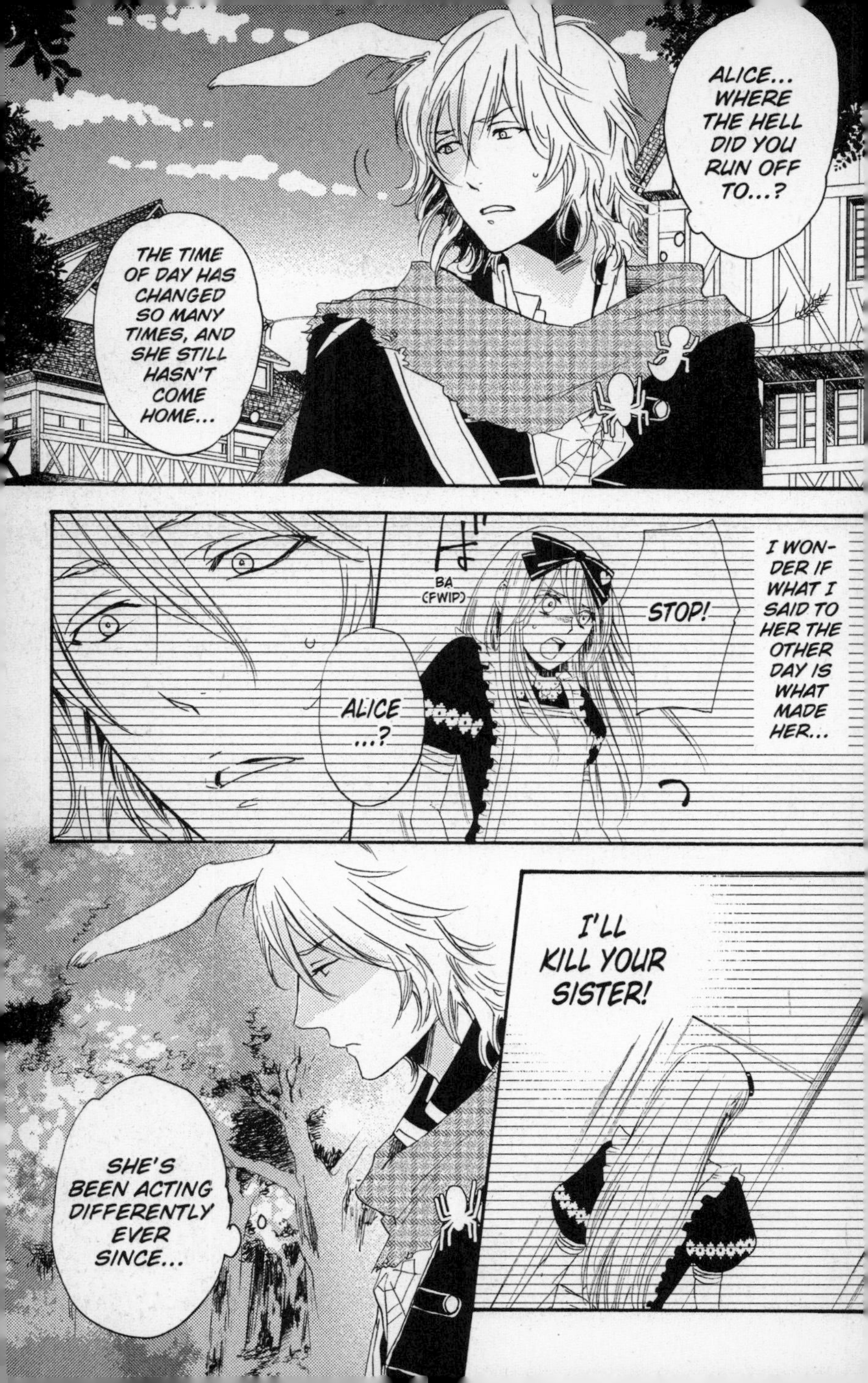
ALICE... WHERE THE HELL DID YOU RUN OFF TO...?
THE TIME OF DAY HAS CHANGED SO MANY TIMES, AND SHE STILL HASN'T COME HOME...
I WONDER IF WHAT I SAID TO HER THE OTHER DAY IS WHAT MADE HER...
STOP!
BA (FWIP)
ALICE ...?
I'LL KILL YOUR SISTER!
SHE'S BEEN ACTING DIFFERENTLY EVER SINCE...

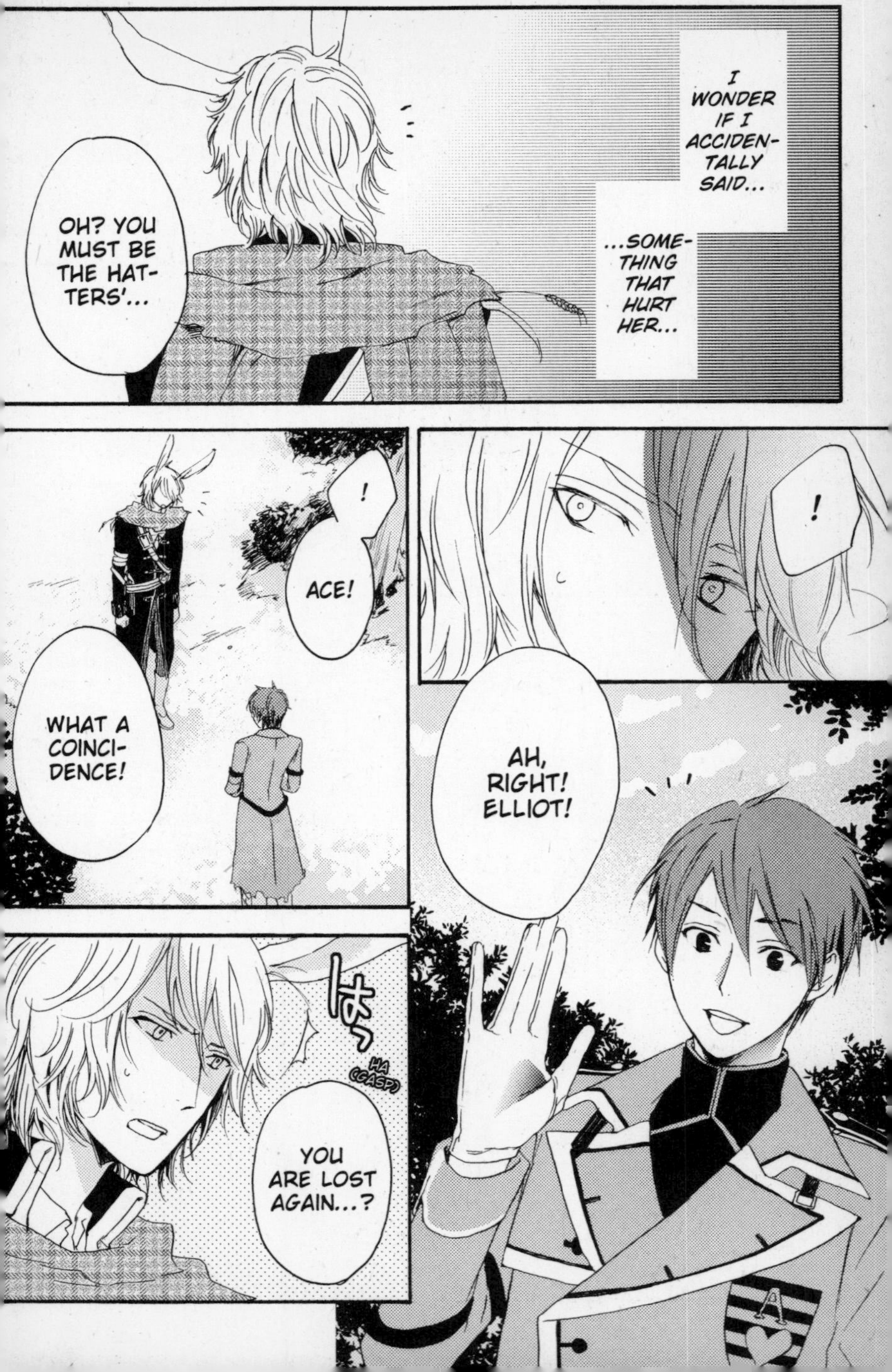
I WONDER IF I ACCIDENTALLY SAID...
...SOMETHING THAT HURT HER...
OH? YOU MUST BE THE HATTERS'...
!
!
ACE!
WHAT A COINCIDENCE!
AH, RIGHT! ELLIOT!
はっ
HA (GASP)
YOU ARE LOST AGAIN...?

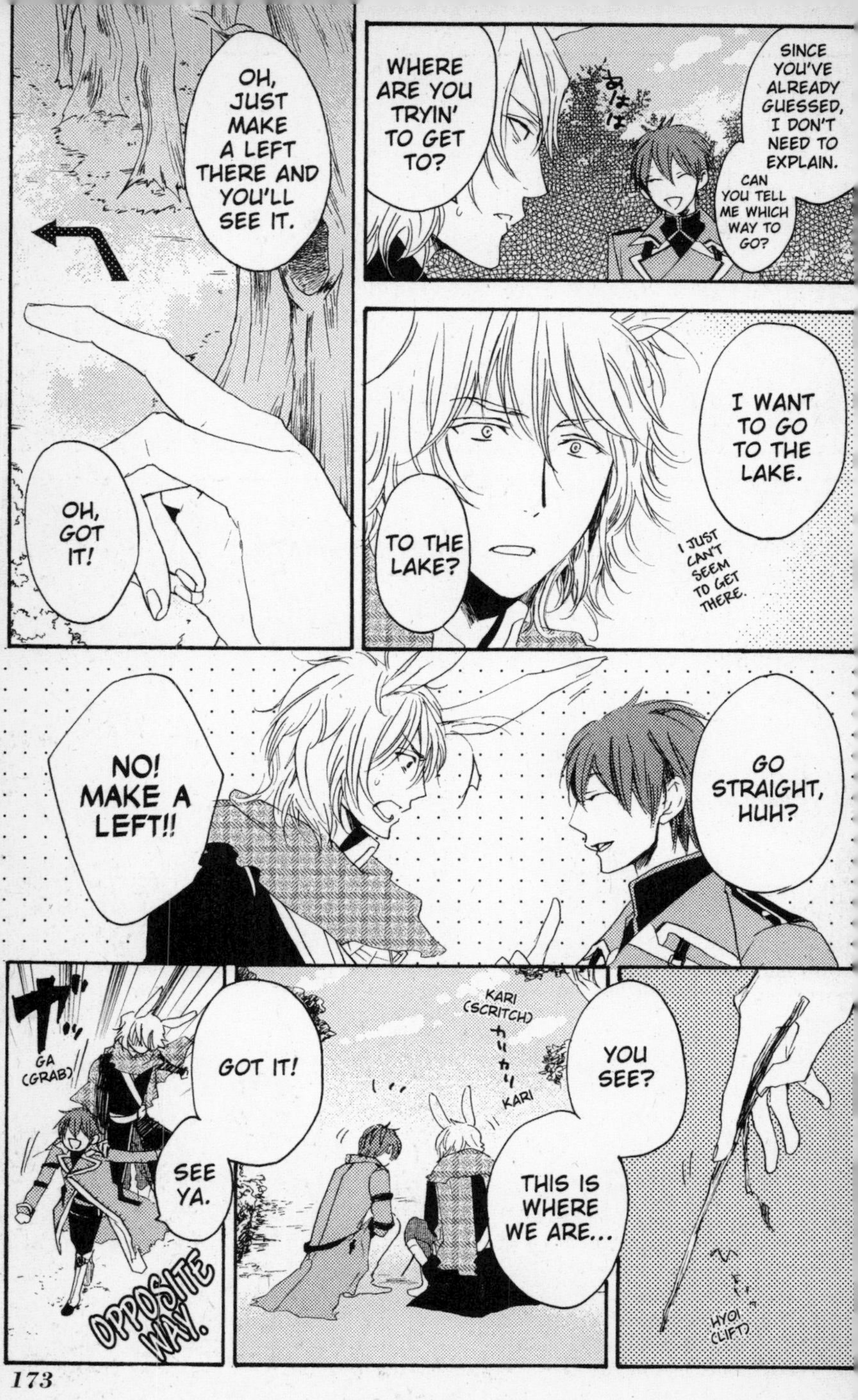

あはは
SINCE YOU'VE ALREADY GUESSED, I DON'T NEED TO EXPLAIN.
CAN YOU TELL ME WHICH WAY TO GO?
WHERE ARE YOU TRYIN' TO GET TO?
I WANT TO GO TO THE LAKE.
I JUST CAN'T SEEM TO GET THERE.
TO THE LAKE?
OH, JUST MAKE A LEFT THERE AND YOU'LL SEE IT.
OH, GOT IT!
GO STRAIGHT, HUH?
NO! MAKE A LEFT!!
HYOI (LIFT)
YOU SEE?
THIS IS WHERE WE ARE...
KARI (SCRITCH)
カリカリ
KARI
GOT IT!
SEE YA.
GA (GRAB)
OPPOSITE WAY.

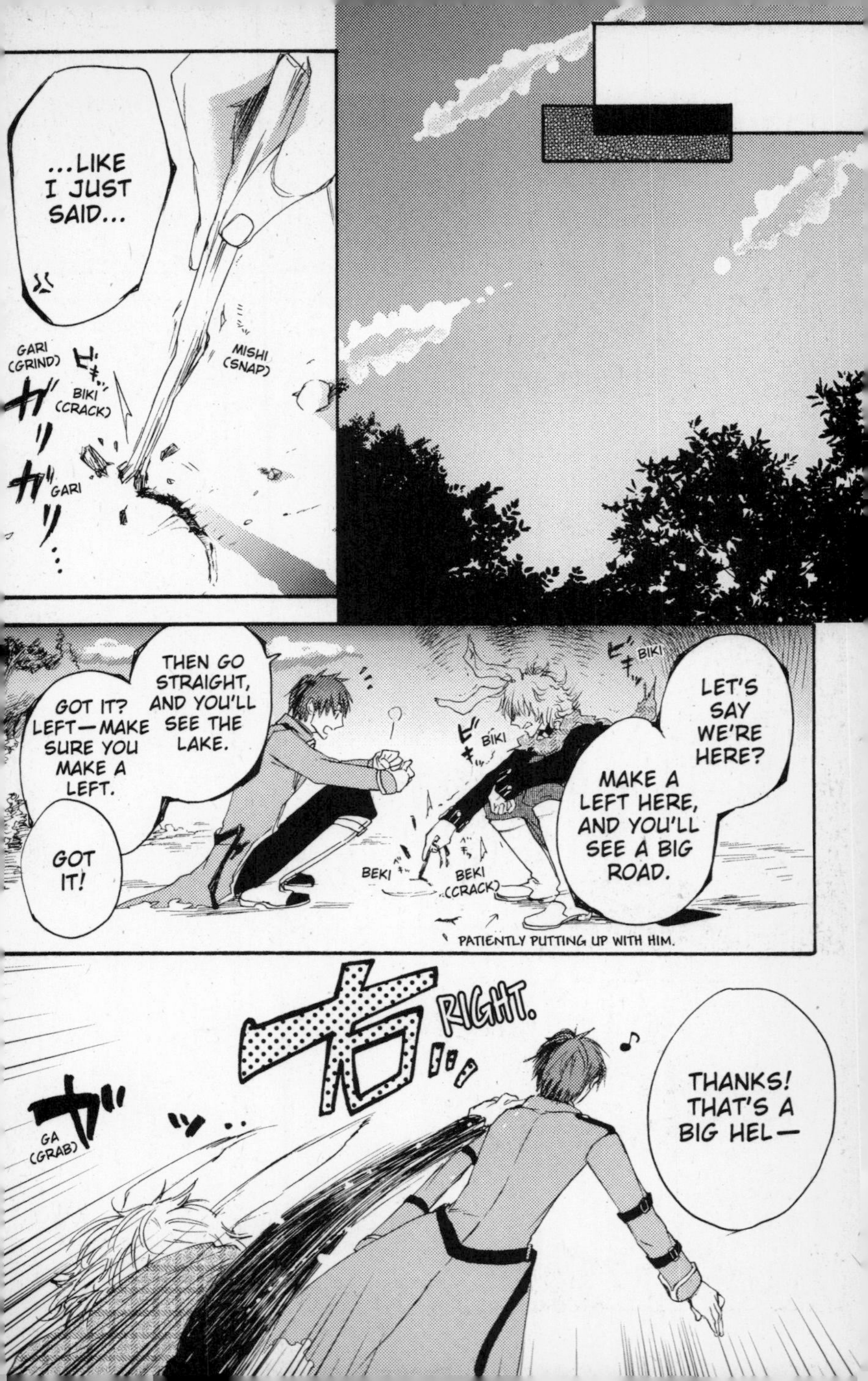
...LIKE I JUST SAID...
MISHI (SNAP)
BIKI (CRACK)
GARI (GRIND)
GARI
BIKI
LET'S SAY WE'RE HERE?
MAKE A LEFT HERE, AND YOU'LL SEE A BIG ROAD.
BIKI
BEKI (CRACK)
BEKI
THEN GO STRAIGHT, AND YOU'LL SEE THE LAKE.
GOT IT? LEFT—MAKE SURE YOU MAKE A LEFT.
GOT IT!
PATIENTLY PUTTING UP WITH HIM.
THANKS! THAT'S A BIG HEL—
RIGHT.
GA (GRAB)

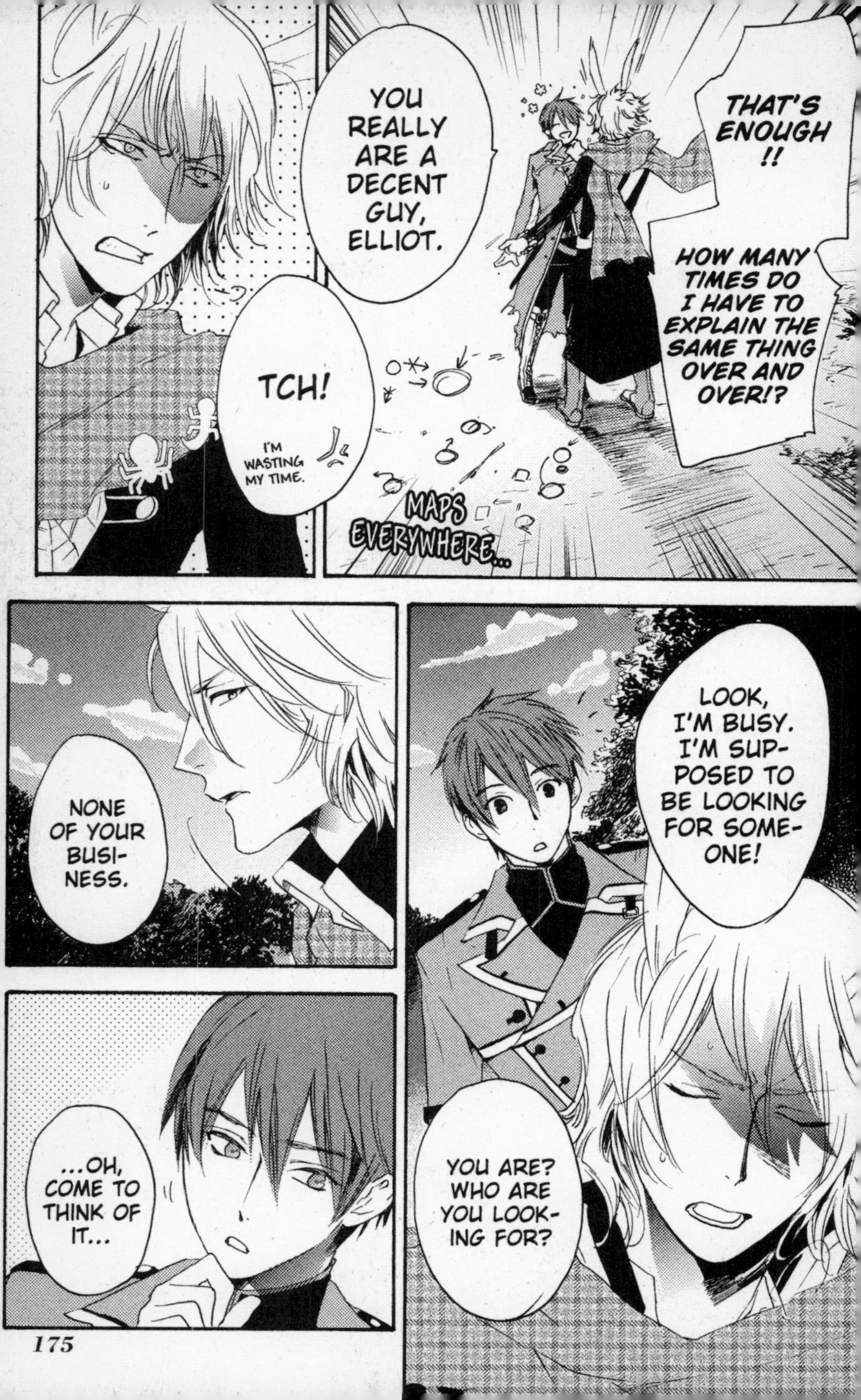

THAT'S ENOUGH!!
HOW MANY TIMES DO I HAVE TO EXPLAIN THE SAME THING OVER AND OVER!?
YOU REALLY ARE A DECENT GUY, ELLIOT.
MAPS EVERYWHERE...
TCH!
I'M WASTING MY TIME.
LOOK, I'M BUSY. I'M SUP-POSED TO BE LOOKING FOR SOME-ONE!
YOU ARE? WHO ARE YOU LOOK-ING FOR?
NONE OF YOUR BUSI-NESS.
...OH, COME TO THINK OF IT...

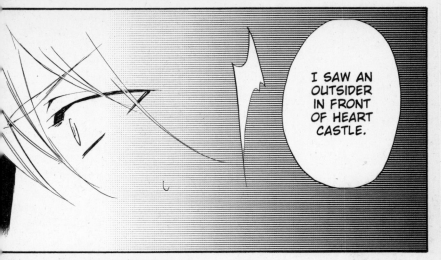

I SAW AN OUTSIDER IN FRONT OF HEART CASTLE.

A GIRL NAMED ALICE.

I WAS SURPRISED TO SEE HER SINCE I'D NEVER MET AN OUTSIDER BEFORE.

OUT-SIDER ....!?

ZA (ZSH)

I THINK PETER TOOK HER INTO THE CASTLE.

PETER!?

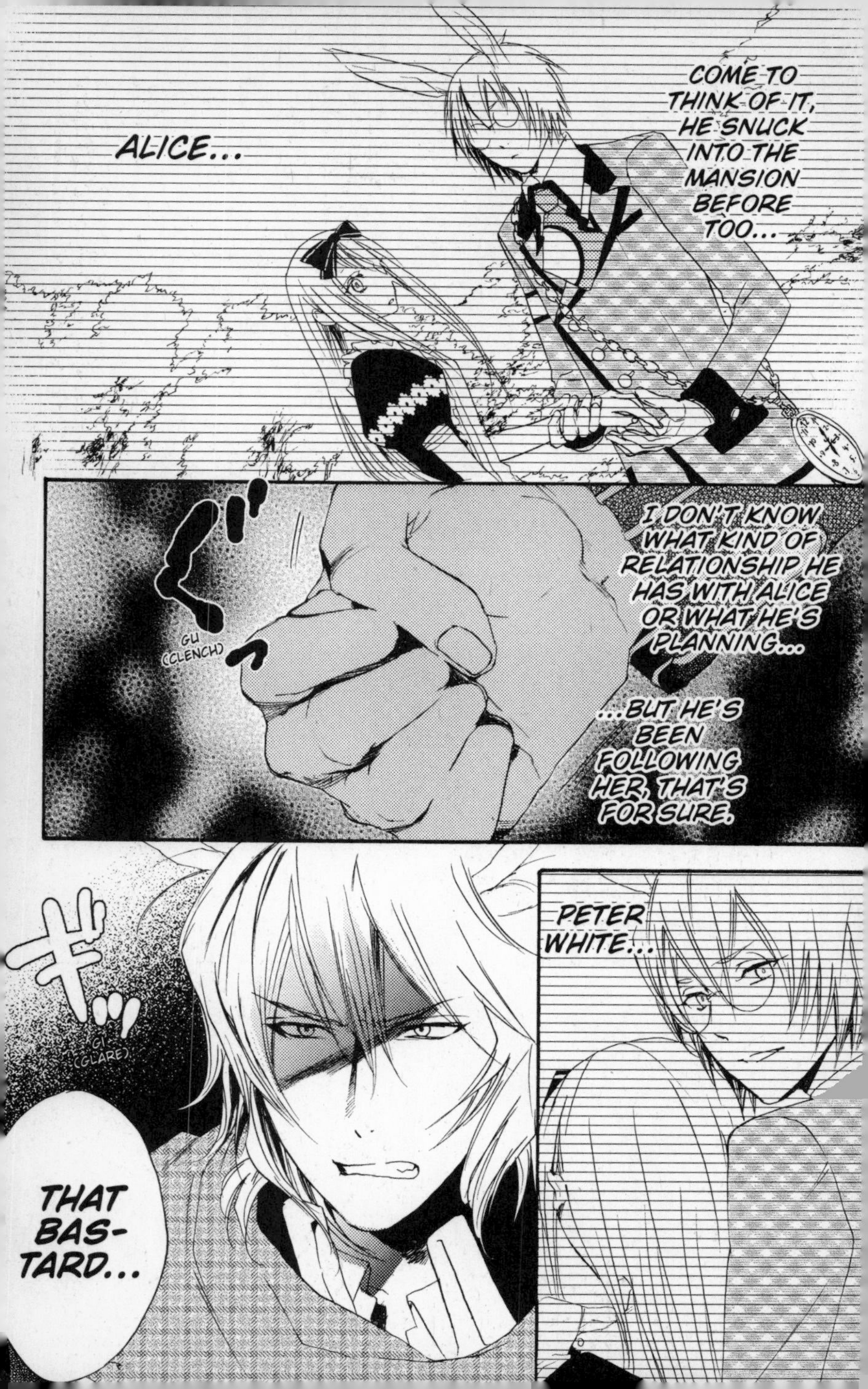
COME TO THINK OF IT, HE SNUCK INTO THE MANSION BEFORE TOO...
ALICE...
I DON'T KNOW WHAT KIND OF RELATIONSHIP HE HAS WITH ALICE OR WHAT HE'S PLANNING...
...BUT HE'S BEEN FOLLOWING HER, THAT'S FOR SURE.
GU (CLENCH)
PETER WHITE...
GI (GLARE)
THAT BAS-TARD...

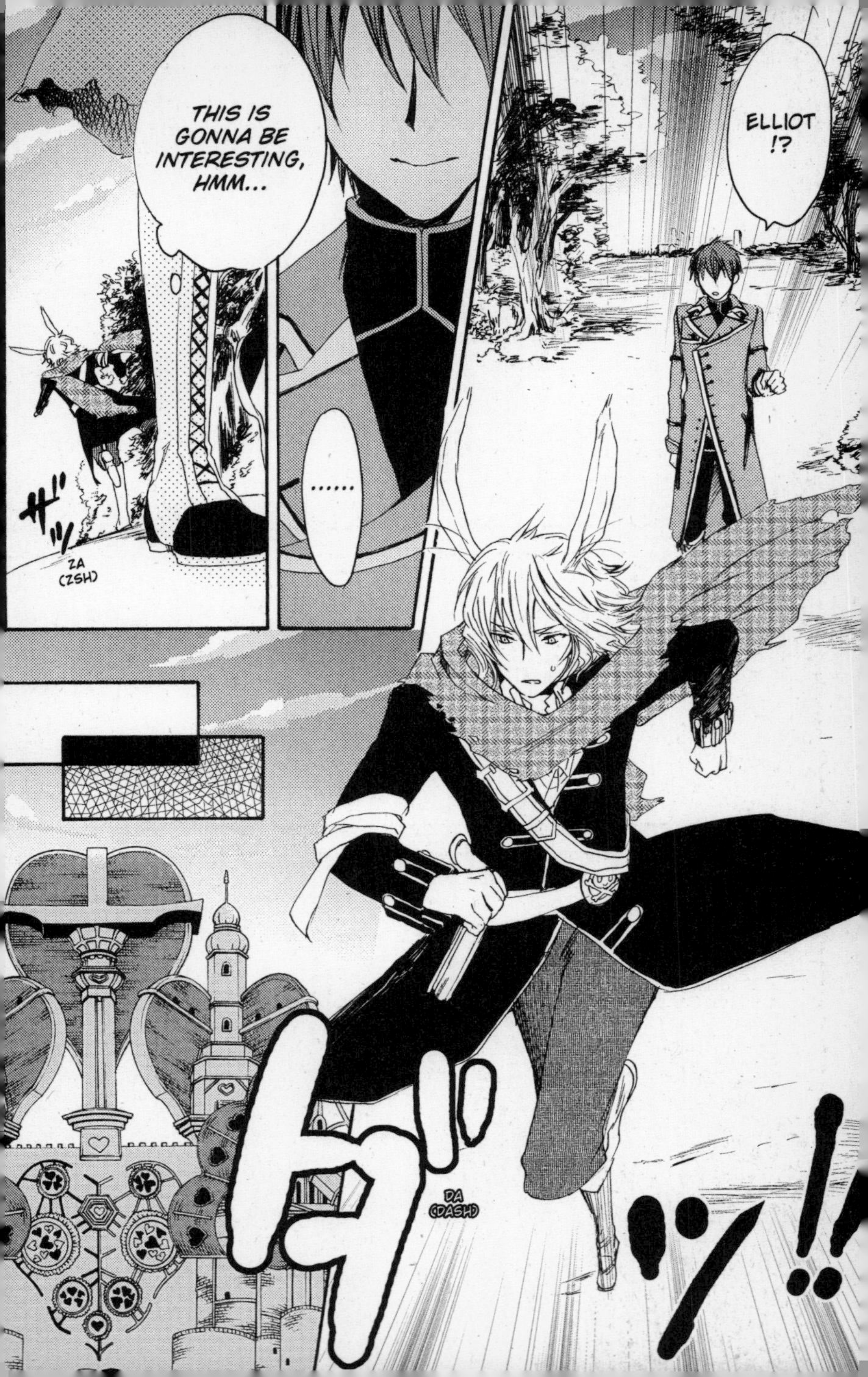
ELLIOT !?
......
THIS IS GONNA BE INTERESTING, HMM...
ZA (ZSH)
DA (DASH)

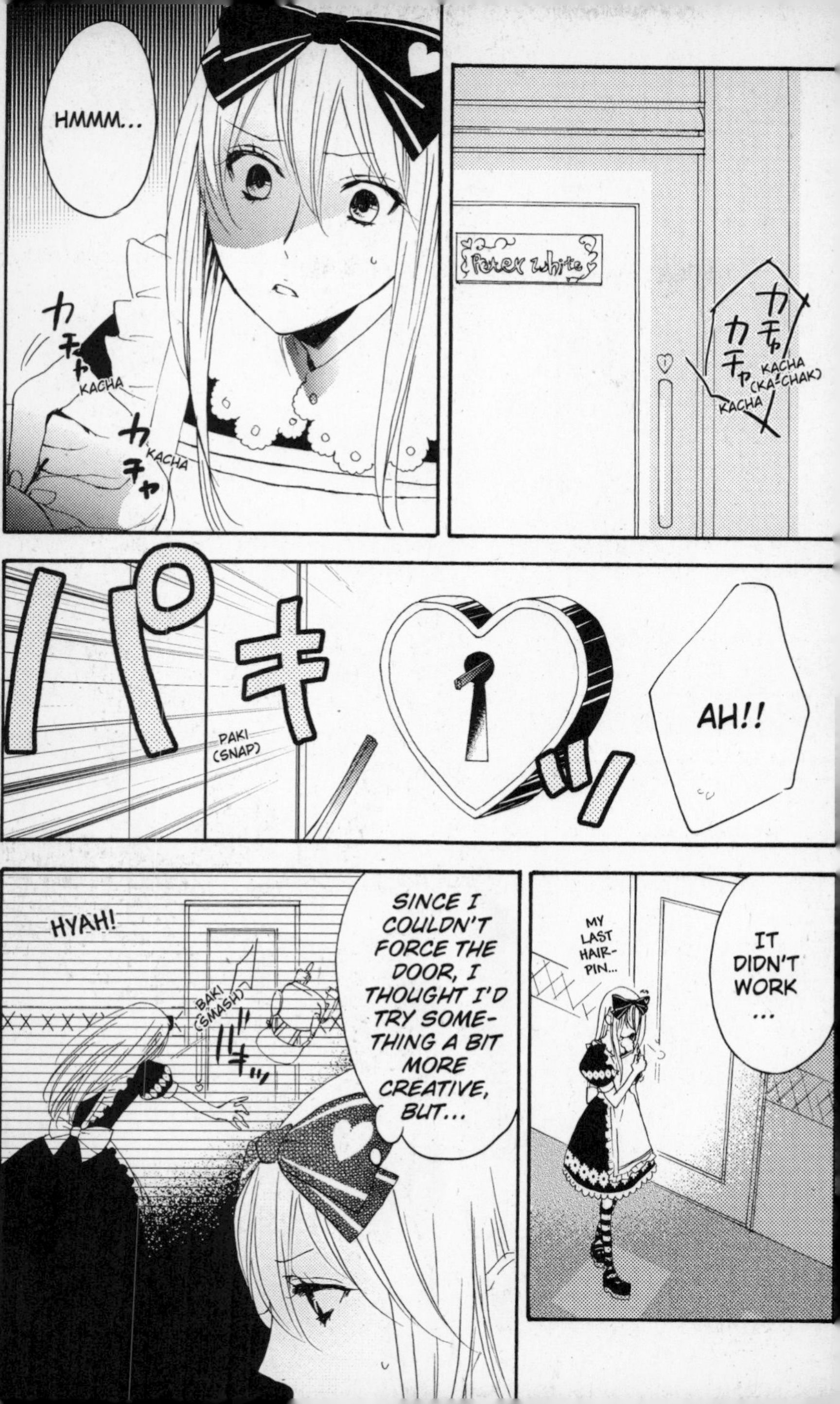

Peter White
カチャカチャ
KACHA (KA-CHAK)
KACHA
HMMM...
カチャ
KACHA
カチャ
KACHA
AH!!
パキ
PAKI (SNAP)
IT DIDN'T WORK...
MY LAST HAIR-PIN...
SINCE I COULDN'T FORCE THE DOOR, I THOUGHT I'D TRY SOME-THING A BIT MORE CREATIVE, BUT...
BAKI (SMASH)
バキッ
HYAH!

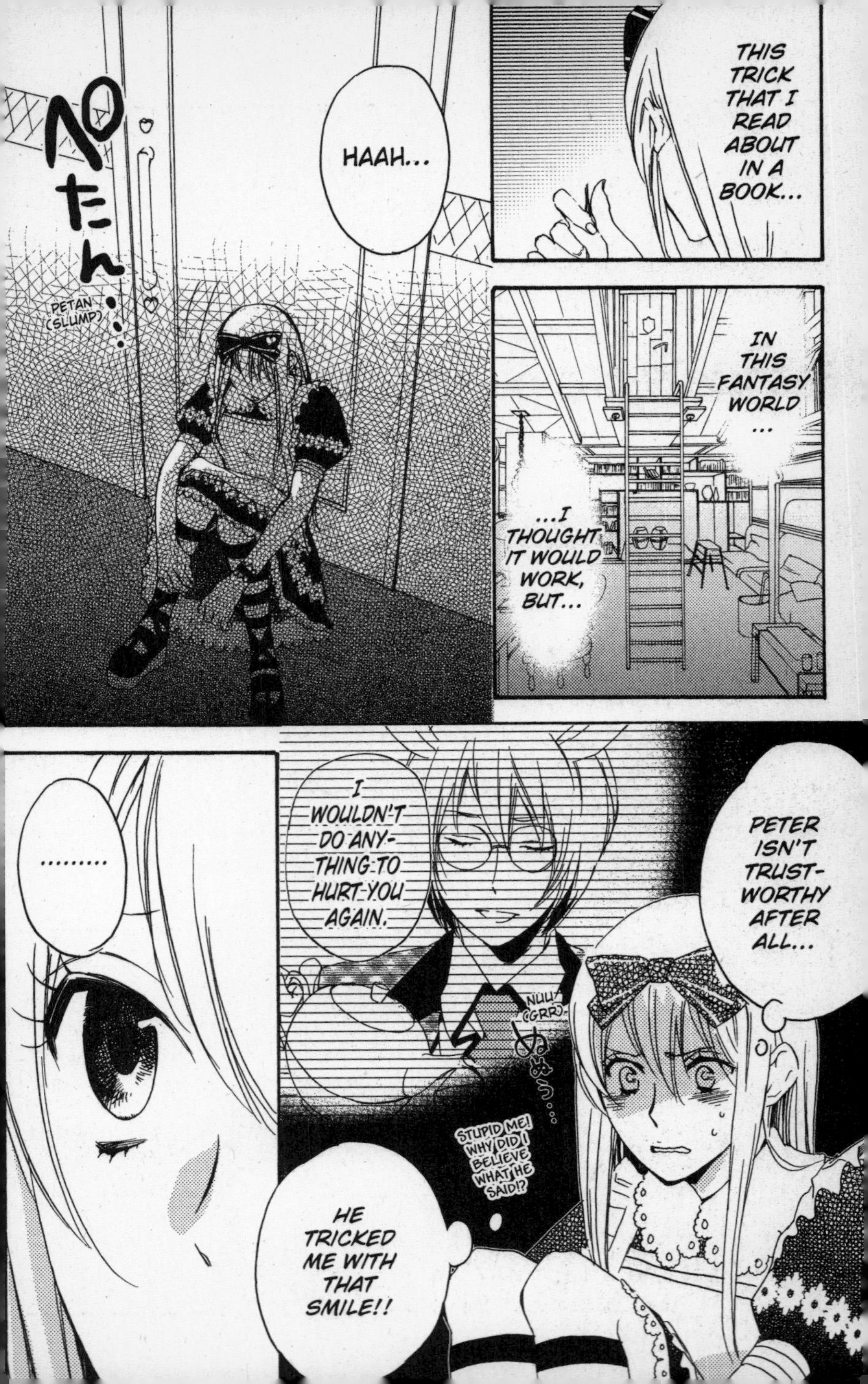
THIS TRICK THAT I READ ABOUT IN A BOOK...
IN THIS FANTASY WORLD...
...I THOUGHT IT WOULD WORK, BUT...
HAAH...
ぺたん…
PETAN (SLUMP)
PETER ISN'T TRUST-WORTHY AFTER ALL...
I WOULDN'T DO ANY-THING TO HURT YOU AGAIN.
NUU (GRR)
ぬぅ…
STUPID ME! WHY DID I BELIEVE WHAT HE SAID!?
HE TRICKED ME WITH THAT SMILE!!
....

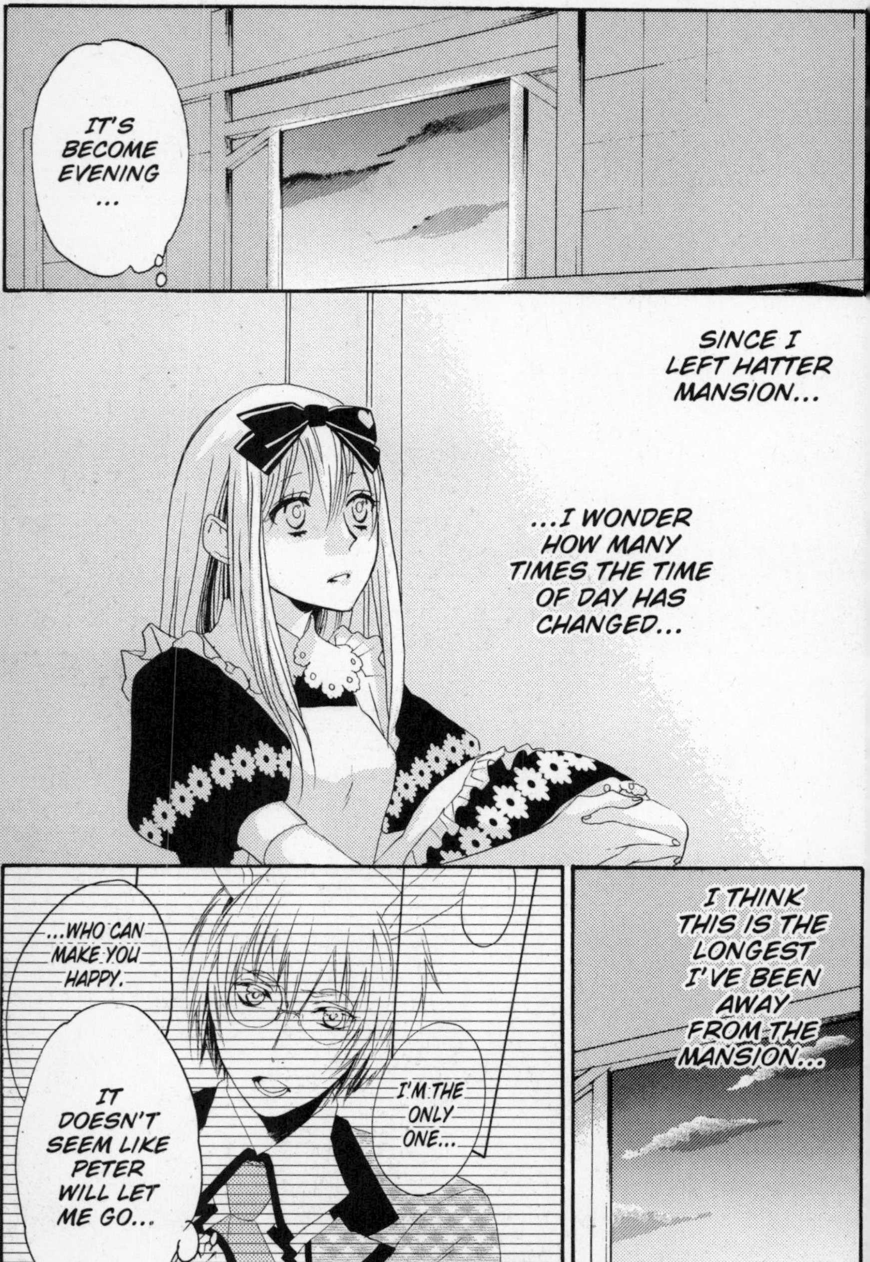
IT'S BECOME EVENING ...
SINCE I LEFT HATTER MANSION...
...I WONDER HOW MANY TIMES THE TIME OF DAY HAS CHANGED...
I THINK THIS IS THE LONGEST I'VE BEEN AWAY FROM THE MANSION...
I'M THE ONLY ONE...
...WHO CAN MAKE YOU HAPPY.
IT DOESN'T SEEM LIKE PETER WILL LET ME GO...

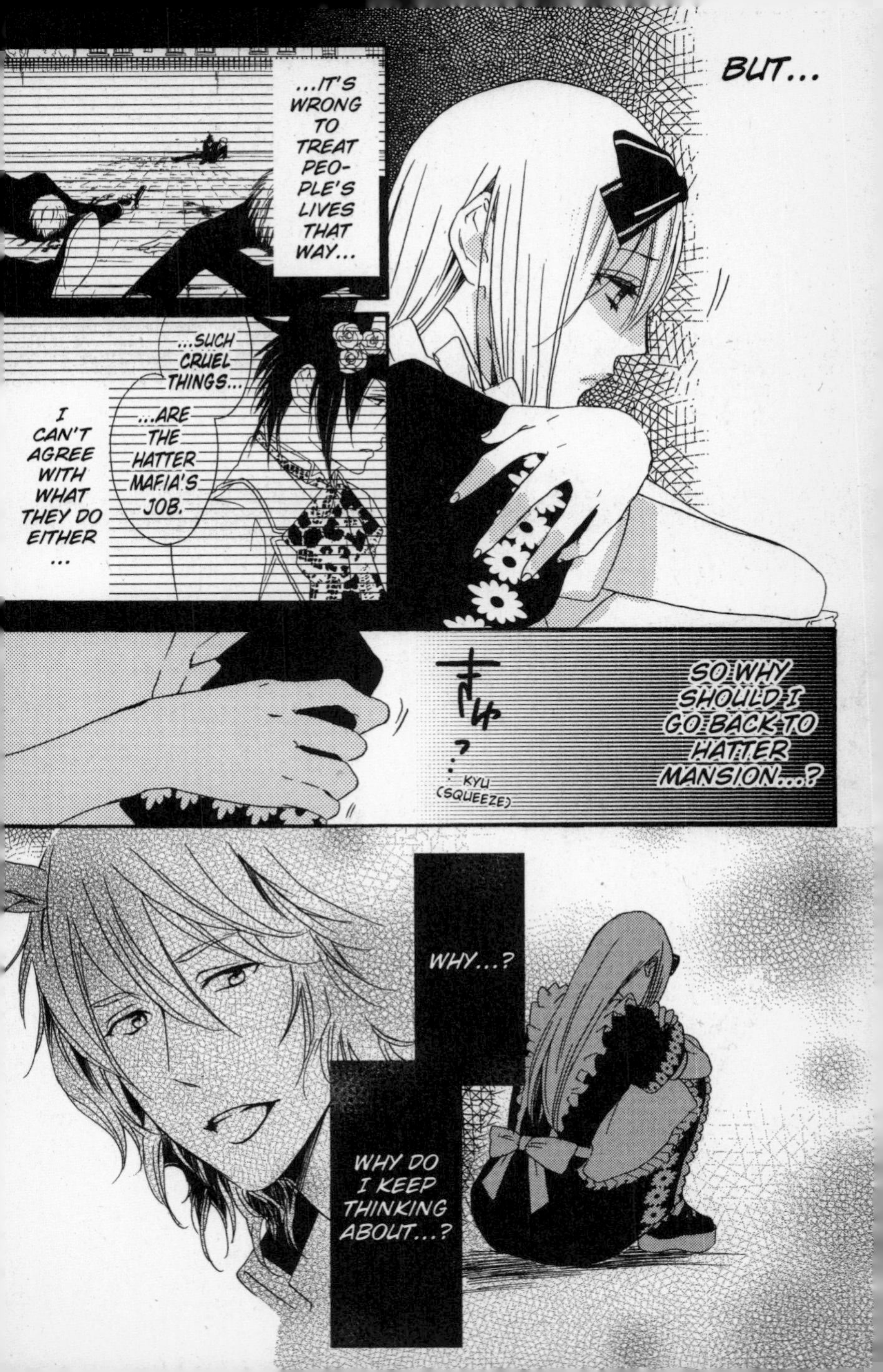
BUT...
...IT'S WRONG TO TREAT PEO-PLE'S LIVES THAT WAY...
...SUCH CRUEL THINGS...
...ARE THE HATTER MAFIA'S JOB.
I CAN'T AGREE WITH WHAT THEY DO EITHER...
SO WHY SHOULD I GO BACK TO HATTER MANSION...?
きゅ
KYU (SQUEEZE)
WHY...?
WHY DO I KEEP THINKING ABOUT...?

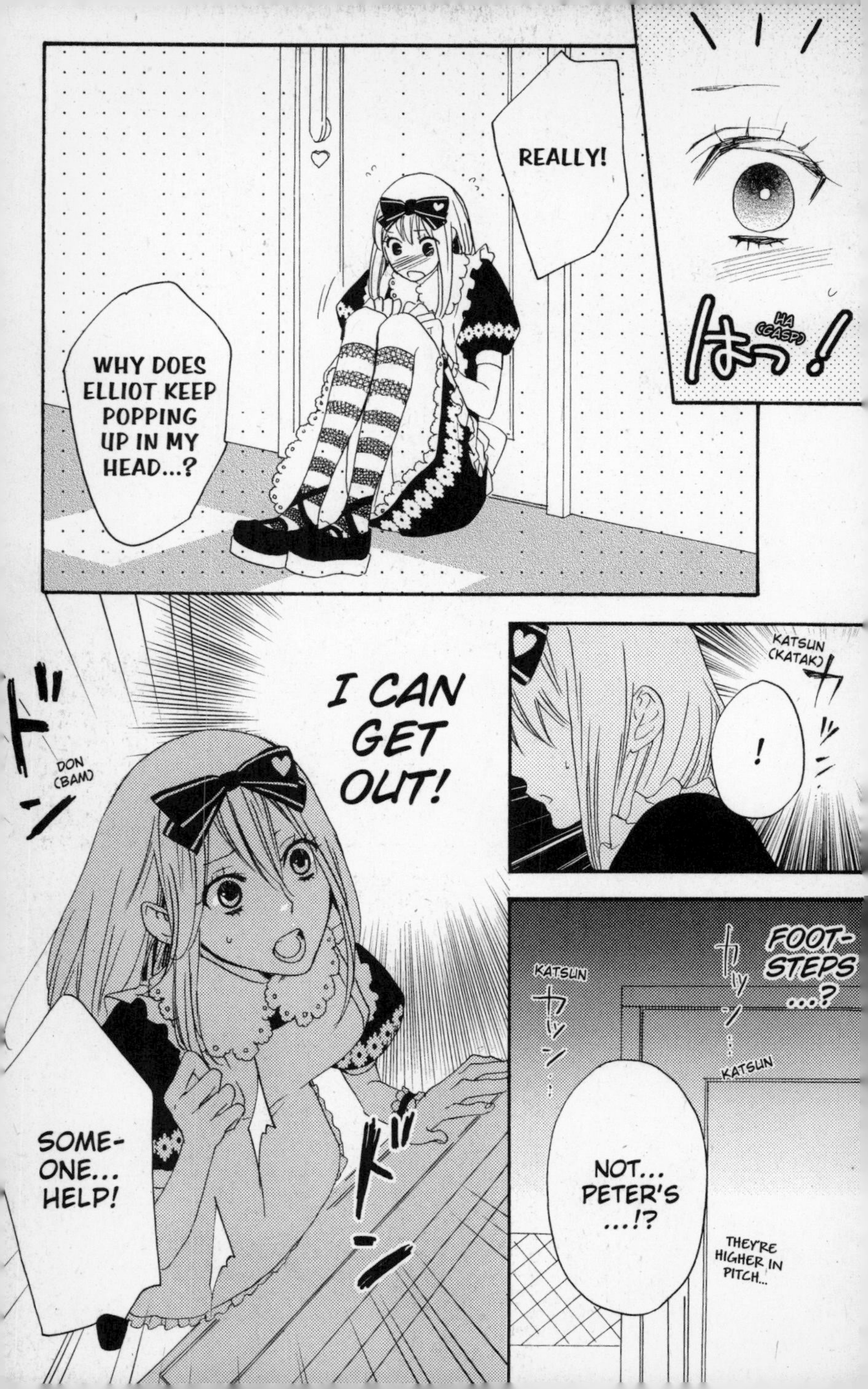
HA (GASP)
はっ!
REALLY!
WHY DOES ELLIOT KEEP POPPING UP IN MY HEAD...?
KATSUN (KATAK)
!
FOOT-STEPS...?
KATSUN
KATSUN
NOT... PETER'S...!?
THEY'RE HIGHER IN PITCH...
I CAN GET OUT!
DON (BAM)
SOME-ONE... HELP!

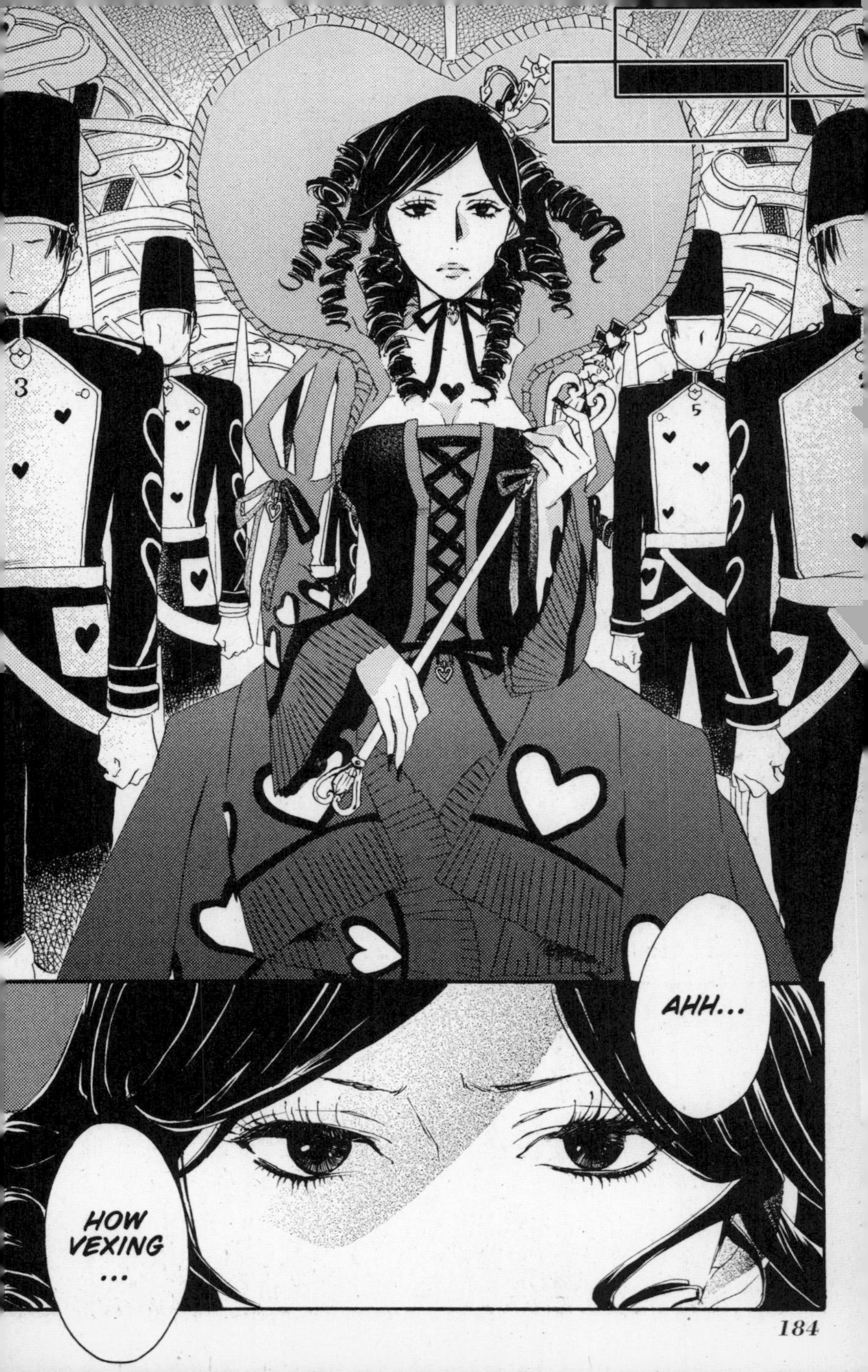
AHH...
HOW VEXING ...

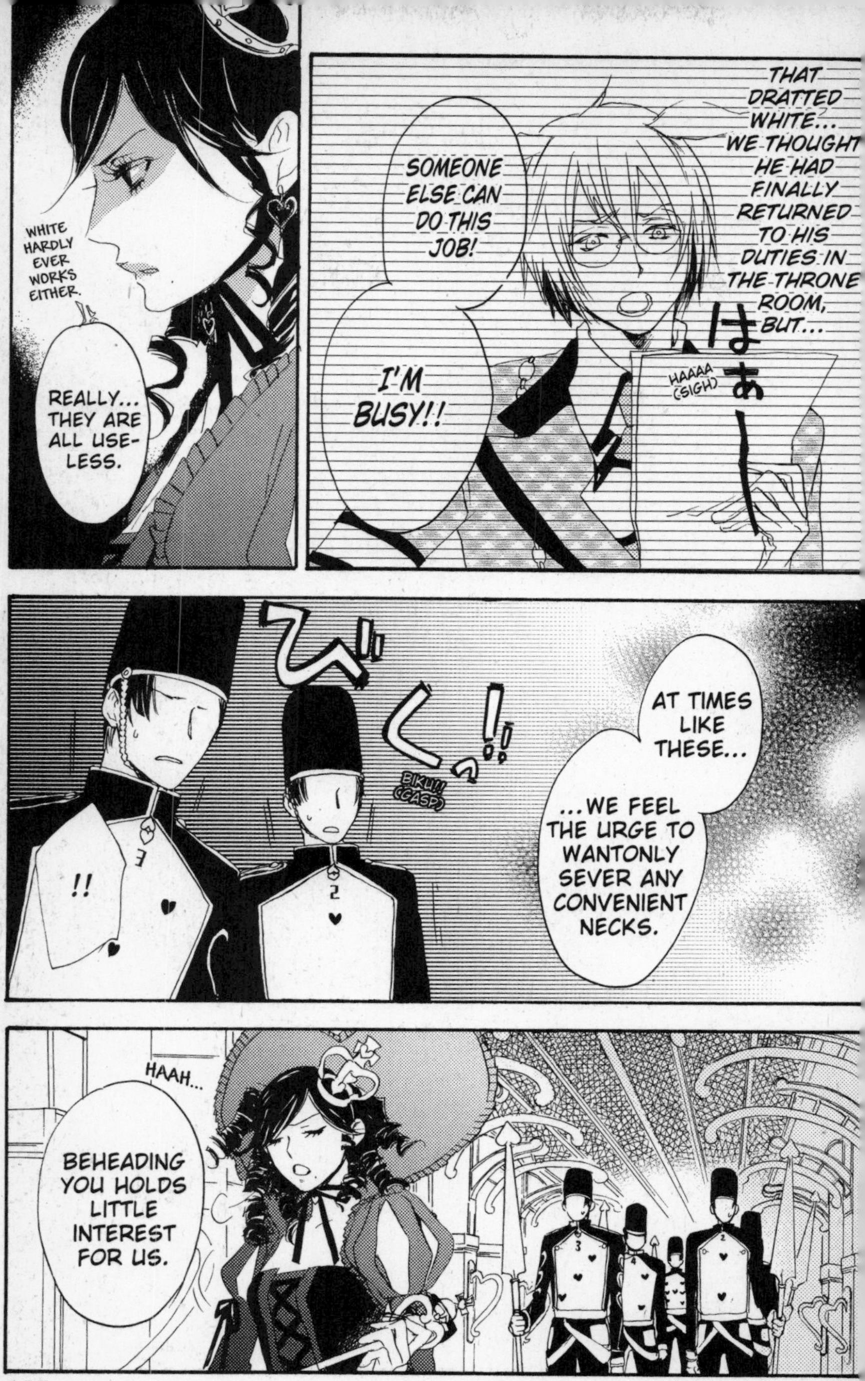
THAT DRATTED WHITE... WE THOUGHT HE HAD FINALLY RETURNED TO HIS DUTIES IN THE THRONE ROOM, BUT...
はぁー
HAAAA (SIGH)
SOMEONE ELSE CAN DO THIS JOB!
I'M BUSY!!
WHITE HARDLY EVER WORKS EITHER.
REALLY... THEY ARE ALL USE-LESS.
AT TIMES LIKE THESE...
...WE FEEL THE URGE TO WANTONLY SEVER ANY CONVENIENT NECKS.
びくっ!!
BIKU!! (GASP)
!!
HAAH...
BEHEADING YOU HOLDS LITTLE INTEREST FOR US.

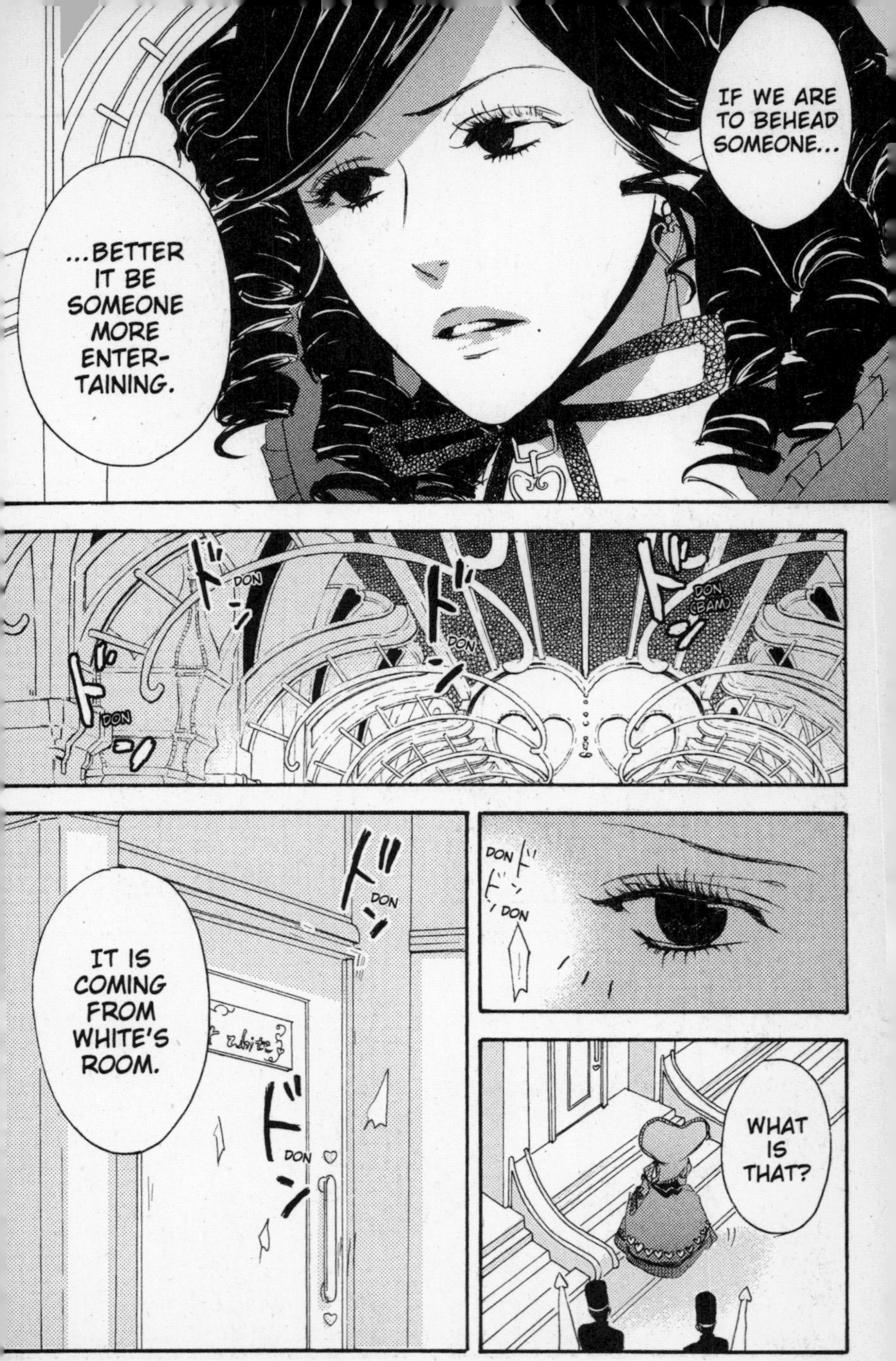
IF WE ARE TO BEHEAD SOMEONE...
...BETTER IT BE SOMEONE MORE ENTER-TAINING.
ドン DON (BAM)
ドン DON
ドン DON
ドン DON
ドン DON
ドン DON
WHAT IS THAT?
ドン DON
IT IS COMING FROM WHITE'S ROOM.
ドン DON

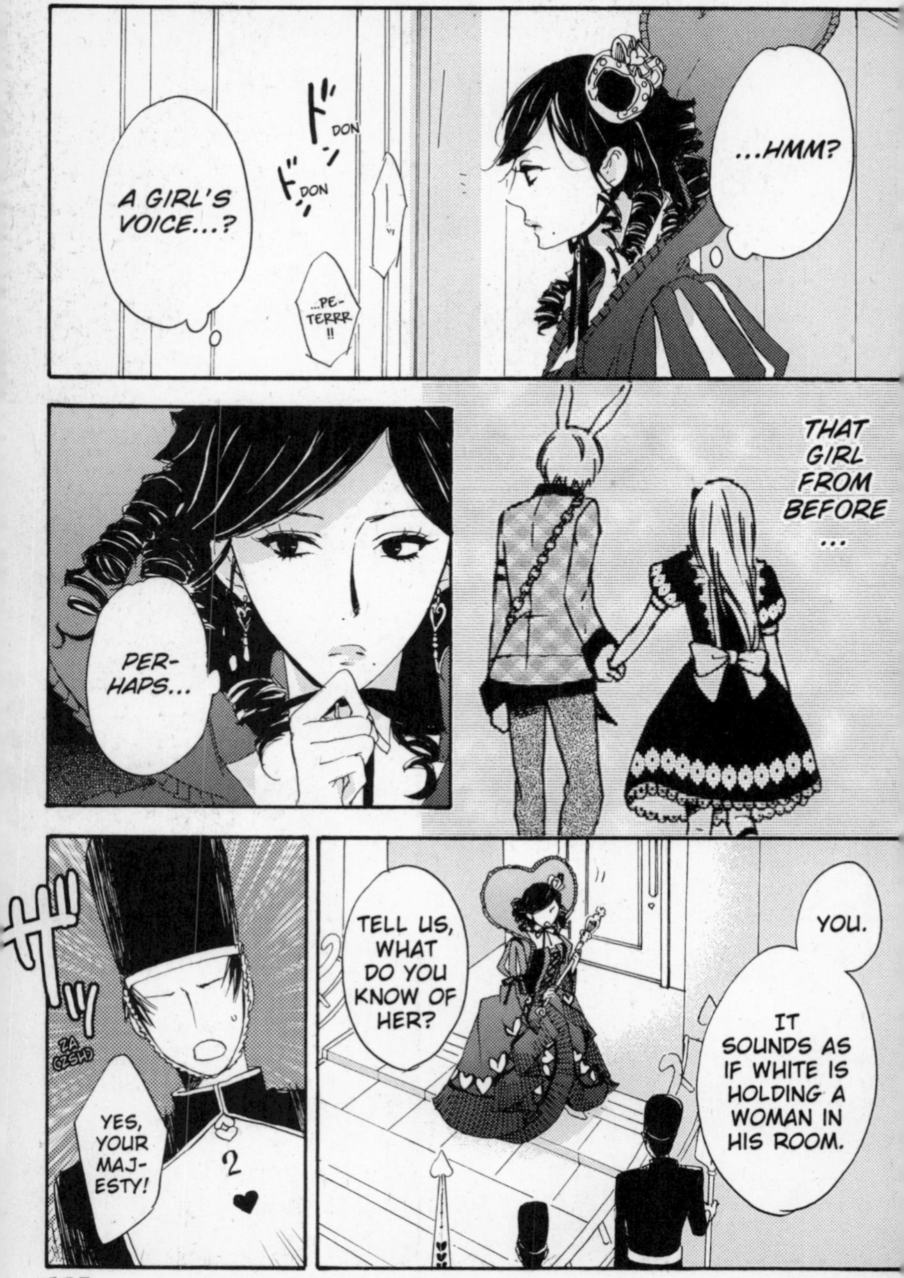
...HMM?
DON
DON
...PE-TERRR!!
A GIRL'S VOICE...?
THAT GIRL FROM BEFORE...
PER-HAPS...
YOU.
IT SOUNDS AS IF WHITE IS HOLDING A WOMAN IN HIS ROOM.
TELL US, WHAT DO YOU KNOW OF HER?
ZA CZSHD
YES, YOUR MAJ-ESTY!

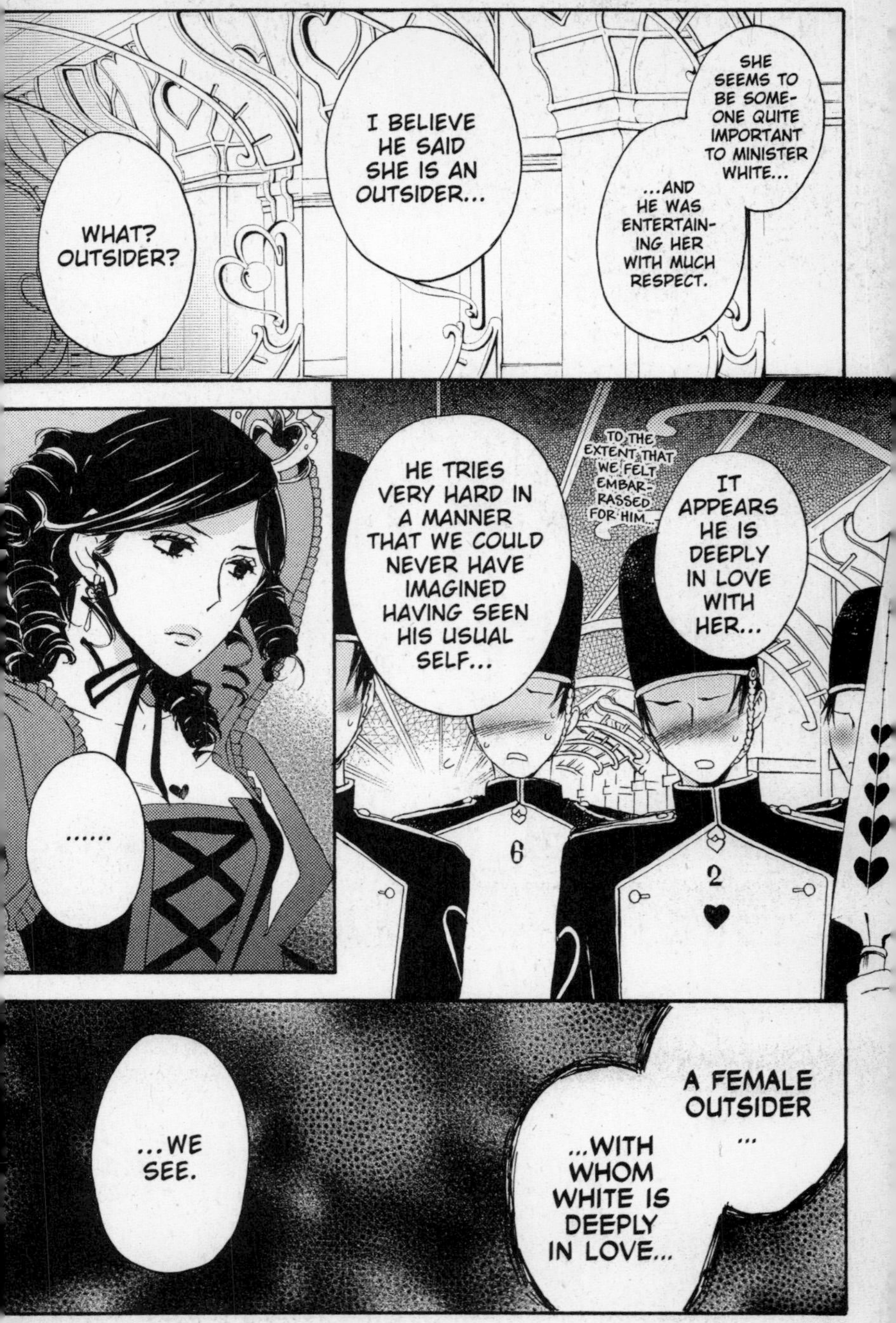
SHE SEEMS TO BE SOME-ONE QUITE IMPORTANT TO MINISTER WHITE...
...AND HE WAS ENTERTAIN-ING HER WITH MUCH RESPECT.
I BELIEVE HE SAID SHE IS AN OUTSIDER...
WHAT? OUTSIDER?
IT APPEARS HE IS DEEPLY IN LOVE WITH HER...
TO THE EXTENT THAT WE FELT EMBAR-RASSED FOR HIM...
HE TRIES VERY HARD IN A MANNER THAT WE COULD NEVER HAVE IMAGINED HAVING SEEN HIS USUAL SELF...
......
A FEMALE OUTSIDER ...
...WITH WHOM WHITE IS DEEPLY IN LOVE...
...WE SEE.

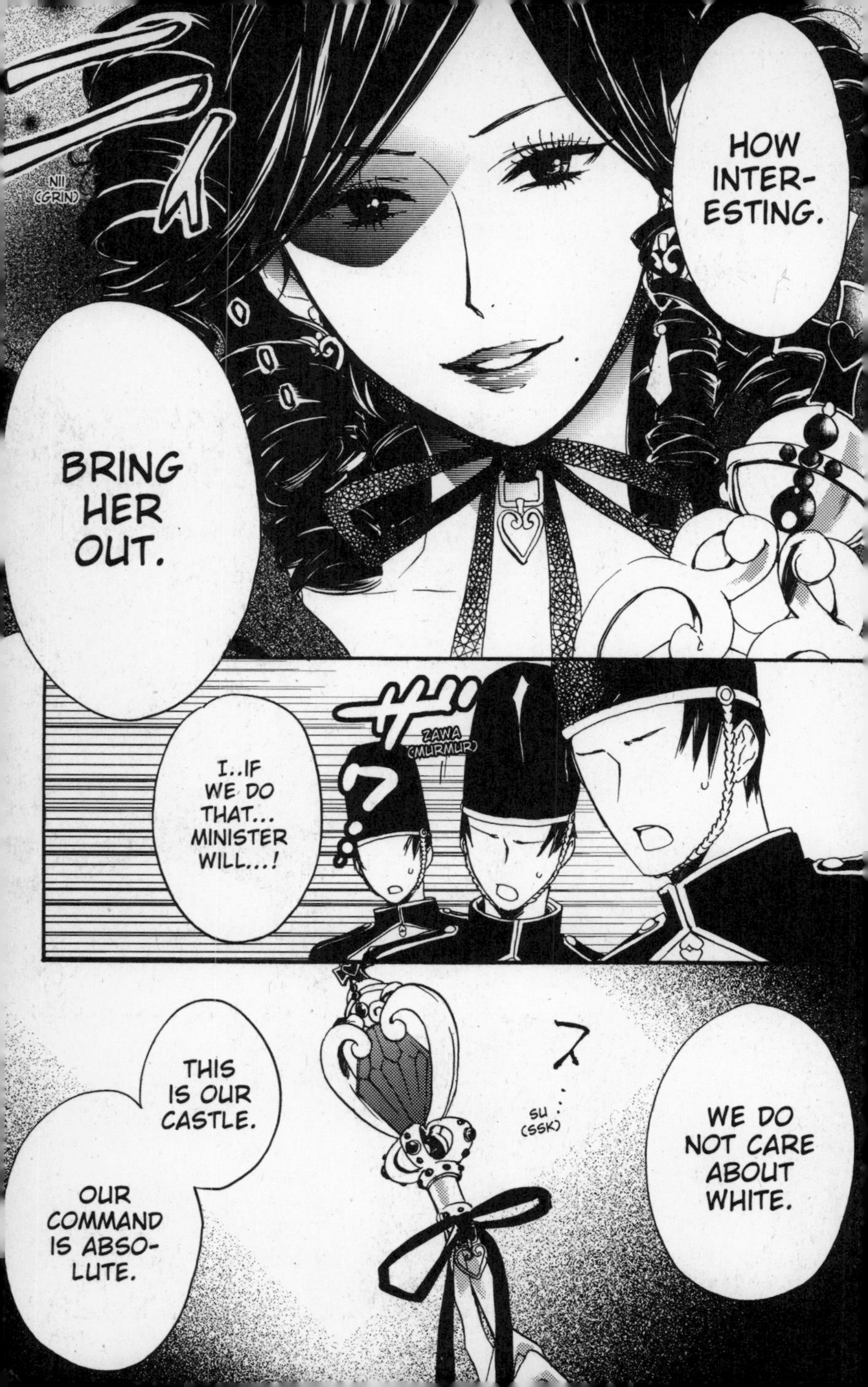
HOW INTER-ESTING.
NII (GRIN)
BRING HER OUT.
ZAWA (MURMUR)
I..IF WE DO THAT... MINISTER WILL...!
WE DO NOT CARE ABOUT WHITE.
SU (SSK)
THIS IS OUR CASTLE.
OUR COMMAND IS ABSO-LUTE.

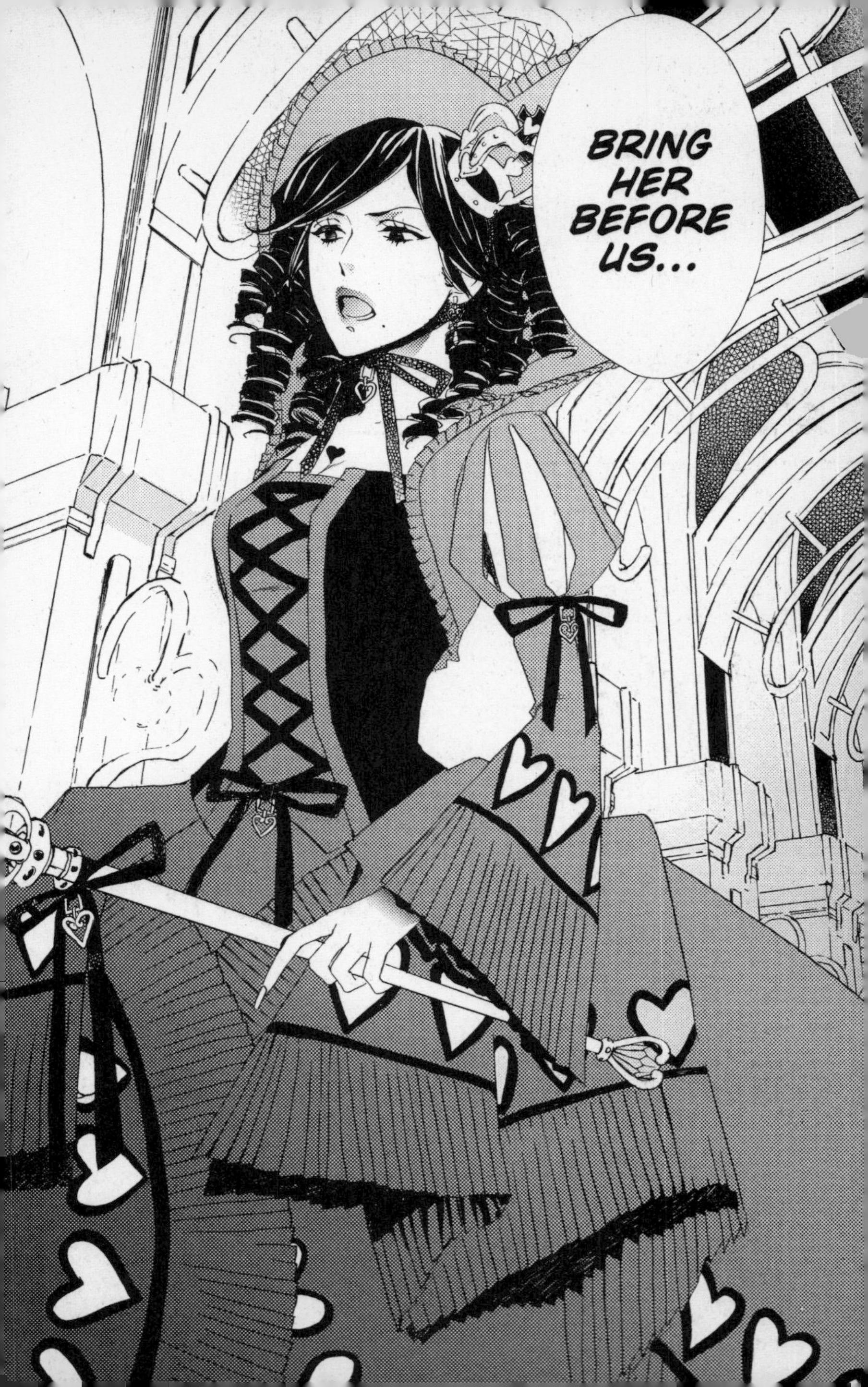
BRING HER BEFORE US...

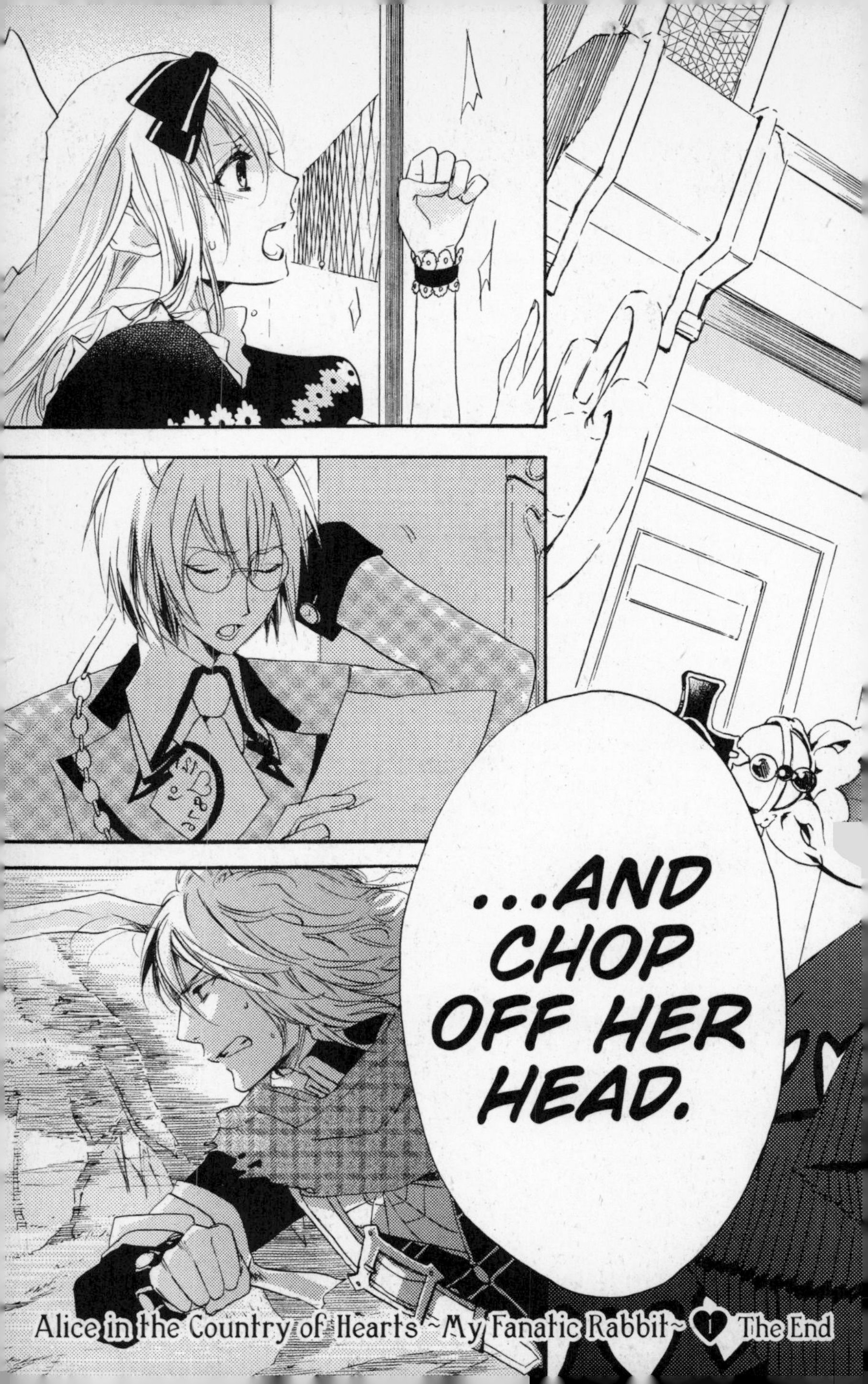
...AND CHOP OFF HER HEAD.
Alice in the Country of Hearts ~My Fanatic Rabbit~ 1 The End

FEB 1 2 2013

ALICE IN THE COUNTRY OF HEARTS
My Fanatic Rabbit
1

QuinRose
Delico Psyche
Owl Shinotsuki

Translation ♥ Ajino Hirami

Lettering ♥ Keiran O'Leary

ALICE IN THE COUNTRY OF THE HEART -My Fanatic Rabbit- Vol. 1 © QuinRose. All rights reserved. © 2010 Delico Psyche. First published in Japan in 2010 by MAG Garden Corporation. English translation rights arranged with MAG Garden Corporation through Tuttle-Mori Agency, Inc., Tokyo.

English translation © 2012 Hachette Book Group, Inc.

Yen Press
Hachette Book Group
237 Park Avenue, New York, NY 10017

www.HachetteBookGroup.com
www.YenPress.com

Yen Press is an imprint of Hachette Book Group, Inc.
The Yen Press name and logo are trademarks of Hachette Book Group, Inc.

First Yen Press Edition: December 2012

ISBN: 978-0-316-22920-3

10 9 8 7 6 5 4 3 2 1

BVG

Printed in the United States of America